STATE-BUILDING: A COMPARATIVE STUDY OF UKRAINE, LITHUANIA, BELARUS, AND RUSSIA

STATE-BUILDING: A COMPARATIVE STUDY OF UKRAINE, LITHUANIA, BELARUS, AND RUSSIA

Verena Fritz

CEU PRESS

Central European University Press
Budapest New York

Published in 2007 by
Central European University Press

An imprint of the
Central European University Share Company
Nádor utca 11, H-1051 Budapest, Hungary
Tel: +36-1-327-3138 or 327-3000
Fax: +36-1-327-3183
E-mail: ceupress@ceu.hu
Website: www.ceupress.com

400 West 59th Street, New York NY 10019, USA
Tel: +1-212-547-6932
Fax: +1-646-557-2416
E-mail: mgreenwald@sorosny.org

ISBN 978-963-7326-90-5

Library of Congress Cataloging-in-Publication Data

Fritz, Verena.
State-building : a comparative study of Ukraine, Lithuania, Belarus, and Russia / Verena Fritz.
p. cm.
Includes bibliographical references.
ISBN 978-9637326905
1. Former Soviet republics–Politics and government. 2. Democracy–Former Soviet republics. 3. Post-communism–Former Soviet republics. 4. Finance, Public–Former Soviet republics. I. Title.

JN6531.F75 2007
320.947–dc22

2006100694

Printed in Hungary by
Akaprint

TABLE OF CONTENTS

ABBREVIATIONS

AC	Accounting Chamber (Ukraine)
BEEPS	Business Environment and Enterprise Performance Survey
BPF	Belarusian Popular Front
BR	Belarusian Ruble
CEE	Central Eastern Europe
CIS	Commonwealth of Independent States
CIT	Company Income Tax (= EPT in Ukraine)
CLI	Confederation of Lithuanian Industrialists
CPI	Corruption Perceptions Index (by Transparency International)
CPSU	Communist Party of the Soviet Union
CPU	Communist Party of Ukraine
EBRD	European Bank for Reconstruction and Development
EPT	Enterprise Profit Tax (Ukrainian CIT)
FDI	Foreign Direct Investment
FPU	Federation of Ukrainian Trade Unions
FTUB	Federation of Trade Unions of Belarus
GDP	Gross Domestic Product
HDI	Human Development Index
IFI	International Financial Institutions
ICPS	International Centre for Policy Studies (Ukraine)
LDDP	*Lietuvos Demokratine Darbo Partija* - Lithuanian Labour Party (ex-Communist → LSDP)
LLS	Lithuanian Liberal Union
LSDP	Lithuanian Social Democratic Party (→ successor to LDDP)
LTL	Lithuanian Litas
NDP	*Narodno-Demokratychna Partiya* - People's Democratic Party (Ukraine)
NIS	Newly Independent States
NPGU	Independent Miners Union of Ukraine

PIT	Personal Income Tax
RUIE	Russian Union of Industrialists and Entrepreneurs
RUR	Russian Ruble
SAI	Supreme Audit Institution
SC	State Control (Lithuania)
SCC	State Control Committee (Belarus)
SMD	Single Mandate Districts
SPS	*Soyus Pravnykh Sil* - Union of Rightist Forces (Russia)
SST	Social Security Tax
STA	State Tax Administration (Ukraine)
STS	State Tax Service (Russia)
TS (LK)	*Tėvynės sąjunga* - Homeland Union (Lithuania)
UAH	Ukrainian Hryvnia
UEPLAC	Ukrainian-European Policy and Legal Advice Centre
UNECE	United Nations Economic Commission for Europe
UUIE	Ukrainian Union of Industrialists and Entrepreneurs
VAT	Value-Added Tax
WDR	World Development Report

LIST OF TABLES AND GRAPHS

ACKNOWLEDGEMENTS

This book could not have been completed without the generous support of colleagues and of many people in the countries visited and studied. My thanks go to Jonathan Wheatley, who has read the entire manuscript at several stages and who has been a good friend and colleague working on post-Soviet countries. Special thanks are due to Philippe Schmitter who helped to launch me on this research. Jan Zielonka and Kataryna Wolczuk as well as Claus Offe and Valerie Bunce provided invaluable comments at various stages of the manuscript. Sarah Whitmore at Oxford Brookes and Hans-Jürgen Puhle at the University of Frankfurt provided me with opportunities to present this research in their seminars, from where I took useful comments and encouragement. I have been able to benefit from numerous discussions with other colleagues and visitors at the European University Institute in Florence.

In the countries studied, I am especially grateful to Larisa Leshchenko who made it possible for me to spend three months at the World Bank office in Kiev in 2000, and to Sergiy Kulyk and Luca Barbone of the World Bank who kindly shared their thoughts. I owe thanks to the public officials, parliamentarians, researchers, and other interlocutors in Belarus, Lithuania, Ukraine, and Russia who were generous with their time, insights, and analysis. Their contribution was crucial for making this study possible. Very warm thanks are also due to my hosts and friends, who welcomed me and helped me to understand the region from their various perspectives. Rainer Lindner of the German Institute for International and Security Affairs, Berlin provided me with good advice and helpful contacts in Ukraine when I first embarked on this research.

Many thanks are due to Cathy Setzer of the Centennial Center of the American Political Science Association in Washington DC, who made it possible for me to spend several quiet weeks in the Center refining and finishing the manuscript. I am grateful to colleagues and friends at the Overseas Development Institute in London—especially David Booth, Alina Rocha Menocal, and Paolo de Renzio—who have a common keen interest in the state, in fiscal issues, and in a political economy perspective, and who have further shaped my thinking on these issues.

Finally, I owe special thanks to Luis Alvaro Sanchez, who has shared his thoughts and insights, and a common interest in the region. He has provided me with the emotional support that makes life worthwhile—and I have to ask his forgiveness for the periods of distraction which the work on this study has inevitably brought.

All errors and omissions are mine.

I. INTRODUCTION

State formation and transformation in the former Soviet Union

Moments of state formation are rare events in history.[1] They are the initial periods of the long term history of a state and the evolution of its capacity. States and their development are important: although today states are no longer viewed as quasi-metaphysical entities, as ends in and of themselves, they still serve as crucial structures through which societies solve their collective action problems. States remain crucial 'loci' of governance which allow modern, complex societies to function and to enhance their welfare—and where states fail or are malfunctioning, the consequences for society are serious and often painful.

To various degrees, and particularly in the case of most post-Soviet countries, state formation occurs in tandem with the transformation of the state's role. In the Soviet system, the state was the owner of most economic entities—factories, farms, services—and the state sought to direct economic activity through a planned process. After 1991 in all post-Soviet countries, the role of the state changed to some degree, and in most, the change was far-reaching.[2] The main share of economic entities was privatized, and the planning system was dismantled. However, the result of independence and of state and economic transformation was not a well-functioning capitalist order, but rather a period of relative chaos, 'wild West' capitalism, rising corruption, and deep social dislocation.

Initial state-building in the former Soviet Union coincided with economic crisis and in many cases with a protracted struggle over the establishment of a new legitimate government. The simultaneity of these challenges deepened and prolonged the crisis. In the face of these challenges, states in the former Soviet Union did not break down—as some states especially in Africa have under the pressure of economic crisis.[3] However, the level of service provision by the state deteriorated sharply, and only a minority of countries moved successfully towards building modern, effective as well as accountable states during the initial 15 years after the end of the USSR.

Issues of state-formation and transformation are crucial for understanding the current developments in the post-Soviet region. The initial debates on the region have focused on political and economic transitions ('democratization', 'marketization'), as well as on issues of national identity, and have tended to neglect the state. Increasingly, however, the weakness of post-Soviet states has been pointed to as a key problem for these other processes.[4] Still, there are few in-depth inquiries of *why* these states are weak or otherwise dysfunctional and into the potential and dynamic of their recovery. The goal of this study is precisely such an inquiry, focusing on state-formation as the dependent variable and seeking to trace the formation of state capacity and to understand its driving factors. To do so, it seeks to capture and to account for variations, i.e. to explain why some states in the former Soviet Union are weaker or more dysfunctional than others, and how state capacity has evolved over time.

The experience of 'failing' economic and political transitions in the former Soviet Union has given rise to controversy about the role of institutions and their relative neglect by social scientists at the outset of transitions. In the early 1990s, international advice by economists focused on the dismantling, but insufficiently on the re-building of institutions—and underestimated the challenges to developing effective institutions especially in less advanced transition countries.[5] At the same time, in the field of political science 'transitologists' tended to focus on transitions affecting the political regime and political institutions, as well as on national identities, but much less on wider state institutions and the process of state-building.[6]

A challenging aspect for analyzing transition as well as state-building in the post-communist region is the speed and degree of change. Economic crisis has been followed by rapid economic recovery in many countries—even though the duration of crisis has varied considerably, and the apparent boom may not be sustained and may not resolve the deep dislocations of the previous period. The far-reaching breakdown of institutional structures has been followed by re-building; however, re-building has resulted in more or less 'good' institutional structures. The challenge for analyzing the state-building process is that the explanatory interpretation has to account for deterioration as well as for re-building, for the differences in the extent and quality of each, and for what drives the changing trends.

The scope and key arguments of this book

The main thrust of this research is to understand how states and state capacity developed in post-Soviet countries. In order to analyze the driving factors, it is first necessary to develop a suitable framework, since state capacity is not easy to assess empirically. Drawing an analogy with transition theory, we see that the question 'What is a democracy?' has been amply debated over the past decade; while the question of 'What is a capable state?' has not received the same systematic attention. Hence, a first aim of this research is to develop a suitable framework for assessing states. Based on such a conceptualization of the state, the aim is then to craft an account of the factors driving state development in the region, and particularly in a sub-set of four cases.

There are two key issues to the conceptualization. One is that a continuum from weak to strong states is one-dimensional and therefore insufficient. States need to be assessed not only based on their strength but also on the quality of their institutions. Compared to states in other middle-income countries, most post-Soviet states are reasonably strong, but they suffer from high levels of corruption and related forms of misgovernance. Furthermore, the size or scope of a state—the extent of its role in the economy, and the share it extracts from the economy via taxation—is not equivalent to high state capacity, or the 'strength of the state.' The region's own history illustrates this well: the Soviet state assumed a very wide role, but nonetheless became increasingly weakened since the late 1970s.[7]

The second element of the conceptualization is that in order to analyze states, it is useful to disaggregate elements of state capacity. In this research, I distinguish three dimensions: the capacity to take decisions, implementation capacity, and the nature of control and accountability relationships. The first two dimensions primarily concern the effectiveness of the state, while the third dimension inquires into the safeguards against misgovernance and about the dominant forms of control and accountability. Especially the first and the third dimensions are closely linked to the nature of the political regime.

The book covers the post-Soviet Union, and from this region, four cases are discussed in depth: Ukraine, Belarus, Lithuania, and Russia. Following a 'most-similar-systems' logic, all four cases are among the more highly developed post-Soviet countries (in contrast to the less developed successor states especially in Central Asia). All post-Soviet countries became independent at the same point in time, and emerged from the same previous institutional order—even if there was some *de facto* variation within the USSR.[8] The findings of this study are based on this particular universe of cases.

Furthermore to analyze state-building processes in the former Soviet Union, this book makes use of a fiscal perspective, inquiring into the development of tax systems, budgeting, and fiscal accountability. In doing so it draws on the tradition of 'fiscal sociology', which puts the inquiry into fiscal systems at the center for understanding the development of the state, society, and state-society relations.[9] A fiscal perspective offers several strengths: taxing and spending is central to any state; and this universality makes it useful for comparative analysis. The centrality of fiscal issues means also that this perspective covers the internal workings of the state, as well as key elements in the relationship between the state and society (extraction and accountability). Moreover, it opens a field that offers a wealth of data which in turn allows for an in-depth empirical inquiry and for bridging the gap between the causal links proposed by theory and possible observations in the empirical world.

The fiscal perspective is adopted here as a fruitful one, which allows an in-depth and rigorous inquiry; but this book makes no claim that this should be the exclusive perspective on the state and state-building processes.[10] It allows the scholar to capture certain important and central aspects of the state, but also screens out others. An unavoidable trade-off in choosing a specific perspective on the state is that other pertinent issues of the state are not or are only marginally addressed, as, for example, the development of internal and external security structures. Importantly, the fiscal perspective is adopted here as a focal point for observing state capacity; while the net for causal or driving factors is cast wide, covering key domestic and external factors which may be presumed to shape the state (see below as well as Chapter 4). Furthermore, the more technical aspects which the fiscal perspective necessarily involves are presented in such a way so as to be accessible to generalist social science readers.

This research considers a range of potential driving factors which promoted or inhibited state-building in the former Soviet Union. The central finding is that differentiation in state-building trajectories is primarily driven by the way in which the political regime was formed at the outset of independence. The restoration of an authoritarian regime, the move to a democratic regime, or prolonged 'hybridity' and uncertainty over the political regime had important implications for how state-building evolved.

A further central assertion is that the degree of institutional erosion at the outset of independence was high across the former USSR which created a situation of partial 'anarchy', or absence of effective governance. Institutional erosion was significantly greater than in Central Eastern Europe. This had important implications for actors at the outset of independence, creating higher uncertainty, fewer constraints on 'piracy' or the lawless acquisition of formerly state-owned property, and consequently different incentives and opportunities for establishing a new institutional order. The way in which a new regime was set up, and the timing of establishing and consolidating of a regime consequently had important implications for overcoming the situation of partial anarchy—including the potential to consolidate the re-distribution of wealth and power which had occurred during the period of institutional erosion.

The research also explores several other putative driving factors, especially the level of development and the relative importance of external linkages and influence. It has been argued that the level and historic 'depth' of development have been key factors for explaining economic and political transition trajectories in the post-communist region.[11] External linkages and external influence—manifest in trade relations and the conditions of international financial institutions (IFIs)—are widely assumed to constrain or inhibit state-building in less developed countries, and may therefore also be assumed to have a negative impact on post-Soviet state-building processes.[12] The putative factors are set out in Chapter 4 in detail, and are then explored in the empirical part of this book (Chapters 5–11).

Case selection: a most-similar-systems comparison of Ukraine, Belarus, Lithuania, and Russia

From the universe of post-Soviet cases, the four 'most similar' cases in terms of general conditions such as culture and level of development have been selected for in-depth study. With the exception of Russia, all had about a quarter of employment and GDP in agriculture, and had a rather high level of human development at the end of the Soviet period (see Table 1 below). All four countries were late developers but underwent large-scale modernization after WWII and had experienced a major push of industrialization during the Soviet period.[13] Furthermore, by the end of the Soviet rule, all these countries had achieved high levels of education, while their industries were largely run by members of the 'titular nationality', rather than by migrants from other republics.[14]

Culturally, there is also considerable similarity: Belarus, Ukrainians, and Russians together form the Eastern Slavic linguistic group. In all three countries Orthodox Christianity is the main religion, despite considerable secularization in Soviet times. Lithuania is the only predominantly Catholic post-Soviet country—a religion arguably closer to the Orthodox Church than either the Protestantism of Latvia and Estonia, or the Islam predominant in

Central Asia. Belarus, Lithuania, and Ukraine are also similar in having been influenced by Polish as well as Russian pre-dominance.

Table 1: Basic structural indicators

	Belarus	Lithuania	Russia	Ukraine	Estonia	Uzbekistan
HDI 1990	**0.808**	**0.814**	**0.823**	**0.793**	**n/a**	**0.693**
GDP per cap in 1985 at PPP	7388	6663	7804	5853	7163	3523
Share of agriculture in GDP 1992	23.8	25.2	7.2	20.3	6.1*	35.4
Employment in agriculture 1980	26	28	16	25	15	40
Literacy around 1900	20.3	48.4	29.3	18.9	94.1	3.4

* 1996 (first available figure); (Estonia and Uzbekistan are included for comparison, marking the upper and lower bound of development in the region).

Sources: UNDP, EBRD, WB; literacy and GDP per cap in 1985: Kitschelt (2001)

Furthermore, during the transition period, none of these cases has experienced ethnic conflict or civil war, with the exception of the Chechnya conflict in Russia (which—despite all its importance—has been more marginal for the country than the civil wars in Moldova, Tajikistan, or Georgia). Thus, in terms of social pre-conditions we are dealing with a most-similar subset of the post-Soviet universe.

This is not to deny that there are considerable differences and important idiosyncrasies of each country which we cannot control for. These include differences in population and geographical size (populations—Lithuania: 3.7m, Belarus: 10m, Ukraine: 48m, Russia: 145m), the different historical trajectory experienced by Lithuania (interwar independence and capitalist development), and the natural resource wealth on the one hand and the federal structure on the other as unique to the Russian Federation. Furthermore, Lithuania is regarded as a country with a very strong national consciousness, while Belarus is at the opposite end of the spectrum, with Ukraine and Russia lying somewhere in between.[15]

A roadmap to this study

This book is organized as follows: Chapters 1 to 4 set out the framework for analysis. Chapter 1 traces some key issues in existing conceptualizations of the state and of state-building processes. In particular, the chapter discusses the notion of state autonomy, and covers key debates about the size of the state and the quality of governance. Chapters 2 and 3 outline a framework for assessing states. Chapter 2 develops a framework for thinking about the two aspects of the state as a source of solutions and as a source of problems ('bad governance'). Based on neo-institutionalist notions of institutional change, Chapter 3 then introduces a framework for investigating the dynamic of state-building. It develops the idea that institutional deterioration is a potentially important but often neglected element of institutional change. Chapter 4 discusses the presumed driving factors and their interaction, and based on these distinguishes four potential state-building trajectories.

Chapter 5 offers an overview of Soviet institutional legacies in the fiscal sphere, and of developments in the 15 successor states. This chapter in particular investigates the relative importance of the level of development and of international influence.

Chapters 6 to 8 trace the development of fiscal institutions and the factors driving this development in Ukraine from around 1992 to 2005. Among the four cases, Ukraine is covered in the greatest depth, as this case serves particularly well in exploring the initial 'rounds' of institution-building and how the process has changed over time. The second largest post-Soviet country after Russia, Ukraine is a case of prolonged regime contestation, between the authoritarian leanings of the 'Kuchma era' from 1994 to 2004 and the second transition to a more democratic regime during the 'Orange Revolution'—with, however, the new democratic regime remaining unconsolidated during the first year of the Yushchenko government. The Ukrainian state became particularly weak and disorganized in the early 1990s. Although state structures were re-built in the late 1990s, due to the hybrid nature of the regime and to the state capture by oligarchic groups associated with it, considerable problems with misgovernance emerged, some of which were deliberately created by the regime. From 2005, post-Orange governments then struggled to redesign the state and to improve the quality of governance, with rather mixed initial success.

Chapters 9 and 10 cover the state-building processes in Belarus and Lithuania respectively. These two neighboring countries provide examples of distinctly contrasting political and state-building trajectories. In Lithuania, a democratic regime which included both a strong reformed communist party and a national-democratic opposition that had emerged from the *Sajudis* movement was consolidated soon after the country gained independence. The reform of the role of the state was rapid, incurring a considerable cost at the outset, but re-building institutions successfully. The EU provided a strong external anchor which guided the institution-building process, and offered models for institutional modernization. Nonetheless, although much more limited than in Ukraine, Lithuania also suffered problems of bad governance and conflicts of interests due to close linkages between business and politics. In contrast to Ukraine, however, there was greater accountability to wider society, and egregious abuses of power had consequences, most prominently the impeachment and removal of president Paksas in early 2004.

Belarus is an unexpected case in several ways. A communist-style state has been restored in Belarus since the ascendancy of Lukashenka to the presidency in 1994. The establishment of one of the most consolidated authoritarian regimes in the former Soviet Union is surprising in a country which is relatively developed, and also bordering countries which have made the complete transition to democracy (Poland and Lithuania). The weakness of nationalism is widely held to account for this, as it has meant that a key conduit for developing a strong opposition was lacking.[16] Fiscally, Belarus is the largest state among those emerging from the Soviet Union. Generally, the state in Belarus possesses considerable capacity and has been relatively less affected by problems of bad governance such as corruption. However, Belarus faces the risks of irrational governance and of stagnation which are associated with hardening autocratic regimes or 'tyranny'. Increasingly, state capacity is used not only for service provision but also for political oppression. At the same time, despite the relative strength of the state, its independent statehood has been called into question, as the political leadership has declared its intention to join the Russian Federation. However, the willingness to forgo statehood has also had real limits as the Belarusian elite appears ultimately disinclined to have its country downgraded to a Russian province.

Chapter 11 addresses the process of tax reform in Russia. The focus of this case study is narrower than the one used in the others for two reasons. First of all, Russian state-building is relatively well covered in the literature, and thus a general account would add relatively little of value.[17] Secondly, tax reform is a particularly interesting aspect for the purpose of this study: the Russian state-building and economic reform process ran aground in the 1998 financial crisis due to a serious crisis of the tax system. Tax reform helped to restart this process, and was one of the key reforms which Putin pursued during the initial years of his presidency. Furthermore, the comparison with Ukraine is particularly interesting: in both countries the debate over tax reform started around the same time, but despite the additional obstacles inherent in its federal system Russia moved ahead with a comprehensive reform several years earlier than Ukraine.

The conclusion draws the various lines of inquiry into post-Soviet state-building processes presented in this study together, revisiting, and condensing the key findings.

Notes

1 State-formation and state-building will be used interchangeably in this study. State transformation is used to refer to the changes in the state's role in the context of transition.
2 Post-communist is used here to denote all transition countries in the Eurasian region. 'Post-Soviet', in contrast, refers to the 15 successor states of the Soviet Union, including the Baltic states. Occasionally, 'the CIS' will be used to connote all non-Baltic post-Soviet states.
3 Rotberg (ed.), (2004).
4 Carothers (2002); Holmes (1997).
5 Popov (2004); Hausner et al. (eds.) (1995), 3-43; Gel'man (2004).
6 See also Grzymala-Busse and Jones Luong (2002).
7 Stark and Bruszt (1998).
8 *De facto* variation in how institutions function is common to many larger and internally diverse countries, such as the US, Brazil, or Italy. Putnam (1993).
9 Goldscheid (1994, originally published in 1919); Levi (1988); Olson (1997); Steinmo (1993).
10 A different, but similarly specific focus is adopted by Evans in his book on the state's role in East Asian development, focusing on those institutions dealing with economic management. Evans (1995).
11 Kitschelt (2001); Norgaard (2000).
12 Wallerstein (1974); Wedel (1998); Leftwich (2005); Grindle (1996), 23ff.
13 On Belarus see Nørgaard (2000), 192.
14 Beissinger (1997), 171.
15 See Beissinger (1992), 141-169; regarding Belarus see also Nørgaard (2000), 193-194.
16 Hill (2005); Mihalisko (1997). See also Bunce (2003).
17 Smith (1999); Sperling (2000); Lynch (2005).

CHAPTER 1.

STATE- AND INSTITUTION-BUILDING – A FRAMEWORK FOR ANALYSIS

The state is undeniably a messy concept.
(Michael Mann[1])

The debate about the role of the state in the social sciences has deep historical roots and is multi-faceted. This first, theoretical part draws on several strands of the debate. It serves to develop a conceptual basis that will support the empirical work of the book, placing the research in its wider theoretical context on the one hand, and providing a conceptualization and operationalization for the empirical study on the other hand.

The part is divided into four chapters. The first chapter gives an overview of some fundamental definitions and debates in the relevant literature, including the emerging debate on stateness in transition countries. The second chapter develops key concepts about the state that will be used in defining the dependent variable of this study. The third chapter addresses the dynamic of stateness based on concepts developed in the new institutionalist literature. In the fourth chapter, I set out the putative factors which are assumed to drive state-building and develop a causal model which considers the interaction among various factors.

1.1. The state and state-building: definitions and debates

States have widely diverged in their appearance—from the emerging states of early modern Europe to the post-WWII welfare states with enormous fiscal resources, to various African post-colonial 'shell' states and failed states. It has been argued that states are dissolving due to the forces of globalization, the primacy of the market combined with increasing international integration. However, in rich, capitalist societies, states still matter, even if their role is continuously undergoing changes; while in poorer, and more conflict prone regions, the experience of weak and failing states has led to a re-evaluation of the importance of capable states.[2]

With regard to post-communist Eastern Europe and the former Soviet Union, social science debates have primarily focused on democratization, economic transition, and issues of national identity. However, since the late 1990s, there has been an increasing interest in the formation and transformation of states in the region, and a recognition of the multiple problems associated with weak and dysfunctional states (corruption, decline in service delivery, etc.).

A central pillar of the academic discussion about states is the experience of European early modern state formation. As part of this discussion, two classic definitions of the state were developed by Max Weber and Charles Tilly. According to Weber

> "The state is a human community that (successfully) claims the monopoly of the legitimate use of physical force within a given territory. [...] If the state is to exist, the dominated must obey the authority claimed by the powers that be. When and why they obey, can only be understood, when one knows the inner justification and external means on which a domination rests."[3]

Tilly's definition is the following: "An organization which controls the population occupying a defined territory is a state *in so far as* (1) it is differentiated from other organizations operating in the same territory; (2) it is autonomous; (3) it is centralized; and (4) its divisions are formally coordinated with one another."[4]

Both definitions stress the structural and organisational aspects of the state. They do not mention any state functions apart from the monopoly of violence in Weber's definition. An important difference between the two definitions is Weber's strong emphasis on legitimacy, understood as the acceptance of authority by the people.

1.1.1. STATE AUTONOMY AND STATE-SOCIETY RELATIONS

Especially Tilly's definition focuses on autonomy as an important aspect of the state. This aspect forms part of a wider debate about state autonomy, embeddedness, and state capture. It was developed against the backdrop of a pluralist paradigm which viewed the state merely as an arena within which social forces struggled and compromised over their interests.[5] State autonomy is also directed against the orthodox Marxist view that the state is a mere "agent of class interest" of the capitalist class.[6] Thus, the question is whether 'the state' can have an active role of its own—acting from a situation of relative independence from various societal interests, but (presumably) nonetheless acting in the (long-term) common interest of society as a whole.

While the recognition that states are important structures and that they are not simply beholden to any one group in most cases is sound, "state autonomy" can be a problematic normative concept: while (highly) autonomous states may sometimes promote general welfare, at other times they may engage in highly destructive or self-interested policies. Furthermore, empirically, few states other than extreme dictatorships are fully autonomous. Studying East Asian states during their phases of strong, state-led economic growth Evans therefore proposed the idea of "embedded autonomy."[7]

The post-communist experience of formerly powerful, but subsequently weakened states deeply affected by problems of corruption led to the use of the concept of "state capture"[8] as a framework for analysis "State capture" in a sense is the opposite of "(embedded) autonomy." A captured state is one which has become distorting, serving the interests of a few "captors," rather than society as a whole; and which consequently is also incoherent, as narrow rather than encompassing interests predominate in decision-making processes. However, the problem of state capture is not exclusive to the post-communist world;[9] and it is also not the only dimension of the stateness problem which post-communist countries face.

A related, pertinent distinction is made by Michael Mann between 'despotic powers' and 'infrastructural powers' of the state.[10] Despotic power is the ability to make decisions arbitrarily or autonomously—on this count early modern states were powerful. Infrastructural power refers to the actual penetration of societies by state bureaucracies and state-sponsored programs such as public education. Mann sees the historic evolution of states towards higher 'infrastructural powers,' but at the same time lowered despotic powers, i.e., towards less or at least more "embedded" and constrained autonomy, as rulers were increasingly bound by accountability to their societies. However, post-Soviet countries inherited a legacy which combined considerable infrastructural powers with a continuation of a despotic exercise of power.

In contrast to many post-colonial states in the post-WWII period in Africa and Asia, post-Soviet states started from rather high levels of state infrastructural penetration of society: many of the basic functions of modern states such as internal and external security structures, as well as health and education systems were in place (while often being in serious need of reform). At the same time, especially during the Stalinist period, the Soviet state had held nearly unbounded despotic powers. Since the 1960s, the exercise of despotic powers lessened and became fragmented, with mid-level power-holders becoming increasingly independent from central command. This trend of continued despotic but increasingly fragmented power was inherited by the newly independent states; together with the infrastructural capacities which had been built during the Soviet period.

This study adopts a basic Weberian perspective, in the sense that it considers the building of a capable state apparatus as an important goal. The central interest of the inquiry is around the change towards or away from this goal. n order to understand why some post-Soviet states became more capable and less dysfunctional than others we have to analyze the political and social foundations of state-building, as well as their interaction with existing or inherited institutional structures. As formulated by Caporaso and Levine, societal actors and state structures are linked in a continuous process of interaction: "The state enters into the constitution of society just as society contributes to the constitution of the state."[11] This basic idea is translated into an operational framework for analyzing post-Soviet states in Chapter 4.

1.1.2. THE ROLE OF THE STATE—NORMATIVE DEBATES

The issue of the size of the state has given rise to considerable debate—which includes both descriptive-analytical and normative contributions. In the 1980s, a debate about "downsizing the state" gathered force. To some extent, this was a reaction to the remarkable expansion of the state since the 19th century, and particularly after WWII, in developed countries. It was also a reaction to the failure of attempts at state-led development outside of East Asia.[12] Advocates of "neo-liberalism" proposed that downsizing the state—through privatization, outsourcing, and other means—was the solution to economic stagnation in the developed world and to "predatory states" and economic decline in the developing world.

However, the results of attempts at 'downsizing' the state have been far from universally positive, especially in less developed countries.[13] In reaction, the World Development Report of 1997—*The State in a Changing World*—brought the importance of state capacity back into the debate. As section 3 in Chapter 2 develops further, this study assumes neither that there is an "optimal" size of the state, nor that the (fiscal) size of the state is equivalent with state capacity or the strength of the state. However, it does assume that expectations of the state in the 21st century are considerable—and hence that states need a substantial fiscal size and general capacity to deliver on these domestic as well as internationally driven expectations.

Today, states are widely expected to provide at least basic health-care and education systems as well as to act as sophisticated regulators of markets. Therefore, even the neo-liberal ideal of a "night-watchman state" which concentrates on setting and enforcing rules for private actors, and rejects redistribution as part of the state's role, requires considerable state capacity—far greater than the one early modern states possessed, or which many weak states in various parts of the world possess today.[14]

1.1.3. STATES AND THE QUALITY OF GOVERNANCE

In recent debates about the role of the state, the idea of "(good) governance" has become increasingly prominent. "Good government" and its opposite are an old concern among societies and political theorists.[15] In contemporary debates "good governance" is widely regarded, explicitly or implicitly, as the goal of state formation and transformation efforts. The meaning of "governance" remains often rather vague.[16] Keohane and Nye define governance as "the process and institutions, both formal and informal that guide and restrain the collective activities of a group."[17] Broadly, we can take governance as the system of rule making, rule implementation and accountability in a given polity.[18]

As reflected in the empirical chapters, state-building in the former Soviet Union involves many problems with regard to the quality of governance: high levels of corruption, hybrid political regimes, disregard for the rule of law, and more. However, the language of 'governance' at times conflates various problems, symptoms and causes. Furthermore, many inquiries into governance are either descriptive (seeking to measure the quality of governance across cases and across time) or normative, prescribing particular models of governance (such as a liberal market system).[19] These two approaches need to be complemented with analytical inquiries into why governance is better in some polities than in others, and what factors drive the development of governance over time.

The relationship between state capacity and the quality of governance which frame this research are spelled out in Chapter 2, sections 1 and 2 below. Thus, the implicit normative 'goal' of this study is not only a capable, but also a 'well governed' state. While differentiating between these aspects of the state, the main line of inquiry is to disentangle the causal relationships which drive post-Soviet states towards or away from these goals.

1.1.4. WAVES OF STATE-BUILDING

A further aspect pertinent to this study is the assumption that state-building differs according to the time-period in which it occurs. Taking a cue from the democratisation literature, we might distinguish different *waves* of state-building.[20] Weber, and even more so Tilly were primarily concerned with the emergence of states in early modern Europe. Hall stresses that later instance of state-building differ due to the pre-existence of a model:

> Perhaps the most fundamental reason why it will always be impossible to establish sociological laws is the simple fact that key transformations have only occurred once. The endogenous emergence of capitalism only happened once, with all other states thereafter imitating something of whose social contours they had a good idea. [...] state formation in the developing world is likely to differ from that experienced by the European heartland.[21]

The last major wave of state-building before the 1990s was the post-colonial wave of the 1950s to 1970s in post-colonial Asia and Africa. A previous and somewhat forgotten wave of state-building in Eastern Europe occurred after WWI.

Within the post-communist wave of state-building there are two or three distinct 'sub-waves': largely peaceful state-building in most of the post-communist realm versus highly conflictual and protracted state-building in the former Yugoslavia (with ongoing and unfinished state-building processes especially in Bosnia-Herzegovina and in Kosovo); and overall successful state-building in those new states which acceded to the EU in 2004 (Slovakia, Slovenia, Estonia, Latvia, Lithuania), versus more troubled state-building and greater weakening of the state in the rest of the former Soviet Union.

The end of the Cold War was an important 'critical juncture' for the development of states especially, but not only in the post-communist region itself: in parallel to post-communist state-building there has been an increase in state collapse (particularly in Africa) and in humanitarian and security interventions (East Timor, Afghanistan, Iraq). As a result, the 1990s and 2000s are marked by a rising concern about "state-building strategies."[22]

All of these current waves of state-building take place in a situation in which state and institutional models are widely available.[23] This is reflected in an active trade in exporting various models to newly independent entities. Foreign experts advise on how to create tax and treasury systems, and promote various models of how to structure and operate a public administration. However, availability of state models is clearly not a sufficient condition for success, as the difficulty of improving state capacity in many countries attests.[24] When sophisticated institutions are created 'on paper' but fail to function in practice, they may even become an obstacle to the state-building effort.[25] The institutional export by the EU to Central Eastern Europe on balance is widely regarded as a success; but similar efforts in the Western Balcans have had less effect.[26] Thus, while the level of external support can play an important role, domestic conditions appear as crucial, and as a likely major source of divergence among cases.

This study is concerned with cases from one particular "(sub-)wave" of state-building. In this sense, the general international environment is kept constant; this environment includes the ready availability of institutional models and the shifting emphasis in the international discourse and advice from a focus on 'marketization' to a focus on capacity building. Furthermore, all cases share the same Soviet legacy, including the experience of people with regard to the state's role during Soviet times.

A further factor which is kept constant in this research is the absence of conflict at the outset of state-building.[27] Many instances of post-colonial state-building have been connected to struggles or even wars of independence—creating particular foundational myths, but often also problems of militaristic constellations in their aftermath, as in 19th century Latin America.[28] In comparison with these instances, winning independence and starting a process of state-building has been relatively peaceful in the post-Soviet space—as well as in the cases of Slovakia and the Czech Republic, but not in the former Yugoslavia, or in Afghanistan and Iraq.[29]

1.2. Fiscal perspectives on the state

Taxes are the sinews of the state.
(Cicero)

The revenue of the state is the state.
(Edmund Burke, Reflections on the Revolution in France)

As set out in the introduction, this research employs a fiscal 'lens' to explore the process of state-building, as fiscal issues are central to state-formation and transformation. In new states there is a need to establish extractive capacity, to learn how to formulate and execute budgets as well as to devise controls over the use of public funds. The way in which revenue extraction and the flow of expenditure is organized legally, formally, and informally defines in fundamental way the state-society and state-economy relationship. The Russian crisis in 1998 is a particularly visible symptom of what can happen when the establishment of a coherent fiscal system is failing.

The fiscal perspective, which this study adopts, is in some sense a narrow one since it blinds out other important areas of stateness, such as the provision of security.[30] However, adopting this particular limited perspective has several key strengths: since the fiscal system is central, it promises to reveal important insights about the state. Since it is a core feature, furthermore, it exists in any state, thus being useful for a comparative approach. Furthermore, fiscal systems are particularly well suited to study the dual aspect of the state, a key concept of this study which is developed in Chapter 2: the fiscal sphere reflects the state both as a necessary provider of solutions *and* as the cause of problems. Finally, a narrow perspective allows us to probe in more depth than a broad perspective does.

An important inspiration for this study are the meta-level accounts using a fiscal perspective, drawing from it major conclusions on the development of societies and states ("fiscal sociology"). Early 20th century meta-level arguments about fiscal issues were made by Goldscheid and Schumpeter. Goldscheid argues that, "the budget is the skeleton of the state stripped of all misleading ideologies."[31] Schumpeter refers to the fiscal sphere as both a dependent variable (of the culture, the social structure) and an independent variable (in its turn shaping the socio-economic structure of a state).[32]

More recent 'meta-level' accounts of taxing and spending have been presented by Margaret Levi and Mancur Olson.[33] Levi assumes that rulers are (always) revenue maximizers, who, however, operate under political and economic constraints (that are specific in terms of case and time period). She argues that historically more consensual forms of rulemaking (parliament) were conducive to higher levels of taxation as they improved (voluntary) tax compliance.[34]

Olson discusses different forms of rule (roving bandits, stationary bandits, and democracy) and the different public financial orders they would produce. His central idea is that roving bandits—i.e., competing lords or oligarchs—tend to over-extract and under-invest in public goods, since they lack an encompassing interest, i.e., security of being able to extract in the long run. A stationary bandit with secure control over the territory and its economy, in contrast, has a rational incentive not to over-extract and to provide those public goods which will enhance economic growth over time thus allowing sustained and increasing extraction. In a democratic polity Olson assumes—in contrast to Levi—that extraction would be less than under a (long-term) revenue-maximizing autocrat, since the majorities in which political leaders are interested do best under a combination of limited public-goods provision and 'keeping money in their pockets.'[35]

Looking beyond this tradition of 'fiscal sociology,' public finance specialists and economic historians have proposed three broad causes for the development of specific taxing and spending systems: (1) economic, (2) institutional, and (3) political. The economic argument holds that the economic base (level of development) limits and shapes the opportunities for extraction. Thus, in a more agricultural and generally a poorer economy, the share of revenue extraction relative to GDP is expected to be smaller than in an industrialized economy.[36] Also, the relative volatility of the economy matters: as Wildavsky has argued, poor countries with volatile economies will find it particularly hard to plan and execute budgets properly because they have fewer resources and reserves to act as a buffer in unexpected circumstances.[37] The relevance of the level of economic development among post-Soviet countries is explored in Chapter 5 which provides a broad tableau of all 15 post-Soviet countries.

A strand of literature has explored the importance of institutions, especially with regard to fiscal discipline (the size of the deficit) and other risks of 'overgrazing the commons' that exist in the fiscal sphere (Alesina, Poterba and Hagen).[38] However, this literature generally focuses on the effects of (different) institutions on outcomes, rather than the dynamic of institutional change itself, which is at the centre of this study and therefore is less directly pertinent.

The political argument is made in various ways, depending on the country or regional context. Steinmo has studied the link between broad social coalitions and the tax system (with a focus on the distribution of the tax burden). In politically less structured countries, tax privileges and budget subsidies are widely assumed to be one of the means by which rulers have to buy political support from narrow but decisive circles such as patronage networks.[39]

In the political economy literature on fiscal issues in Eastern Europe, attention has been focused on Russia on the one hand, and on Central Eastern Europe on the other. Particular attention has been given to the Russian financial crisis, triggered by a collapse of the revenue system, and the subsequent tax reform. Easter argues that Russian political elites early in the transition were pressured into bargaining with powerful groups (regional governors, corporate directors and private financiers), in order to ensure continued extraction;[40] however, this short-term ability to extract was bought at the price of losing more and more extractive powers in the longer term.[41]

Treisman and Shleifer claim that 'reform entrepreneurs' in government generally used the method of co-opting and buying-off opponents to various reforms—but failed to achieve this with regard to tax reform in the 1990s.[42] Jones Luong and Weinthal propose that subsequent to the 1998 crisis tax reform in Russia did become possible due to the vulnerability inflicted both on key economic actors and on government by global markets, which fostered "a desire for formal rules."[43] In this study, I consider the experience of tax reform in Russia (Chapter 11) in contrast to the more muddled and incremental process of reform in Ukraine (Chapters 6 to 8); and as reflecting the different ways of re-developing state capacity in these two countries.

Most comparative accounts of fiscal systems in transition countries have concentrated on the CEE region. Brusis and Dimitrov study the relationship between the set-up of the central executive and fiscal performance, defining 'fiscal performance' as a combination of "aggregate fiscal discipline and the predictability of the budgetary process."[44] They find that greater centralization (i.e., more power granted to prime ministers and ministers of finance) led to better fiscal performance. Similarly, analysing fiscal reforms in Poland, the Czech Republic, and Hungary Bönker concludes that "embedded autonomy" of the executive produced the best results in terms of fiscal reforms.[45] Furthermore, he finds that external actors—the IMF and the EU—played an important role particularly during the consolidation phase of reforms. The literature on CEE countries focuses on institutional arrangements and administrative capacities and largely ignores the issue of powerful interest groups, while the literature dealing with Russia tends to do the opposite.

Overall, the fiscal perspective adopted here follows a longer tradition of 'fiscal sociology' and political economy which considers the fiscal system as a key aspect of the state. This approach also has the advantage of allowing a detailed empirical analysis of the dependent variable and to explore some widely accepted propositions such as the relative importance of the level of economic development. At the same time, this is not meant to be an argument for exclusivity: this is one cut into the cake of state capacity; but it is the combination of perspectives which ultimately provides a full picture.

1.3. Regimes and states: the missing link in the transition debate

> The most important political distinction among countries concerns not their form of government but their degree of government. [...] Communist totalitarian states and Western liberal states both belong generally in the category of effective rather than debile political systems. The United States, Great Britain, and the Soviet Union have different forms of government, but in all three systems the government governs.
>
> *(Samuel Huntington[46])*

As O'Donnell has pointed out, the relationship between "degrees and forms of government," that is between states and regimes, is not well conceptualised.[47] On the one hand, transition theorists have focused on the impact of stateness problems on the prospects of democratization. Statist theorists, on the other hand, have tended to be primarily concerned about the impact of state interventions on economic development. Post-Soviet countries, in which the relationship between states and regimes, and between state-building and political transition is not constant either over time or across cases call for a further conceptualization of this relationship.

In this research, the key focus is on the effects of political regimes on the state-building process and especially on the dynamics at work—i.e., the effects of regime changes on the state-building process. Stressing this causal direction also draws attention to an important temporal logic: generally, political systems can be changed and political power can be consolidated in shorter periods than states and state capacity can be built, transformed and/or consolidated. Chapter 4 elaborates on the causal factors which presumably shape the building of capable and well-governed states, giving prominence to the role of regime change and the relative stability of regimes in this regard.

Among transition theorists on the one hand, Linz and Stepan, have argued that the pre-existence of a state is a requirement for the successful development of democracy.[48] Similarly, Lynch and Bunce have argued that the weakness of the Russian state is a key problem for its process of regime transformation—as well as for the prospects of economic growth.[49]

Authors focusing on the state, on the other hand, tend to leave the regime dimension out of their analysis: Evans, in his discussion of the state's embedded autonomy in East Asia does not inquire about the nature of the regimes. Accounts dealing with the state in developed countries generally assume *a priori* that they have democratic regimes.[50]

However, an insight which can be drawn from Evans as well as from Huntington is that effective states can occur both in democratic and in non-democratic regimes. Bunce has argued furthermore, that strong regimes and strong states are closely associated and that "[w]hen regimes are strong, they can lend power to states."[51] Robinson has sought to explain state-building problems in Russia due to the evolution of its political regime since tsarist times.[52]

In the early 1990s, questions of identity and nation-building stood in the foreground of the debate about post-Soviet countries. Only later did the building of state structures, including democratic and economic institutions begin to receive increasing attention.[53] Still, while many authors identified weak state capacity as a problem, treating it as an independent or an intervening variable, there were initially rather few attempts to treat the state as the dependent variable and at explaining the pre-conditions and pathways of state-building in the post-Soviet realm.[54] Often states are still designated as 'weak' while a deeper comparative inquiry about the relative degree of 'weakness,' and about causes, pathways, and dynamics is missing.

As a result, academic inquiry into the depth and dynamic of various 'stateness' problems emerged only rather late into the transition process. This has also held back a deeper analysis of how to improve stateness from a given status quo and about the potential avenues and possible pitfalls of external support of such processes.

Alongside the academic discourse on stateness, the concern about the state has also been taken up within post-Soviet societies themselves, as well as among international agencies involved in the promotion of state capacity and good governance in the region.[55] After an initial focus on 'liberalization,' international institutions paid increased attention to institution-building and the need to improve state capacity since the late 1990s.[56] In particular, IFIs funded major surveys on the interface between the state and economic and social actors.[57] The results show that relative to their income levels, post-communist and in particular post-Soviet countries were the most corrupt and provided the least public goods by inter-regional comparison in the late 1990s; while the situation appeared to have improved to some extent by 2002.[58] Regarding the focus of wider foreign assistance, Carothers has criticized that state-building was treated as a secondary problem. He furthermore raises the issue that promoting democratization by emphasizing power diffusion (decentralization, weakening the relative power of the executive branch) may have negatively affected state-building.[59]

Within post-Soviet societies, discussions about stateness problems frequently point to the need for a 'strong hand' approach: especially among state elites in Russia and other post-Soviet countries a preferred solution to stateness problems has been to strengthen so-called 'presidential verticals.'[60] The new Yushchenko government in Ukraine, in contrast, promised to remodel the state towards serving the people in its 2005 program (see Chapter 8).

Thus, this study has a dual thrust: firstly it seeks to bring the inquiry about processes of state formation more prominently into focus. Secondly, it seeks to raise the profile of interactions between political transitions and the capacity and quality of the state. Creating capable and well-governed states which are based on democratic regimes is a challenge for societies and elites; and when this challenge is not met over a period of time, the attractiveness of authoritarian alternatives rises, not least out of the perceived need to address stateness problems. Going down this route, societies might find themselves then trapped in a stronger, but still badly governed state with less flexibility for experiment and adjustments which are essential for broad-based social development (see also Chapter 4 and the empirical chapters on Belarus and Russia below).

1.4. Potential contributions of post-Soviet cases to general theories of state-building

As Hall and others have stressed, waves of state-building differ significantly from one another. Thus, each new wave can contribute to reconsidering existing debates on state-formation.[61] In this sense, exploring post-Soviet state formation provides further insights about the conditions for success and failure and about processes of state formation in various regions and at various times.

Furthermore, observation of post-Soviet cases are also pertinent for debates about the role of states. The poor functioning of many post-Soviet states contributes to generating a renewed recognition of the importance of states (and of institutions in general) for the functioning of societies and markets. Consequently, post-Soviet cases are stimulating research into how states operate, how they are created and changed, destroyed and consolidated. This concern is even more marked with regard to cases of 'fragile states' and 'failed states' in the developing world, and in the new 'quasi-colonial' areas from Bosnia-Herzegovina to Iraq.[62] The rapid shift of Eastern European countries more generally from socialist systems to a mix of liberalism and social democracy (marked by low tax rates, and the charging of formal and informal fees for many public services) also provides a challenging counterpoint to the ongoing and contested efforts at (welfare) state reform in Western Europe.

An especially fruitful angle for comparison between developing and transition countries is the relationship between regimes or regime change and state formation, as laid out in the previous section. This relationship has largely been neglected both by the statist literature and by the literature on democratic transitions; but it is an important one for many countries both in the post-Soviet region and beyond.[63] Post-Soviet cases provide an opportunity to explore different combinations of state capacities with democratic, authoritarian, and various hybrid regimes as this study will show.

Whereas state-formation occurs rather rarely, institution-building and institutional change are common phenomena. When we frame post-Soviet state-formation and transformation in institutionalist terms, they offer vast material on non-incremental institutional change (while in more stable Western cases incremental changes predominate), on the role of legacies, as well as on how institutions (and systems of institutions) are established, maintained, undermined, etc. In particular, post-Soviet countries serve to remind us that state-building is not a linear-progressive process but may be seriously derailed—even in relatively "developed" areas of the world.

Finally, from a methodological point of view, the post-Soviet area offers a quasi-experiment, since 15 countries embarked on state-building at the same time starting from a formally homogeneous system. This offers fruitful material for comparative research.[64] In particular, it allows us to test assumptions about potentially homogenizing factors (common legacies, the shared current international environment), against factors which could explain divergence (level of development, elite constellations, elite-society relations).

Thus, while this research does not strive to provide a general notion of state-building which would be valid at all times and in all cases, it strives to provide building blocks for the broader debate in comparative politics on institutional change and creation by using material from new and still under-researched cases. Moreover, regarding the region itself and its overall transition process, this study seeks to offer deeper insights into the causes of weak state capacity and the chances of overcoming this key problem.

Notes

1 Mann (1994), 333.
2 See Thomson (1995), 215; Fukuyama (2004).
3 Weber (1966), 27-28.
4 Tilly (1975), 70.
5 See Caporaso and Levine (1992), 181-196.
6 Caporaso and Levine (1992), 186.
7 Evans (1995).
8 Hellman, Jones, and Kaufmann (2000). "State capture is defined as shaping the formation of basic rules of the game (i.e. laws, rules, decrees, and regulations) through illicit and non-transparent private payments to public officials."
9 Olson (1982).
10 Mann (1994).
11 Caporaso and Levine (1992), 192.
12 Bates (1981); Grindle (1996).
13 Van de Walle (2001); Grindle (1996), 5.
14 Nozick (1975).
15 See, for example, the frescoes in the *Sala della Pace* in Sienna (14th century) depicting the good and bad government (*buon e mal governo*), also mentioned in Braithwaite and Levi (eds.) (1998), 1; as well as historic treatments such as Nicolo Machiavelli, *The Prince* (first published in 1515); Kautiliya, *Arthashastra* (an Indian treatise on statecraft written in the 4th century BC); Ibn Khaldoun, *The Muqaddimah* (1377).
16 For a good overview over the debate on 'governance' and various usages of the term, see Kjaer (2004).
17 Keohane and Nye, "Introduction," in: Nye and Donahue (eds.) (2000), 12. Another definition, which is similar but with a more explicit reference to power: "Governance refers to the process whereby elements in society wield power and authority, and influence and enact policies and decisions concerning public life, and economic and social development." From: www.gdrc.org/u-gov/work-def.html (The Governance Working Group of the International Institute of Administrative Sciences) [accessed: July 30, 2002].
18 Kjaer, (2004).
19 World Bank Institute, Governance Indicators, at http://www.worldbank.org/wbi/governance/govdata/; Hyden and Court (2004). A normative approach is taken for example by: The Heritage Foundation Index of Economic Freedom, http://www.heritage.org/research/features/index/.
20 On waves of democratisation, see Huntington (1991).
21 Hall (ed.) (1994), vol. II, 217.
22 Fukuyama (2004), Chapter 3. There was also a marked increase in UN membership: while in the course of the 1980s, membership grew by 5, over the 1990s it grew by 30 new members.
23 See Krasner (1984), 241.
24 DiMaggio and Powell (1983); Evans (1998).
25 This point is emphasised by Hausner, Jessop, and Nielsen (eds.) (1995), 17.
26 See White et al. (2003); Broadman et al. (2004).

27 The term 'mode of extrication' is borrowed from democratisation theory. See Fish (1999).
28 See for example, Wolf and Hansen, "*Caudillo* Politics: A Structural Analysis," in: Hall (1994), 219–230. Krasner (1999), Chap. 7: States after 1945.
29 There have been conflicts in some post-Soviet states such as Armenia and Azerbaijan (Nagorno-Karabakh), Moldova (Transnistria), Tajikistan, and Georgia (Abkhazia and South Ossetia). However, none of the post-Soviet states gained independence *as the result of armed conflict*; furthermore, the cases we select here for 'closer scrutiny' (Ukraine, Belarus, Lithuania, and Russia) were not engaged in armed conflict at the time of becoming independent, and except for Russia have not experienced armed conflict since then.
30 Furthermore, this study focuses on the national level and does not address intergovernmental (fiscal) relations or the local level itself.
31 Schumpeter, quoting from Goldscheid. See Schumpeter (1991), 100; from: Rudolf Goldscheid, *Staatssozialismus oder Staatskapitalismus*, 1917.
32 Schumpeter (1991), 100–101.
33 Levi (1988); Olson (1997).
34 As Chapters 5 and 9 show, this proposition is not borne out in the current constellation of post-Soviet countries. Some of the most authoritarian countries have the highest rates of extraction.
35 Olson (1997), 15: "The majority's interest in its market earnings induces it to redistribute less to itself than an autocrat redistributes to himself."
36 Ardant (1975). For a more detailed discussion of this relationship, see Burgess and Stern (1993). An adjacent stream of economic argument is that the type of economy is important: thus, it is important whether the economy is primarily based on natural resources, on foreign trade, or on domestic production and consumption. The first two provide particular opportunities for raising revenues, with implications for the way in which state and society interact (see Karl 1997; Moore 2004). In general, different tax 'handles', i.e. options for the state to collect revenues, are available in different types of economies.
37 Wildavsky and Caiden, "Prologue to Planning and Budgeting in Poor Countries," in: Wildavsky (2001), 199–213.
38 Alesina et al. (1999); Poterba and von Hagen, (1999).
39 Alfredo Baldini, "Parliamentary Dynamics and Fiscal Policy," in: Strauch and von Hagen (2000), 19–60; Robert Franzese, "Electoral and Partisan Manipulation of Public Debt in Developed Democracies," in: Strauch and von Hagen (2000), 61–85; Steinmo (1993); Ames (1987).
40 Easter (2002).
41 Piroska Nagy argues in a similar vein. Nagy (2000), see in particular 64–66, 88–106.
42 Treisman and Shleifer (2000). However, eventually tax reform was actually undertaken in Russia as discussed in Chapter 11.
43 Jones Luong and Weinthal (2002). A similar argument is suggested, but not elaborated in detail, in the 2002 EBRD Transition Report. EBRD, *Transition Report 2002*, 30.
44 Brusis and Dimitrov (2001).
45 Bönker (2000).
46 Huntington (1968).
47 O'Donnell (1993).
48 Linz and Stepan (1996), 16–24.
49 Lynch (2005); Bunce (2004).

50 See for example, Peters (1991); Evans (1995).

51 Bunce (2004), 217.

52 Robinson (2002).

53 According to Grzymala-Busse and Jones Luong, "One of the more curious, and persistent, missed opportunities in comparative politics is a productive dialogue between scholars of post-communist transitions and of the state." Grzymala-Busse and Jones Luong (2002), 529.

54 For a recent comparison of Kazakhstan and Kyrgyzstan, see Cummings and Norgaard (2004). On Russia see Sperling (2000); Smith (1999); and Lynch (2005). On the state in the wider post-communist region, see Nunberger (1999) regarding the administrative dimension; and Whitmore (2004) and Wolczuk (2001) on specific aspects of state- and institution-building in Ukraine (parliament; constitutional development). On Ukraine, see Kuzio (1998).

55 See Russell Bova, "Democratization and the Crisis of the Russian State," in: Smith (1999), 27-29.

56 These recommendations include among others the World Development Report 1997 *The State in a Changing World,* a chapter on "Governance in Transition" in the 1999 EBRD report, and Stiglitz (1998).

57 For example, the Business Environment and Enterprise Performance Survey (BEEPS), jointly by the EBRD and the World Bank, in which 6000 firms across 26 countries in the region were surveyed.

58 Hellman et al. (2000); Hellman, Jones, and Kaufmann (2000). EBRD (2002), 17-31. (chapter 2: "Progress in Transition and the Business Environment").

59 Carothers (2002), 17.

60 See Paul Globe, "A New Vocabulary For An Old Agenda," *RFE/RL NEWSLINE,* January 28, 2000. Paul Globe, "Strong and Weak," *RFE/RL NEWSLINE,* March 10, 2000; on Ukraine: "Ukrainian President says Referendum only Solution to Parliamentary Crisis," *RFE/RL NEWSLINE,* February 22, 2000; on Belarus: "Belarusian Administration Shake-up," *RFE/RL NEWSLINE,* November 28, 2000. For a good analysis about moves to strengthen the executive see Fish (2000).

61 See also Grzymala-Busse and Jones Luong (2002) on potential contributions from post-Soviet state-building to the general 'statist' literature.

62 Fukuyama (2004), Chapter 3.

63 See for example, Evans (1995). Evans does not discuss in depth the question of regimes and regime transition in the context of state capacity; see also, Carothers (2002).

64 Bunce (1999b).

CHAPTER 2.

A FRAMEWORK FOR ASSESSING STATES: SIZE, CAPACITY, AND QUALITY

This chapter provides a conceptualization of the state, developing a framework for empirically assessing different states. Understanding which states are more capable or are better governed than others, and establishing concrete indicators on which such an assessment can be based, is an essential first step. On this basis we can then inquire into the causes for the different development of states. Section 1 of this chapter sets out the three aspects of size, capacity, and quality. Section 2 focuses on the quality of the state and how it is related to the political regime. Section 3 discusses the size of the state, especially with respect to the fiscal sphere; and section 4 presents a more detailed framework for analyzing state capacity.

2.1. The three aspects of the state

The most frequent attribute for states is 'weak' or 'strong'; and some participants in the debate about post-communist or post-Soviet states have inquired whether (some of) these states have become too weak.[1] However, as Darden has pointed out, post-Soviet states can be relatively strong, but (very) badly governed, and some practices of bad government actually support the power of the state.[2] At the same time, when we look at fiscal developments or also at the provision of public services, the size of post-Soviet states has changed considerably compared to the state during the Soviet era, and has undergone considerable variation throughout the post-Soviet period.

The broad labels of a 'weak' or 'strong' state are therefore insufficient to assess the nature of a state. In order to assess states, it appears helpful to distinguish between three different aspects: the size of the state, the capacity of the state, and the quality of the state. The *size* of the state refers to the scope or extension of the state, i.e., the share of GDP it collects in revenues, the number of people the state employs, and the scope of tasks and responsibilities it assumes. A large size is not necessarily equivalent to a strong state—in the late USSR, the state was certainly very large, but it still lost the capacity to adopt and implement effective policies (see section 2 below).

State *capacity* is more precisely 'weak' or 'strong.' State capacity is framed here as the capacity to take decisions, to implement policies, and to exercise (managerial) control (see section 4 below). A further distinction can be made between the 'despotic capacity' and 'infrastructural capacity' of the state (drawing on Mann's terminology as discussed in Chapter 1). The main focus of this study is on the development of 'infrastructural capacity'—which is the aspect of capacity essential to supporting the social and economic development of societies. However, in many post-Soviet states, governments still rely to a considerable extent on 'despotic capacities', privileging the exercise of command over rules and procedures—which can also hinder the development of 'infrastructural capacity,' as the empirical chapters show.

The third aspect is the *quality* of the state. States which (still) rely to a considerable extent on despotic rather than infrastructural capacity are more likely to be affected by bad governance. However, the quality of the state may also suffer due to populist policies, or due to the power of 'opaque networks' and resulting state capture (see Chapter 4). There are several potential mechanisms for 'protecting' or improving the quality of the state: the presence of a 'benevolent dictator' or in a sense a 'single owner' of the state (as, for example, discussed by Olson; but involving the risks of tyranny, as pointed out in section 2), effective checks and balances between several power holders, and democratic accountability between elites and citizens.

The three aspects of the state are linked: weak or declining infrastructural capacity, as well as mismatches between the scope of the state and actual capacity, are assumed to have negative implications for the quality of the state and ultimately for societies (e.g., the state assumes to provide universal free health-care, but has not enough resources to finance the system adequately, which in turn promotes corruption). The following sections discuss these three aspects of quality, size, and capacity in more detail.

2.2. States as problems and solutions under various regimes

If men were angels, no government would be necessary. If angels were to govern men, neither external nor internal controls on government would be necessary. In framing a government which is to be administered by men over men, the great difficulty lies in this: you must first enable the government to control the governed; and in the next place oblige it to control itself. A dependence on the people is, no doubt, the primary control on the government; but experience has taught mankind the necessity of auxiliary precautions.

(Alexander Hamilton, James Madison, "On a Just Partition of Power," The Federalist Papers, 1788.)

A fundamental distinction in the thinking about states is that between *the state as a problem* versus *the state as the solution* (Evans).[3] The basic conflict between the need for some form of governance (as a solution to the problems of anarchy or anomy) on the one hand, and the risks of bad governance on the other hand is an old one in the social sciences and social philosophy. Hobbes argued particularly strongly for the need for a state, regarding any government as better than none

How many throats hath this false position cut, that a prince for some causes may by some certain men be deposed? [...] Lastly, how many rebellions hath this opinion been the cause of which teacheth that the knowledge whether the commands of Kings be just or unjust, belongs to private men, and that before they yield obedience, they not only may, but ought to dispute them?[4]

The 'state-as-solution-perspective' has been particularly strongly embraced by those who view the state as the main collective actor in bringing about fast economic growth in 'backward' countries, an idea initially proposed by Gerschenkron, and more recently elaborated by scholars focusing on the 'developmental state' in East Asia.[5]

In contrast, as Bastiat and others have observed, the state can also be regarded as a source of problems: "The state is the fictitious entity by which everyone seeks to live at the expense of everyone else."[6] While there is a cost attached to any state, there is considerable variation in the extent that the state becomes a source of problems. Empirical research on post-Soviet states and states in the developing world has pointed to the numerous ways in which the state can become a source of problems—through corruption, the skewing of the economic playing field in favor of politically influential groups and more generally through the abuse of the public domain for personal enrichment and the weakening of potential political competitors.[7] The perspective of the 'state as a problem' hence points to the range of risks associated with 'bad governance.'

Ensuring the quality of the state is a key challenge of state-building. Graph 2.1 maps the dual challenge of building capable states and ensuring that the potential negative aspects of the state are contained.[8] Some strands of thinking associate a larger scope or size of the state with a higher prevalence of the 'state as a problem' (see Chapter 1, section 1, and section 3 below). However, as the examples of the states emerging from the Soviet Union show, downsizing the scope of the state does not automatically result in a reduction of the 'state as a source of problems' or what we may call the dysfunctional aspects of the state. In fact, key aspects of downsizing the state, such as rapid privatization, involve considerable risks as powerful economic actors can emerge which subsequently 'capture' the state.

As Graph 2.1 depicts, the ideal is to develop a state which would fall into quadrant A, where the state is capable and where the state as a source of problems is kept in check. The worst situation is quadrant D, where the capacity of the state is low or moving towards state failure and where whatever capacity exists is more a source of problems than solutions and hence is dysfunctional from the perspective of society.

However, states may also fall into quadrant B, where some or even considerable state capacity exists, but state capacity is nonetheless primarily a source of problems rather than solutions (while quadrant C would be a situation of pre-state societies solving collective action problems without a state structure).[9]

The risks to the quality of the state, and the options for pursuing a well-governed state are closely linked to the nature of the political regime (matrix 2.1). As discussed in Chapter 1, section 2, Olson sees a 'benevolent dictator' or what he calls a 'stationary bandit' who takes an encompassing interest in the state as the best way to ensure the quality of the state. A stationary bandit who is secure in his rule can take a long-term interest in the economic welfare of the country (so as to maximize long-term revenue from it), and hence has an interest in building a state which promotes overall prosperity. However, in many situations, either no single ruler is able to secure his rule and so this is not an available option, or a more or less absolute ruler engages in tyrannical rather than benevolent rule.

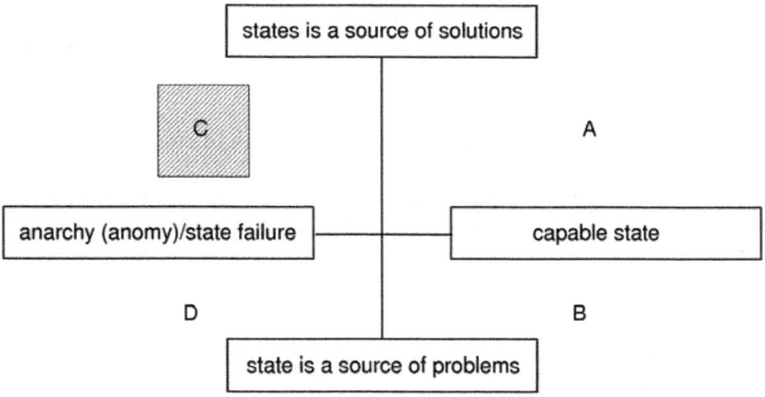

Graph 2.1: The dual challenge of state-building

(The left hand box refers to 'anarchy.' The more precise, but less commonly used sociological term is anomy. In its original meaning, 'anarchy' refers to the absence of a ruler, while 'anomy' refers to the absence of rules. In failed states, there may still be competing rulers, but rules have broken down.)

Democratic accountability is a second principle route for ensuring the quality of the state. The main mechanisms in this situation are bottom-up accountability, or the constraint the ruled can exercise on the ruling, and horizontal accountability (or 'checks and balances') within the political and state realm, in which different institutions and power-holders balance each other, usually based on a pre-defined set of rules.[10]

In unconsolidated, and/or hybrid regimes, in contrast, there may be some accountability, but it will be compromised or ineffective, or limited to certain groups whose interests 'steer' the state in ways which compromise its quality for society at large. Matrix 2.1 sets out these three broad regime options and the assets and risks with regard to the quality of the state.[11]

As the matrix points out, the range of risks is assumed to be especially broad in countries with hybrid political regimes; while the main advantage of hybrid regimes is that compared to authoritarian regimes they reduce the larger risk of tyranny—i.e., the risk of a state focused on the irrational goals and obsessions of a single leader or a small leadership clique (e.g., Albania under Enver Hoxha, or Turkmenistan under the leadership of Niyazov 'Turkmenbashi').

The main asset of a consolidated democratic regime with regard to the state is the existence of democratic accountability which helps to ensure that the state is predominantly a source of solutions, while the main risks are that politicians pursue populist decisions, following the short-term demands of groups or even majorities often in order to win elections, rather than ensuring that longer term challenges are addressed.

Matrix 2.1: Regime types and their assets and risks for the state realm

Regime type	Assets for state realm	Risks for state realm
consolidated authoritarian regime	autocrat (or single party) *may* have an encompassing interest ('benevolent dictator') – however, this is the exception rather than the rule	state (especially security apparatus) is used for oppression/risk of tyranny state benefits small circle/small oligarchy
hybrid/non-consolidated regime	risk of tyranny is lower than in consolidated authoritarian regime	state benefits a broader/competitive oligarchy state (administrative apparatus) is used for more or less hidden oppression to maintain the status quo endemic corruption higher risk of political instability/ low state capacity
consolidated democratic regime	democratic accountability helps to ensure that the state is (predominantly) a source of solutions	populist decision-making overload of particularist interests

2.3. The size of the state

The share of the budget relative to GDP is often used as a quantitative measure of the state. However, while variations in size are important, fiscal size is not equivalent to state capacity. States with a small to medium fiscal size such as South Korea (with a budget of 20 per cent of GDP in 1998) are regarded as the model of a capable developmental state; while the Russian Federation with a somewhat larger budget size has been perceived as a (dangerously) weak state (see Graph 2.2 below).[12] Furthermore, even fiscally large (or maximalist) states may be perceived as tied down like 'Gulliver' by numerous demands as Stark and Bruszt claim that late communist states were.[13]

However, I agree with Skocpol and others that the size of revenues is one important condition of state capacity. "A state's means of raising and deploying financial resources tell us more than could any other single factor about its existing (and immediately potential) capacities [...]."[14] A minimum size is a prerequisite for capacity because modern states assume a rather broad range of functions which require substantial staffing and funding: judges, teachers, and administrators have to be spread around often rather large territories, and they need to be paid sufficiently well if dysfunctional aspects of the state, such as corruption, are to be contained.

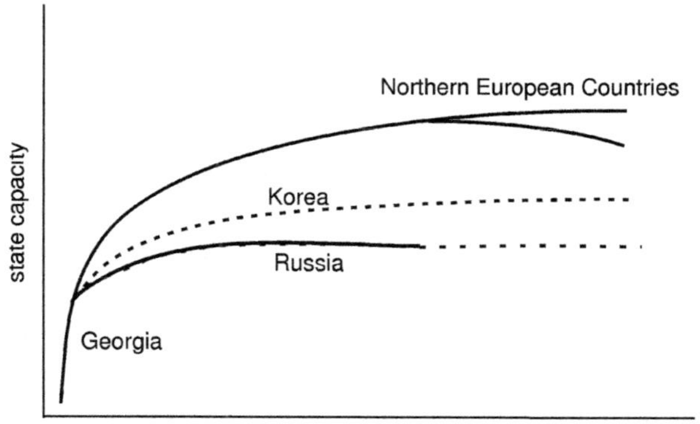

Graph 2.2: Assumed relationship between state revenues and state capacity

As the graph illustrates, a state with no or very low revenues (e.g., Georgia in the early 1990s) cannot be capable—so at the low level there is a close relationship. However, after revenues have reached a certain level, their further increase ceases to be a direct indicator of state capacity: in fact state capacity may even decline despite increases in size.

Furthermore, the input and output size of states may be mismatched. In the fiscal sphere, this results in a sizable and prolonged budget deficit. In a global perspective, considerable budget deficits emerged in the 1970s in many states, while since the 1990s there has been an international wave of reining in deficits.[15] The empirical chapters trace the evolution of fiscal size in post-Soviet states over time (for an overview see especially Chapter 5); including changes in the size of the fiscal deficit. Observing changes in fiscal size and in the (mis)match between the expected scope of the state and available resources—and how these are handled by political actors—provides an 'embedded' view of fiscal size, while avoiding confusing it superficially with state capacity.

2.4. State capacity: decision-making, implementation, and control

As set out in section 1 above, we can disaggregate three dimensions of state capacity: (1) the capacity to formulate policy (decision-making), (2) to implement policy effectively, and (3) the capacity to exercise (managerial) control. This section discusses each of these dimensions, and points to some of the key observations in the fiscal sphere which allow us to assess the relative capacity of a state.

2.4.1. DECISION-MAKING CAPACITY

The ability to make decisions is a fundamental aspect of state capacity which may, however, suffer from a number of problems. A common problem in stable, democratic societies is the blocking of reform decisions by numerous interest groups who expect to lose from the reforms sought.[16] In post-Soviet countries, we are confronted with three further problems. Firstly, in several post-Soviet countries, different branches of power (the president, the cabinet of ministers, the parliament) have engaged in competitive rule-making generating a situation in which rules were no longer taken as binding. This potential problem is also captured by the definition of a state by Tilly quoted in Chapter 1 which requires that different parts of the state have to be formally integrated. Therefore, one benchmark with regard to decision-making is whether decisions are treated as binding.

Secondly, there has often been a prolonged deadlock between the legislative and the executive in various post-Soviet countries (for example, in Ukraine and in Russia). This deadlocking was more fundamental than normal veto-playing since it was due to constitutional uncertainty and competition. It prevented the adoption of urgent reforms often for years in a situation of economic crisis. Both of these capacity failures (no integration; deadlock related to constitutional redefinition of roles) can impose considerable costs on private actors who either have to adjust to constant shifts or have to live with policy gaps.

A different problem is that decisions may be highly partial and benefiting particular and powerful interests, while hurting the interests of society at large. Partial decision-making can occur in more as well as less capable states, but it implies that for the majority of society the state becomes more of a problem and less of a provider of solutions.

Finally, post-communist states may also be *more* capable with regard to decision-making than stable OECD states, precisely because economic crisis, transition, and independence reduced the capacity of many groups to resist change. The volume and scale of decisions taken in post-Soviet countries which remodeled their economies, polities, and states has been astounding in some cases. In the post-Soviet universe, the Baltic states are examples of fundamental and overall rather successfully managed change based on many and fundamental decisions.

Decision-making capacity is closely linked to the political regime, since it occurs in the political realm—in the government and in parliament. The problems of competitive decision-making and of deadlock in particular are related to the situation of a hybrid and contested political regime; while they are less prevalent in post-Soviet countries which early on developed consolidated democracies or which re-created authoritarian regimes. In authoritarian Belarus, decision-making was centralized in the hand of the president, thus preventing deadlocks between parliament and president; while in Russia, Putin created a much more pliant legislature from 2000 onwards. While under an authoritarian regime decision-making as such is usually not a problem (since veto-players are excluded), decisions may nonetheless be partial, benefiting a small clique, or they may reflect the risk of tyranny, i.e., when decisions are based on the whims of a ruler although they hurt the interest of society (such as the decision of the Turkmenistani government to reduce the number of years of schooling).[17]

In a fiscal perspective decision-making capacity can be observed around various instances: regular decisions, such as yearly budgets, and 'big' decisions, such as major tax reform (and their preceding gestation period). With regard to annual budgets, good decision-making capacity would mean that these are adopted on time and are realistic (within the boundaries of a highly uncertain situation); and that different institutions interact constructively in the budgeting process. With regard to 'big' decisions—such as tax reform or the adoption of new budgeting practices—we can observe whether these are taken at all, how long they take to come to fruition, and what kind of trade-offs they entail (i.e. sometimes only the 'easy' parts of a reform are adopted, leaving the difficult questions unresolved and/or hiding the costs). Indicators for the prevalence of multiple and competing decision-making are the intensity of rule-making activities by different bodies; while decisions about tax privileges, for example, offer an opportunity to observe the degree to which decision-making is driven by particularistic versus encompassing interests. Overall, the fact of whether or not decisions are taken without prolonged deadlock and in a binding manner informs us about the sheer level of capacity, while the kinds of decisions which are taken, and the interests which motivate them can tell us something about whether they support more the aspect of the state as a solution or the state as a problem.

2.4.2 THE CAPACITY TO IMPLEMENT POLICY CHOICES

> Freedom cannot produce its best effects, and often breaks down altogether, unless means may be found of combining it with trained and skilled administration.
>
> *(John Stuart Mill, Considerations on Representative Government, Utilitarianism and Other Essays)*

The capacity to implement policy hinges upon the availability of effective institutions, i.e., bureaucracies willing and able to implement the tasks formulated by political elites. To be effective—as Evans has stressed repeatedly—bureaucracies need to be able to attract good bureaucrats, which in turn requires resources. As with state size, there is a matching issue: capabilities need to be matched to assumed roles.[18]

As we will see in the empirical chapters, implementation has posed serious challenges in post-Soviet countries. On the one hand, post-Soviet countries inherited considerable 'infrastructural' and implementation capacities developed during the Soviet era. On the other hand, the challenge of state-building in post-Soviet countries coincided with severe economic crisis, and (in a majority of countries) of transforming the role of the state. These all contributed to reducing the resources available for the state. The contraction of resources was greatest in the poorer, non-resource rich republics in the Caucasus and Central Asia, which had previously benefited from subsidies within the USSR.

The transformation of the state's role tends to reduce implementation capacity, at least initially: for example, when the banking sector is liberalized and enterprises are privatized, financial flows become harder to monitor, and the creation of new capacities in the tax administration is required. Thus, we can observe whether the gaps opened by transformation are addressed by developing new administrative capacity.

Furthermore, for overall state capacity, a close match between decisions and implementation is required. It is at the stage of implementation that we can observe whether or not decisions are in fact treated as binding. With regard to taxation and budgeting, we can particularly well observe whether decisions (set down in formal rules) are implemented fairly and consistently.

The linkages between decision-making and implementation capacity are likely to vary depending on the development of the political regime: for example, in an autocratic system, there may be few effective veto-players at the decision-making stage, which may facilitate decision-taking. However, it may be either not possible to implement decisions, or they may be damaging to society due to the inherent risk of tyranny. In a weak, unconsolidated democratic regime, in contrast, decision-making may be difficult, due to the reasons outlined above; while at the implementation stage decisions may be ignored or only partially followed, especially if there are competing decisions, and when the risk of reprimand for incomplete compliance is low.

An important issue in implementation in post-Soviet countries is finally, whether implementation is intentionally selective, i.e., whether and to what degree the administrative apparatus is (ab)used for political purposes—for example to punish independent media or businesspeople supporting opposition parties. Such abuses tend to reinforce problems of dysfunctionality (or the 'state as a source of problems') as outlined above.

As for the decision-making dimension, the fiscal perspective offers good possibilities to empirically observe implementation capacity; both on the extraction and on the expenditure side. We can observe the degree to which formal tax rules are complied with, including the degree of voluntary *versus* enforced compliance.[19] Furthermore, we may observe the institutional development of the tax administration as such; how this administration is perceived by the business community and the population (with a view to the issue of selective implementation and dysfunctionality). With regard to budgets, implementation capacity implies that budgets are fulfilled largely as planned, both overall and with regard to individual spending categories, or are adjusted according to existing rules.[20]

2.4.3. CONTROL

A dominion then, whose well-being depends on any man's good faith, and whose affairs cannot be properly administered, unless those who are engaged in them will act honestly, will be very unstable. On the contrary, to insure its permanence, its public affairs should be so ordered, that those who administer them, whether guided by reason or passion, cannot be led to act treacherously or basely. (Baruch Spinoza, *Political Treatise*, Chapter 1, 6)

"*Governor*: I have called you together, gentlemen, to tell you an unpleasant piece of news. An Inspector-General is coming.

Luka Lukich: But why, Anton Antonovich? What for? Why should we have an Inspector?

Ammos: The Government is shrewd. It makes no difference that our town is so remote. The Government is on the look-out all the same—" (Nikolai Gogol, *Revisor*, 1836)

The (managerial) control function in the state generally serves to check whether implementation has actually followed the decisions taken. Control can be embedded in a wider system of accountability (especially in states based on democratic regimes).[21] However, under any form of government, there is a necessity for top-down, or 'managerial' control which the top executive exercises over the administration at large.[22] Even if bureaucrats are not assumed routinely to seek private material gain, controls need to be in place in order to ensure that they indeed predominantly serve the public good.

Similar to the decision-making dimension of state capacity, the political regime influences in important ways if and how control is exercised. Hierarchical control from above is the dominant form of control in authoritarian systems—including the Soviet Union, where appeals to Moscow were often the only possible avenue to act against local or regional level corruption.[23] In democracies by contrast, managerial control is embedded in a wider system of accountability of the governing to the governed, which works through elections, a free press and wider public debate. Importantly, in modern democratic states with a sound rule of law, managerial control also involves the governed directly, especially via formal avenues of complaint such as ombudsmen, administrative courts, charters of tax-payers rights, etc.

Dedicated institutions—such as audit institutions—involved in horizontal control are important as well, since they collect evidence on actual practices of the administration. These principally 'horizontal' institutions are shaped by the political regime and the wider set of accountability relationships: thus, in an autocratic system, audit institutions may exist, but report primarily to the head of state, while in a democratic system, such institutions report to parliament and the public.

Importantly, control over the public administration can be exercised following a 'defensive' or a 'supportive' logic. According to the 'defensive' logic, the main aim of the public administration is to support the preservation of existing power structures. Accordingly, the administration may be used to prosecute political opponents or public activists, and even corruption may be deliberately fostered, since it allows the usage of threats against potentially disloyal bureaucrats later on. The 'supportive' logic of control, in contrast, seeks to ensure that the administration works according to established rules and supports public policies. Thus, under this logic the effort is to limit and reduce, rather than exploit the problem of public sector corruption and arbitrariness.

Exercising control based on a 'defensive logic' involves risks for implementation capacity and for the legitimacy of the state: the corruption which is tolerated or fostered can undermine the whole system of governance over time (i.e. 'slip out of control'), and citizens may resent and seek to evade the control of a state which is perceived as deeply corrupt, which can have a negative effect on the state's capacity to tax (since under a corrupt bureaucracy bribery can protect those who break rules).

In many post-Soviet states, the two logics may be followed in parallel: on the one hand, there are attempts to ensure the regular working of the administration, while on the other hand, control is also exercised in order to preserve power. Such duality tends to damage state capacity. The dual logic can also be a source of discrepancies between formal institutions and *de facto* practices: as Rose-Ackerman has pointed out in her study on corruption and government, even if institutions of control—such as audit chambers or anti-corruption commissions—are in place they need not necessarily work well, since they are not fully meant to.[24]

The fiscal perspective allows a number of ways in which to observe the existence of effective control and the logic that it follows. Generally, tax administrations are among the most corruption-prone institutions of a state, so a relatively 'clean' tax administration is an indicator of effective control, operating on the base of 'supportive logic.' A tax administration which is used for political purposes, and which, for example, imposes fines on businesspeople known to support the political opposition, reflects that control in the state is based on a 'defensive logic.'

With regard to expenditures, we can observe internal and external control and audit mechanisms. These mechanisms may be more or less effective—for example, an audit institution may report mishandling of funds, but these reports are not followed up on. Like tax administrations, mechanisms for control over public expenditures can also be used to punish opponents—primarily those within the administration itself, who can be found guilty of misusing funds.

As Chapter 3 will develop further, for understanding post-Soviet state-building it is important to note that the capacity and the quality of the state had been hollowed-out during the late Soviet period, and had eroded even further during the Soviet Union's protracted break-up (see also Chapter 5, section 1). During the Soviet period, key decision-making had been located at the center in Moscow. Thus, the new post-Soviet entities found themselves in a situation of having to create new 'heads' for their states, while inheriting an administration which had been created under the old system. In addition, economic crisis and shrinking revenues meant that the new states had little resources to maintain and rebuild their administrations properly. Furthermore, the prevalence of informality was not reduced by independence and market liberalization as may have been expected,[25] but rather tended to grow as formal institutions weakened; and contributed to the weakening of implementation capacity.

Notes

1 Holmes (1997); Way (2003).
2 Darden (2002).
3 See Douglass North, "A Framework for Analyzing the State in Economic History," in: Hall (1994), 326. The terminology is taken from Evans (1992).
4 Thomas Hobbes, *De Cive*, [On the citizen], Author's Preface to the Reader.
5 Gerschenkron (1962); Haggard and Kaufman (1992); Woo-Cumings (1999).
6 Frederic Bastiat, *The State* (Selected Essays on Political Economy, § 5.20) (1995).
7 Ames (1987).
8 North explicitly acknowledges this duality of states but similarly to Hobbes emphasizes the state as solution: "[...] it is still essential to stress that the basic precondition for all economic progress is the existence of a state and that throughout history, individuals given a choice between a state—however exploitative it might be—and anarchy have decided on the former." North (1994), 328.
9 Quadrant C would also be the 'ideal' of an anarchist utopia.
10 Schedler et al. (1999).
11 The classification of three broad regime types—consolidated authoritarian, hybrid, and consolidated democratic—is deliberately kept simple for reasons of parsimony.
12 In this analysis, strength only refers to domestic strength and not to the international role of a state.
13 This is sometimes ignored by analysts who equate revenues with strength. See Easter (2001), 14; "in short, revenue enhances state strength, and strong states claim more revenue."
14 Evans, Rueschemeyer, and Skocpol (eds.) (1985), 17.
15 For example, the European stability pact.
16 Germany and France in the 2000s. On the theory of veto-players, see Tsebelis (2002).
17 See "Turkmenistan's Education System in Downward Spiral," *Eurasianet*, May 5, 2004.
18 World Development Report (1997), 3-7.

19 A high degree of voluntary compliance is preferable since it reduces the cost of tax collection. See Leitzel (2003).
20 In this regard, economic volatility and shocks can weaken implementation capacity.
21 Schedler, Diamond and Plattner (eds.) (1999).
22 See also White and Hollingsworth (1999), 168–69.
23 Willerton (1992); Christian (1982).
24 Rose-Ackerman (1999), 163 (Chapter 3).
25 See Leitzel (1995).

CHAPTER 3.

THE DYNAMIC OF CHANGE: STATE-BUILDING AS INSTITUTION-BUILDING

> In a country such as the former USSR, there existed only one interest—the interest of a totalitarian state. [...] And now the state—the monopoly—suddenly and irrevocably falls. Immediately, hundreds, thousands, of various interests, large and small, private, collective, national, rear their heads to [...] identify themselves, define themselves, and emphatically demand the rights long denied them. In a democratic state there is of course also a multitude of various interests, but the contradictions and conflicts between them are resolved or softened by experienced, well-tried public institutions. Whereas here there are no such institutions (and there won't be any anytime soon!).
>
> *(Ryszard Kapuscinski, Imperium, 1994)*

This chapter shifts the perspective from the state as a static entity to the *processes* of state formation and transformation. Section 1 introduces the notion of the state as an institutional structure and frames state-building as a specific form of institution-building. With a view to the experience of post-Soviet state-building it is stressed that institutional change may involve phases of deterioration as well as transformation or restoration and re-building.

In sections 2 and 3, I address three aspects of institution-building and institutional change: costs, types, and sequences/results. In section 2, I discuss the different costs and benefits of institution-building via change or via restoration. In section 3, I argue that there are four types of institutional change which involve different degrees of difficulty to achieve. Section 4 considers the discrepancies between formal and informal institutions widely observed in post-Soviet states.

3.1. State-building as institutional change —deterioration and re-building

States can be regarded as institutional meta-structures or as institutional 'machineries' as Claus Offe has called them.[1] This institutionalist view of the state has been explored in the context of post-Soviet state-building by Sperling and others;[2] and has also gained attention from international financial institutions engaged in institutional reform.[3]

Initially, the institutionalist literature was primarily concerned with demonstrating that institutions matter—pitting this argument against neo-liberal discourse and concentrating on the effects of institutions on outcomes. Theoretical and empirical research into how institutions originate and change is still evolving as North, Bates and others point out.[4] Research by Thelen and others provides us with a basis for conceptualizing institutional change, while, as Schedler reminds us, research on the origins of institutions has been carried out in many variations also outside the realm of the current 'institutionalist' literature.[5]

The institutionalist literature originated around research on the EU and OECD countries, i.e. around systems which are relatively stable. When applying institutionalist thinking to post-Soviet (and other non-OECD) countries, there is greater variation in institutional features and development and hence a need to adapt the analytical framework. This concerns especially the direction of change, which is not necessarily progressive. State-building in post-Soviet countries starts with the bits and pieces of the previously existing structure and involves institutional destruction as well as institutional change.[6] Thus, in this context, we can distinguish institutional destruction ('de-institutionalization'), institutional transformation (altering existing institutions), and institutional creation (building new institutions) as different potential elements of 'institutional change.' Apart from destruction, transformation, and creation, we may furthermore, talk about 'institutional restoration' when ex-Soviet institutions, which had deteriorated but not dissolved during *perestroika*, are reinvigorated. Depending on the extent of change versus restoration, informal rules and the wider environment are being transformed as well.[7]

Institutional deterioration involved several elements: the break-up of the Soviet Union decapitated the institutional structures of the successor states by cutting off the Union-level institutions—which had performed important functions ranging from policy formulation and decision-making to exercising control over republican level institutions.

The end of the USSR furthermore also ended the monopoly of the Communist Party which had been the key institution providing integration, coordination, and control, albeit with decreasing effectiveness. The CPSU was not an intermediary organization in the sense of a party in a polyarchy. Rather, it was at the center of the edifice of governance. It was within the Party structures that the two capacities of decision-making and of control had their ultimate arbiter, while state structures 'proper' were primarily left with the task of implementation.[8] Hence, its collapse had enormous repercussions for the system as a whole.

Moreover, the breakup of the USSR had been preceded by a prolonged period of deterioration in the late Soviet period. Both state and Party structures of governance had been seriously eroded due to falling credibility (legitimacy and threat of punishment), and due to deliberate policy changes which devolved power and gave more freedom to economic and social agents. This period culminated, as has been described by Solnick, in a "bank run" when—in anticipation of the USSR's dissolution—agents of the state apparatus began to expropriate state resources for private gain at an accelerating pace.[9] Thus, at the start of independence, the level of institutionalization or the "degree of governance" in post-Soviet countries had been significantly eroded.[10]

The overall process of post-Soviet 'state-building' involves the elements of institutional deterioration, re-building, and restoration to different degrees over various time periods. As we will see, some post-Soviet countries preferred state formation over the transformation of the state's role, primarily via institutional restoration (as, for example, in Belarus and Uzbekistan). In others, considerable institutional destruction took place, but subsequent processes of institutional creation were derailed. I will return to these points when discussing types of institutional change as well as the question of divergent pathways in Chapter 4 below.

3.2. The costs and risks of institutional change

Institutions and institutional systems create an incentive structure and stimulate system-specific investments. Thus, if the institutional system creates incentives for piracy, then people invest in becoming good pirates.[11] As a consequence, institutional change is difficult and, moreover, it is costly.[12] According to North, "[s]tability is accomplished by a complex set of constraints that include formal rules nested in a hierarchy, where each level is more costly to change than the previous one."[13] Thus, the deterioration and the transformation of a whole institutional structure from top to bottom are extremely costly. Furthermore, institutional transformation involves risks, such as "getting stuck" with a poorly functioning institutional system. When an old order is thoroughly eroded and dismantled it cannot be clear at the outset whether the society involved will be able to build something better in its stead and how long this process may take.[14]

Surprisingly, the cost of institutional change has received relatively little attention. Popov addresses the issue:

> To put it differently, Gorbachev's reforms of 1985–91 failed not because they were gradual, but due to the weakening of the state institutional capacity leading to the inability of the government to control the flow of events. Similarly, Yeltsin reforms in Russia, as well as economic reforms in most other FSU states, were so costly not because of shock therapy, but due to the collapse of the institutions needed to enforce law and order and carry out manageable transition.[15]

In a similar vein, a UNDP report on *The Shrinking State* in post-communist countries warned in 1997:

> This is not to deny the importance of macroeconomic and financial stability, fiscal adjustment and reform of public finance, but rather to point out that such reforms could be costly in terms of loss of government capacity to oversee the process of transition and market-building. When carried out in a rapid manner and with no support for building governance capacity, fiscal policy reform could reduce government effectiveness at a time when in fact more of it is needed as the State in transition is required to undertake the new and complex functions of market-building and market regulation.[16]

While this study does not attempt a rigorous assessment of the costs of various paths of institutional change, it draws attention to the importance of costs and risks. For example, there seems to be an association between the pathway of institutional change chosen and the scale of GDP that was lost during the transition recession. Those countries which chose to restore the previous system initially retained a much higher level of their previous GDP than the others (see Chapter 5, and Appendix, Table I.1.1).

Institutional creation may be more costly than restoration at least in the short to medium term since the creation of new institutions requires adjustment and re-tooling (from pirates to shipbuilders, for example), the costs of abandoning the old infrastructure, etc. Furthermore, since creation involves the agreement on a new and unknown model—and agreement on the model to chose may take time—this path tends to be more challenging than institutional restoration. As the empirical observations in this study will show, sometimes sub-optimal institutions are further improved later on, while sometimes they remain in place for considerable periods of time.

Furthermore, the cost and gains of institutional change are unequally distributed in a society; and institutional deterioration in general tends to increase inequality since it involves a reduction in redistribution mechanisms. The unequal distribution of costs and benefits during the initial transformation opens up a gap in wealth (especially due to privatization) and income. The extent of inequality emerging during transition may also have an impact on the kind of new institutional system which is eventually established.

3.3. Types of institutional change

As described in the previous section, 'institutional change' can include processes of deterioration as well as of re-building. Furthermore, we can distinguish different types of institutional change, i.e., whether institutional change is intentional or unintentional, whether it is a 'big leap' or incremental (evolutionary) change, and whether it involves distributional issues or rather not.[17] The combination of these characteristics can inform us about the likely level of difficulty involved.

'Big leap' institution-building refers to large-scale reforms, such as reforming the administrative order of a country, or adopting major new laws (such as tax codes). Big leap institutional change is necessarily intentional (while it may have important unintended consequences); furthermore, it will require explicit agreement on a model to follow (a 'focal point') and the overcoming (or cooptation) of veto-players. 'Big leap' institutional reform should be most difficult when it is concerned with major distributional issues—at least as long as the losers of the change have any veto power.[18] Since such 'big leap' reforms are difficult, they are likely to occur in 'fits and starts' rather than in a linear and easily predictable fashion. Furthermore, 'big leaps' require decision-making capacity to be achieved.

Evolutionary institutional change appears to be relatively less difficult; it will often be subject to processes of learning and does not require the same broad agreement; it may not even be intentionally pursued by particular actors. Evolutionary change should be least difficult when few distributional issues are at stake (or are obvious for the actors involved), when Pareto-improving solutions are available and the up-front costs of the institutional change are small. Thus, for example, new governments and new parliaments may agree over time to better procedures for budget negotiations—these may improve the efficiency both of bureaucrats and of MPs (i.e., they are Pareto improving). Such agreements are likely to be easier to come by in parliamentary systems in which important committee members and members of the government belong to the same party (i.e., no major distribution of power issues are involved) and somewhat more difficult in semi-presidential systems where the distribution of power between the executive and parliament tends to be more deeply contested.

Matrix 3.1: Types of (positive) institutional change

	Big leap	Evolutionary
Distributional	most difficult	intermediate
Distributional issues not obviously involved	intermediate	least difficult

"Positive" institutional change signals that these are changes which seek increases and/or improvements, rather than decreases in levels of institutionalization. Positive change tends to be more difficult than "negative" change, i.e., the dismantling of institutions.[19] In the early stages of transition the dismantling of institutions—the abolition of price controls, the abolition of licensing systems for foreign trade, etc.—stood in the foreground. Advocates of shock therapy advised to undertake as many 'big *bang*' changes—that is, efforts at dismantling the old order—at the beginning of the transition period as possible, when it was difficult to calculate their effects, and resistance was presumed to be weakest. A crucial idea was that this would change incentives for economic agents who would rapidly react and start to re-build the economy on new foundations.

In several CEE and in the Baltic states this succeeded; but it did so since dismantling was combined with fundamental capacities of the state to steer institutional change and, especially in Poland and in Hungary, to organize redistribution on a considerable scale to those groups who were made worse off. In the former Soviet Union, in contrast, the intentional 'big bang' coincided with an ongoing process of unintentional long and deep institutional erosion.[20] Consequently, the capacity for digesting institutional change and creating a new institutional structure was weaker.

Thus, intentional negative institutional change can work in a situation in which many other parts of the institutional machinery are relatively robust, but it involves especially high risks in situations where they are not. Particularly in such situations, the re-building of new institutions may turn into a protracted and muddled process.

3.4. The importance of formal-informal discrepancies

A state functions based both on formal and informal rules. In many situations, informal rules are broadly supportive of formal rules. When the two diverge and become conflicting, in contrast, this signals a general deterioration of institutional capacity, and is usually associated with a rise in the dysfunctionality of the state. Discrepancies between formal and informal rules can increase due to a loss in state capacity, as well as due to intentional efforts at preserving the distribution of power by perverting the public administration as discussed in Chapter 2, section 4.

As North points out in his seminal book, *Institutions, Institutional Change and Economic Performance*, informal institutions are crucial for the functioning of any formal set of rules.[21] Informal institutions *enable* formal institutions to function: "Informal constraints... allow people to go about the everyday process of making exchanges without having to think out exactly the terms of an exchange at each point and in each instance."[22]

During the Soviet period, informal rules allowed the system to function; but at the same time, there was a particularly stark contradiction between the formal and the informal.[23] Officially, market exchanges and profit-making were forbidden while at the same time the informal or "second" economy eased the shortages of consumer goods as well as production inputs.[24] Moreover, as Willerton has argued, there was a "second polity" of patronage networks which were "publicly decried" while at the same time "few [countries] have been as influenced by it [patronage relations] as the Soviet Union."[25] The rigidity of communist ideology (in its demands and depiction of how elites should behave, in its denial of profit-seeking) on the one hand, and the suppression of a free press and an open opposition able to expose discrepancies on the other, fostered an increasing divergence of formal rules and actual behavior. Similarly, as Jowitt has pointed out, an important legacy of communism was the sharp division between the realms of the official and the private, the pervasive evasion of formal rules, and the high level of distrust towards the state.[26]

This implies that there is a strong tradition of distrusting the state and subverting formal rules.[27] This discrepancy between formal and informal rules has continued among post-Soviet countries—but to varying degrees. Black or shadow economies are estimated to be large in most post-Soviet countries.[28] Gaining independent statehood, allowing market forces to operate (in most post-Soviet countries), and establishing a democratic system of governance (in some post-Soviet countries) might be assumed to have brought formal and informal institutions into greater congruence. However, this is not necessarily the case as weakness in state capacity on the one hand, and abuses of the formal system driven by a 'defensive' logic of government on the other hand, maintain or even increase such discrepancies.

Observations about formal-informal discrepancies are therefore supplementary indicators for the capacity and the quality of the state, or the degree to which the state is a source of problems. There are several comparatively collected indicators about the degree to which such formal-informal discrepancies exist in post-Soviet countries. These include estimates about the size of the shadow economy relative to GDP, and various types of surveys such as the BEEPS and the Corruption Perceptions Index (CPI) indicating levels of corruption. Furthermore, surveys about trust in public institutions indicate the extent to which the societies of these countries see various parts of the state as functioning.[29] While formal-informal discrepancies are hard to measure precisely, and hence such indicators need to be used with some caution, considering a set of such indicators rather than individual ones can help us to assess at least broad trends and the relative position of a particular case.

In the empirical chapters, this study stresses the frequently neglected aspect of institutional deterioration and its implications for the subsequent trajectories of institutional change. It addresses the long and rather tortuous period of re-building which followed from this starting phase. The processes of institutional re-building were not linear and even partial results often remained contested and unclear in their effects.

In general, the fiscal sphere reflects the different degrees of the various types of institutional change rather well: it involves incremental changes as well as (attempts at) 'big leap' reforms. Some improvements in the budget process were evolutionary, involving learning, changes of personnel over time, etc. Tax codes and budget codes, in contrast, are 'big leap' reforms, and tax codes in particular necessarily involve major distributional issues. Generally, 'big leap' reforms play a bigger role in countries engaging in economic reform than in those which pursued a restoration of the old order, such as Belarus. Some changes brought overall improvements, while some institutions remained rather ineffective, or involved the development of major dysfunctionalities (e.g. tax administrations). Thus, the fiscal sphere provides a number of important indicators which reflect the various elements of a broad process of institutional re-building.

Notes

1 Offe (1996), 62.

2 Sperling (ed.) (2000), 3. See also Clemens and Cook (1999) 25, 443: "Disaggregating the monolithic entity of 'the state' also facilitates exchanges with institutionalist arguments developed in organizational analysis, social psychology, and simulation studies of social dynamics."

3 See EBRD (2000), 26.

4 Waldner (1999), 5; Robert Bates "Macropolitical Economy in the Field of Development," in: Alt and Shepsle (eds.) (1990), 48; Jack Knight and Douglass North, "Explaining the Complexity of Institutional Change," in: Weimer (ed.) (1997), 349-354.

5 Thelen (2002); Andreas Schedler, "Restraining the State: Conflicts and Agents of Accountability," in: Schedler, Diamond and Plattner (eds.) (1999), 336.

6 Von Beyme (2001), 8.

7 Considerable interest in institution-building and institutional change in Eastern Europe has developed. See, for example, Elster, Offe, and Preuss (1998); Nørgaard (2000); von Beyme (2001).

8 See Srivastava (1999).

9 Solnick (1998); Solnick (1996).

10 Jones Luong has stated this for Russia: "The fact that the Soviet Union was itself a collapsed state when the Russian Federation emerged as its chief successor is crucial to understanding the elite attitudes and behavior [...]" Pauline Jones Luong, "The 'Use and Abuse' of Russia's Energy Resources: Implications for State-Society Relations," in: Sperling (2000), 31. See also Helmut Wiesenthal: "Die Politische Organisation des Unwahrscheinlichen [The Political Organization of the Improbable]," in: Hinrichs, Kitschelt, Wiesenthal (eds.) (2000), 197.

11 Pierson (2000a), 256, citing North.

12 Pierson (2000a), 256; and Pierson (2000b).

13 North (1990), 83.

14 See Clifford Gaddy and Barry Ickes, "An Evolutionary Analysis of Russia's Virtual Economy," in: Cuddy and Gekker (2002), 76.

15 Vladimir Popov, "Strong Institutions are more Important than the Speed of Reforms," in: Cuddy, and Gekker (eds.) (2002), 65.

16 UNDP (1997), 1.

17 The term 'big leap' change is chosen to signal a big (non-incremental) institutional improvement; in this sense, the 'big leap' is the opposite movement to the 'big bang' advocated by shock therapy in the early 1990s.

18 See Schedler (1999), 333; Knight in particular has stressed the importance of whether institutional changes have distributional effects or not and that distributional conflicts may

affect institutional change as much as or more than the search for better (functional) solutions. See Knight (1992).

19 Grindle (2002).

20 See also Johnson (2001).

21 North (1990), 83.

22 North (1990), 83, 88.

23 "In real life, an enterprise, having received its authorization and needing the right goods on time and in sufficient quantity, as a rule is compelled to resort to corruption." Simis (1982), 97.

24 Wittkowsky (1998), 98: "The roots for the illegal economic activity lie also in the deficiencies of the planned economy. [...] Since most economic plans were inconsistent, strategies for achieving the fixed production goals had to be developed at the enterprise level [...]. In the illegal procurement markets, bribery and corruption became conditions for success in the day-to-day activity [of enterprises]."

25 Willerton (1992), 9.

26 Jowitt (1992).

27 UNDP (1997), 5.

28 Schneider and Enste (2000), Table 3.

29 While the CPI and the BEEPS provide comparative data, surveys on trust collected in individual countries are not fully comparable across time and cases. However, data tends to be sufficiently uniform to allow for simple comparisons on broad trends.

CHAPTER 4.
A MODEL OF POST-SOVIET STATE-BUILDING TRAJECTORIES

The fiscal perspective on post-Soviet state-building presented here involves two analytical steps. The first is to use observations from the fiscal sphere to evaluate the progress of building state capacity, i.e. to assess states and state-building processes as set out in Chapters 2 and 3. The second is to analyze *causes*: What drives some post-Soviet states to be more capable and to be better governed than others? And what causes individual post-Soviet states to develop in certain directions over time?

As elaborated in Chapter 3, when analyzing state-building and institutional change, we are interested in a process and its results. Apart from the Baltic states, post-Soviet state-building is widely judged to be seriously defective. Problems with dysfunctional aspects of the state abound; and a number of post-Soviet countries have reverted to more or less authoritarian political systems, not least in order to shore up state capacity.

Section 1 of this chapter presents a causal model of state development. Section 2 then offers a more detailed discussion of the presumed individual causal factors and the ways in which they are assumed to affect state-building. Section 3 focuses on the central interaction between institutional deterioration (as a key feature of the 'starting point'), and the degree, timing, and type of political consolidation. Based on this I outline four trajectories of post-Soviet state development.

4.1. The causal model

The process of state-building and the evolution of state capacity are shaped by a number of factors and their interaction. The key interaction which this research focuses on is that between institutions on the one hand and actors in the political sphere and in wider society on the other hand. A macro model of these interactions is presented in Graph 4.1 below. Overall state capacity and the quality of the state are the dependent variables.

Institutions (box II) undergo far-reaching change in post-Soviet countries, so the incentives and constraints they provide for actors are in a process of fundamental reconfiguration (arrow 1). As set out in Chapter 3, section 1, this institutional deterioration (resulting from the erosion and break-down of the Soviet Union) has an initial important impact. Some actors—especially those holding high political office, or controlling substantial economic resources and organized groups in society—can seek to influence the process of institutional re-configuration (while others lack the power and resources to do so) (arrow 2). Furthermore, structural factors have an impact on institutions and actors (arrows 3 and 5). This study considers the level of development and to some extent the prevalence of nationalism, but does not explore the impact of conflict on state-building, since it concentrates on four cases in which conflict played no major role. External influences can also be important. Chapter 5 will in particular explore whether international influences are likely to prevent successful state-building in a 'peripheral' region.

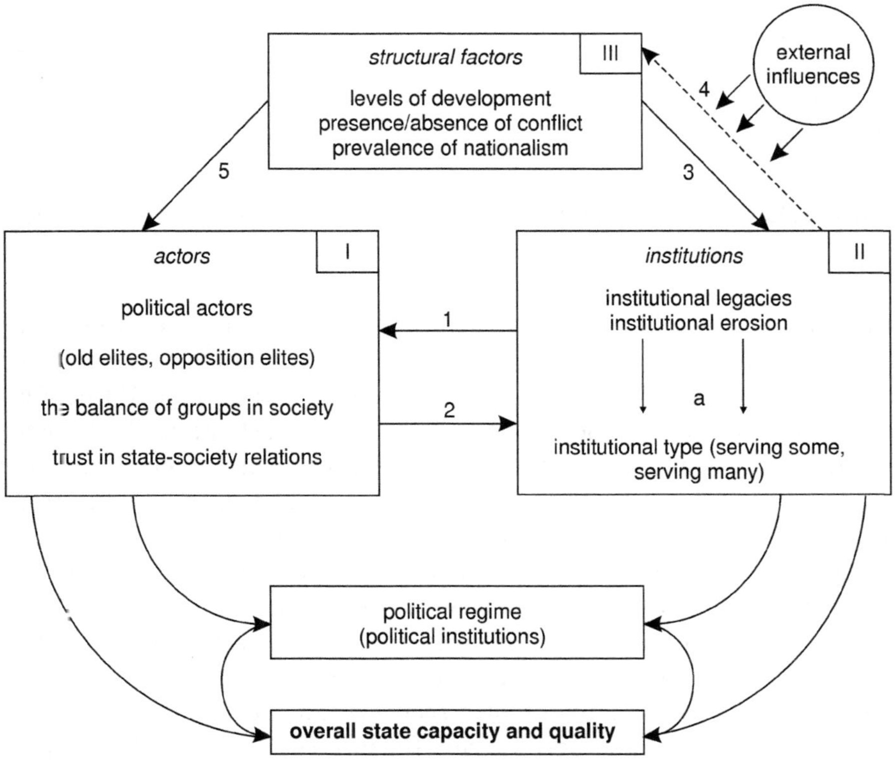

Graph 4.1: Macro model of factors shaping state formation

Eventually, institutions can have an impact on structural factors, in particular on economic development (i.e., better institutions will in the long run result in higher prosperity) (arrow 4). However, this arrow is largely outside the empirical research conducted here.

Furthermore, as Graph 4.1 indicates, actors are involved in shaping specific institutions, for example, the tax administration, or the constitutional court, or the rules for holding elections. The aggregate set of these institutions is the political regime on one level, and the overall capacity and quality of the state on the other level (neither of which may have an overall shape which any one actor intended). The interaction between actors, institutions, structural, and international factors affects the overall capacity and quality of the state both directly and via the political regime. The effects of regime developments on how states are formed are a central theme of this study.

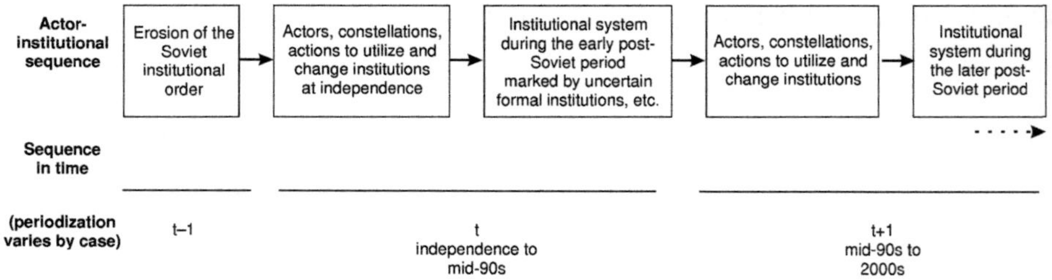

Graph 4.2: Mutual constitution of actors and institutions – schematic sequence

The key interaction between institutions and actors is iterated over time. A stylized sequence of this iteration is set out in Graph 4.2. At the outset of transition, actors 'play' within the situation of a deteriorated institutional structure and at least some try to influence the building of new institutions. Following this situation of institutional deterioration at independence, an initial new order takes shape in the early 1990s (t), providing an evolving, and not yet firm set of institutions for actors. Especially since institutions are still fluid an intense game continues among actors, eventually resulting in a further evolved set of institutions. At t+1, the initial new set of institutions itself then turns into an independent variable, influencing the choices available to actors. While initial periods of the sequence are marked by a rather rapid process of change, eventually the duration of each sequence extends and the degree of change lessens, if and when new systems stabilize (i.e., at t+2, t+3, and beyond).

As the overall causal model and the sequence of institutional re-building reflect, the development of states is presumed to be primarily driven by the interaction between (powerful) actors and institutions. A key point of the sequence is that early on a fundamental change with regard to the institutional constraints on actors occurs. This initial lowering of institutional constraints means that all emerging post-Soviet states had to address some problems commonly associated with 'anarchy' (or more precisely, anomy), i.e., a rise in the relative power of the most unscrupulous actors and at least a partial breakdown in law and order.

Furthermore, influential actors are at the same time engaged in shaping the political regime and the state. Therefore, this study is built around the assumption that the political regime which emerges from the relative weight between different groups of actors has an important impact on the capacity and the quality of the state.

4.2. Individual causal factors

This section describes the key individual factors captured in the macro model in more detail. The six putative factors considered are: 1) the level of economic development; 2) external influences; 3) institutional legacies and the process of institutional erosion and subsequent re-configuration; 4) the importance of regime consolidation with regard to creating a clear set of actors who can engage in state-building; 5) the structure of groups in society, especially with regard to the type of institutional system which is being built; and 6) trust and expectations which society at large has regarding state institutions.

Factors 4, 5, and 6 concern the nexus of the political regime, the way in which society is structured and organized, and trust and expectations as an important aspect of state-society relations. As Knight has argued, political and wider social power shape institution-building.[1] The mutual constitution of states and societies has a long tradition and has also played a prominent role in the analysis of previous waves of state-building.[2] All six putative factors are regarded as potentially linked and interacting, rather than as mutually exclusive. The empirical research will assess which factors are more important than others and at what points of the state-building process they occur, both by considering the overall post-Soviet space and by a detailed tracing of the development in individual cases.

4.2.1. THE LEVEL OF DEVELOPMENT

Among structural factors the level of economic development—measured roughly as the level of GDP per capita—can be presumed to have an important impact on the development of the state. A richer economy offers more opportunities for the state to extract. At the same time, the level of development would not affect all aspects of the state equally. An assumption widely shared in the literature is that states in countries with richer economies not only extract more in absolute but also in relative terms.[3] Thus, the level of development would affect the size of the state. However, in international comparison this is a loose rather than close relationship, i.e. there is still considerable variation within any given 'bracket' of development (e.g. between Sweden and Switzerland, or between Poland and Mexico).[4] Kitschelt furthermore argues that the level and historical 'depth' of development affects the chances for successful political and economic transition.[5]

Among the three dimensions of state capacity, the level of development can most obviously be assumed to affect implementation capacity, since this is the most 'resource intensive' dimension of capacity (see Chapter 2, section 4 above). There may also be a link to the quality of the state: a higher level of resources can make it easier to provide adequate pay for public servants, and hence can be a factor with regard to certain problems with the quality of the state, especially widespread petty corruption.

At the same time, there are also good reasons to expect that the level of development does not have a *determining* influence. Basic decision-making capacity does not depend on the level of development. Furthermore, as with regard to the size of the state, it is likely that the capacity and the quality of the state can vary substantially at any given level of development. Finally, some states have proven to be capable of supporting a rapid expansion of the economic base (e.g., South Korea), while others have not.

4.2.2. EXTERNAL INFLUENCES: INTERNATIONAL ECONOMIC INTEGRATION

External influences have a potential impact on state-building processes. Dependency-theory and similar approaches have assumed that state-building in peripheral regions is bound to be limited by dominant external factors emanating from increasingly internationalized markets.[6] External influence may be associated with identifiable agents (such as international financial institutions or the bilateral policy of a 'hegemonic' country), or may be more diffuse and associated with 'anonymous' structural forces. Key examples of the latter are increasingly powerful global financial markets which are assumed to constrain domestic institutional choices, and especially to limit the possible size of the state.[7]

More direct external influences can be the advice and conditionality of identifiable agents (such as the IMF and the WB, or the EU). For example, Holmes argues that outside advisors led Russian reformers to focus for too long on reducing the power of the formerly authoritarian state, but in doing so also furthered (or neglected to prevent) the erosion of state capacity.[8] However, while their demands may be clearly stated, the real leverage of these identifiable external actors is not always clear or clearly addressed.

One avenue of leverage is conditionality for receiving certain benefits (new loans at favorable rates; accession to a club like the WTO). Such conditions frequently focus on certain areas of the state (e.g., a reduction of the budget deficit), including keeping the state as problem in check (e.g., combating corruption). Also, identifiable external agents may actively promote certain institutional models (such as promoting the adoption of a treasury model, or adopting specific procurement and competition rules).

Especially with regard to Central Eastern Europe, and in contrast to assumptions about how external factors affect state capacities in most other regions, there is also the contrary assumption of a very positive external effect, namely EU accession.[9] EU accession is presumed to provide an 'external anchor' and guidance to the overall process of institutional reform. However, except for the Baltic states former Soviet countries have been excluded from membership, while some have received a 'neighborhood' status in the early 2000s; so they would only be weakly or even negatively be affected by EU enlargement.

Beyond international economic integration, there are various 'bilateral' influences, i.e. the policies especially of Russia and the US vis-à-vis the countries of the former Soviet Union.[10] However, these bilateral relationships vary by country and also over time—for example, the US became particularly interested in Central Asia after September 2001; while Russia was initially preoccupied with internal turmoil, but then sought to re-assert its influence from around the same time. The bilateral relationships will be touched upon in the case studies (especially Chapter 9 on Belarus) but are not explored in depth in this research.

The main focus here is on seeking to assess the relative importance of 'global' international economic integration. If economic integration is so important for shaping state capacity, then there should be some common trends observable among the post-Soviet states, which all opened up to international markets at the same time after a previous common experience of being part of a separate economic bloc. Furthermore, if international integration in general has a negative impact on state-building, then we would expect the state to be particularly weak in those countries which are most open to trade or particularly dependent on external financing.

4.2.3. INSTITUTIONAL LEGACIES AND THE IMPORTANCE OF INSTITUTIONAL EROSION

As set out in Chapter 3, this study especially considers the importance of institutional erosion for the subsequent process of state-building on the one hand, and the importance of institutional legacies on the other. Legacies are widely assumed to have shaped post-communist and post-Soviet developments. However, there is a variety of ways in which legacies are used to account for explaining post-communist developments. Some versions of the legacy argument focus strongly on communist institutional legacies.[11] Thus, Jowitt wrote in 1992: "Whatever the result of the current turmoil in Eastern Europe, one thing is clear: the new institutional patterns will be shaped by the 'inheritance' and legacy of forty years of Leninist rule."[12] Crawford and Lijphart similarly assume that the Leninist past and its "social, cultural, and institutional structures" would shape the post-communist institution-building process. Jowitt, as well as Crawford and Lijphart focus primarily on the chances of establishing liberal, capitalist democracies, and the prediction was pessimistic.[13]

Observing the divergence among post-communist states, Bunce finds that a strong 'legacy' hypothesis about communism is untenable and that rather the different features of communism across countries led to a variety in subsequent developments.[14] Lynch stresses the importance of longer historical 'roots' and includes the pre-Soviet experience among the legacies driving post-Soviet state development.[15] Johnson, in contrast, has cautioned against an overly deterministic view of post-communist development and instead proposes the concept of 'path contingency' as an alternative to 'path dependency.'[16] Outside the context of post-communism, Farrell and Crouch have similarly argued against a too deterministic approach to institutional development in general.[17] Still, the reference to legacies remains widely used to explain outcomes in individual cases.[18] However, the many different arguments about legacies risk arbitrariness: current developments can somehow be casually related to the past.

This study explores two particular arguments: the importance of Soviet institutional legacies, and the importance of institutional erosion. All post-Soviet countries shared common formal institutional structures for at least four decades.[19] While other legacies may have differed—informal institutions, the pre-Soviet experience of independent statehood, etc.—these shared structures may reasonably be assumed to have a substantial impact on post-Soviet developments. If Soviet institutional legacies are important, this should be reflected in some subsequent common developments (or systematic similarity), and these developments should have some clearly recognizable similarity with the previous system (otherwise similar developments could be driven by similar external pressures, for example).

A second assumption about endogenous institutional factors is the relative importance of institutional erosion in the late Soviet period as developed in Chapter 3, section 1. Institutional erosion means that one order—the Soviet political, bureaucratic, and planned economy system—becomes porous and crumbles, without a new order immediately taking its place. Institutional erosion therefore marks a shift towards semi-anarchy and 'wild capitalism,' rather than towards a modern, democratic, and capable state. Institutional erosion is assumed to result in substantial shifts in the constraints on actors, and in greatly increasing the uncertainties they face.

The proposition is that institutions in post-Soviet countries have evolved in *reaction* to the erosion of formal institutions in the late 1980s and early 1990s; and that this 'logic' of a response to erosion has different effects than 'path dependency' would lead us to expect, i.e., the development of institutions which closely resemble the previous system.

Deep institutional erosion is assumed to weaken institutional legacies in several ways; for example, the terrible budget crises of the 1990s in the former Soviet Union eroded Soviet legacies of welfare provision (and more so than in Central Eastern Europe where institutional erosion was far less prevalent). If institutional erosion matters, then we should observe a general, considerable weakening of formal rules, and eventually, specific reactions to this situation. At the same time, as proposed in the next factor, there may be considerable variation in the pathways and timing of recovering from institutional erosion.

4.2.4. THE ALLOCATION OF POLITICAL POWER: REGIME CONSOLIDATION VERSUS CONTESTATION AND FRAGMENTATION

Political institutions can be conceived of as the nucleus of wider institutions of the state (see Graph 4.3). Therefore, the links between regime change and state-building are a key focus of this research, as set out in Chapter 1, section 3. A political regime is the set of formal and informal *political* institutions operating in a country. In post-Soviet countries political institutions had to be established upon gaining independence and it had to be determined which type of regime to adopt—in parallel to embarking on state-building. In some post-Soviet countries, political actors either agreed upon a new set of political institutions quickly (democratic consolidation), or political power was effectively monopolized (authoritarian consolidation). In others, a prolonged struggle among various political actors ensued over the nature of the political regime.

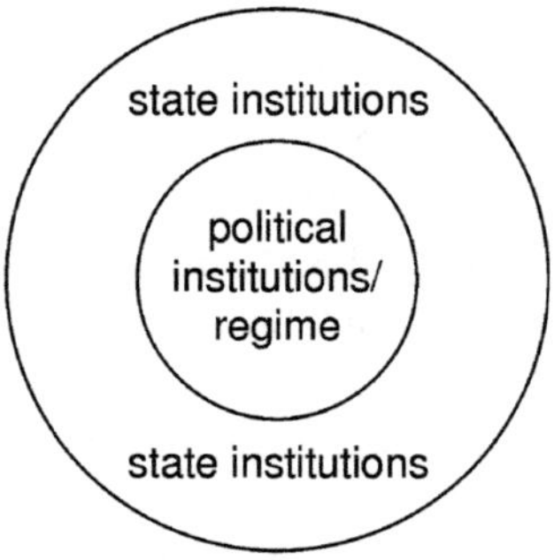

Graph 4.3: Political regime and state institutions

McFaul, Bunce and others have pointed out that the consolidation of a political regime—democratic or authoritarian—is an important factor for the development of transition countries.[20] Roberts and Sherlock consider the political causes of weak state capacity in Russia and suggest that polarized elite conflict, and a lack of cooperative links between state and society and 'social capacities' (i.e., social capital) are key factors which weakened the state in the 1990s.[21]

The basic assumption made in this study is that the consolidation of a political regime facilitates state-building, whereas political contestation and fragmentation will tend to impede it. The term 'consolidation' is used here to refer to the consolidation of any political regime, whether democratic or authoritarian.[22] In a consolidated regime the (formal and informal) rules according to which power is allocated are uncontested, although there may well be a contestation over who actually receives power within the framework of these rules (especially in democratic regimes, but also during periods of succession in authoritarian regimes). The *de facto* acceptance of how political power is allocated in turn allows for a concentration on building the various elements of a state apparatus.

Consolidated authoritarian regimes can be akin to Olson's stationary bandit who engages in building capable structures which allow long-term revenue maximization. State- and institution-building have been successful in some consolidated authoritarian regimes (South Korea during its developmental state period; post-Mao communist China; Uganda during the early Museveni period). However, authoritarian consolidation inevitably involves the risk of irrational leadership, particularly when the regime is highly personalistic or "sultanistic" (for example, Mugabe in Zimbabwe, Kim Jong-Il in North Korea, or Niyazov in Turkmenistan) which may involve leaders building (powerful) states that are predominantly used to control or even destroy society. Furthermore, when authoritarian regimes come under threat of 'deconsolidation,' they rely on their 'despotic powers' to maintain control, violating human rights and shifting resources away from providing public goods, and into building up an oppressive apparatus.

In a consolidated democratic regime, basic democratic rules have become the 'only game in town,' according to the definition by Linz and Stepan.[23] Thus, in a democratic system, political consolidation is achieved if democratic rules have been designed, have been agreed upon, and are continuously followed (both with regard to changes in power and to policy making processes).

When the political regime is contested or power is fragmented among a number of 'roving bandits,' attention will be focused on contesting, gaining, or holding on to power. Fragmentation implies that power is held by multiple actors, in its more problematic forms outside any agreed system; and contestation implies that these multiple actors seek to increase their respective share of power outside mutually agreed rules (rather than just accepting a situation of fragmentation).[24]

Frequently in situations of fragmentation and contestation the development of state capacity is likely to suffer, no power holder is able to summon sufficient resources to build an integrated institutional structure. In its most extreme form, political contestation can turn into civil war among multiple warlords (for example, China in the 1940s, Somalia in the 1990s, Tajikistan in the early 1990s) with a complete destruction of existing institutional systems as a consequence.

In situations of more limited fragmentation and contestation, central power-holders have to shore up their rule, and a common means of doing so is by dispensing various forms of privileges. Such practices in turn risk undermining state capacity piece by piece and especially tend to worsen the quality of the state.[25] Contestation over the political regime also tends to shorten time horizons, as actors cannot be sure how long the current set of rules will last. Furthermore, each power-wielding group may try to bring lower-level institutions under its command. In hybrid political systems, contestation can involve abuses of various state institutions for covert oppression of the political opposition (rather than using the security apparatus outright). Such mechanisms hinder institutional integration and coordination, and they also tend to undermine the legitimacy of the state in the perception of citizens.

Moreover, if institutional erosion is an important factor at the start of the post-Soviet state-building process, as proposed above, then the consolidation of a political regime is an important step to reverse this erosion, while political contestation and fragmentation tend to prolong and deepen it. In this way, the emerging political regime is an important crux between the various factors driving erosion and the results of state-building, as depicted in Graph 4.1 above.

Consequently, establishing a consolidated regime rapidly after independence is presumed to be advantageous to the state-building process. Regime consolidation is particularly relevant in a situation of new statehood and unstable state capacity when many decisions have to be taken and when many elements of a new order have to be built. However, early consolidation is not necessarily the 'end of history,' and challenges may occur later on. Vice versa, initially unconsolidated regimes may change track towards either democratic or authoritarian forms of consolidation later on.

4.2.5. GROUPS, INTERESTS, AND INTERMEDIARY ORGANIZATIONS

The configuration of groups and individual actors in post-Soviet societies interacts with the institutional changes in the realm of the political regime and of the state. The causes for why post-communist societies developed certain regimes are extensively debated in the transition literature.[26] The reconfiguration of actors and especially the entry of new elites is widely seen as an important proximate cause.[27] Thus, early political consolidation would appear more likely as a consequence of either fundamental or no reconfiguration. If early reconfiguration is partial, on the other hand, this can result in a challenge to, but not an outright change of the rules, leading to a situation of continuous contestation. In turn, actors are affected by and adjust their behavior depending on the changes in the institutional structure, as reflected in Graphs 4.1 and 4.2, in this way also influencing the further reshaping of institutions.[28]

Society at large is widely assumed to be relatively weak and weakly structured in post-communist countries.[29] However, there are nonetheless important groups based on interests (e.g., ideological, or economic) and/or regional networks. In general, groups can have narrow or more encompassing goals, be 'visible' or 'opaque,' and have a voice or be shut out.[30] Importantly, most post-Soviet societies are marked by the importance of relatively small elite groups and by intra-elite struggles, while the majority of society has relatively little clout and has had to struggle with vastly increased economic uncertainty and a spread of poverty (with some reversal of this trend since the early 2000s).

In post-Soviet societies, 'visible' structures representing broader interests tend to be thin: political parties have few members and are organizationally weak.[31] Trade unions formally often still have a large membership but are ineffective and enjoy little trust given their pre-history of being 'transmission belts' for orders from above.[32] Civil society—in the sense of modern associations, NGOs, and also more broadly of a wide-spread engagement of citizens—has lacked roots in society, but has evolved to varying degrees.[33]

Some theorists have argued that a weakly organized society is beneficial for building capable states; and also for achieving radical economic transformation.[34] However, as pointed out in Chapter 1, high levels of elite autonomy foster successful state formation and transformation *only under certain conditions*. If these are not present, then the weakness of society may simply be a feature of a period of disorientation and elite enrichment. Thus, in post-Soviet countries, the weakness of society appears more as part of the problem than as part of the solution to weak and dysfunctional states.

This is especially the case since there are strong 'opaque' networks—patronage networks, including 'old boys' networks uniting former *Komsomol* and former communist party members, and networks based in certain industrial regions. These opaque networks generally represent narrow rather than broad societal interests. While opaque networks are present in many societies—whether it is the 'oil interests' in the US or 'the mafia' in Italy— they pose a more serious problem the less they are balanced by a well-developed structure of 'visible' groups. Visible groups can become public participants in political bargains. Opaque groups usually cannot become part of such bargains and hence are also not bound by them.

Where intermediary organizations representing broader societal groups are weak, institution-building remains a game played amongst elites. Such weakness also reduces the capacity of society to exercise control over the state elites and to keep the 'state as a problem' in check through democratic accountability—since society's 'voice' in the Hirschmanian sense is reduced. Moreover, the weakness of intermediary organizations on the one hand and the strength of 'opaque' networks on the other hand is presumed to increase the likelihood that a state emerges which serves the interests of narrow groups, but not wider society, and which is marked by significant distortions.

Strong encompassing and 'visible' groups, in contrast, are likely to support a better state-building path: under an authoritarian regime, a more encompassing form of interest organization and representation would be expected to lead to 'embedded' authoritarianism as described by Evans. In the context of a democratic regime, such interest organizations are likely to promote an inclusive state providing benefits for many citizens. Furthermore, encompassing groups would be more likely to ensure accountability in society-elite relations and keep the state-as-a-problem in check.[35]

As the consolidation of the political regime, the structure of groups in society evolves over time. In most post-communist countries, narrow, opaque groups play an important role, but in some they appear to become more balanced by visible groups. The 'follow-up transitions' in Georgia and Ukraine mark attempts to move from hybrid regimes with strong overtones of state capture and oligarchic structures to democratic regimes with pluralistic interest representation. In Russia, in contrast, the movement may be more one from a situation of semi-democratic state capture to an authoritarian regime which has some features of embeddedness, as well as of an oligarchy which seeks to limit society's potential voice.

4.2.6. PERCEIVED LEGITIMACY: TRUST AND EXPECTATIONS IN STATE-SOCIETY RELATIONS

As Levi and others have argued, trust matters for governance. Low trust can be assumed to decrease the capacity to govern for various reasons.[36] In the fiscal sphere, mutual distrust between the state and society lowers voluntary tax compliance which makes extraction more costly (raising monitoring and enforcement costs), while high levels of trust are associated with fiscally large and well-functioning states.[37]

Moreover, trust is closely related to neo-Weberian notions of perceived legitimacy.[38] Perceived legitimacy means that people accept the current order—for reasons which may be intrinsic to a particular society. When trust in state institutions is (extremely) low, perceived legitimacy is in jeopardy. Public opinion surveys concerning political elites, various state institutions and, in particular, fiscal institutions such as the tax administration offer an opportunity to observe how the perceived legitimacy of post-Soviet states has evolved over time.

Lack of trust in a state may create problems in the fiscal sphere—as taxation has to rely on some degree of quasi-voluntary compliance and distrust of the state is widely assumed to be damaging for extractive systems.[39] Furthermore, the level of trust is likely to have indirect effects on institutional change: distrust may make it more difficult to agree on models of change, as it fosters the suspicion that the other side is seeking distributional gain and cannot be trusted to offer a fair compromise. Thus, state capacity as well as the ability to develop capacity is reduced.

Perceived legitimacy of a state involves not only the level of trust but also the match between trust and expectations, and expectations and actual policies. Trust and expectations may be combined symmetrically (i.e., both trust and expectations are low) or asymmetrically (low trust but high expectations). The latter combination would generally be regarded as more difficult, particularly for combining state formation with state transformation (i.e. the need to win trust in the state while expectations are disappointed due to the transformation of the state). As will be recounted in the empirical chapters, post-Soviet citizens tend to have rather socialist-type expectations of the state—preferring the state to remain the owner of large industries, and the state to provide social welfare.

We need to pay attention to the possibility that trust is part of a feedback loop: while trust is a factor that improves governance and is likely to ease institutional reforms, trust is also the result of institutional performance (see also Chapter 3, section 4 above).[40] In this perspective, trust would be more an indicator of existing state capacity than a driving factor.

4.3. Four state-building trajectories

State-building is a long-term process—even though in post-Soviet countries it occurs in a rather condensed form.[41] Within the limited time-period of post-Soviet state-building that we are able to observe, we can *provisionally* distinguish three phases: the phase of shock, i.e. the immediate aftermath of independence (early 1990s), the initial phase of realignment (late 1990s) and the secondary phase of realignment (early to mid 2000s). This delineation is provisional, and in individual cases the pace of phases varies.

In Graph 4.2 above, a generic sequence of interaction between institutions and actors was presented. In the initial phase of state-building, the sequence of interactions occurs at a rapid pace as actors are engaged in developing (and then testing out) new or amended institutions at relatively short intervals. As the situation moves towards a new stable state, the pace of change slows down. However, new periods of more rapid change may emerge, for example, as a consequence of 'follow-up' transitions (e.g., the 'Orange Revolution' in Ukraine).

Graph 4.4 below proposes four 'stylized' trajectories of initial state-building in post-Soviet countries up until the early 2000s: autocratic regime consolidation, democratic regime consolidation, and uncertain regimes (veering more to the autocratic or more to the democratic side). All countries start from the (common) departure point of Soviet institutional erosion; while the type and the degree of regime consolidation is the main differentiating factor putting individual cases on one or another trajectory. The graph focuses on the domestic political nexus, leaving especially the two proposed structural factors—the level of development, and external influences—aside. In particular, it focuses on the interaction between institutions and actors, as mapped in Graphs 4.1 and 4.2 above. While on the institutional side the initial deterioration marks the starting point, on the agency side the starting period evolves around the degree of elite reconfiguration, as discussed in the previous section.

Starting from the top, the first trajectory is that of early authoritarian consolidation. In those countries where new elites were able to have only a minimal impact a consolidated authoritarian political regime tended to develop. Early authoritarian consolidation was to some degree associated with restoring features of the communist institutional system (albeit to varying degrees and with modifications). Autocratic governments may or may not be benevolent in the sense of seeking to provide public goods, but they are all interested in consolidating those aspects of the state which allow the autocrat to continue in power.

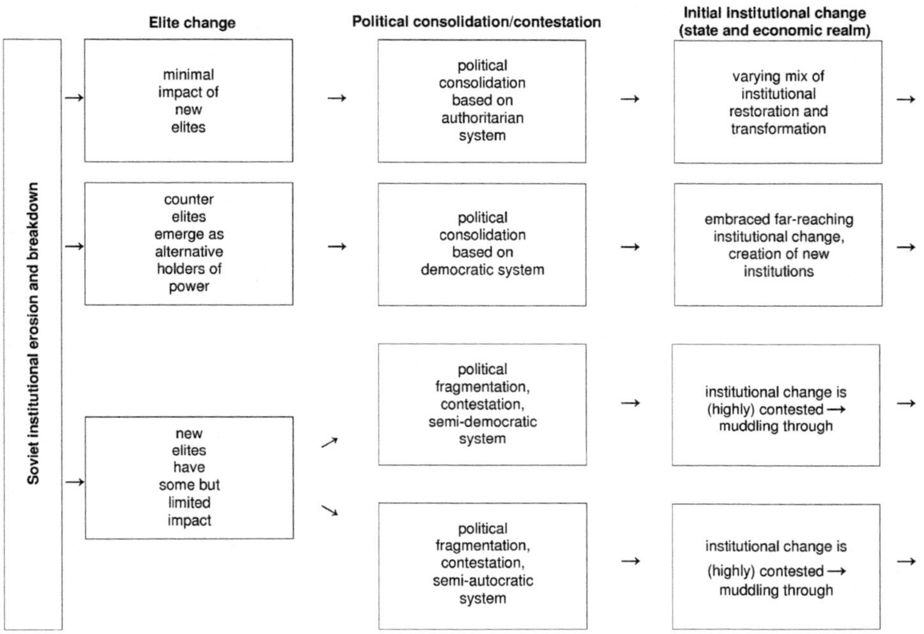

Graph 4.4:

Initial take-over of the reigns of government by new elites, in contrast, has tended to be followed by consolidation of a democratic regime. A necessary condition is that the democratic election of governments is widely recognized as legitimate, which bolsters the government's power to implement institutional re-building. Empirically, it appears that in those post-communist countries which have embarked on full democratization, progress in institution-building has been rather steady and overall most successful.[42]

Where new elites made some inroads but did not take over government, this tended to be followed by various forms of prolonged incomplete transitions (the two bottom trajectories).[43] In countries with such uncertain regimes efforts at state-building would suffer; as the political game would be focused on the contestation of political rules rather than on contestation within certain rules, weakening and distorting efforts at building the wider institutions of the state.

Initial elite reconfigurations occur during the first phase of independence (see the first column in Graph 4.4). The subsequent three factors, regime consolidation, choices about institutional change in the state and economic realm, and the re-balancing of groups in society occur over time and interact

Re-balancing of groups in society	Resulting capacity and quality of the state	Problems/risks and potential solutions
opaque groups remain weak (no privatisation; successful monopolization of power by a single leader: stationary bandit) →	early recreation of state capacity; (particularly: decision-making, implementation) state dysfunctionalities are (at least initially) contained →	*potential problems:* erratic leadership; oppression at the expense of 'state as solution'; leadership succession, contestation of authoritarian regime
opaque groups are contained by emergence of visible, encompassing groups; free press →	early recreation of state capacities (particularly: decision-making and control; implement. suffers temporally from system change); state dysfunctionalities low by inter-regional comparison. →	*potential problems:* later extreme fragmentation (secondary destabilization of the party system); containable if institutional system is already well-established
opaque groups are strengthened (privatization), weakly balanced by visible, encompassing groups and/or free press →	recreation of state capacities is slow, lack of integration of different institutional elements; state dysfunctionalities high →	*problems/risks:* continuously weak institutions; risk of institutions serving some rather than all is high; *potential solutions:* secondary regime change through 'colour revolution' or through creeping authoritarianism; transformation of opaque groups, into more visible interests
opaque groups are strengthened (privatization), not balanced by visible, encompassing groups and/or free press →	recreation of state capacities is slow, poorly integrated; state dysfuntionalities very high →	*problems/risks:* continuously weak institutions; risk of institutions serving some rather than all is high; *potential solutions:* secondary regime change through 'colour revolution' or through creeping authoritarianism; transformation of opaque groups into more visible interests

Model of four state-building trajectories

throughout subsequent phases of state-building. As syndromes, these interacting factors affect the creation of state capacities. In the last column, the problems, risks, and potential solutions to each of these four initial state-building trajectories are captured.

Those countries which initially built states based on authoritarian consolidation were generally able to regain institutional capacity relatively quickly (the uppermost trajectory). However, these cases—Turkmenistan, Uzbekistan, Belarus—to a greater or lesser degree suffer from an increasingly erratic leadership; and they may experience a cataclysmic moment at the point of the leadership succession.

Countries which achieved political stabilization via early full democratization—the Baltic states—began to rebuild institutional capacity relatively quickly (the second trajectory from the top). Furthermore, they have built state capacity by embracing a process of modernization and changing many aspects of how their states operate.

The initially most difficult trajectories are those of countries where the regime remained uncertain for some time after independence. In these uncertain regimes, economic reforms were initiated under conditions of a weak political regime and weak state institutions, which in turn promoted ‘oligarchization’—the rise of strong narrow and opaque groups. The model distinguishes between those unconsolidated pathways which show more traits of a semi-democratic regime and those showing more traits of a semi-autocratic regime. I assume that in an autocratic system lacking political consolidation, the likelihood of extremely high state dysfunctionalities is even greater than in a semi-democratic setting: while the discipline of a ‘stationary bandit’ (i.e., a single strong ruler) is lacking, potential pressures for better governance from below and from external actors can have even less impact. With regard to both the last two trajectories, a potential solution appears to be a later regime consolidation, based either on greater democratization or on the emergence of an autocratic ruler.

In the longer run, all four initial regime configurations are liable to undergo further changes. The most stable trajectory is likely to be that based on democratic consolidation. Consolidated authoritarian regimes could be stable for considerable periods but come under pressure at moments of leadership change, as well as due to eruptions of popular discontent, particularly if the balance of their institution building is heavily tipped towards oppression and against adequate provision of public goods.

Shifts towards greater regime consolidation over time are an important exit path from initial problems with building state capacity. Still, ‘late consolidators’ may face greater obstacles to successful state-building since more deterioration has taken place than in ‘early consolidators;’ in particular with regard to reigning in dysfunctionalities which emerged during earlier phases. Since there is a cost associated with having poor institutions, late consolidation would be expected to be associated with a higher social and economic cost than early consolidation; but better than continuous non-consolidation. Furthermore, in some cases, regime consolidation is likely to remain elusive. Particularly where this is associated with a lower level of development, state capacity may remain weak for long periods of time.

The “color revolutions” which occurred in Georgia, Ukraine, and Kyrgyzstan in the early 2000s are examples of later regime shifts towards greater democratization. However, there is no certainty that such revolutions will result in *consolidated* democratic regimes; and in fact, the subsequent development of the earlier of these “revolutions”—in Georgia and (outside the FSU) in Serbia—suggests that regime consolidation can remain elusive particularly when the challenge of regime consolidation is compounded by conflicts over the territorial extension of the state.[44]

Three factors set out in section 2, trust, external influences, and the level of development, are not captured in Graph 4.4, as it is focused on the presumed core interaction. However, we can make assumptions about how they are linked. Trust—as a sign of perceived legitimacy—is likely to be closely associated with the degree of regime consolidation and resulting state capacity; i.e., expected to be higher both in consolidated autocratic and in democratic regimes than in cases with uncertain regimes.

The importance of international factors will vary: in general, international integration would grow over time, as trade and financial relationships with the world beyond the former USSR intensify. However, there is likely to be variation as some countries became highly indebted, while others avoided debt, or could pay external debts off due to rapidly rising prices for natural resources in the early 2000s (see especially Chapter 11 on Russia). For the Baltic states the EU became an important and overall positive external influence; while the Central Asian states are subject to revived 'great games' and to destabilizing influences from their southern neighbors.[45] Furthermore, external *leverage* may be subject to swings: it is likely to peak during periods when accession or new disbursements of an (official) loan are negotiated, but will fall once accession or disbursement has occurred.[46]

The level of development is expected to have an impact potentially at several points: on the likelihood of certain elite configurations, but also directly on the potential for building capable states, via the avenues discussed in section 2 of this chapter. As set out in the introduction, this study concentrates on four cases which were relatively similar with regard to their level of economic development at independence. Among these four cases, the initial level of development is therefore not a key distinguishing factor. However, within the overall universe of post-Soviet states the level of development at the outset varied considerably—with Tajikistan at the low end with an estimated annual per capita income of 2,900 USD in 1989 to Russia at the high end with 10,300 USD (both in purchasing power parities).[47] The relative importance of the level of development will therefore be analyzed in Chapter 5, before embarking on the examination of the four selected cases.

4.4. Summary

This first part (Chapters 1-4) has served to lay out the framework for this study. Chapter 1 provided a brief summary of key concepts and controversies of the state and of state-building. The concept of what an 'ideal state' is has been contested, especially with regard to the two dimensions, the size of the state and the degree of state autonomy (section 1). However, there is broad agreement that considerable state capacity is needed in modern societies, and that it is important to strive for a state which provides good government. Section 2 retraced some of the works in the vein of 'fiscal sociology'—an approach of looking at the development of societies and states from a fiscal perspective. While this is not an exclusive way to consider states and their development, it can be a fruitful one, and for this reason is adopted here.

Section 3 draws the link of this book to the wider transition theory literature; arguing that debates about transition have for a long time neglected the state and the interdependencies between regime change and state-building processes. While state-building was less pertinent for the transitions in Central and Eastern Europe, it was central for all the countries of the former Soviet Union, including the Baltic states, as well as for the countries of the former Yugoslavia. Moreover, while the transition literature offers some inquiry into the *effects* of stateness on political and economic reforms, the *causes* for weak and misgoverned states have received less attention—including the ties between different trajectories of regime change and the state-building effort which are the central focus of this study.

Section 4 reflects on how the study of post-Soviet state-building processes may contribute to wider research on states and institutions: in particular, to the comparative view of different 'waves' of state-building, to conceptualizing institutional deterioration and non-incremental institutional change, and to the study of the relationship between processes of state formation and (political and economic) transformation.

Chapter 2 embarked on the presentation of the conceptual model and its operationalisation for the empirical study. Section 1 sets out that rather than distinguishing crudely between 'weak' and 'strong' states, we should distinguish three aspects of the state: size, capacity, and quality. The size of the state refers to its scope as reflected, for example, in the share of GDP that the state collects in revenue, and the range of tasks that it assumes. The capacity of the state refers to whether the state can actually 'get things done'. The quality of the state is the aspect which is often referred to as 'governance'. It is described here as the degree to which the state is a source of solutions versus a source of problems for society.

The subsequent three sections of Chapter 2 trace these aspects of the state in greater detail. Section 2 considers the quality of the state. It argues that ensuring the quality of the state during processes of state-building is a key challenge. Furthermore, it proposes that different types of (emerging) political regimes are related to different assets and risks with regard to the quality of the state.

Section 3 considers the size of the state, emphasizing that a larger size of the state cannot be equated with greater capacity. Some very capable states, such as South Korea have been relatively small in terms of (fiscal) size. Section 4 looks in greater detail at the issue of state capacity, and argues that it is composed of three dimensions: decision-making, implementation, and the nature of control and accountability relationships. The section outlines some of the problems which we expect to find with regard to these dimensions of capacity, and how these are reflected in particular in the fiscal sphere.

Chapter 3 turns to the dynamic of state-building. How do states arrive at certain levels of capacities? Concepts of neo-institutionalism provide a useful framework to think about this dynamic. When addressing 'institutional change' in general, we need to distinguish between institutional destruction ('de-institutionalization'), institutional transformation (altering existing institutions), and institutional creation (building new institutions) (section 1). The section also stresses the relevance of the fact that post-Soviet state-building occurred from a starting point of institutional erosion and breakdown of the Soviet order.[48]

Section 2 points to the costs and risks of institutional change, which tend to be neglected. Large-scale institutional change involves considerable costs as well as the risk that no better institutional equilibrium is found at least for a number of years and that a country may get 'stuck' on a defective institutional path.

Section 3 distinguishes between different types of institutional changes—large-scale versus incremental change, as well as change with distributional effects versus change without such effects. Combinations of the former (large-scale plus distributional) are assumed to be the most difficult to achieve. It furthermore emphasises that building institutions is generally more difficult than dismantling existing institutions—which was the early thrust of 'pro-market' reforms.

The relationship between formal and informal institutions is the subject of section 4. Discrepancies between formal rules and de facto behaviour were strong during the late Soviet period; and this discrepancy has grown in many instances in the post-Soviet period. Generally, growing divergence and conflict between formal and informal rules can be read as a signal of problems with state capacity, as the formal rules set by the state are for one reason or another not treated as binding at least by certain parts of the population.

Chapter 4 develops the causal model for this study. The central focus of this model is the interaction between any current status of institutions, and how actors deal with them (section 1). The sequence of these interactions in the process of post-Soviet state-building begins with the institutional deterioration marking the erosion and breakdown of the USSR. The initial institutional shape of the mid-1990s was usually a transitory state, followed by further adjustments over time. Furthermore, the model also covers the potential importance of structural factors and of external influences; and it also includes a perspective on the wider state-society relationship, especially with regard to trust in and expectations of the state.

Section 2 describes the individual putative factors covered in the model in greater detail. The section especially takes a closer look at the potentially important actors and their leverage and interests in shaping the new institutional order. The extent of initial elite reconfiguration as well as the relative weight of opaque groups—post-Soviet mafias and oligarchs, including some emerging from the old elite—and their ability to exploit the situation of weak institutions are important for how actors set out to shape the political regime, and consequently wider state institutions.

Section 3 suggests four hypothetical state-building trajectories. All four trajectories start from the same point of Soviet breakdown, while the initial impetus for differentiation is the degree of elite reconfiguration and subsequent regime change. This leads to different choices in the degree and direction of institutional change (restoration versus the building of new institutions), and also to different processes of re-balancing groups in society (implicitly through several consecutive rounds as pointed out in section 1). The model concludes by pointing to the potential risks inherent in each trajectory. The presumed risks are lowest in those states based on consolidated democratic regimes. States based on consolidated authoritarian regimes would generally have maintained relatively high levels of state capacity, and in this sense are considered to have an advantage over states with non-consolidated regimes. However, it is assumed that they face a considerable risk over time—of erratic leadership, of increasing oppression and decreasing provision of solutions by the state, and of contestation during moments of leadership change.

The empirical chapters which follow are based on this theoretical groundwork. They begin with a review of the Soviet fiscal system, and an overview of state-building in all post-Soviet countries from a fiscal perspective. This is followed by the chapters on Ukraine, Belarus, Lithuania, and Russia.

Notes

1 Knight (1992), 123.
2 Kohli, Migdal, and Shue (1994); Migdal (2001); Stepan (1978).
3 Ardant (1975). For a more detailed discussion of this relationship, see Burgess and Stern (1993).
4 Sweden: per capita GNI: $28,840, government revenue: 40 per cent of GDP; Switzerland: $39,880 - 25 per cent; Poland $5270 - 32 per cent; Mexico: $6230 - 13 per cent. World Bank, World Development Indicators.
5 Kitschelt (2001).
6 See Hobson (2000), 134–142; Laidi (2002); Onis and Aysan (2000).
7 See as the seminal expression of this theory: Wallerstein (1974).
8 Holmes (1997). See also: Markwick (1999).
9 Vachudova (2005), especially Chapter 7.
10 Kobrinskaya (2004); Valovaya (2005).
11 See, for example Hausner et al. (1995).
12 Jowitt (1992), 285.
13 See Crawford and Lijphart (eds.) (1997), 2.
14 Bunce (1999b); Kitschelt has argued that *pre-communist* and *structural* rather than *communist institutional* legacies matter and differences in current trajectories can best be explained in light of these. Kitschelt (2001).
15 Lynch (2005).
16 Johnson (2001).
17 Farrell and Crouch (2002).
18 For example, Gordon, "Institutions, Economic Interests and the Stalling of Economic Reform," in Robinson (ed.) (2000), 106–129.
19 Taking into account that some territories were included into the Soviet Union only after WWII.
20 See McFaul (1995), 238–242; and further in McFaul (2004).
21 Roberts and Sherlock (1999).
22 Schedler (1998).
23 Linz and Stepan (1996).
24 Power can also be "fragmented" in a federal, de-centralized system, but based on clear rules and without an intention of actors to challenge and usurp the domain of other power holders.
25 See Ames (1987); Roberts and Sherlock (1999), 489, on post-communist states.
26 Fish (1998); Norgaard (2000).
27 I prefer the term reconfiguration to 'elite change,' since it primarily involves the entry of new elite groups, but not necessarily the exit of previous elite groups.
28 As Putnam has shown, social structures are essential for understanding how societies 'use' institutions. Putnam (1994).
29 Lynch (2005), 5.
30 See Olson (1965), and Hirschman (1970).
31 This is even true for many 'parties of power' which were created from above, but lack a membership base.

32 See Hausner, Jessop and Nielsen (1995), 28: "Late communism [...] is characterized by relatively unconstrained bargaining [...] The role of interest groups changed from transmission belts to bargaining agents in the actual functioning of central planning."
33 Mendelson (2001); Kubicek (2000).
34 Migdal (1992); Aslund (1994).
35 See also Ganev (2001), 21-23.
36 Kornai and Rose-Ackerman (2004); Braithwaite and Levi (1998).
37 Pirrtellää (1999); Steinmo (1993), 199 (fn. 7).
38 Wang (2005); Sil and Chen (2004).
39 See Levi (1988), Chapter 3: "Creating Compliance;" Tanzi (1998), 14.
40 See Mishler and Rose (1998).
41 See also Gryzmala-Busse and Jones Luong (2002).
42 Compare, for example, the ratings of Freedom House reports (Nations in Transit) with the 'Estimates of Governance' given by Kaufmann, Kray, and Zoido-Lobató (2002), 19-25. EBRD (2001), 18.
43 McFaul (2004).
44 Both Serbia and Georgia are faced with secessionist challenges—Serbia in Kosovo and Montenegro and Georgia in Abkhazia and South Ossetia.
45 Halbach (2004). Destabilizing influences include drug trade which is increasingly passing through Central Asia, as well as neighboring fragile states (Afghanistan, Iraq).
46 External influences can also be directed at the political regime itself. Attempts at such influence have tended to increase over time. See also Chapter 8 on the 2004 election campaign in Ukraine.
47 World Bank, World Development Indicators (2002).
48 This institutional erosion was considerably deeper than in most CEECs.

CHAPTER 5.
STATE-BUILDING IN THE POST-SOVIET REGION

This chapter offers an overview of the fiscal system during Soviet times, during the period of disintegration, and during the post-Soviet period across the 15 successor republics. The first section covers potential legacies, and summarizes how the Soviet fiscal system differed from fiscal systems in market economies. Section 2 covers the period of institutional breakdown during the late Soviet Union, based on the assumption set out in Chapter 4 that it matters whether institutional change and state-building start from a situation of relative stability or rather after periods of institutional deterioration. The third section looks at post-Soviet developments, mapping the development of fiscal rules and results; and analyzes the effects of the level of economic development and of the degree of political consolidation with regard to several indicators related to state capacity. Altogether, this chapter provides an initial testing of several variables discussed in Chapter 4, and sketches the range of empirical trajectories among the post-Soviet 'universe.'

5.1. The Soviet state and its fiscal system

The Soviet fiscal system was fundamentally different from that of a market economy, since the state acted as an owner-state rather than a tax state.[1] During the 1920s and 1930s, the phase of the creation of this owner-state-cum-command-economy, the new Soviet state extracted revenue heavily in order to pursue its dual goal of expropriation and collectivization and of acquiring resources for its industrialization drive.[2] In the 1930s in particular, the administration extracted revenue from the rural population to the point of mass starvation.[3] After WWII the system of an owner-state and a command economy became firmly established, and remained relatively stable until the mid-1980s.[4]

While according to the original Marxist vision, the state had been expected to wither away, under 'real socialism' it never did.[5] However, it differed markedly from states in a market economy. The state not only had fiscal instruments to allocate resources to itself, but it actually controlled the entire economy, including prices, wages, allocation of credit and investments for enterprises.[6] The state could suppress private demand and allocate resources to investment by limiting the production of consumer goods; or it could keep wages low and spend more on the defense sector, etc.

The fiscal boundaries of the state were never clearly defined in the USSR, as Hutchings and Nove, and later Cheasty and Davis point out.[7] The budget would expand when the state took more from enterprises and then channeled more money back to them in the form of investment grants; and at the same time, enterprises performed many social service functions which in market economies are either financed through the budget or left to individual citizens.[8]

Budgeting and agencies dealing with the control and execution of the budget were subordinate to the physical planning process.[9] The tax system was less based on general rules and more on negotiations:

> [T]urnover tax rates were not 'parametric:' there were generally thousands of separate rates of the turnover tax. There was also a considerable degree of policy discretion in taxing enterprise profits as it was normal practice for such taxes to be negotiated.[10]

Despite this, tax collection was relatively simple because taxes were primarily collected from enterprises rather than from individual citizens and because all enterprises had to use accounts with state banks.[11] As Tanzi writes:

> The average citizen *qua* citizen was never confronted by the tax system or tax inspectors. He never had to file a return and, in most cases, was not even aware of the existence of taxes. For the average citizen of these countries taxes are a negative externality brought in by the transition to a market economy.[12]

The budgetary system was highly centralized, limiting the experience of republican-level decision-making on fiscal issues and allocating responsibility for decisions to Moscow: for example, in Ukraine the decline of coal mining in the Donbas region was blamed on central decision-makers who had (unfairly) decided to invest more in Siberian mines, without a reflection of whether declining deposits of Donbas-coal actually justified such shifts in investment.[13]

Although large parts of the population benefited from the existing system of free social services, and relative economic security, it cannot truly be labeled as a 'social contract' between the governing and the governed. Personal and political freedom was very much curtailed and there were no channels for aggregating the interests of citizens. To some extent, it was an implicit contract since from the 1960s onward the state relied increasingly less on force and more on tacit acceptance, if not endorsement.[14] At the same time, it was a system in which policies and the overall role of the state was determined from above rather than negotiated with an electorate or openly defined interests groups.[15]

While the system worked in general, it was not without its problems. Firstly, as Brunner has pointed out, the Soviet economic administration was subject to growing fragmentation, leading to an increasingly fierce struggle over budgetary funds.[16] Secondly, managers routinely falsified production figures in order to obtain additional bonuses, more investment inputs, lower plan quotas, *et cetera*.[17] This undermined both the physical and the financial planning process. Connected to this was a considerable and growing black economy which, however, until the late 1980s did not undermine the basic extractive capacity of the state.

Thirdly, there was considerable informal extraction. Simis describes in detail how the ruling elite used its position of power to extract additional resources—be it herds of sheep in Uzbekistan or housing repairs made at the expense of district construction offices. He also shows that "the district mafia" was relatively secure in extracting these rents:

> [The] lower stratum comprises tens of thousands of Party and state functionaries who represent power in the provinces [...] They are the main buttress of central power. Consequently, the supreme authorities have to accept the fact that the local authorities compensate for their lack of official prerequisites [which the state budget cannot afford] by accepting payments, in money and in kind.[18]

In general, informal rules in the Soviet Union stood in a starkly hypocritical relationship with formal institutions. In any system informal institutions exist which are not for 'public consumption' as they may include backroom deals and corruption, but the contradictions between the formal and informal sphere was particularly sharp in socialist countries. While the official ideology stressed collectivism, equality, and, to some extent, frugality, the system relied on underpaid local officials who were informally expected to fend for themselves—rewarding those with the least scruples. Some of the informal practices which the Soviet system bred—such as informal searches for production inputs—provided the necessary 'grease' for the formal system to function. But it was especially the widespread misreporting of production figures which undermined economic planning, negatively affected the formal system.

A further defining feature of the Soviet state system was the authoritarian mode of control.[19] Extreme authoritarian force had originally established the economic institutional structure and the system of an owner-state. Abolishing private ownership, restricting freedom of movement, forcing enterprises to use the state-controlled banking system, and so on, greatly facilitated revenue extraction. Authoritarian forms of control were used to keep informal practices within boundaries, while the informal practices of the governing elite were kept as much as possible from public discussion by means of a controlled press.[20]

The state security police (before 1934, the 'VeCheKa;' from 1934, the NKVD; and after WWII, the KGB), other control organs (including a strong procuracy and various 'people's control' organs) provided strong instruments of top-down hierarchical as well as pervasive control.[21] Finally, there was the party itself which "has always exercised extensive supervisory functions."[22] While the regime, especially during the Stalinist years, had elements of an irrational tyranny (as set out in Chapter 2), it was a particular tyranny, bent on creating a powerful state in order to reshape the social and economic base of the former Russian empire.

As reflected in this account, the Soviet state developed into a rather capable state over the first two decades of its existence: decisions were taken and policies were implemented even if they disrupted the lives of millions of people, such as the policy of forced collectivization.[23] However, two fundamental problems beset the Soviet state. First of all, it was highly 'autonomous' but lacked embeddedness—i.e., effective feedback mechanisms which could have fostered continuous adjustment of the state to changing circumstances and requirements. Secondly, the organizational structures of the Soviet state were bureaucratic but not rule-based.[24] Instead, strong personalistic elements remained, both in the administration in "the trenches" and in the control over the administration by the "top echelons."[25] This manifested itself in a continuous weakness of infrastructural powers and ultimately, it meant that the state was strong only as long as the top leadership was willing and able to employ its despotic powers—the power to use force outside any due process of law.

A further peculiarity of the Soviet state was the central position of the Communist Party. Crucial decision-making and control functions were organized within the Party rather than within the government. As long as the Party 'worked' this represented a way of creating and maintaining an integrated power system—particularly after the end of the Stalin period. However, when the Party was eventually dissolved during the break-up of the USSR, this posed an additional problem for state capacity, since the Party had been such a central element in the institutional system.[26]

During the Brezhnev years, the Soviet state appeared in its most stable phase. However, the policy of 'stability of cadres' meant that the central government gradually lost control over the public administration especially at regional and local levels.[27] Capacity for control and for the implementation of decisions taken at the centre eroded. This lack of state capacity became accentuated when Gorbachev attempted to initiate reforms. While he and the Politburo could take decisions, they could not ensure implementation or effectively punish non-implementers. The following section takes a closer look at the period of deterioration of the Soviet equilibrium and its effects on the fiscal and budgetary system.

5.2. Institutional deterioration: *perestroika* and the break-up of the Soviet Union

During the *perestroika* years, major changes were initiated in the revenue and expenditure system. In the mid-1980s, the government sought to stimulate a new phase of development by sharply increasing investment expenditures. Then, from 1987 onwards, through the introduction of a new "full cost-accounting and self-financing" (*khozraschet*) system, enterprises received more control over their funds and more incentives for profit maximization.[28]

As a result, the state received less revenue from state enterprises: between 1986 and 1990, budget revenue from state enterprises declined from 16.2 per cent of GDP to 11.7 per cent. At the same time, other sources of revenue were reduced as a side-effect of other policies. Wholesale prices were partially liberalized, but retail prices were still kept under administrative control, causing revenues from turnover taxes to drop. Gorbachev's anti-alcoholism campaign, initiated in 1985, reduced revenues from turnover taxes by 2 per cent of GDP. While revenues were declining, political liberalization prompted more populist policies, including higher wages and an expansion of social programs.[29]

The government tried to contain the growing fiscal imbalance through initiating new taxes in 1991—aimed at increasing the share of government revenue from the previous 40–45 per cent of GDP to 55 per cent. However, this proved impossible as the Soviet Union was rapidly disintegrating. Republican governments engaged in intense competition for control over enterprises and revenue shares, keeping resources within their respective republics, while still drawing subsidies from the central Soviet government. Together with unchecked monetary emissions at the republican level during the period of 1990–1991, this amounted to a "genuine civil war in finance" according to Strcev et al.[30] As a consequence, the USSR as a whole finished the last year of its existence with a fiscal deficit of over 10 per cent of GDP.[31]

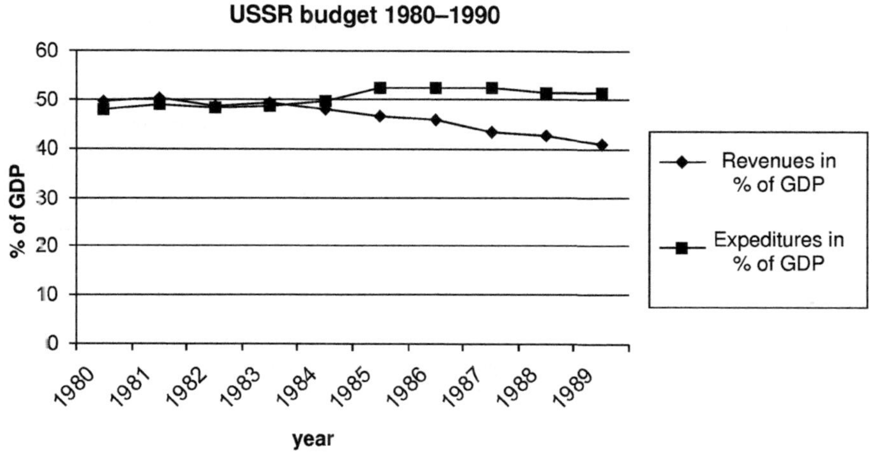

Graph 5.1: Soviet budgets 1980 to 1990

Source: Selnikov and Reznikov (1995), 6.

The fiscal deterioration was part of the system-wide decline. Both hierarchical control and system-wide policy integration were increasingly eroding. Gorbachev had hoped that "socialist pluralism" of opinions would provide a stimulus to overcome the period of *zastoi* (stagnation), but at the same time could be contained. In fact once pluralism was introduced, it rapidly led to the breakdown of the already hollowed-out system.[32] In early 1990, the power monopoly of the Party was abandoned.[33] Given the central role of the Party, the decline and eventual dissolution of the CPSU had enormous consequences for the functioning of the state apparatus. As Srivastava writes: "The worst nightmares of the conservative sections [about destroying the integrity of the Soviet system] expressed during the course of the entire political-ideological conflicts throughout Perestroika proved to be true."[34]

Solnick has used a neo-institutional approach to characterize this situation as a system-wide run on the bank. "[T]he loss of confidence in the institution [the Soviet system] makes its demise a self-fulfilling prophecy."[35] As the Party began to lose its monopoly on power and its continued ability to control agents seemed uncertain, lower level bureaucrats began to grab whatever assets of the system they could. Often, bureaucrats acted in cooperation with semi-legal entrepreneurs who had emerged in the 1980s.[36] The run on the bank, furthermore, had several components, as it was not only about grabbing immediate economic assets, but, at the level of the republics, it was also about grabbing autonomy and eventually independence from the center.

By the time the 15 republics became independent, they emerged from a crumbling system in which decisions were still taken but were no longer implemented, and in which individual agents of the state or the (quasi-governmental) Party were no longer controlled by an overarching institutional structure. As Kuzio put it, from 1990 to 1991 the "Soviet economy and ministry system descended into utter chaos."[37] Hierarchical control had dissolved. As the former empire disintegrated, it was up to the newly independent republics to pick up the threads of a dissolved order.

5.3. State-building in the post-Soviet 'universe'

In the following sections the broad range of trajectories of the 15 successor states is outlined from a fiscal perspective. They discuss the degree of divergence and common developments among the newly independent states. As this broad comparative panorama indicates, the legacies outlined above translated into some common problems, while the solutions and the pathways to solutions differed. The scale of fiscal crisis also differed: it was especially severe in countries experiencing secessionist movements and civil war (Armenia, Georgia, Tajikistan), and in the less developed successor republics without natural resources. While structural factors (the level of development, natural resources) account for the general conditions of the emerging fiscal systems, factors related to the political transition and to the political regime had a decisive impact on how the new states coped with these conditions. An overview of these issues is presented here; followed by the qualitative chapters which cover a particular sub-set of post-Soviet countries in depth.

5.3.1. RULES AND RESULTS: TESTING THE ROLE OF LEGACIES AND INTERNATIONAL FACTORS

As a starting point, I consider fiscal rules and results across the universe of post-Soviet countries. This data reflects a number of trends: a substantially shrinking size of the state across the region, but to varying degrees and at varying speeds; an (again varying) discrepancy between fiscal rules and actual revenue; and its decrease over time as tax rates were reduced considerably in all countries, and the transition from fiscal crisis to greater stability in the late 1990s.[38] Table 5.1 presents basic tax rates and their evolution in the 15 post-Soviet countries. Graphs 5.2 to 5.6 show the development of revenue, expenditure, and deficits for the decade from 1993 to 2003, by individual country, and grouped into three broad regions, (Caucasus and Central Asia, Western/Slavic, and Baltic countries).

Considering this data on fiscal rules and results, several observations emerge with regard to the driving factors for state-building discussed in Chapter 4; and in particular with regard to the role of legacies and international factors.

1) Legacies. From Table 5.1 it appears that tax rates moved in waves: they differed quite significantly in 1992 and in 2001, but were more similar in 1997 and 2004; that is after a first and a second wave of reforms had spread throughout the region. The changes in tax rates include rather radical changes, such as the introduction of a flat rate for personal income taxation, which was started in the Baltic states and in Russia, but then also spread to several other countries. By 2004, all post-Soviet countries had (significantly) lower tax rates on nearly all taxes than in 1992.

As postulated in Chapter 4, common changes across the region suggest that legacies may play a role. However, the trend of lowering tax rates—which also extends to Central and Eastern Europe—cannot be taken as a *direct* legacy of communism (and would not have been predicted as a likely development in the early 1990s). Rather, two broad but different *reactions* to communist legacies and the effects of institutional deterioration appear to have coincided: in the more advanced transition countries, a desire to reduce the role of the state in order to speed up growth and attract investment; and in the weaker CIS countries, a reaction to sharply decreased state capacity associated with the erosion and breakdown of the USSR, which induced governments to reduce formal tax rates in order to bring more parts of the economy into the tax nets.

Table 5.1: Rules—basic statutory tax rates 1992 to 2004

	1992			1997			2001				2004			
	VAT	CIT	PIT	VAT	CIT	SST	VAT	CIT	PIT	SST	VAT	CIT	PIT	SST
Armenia (1)	28	25	na	20	30	38	20	20	20	18	20	20	10, 20	25–5r
Azerbaijan	na	35	55	20	32	39	18	27	35	32+1	18	24	14–35	29
Belarus	28	30	50	20	30	37	20	30	9–30	35	18	24	9–30	35
Estonia	18	35	50	18	26	33	18	0	26f	33	18	0,26k	26f,k	36.5
Georgia (2)	28	na	na	20	20	34	na	20	12–20	28	18	20	12f	20
Kazakhstan	28	35	30	20	30	32	16	30	5–30	21	15	30	5–20	20–7r
Kyrgyzstan	28	35	na	20	30	37	20	10*	20*	29*	20	20	10, 20	33
Latvia	12	35	35	18	25	37	18	22	25f	36	18	15	25f	~43
Lithuania	18	30	33	18	29	31	18	24	33f	34	18	15	33f	31
Moldova	28	48	na	20	32	40	20	28	10–25	31	20	20	10–22	30
Russian Fed.	28	18	40	20	35	39.5	20	24	13f	35.6–5r	18	24	13f	35.6–2r
Tajikistan (3)	28	45	na	20	40	38	20	30	10–20	25	20	25	8–13i	25
Turkmenistan (4)	28	na	na	20	25	31	20	25–35	25	na	15	8, 20	12f	na
Ukraine	22	18	50	20	30	40	20	30	10–40	~ 40	20j	25	13f,ii	~40iii
Uzbekistan (1)	30	45	50	17	37	43	20	26	15–45	na	20	20	36	37.2

CIT Company Income Tax;
PIT Personal Income Tax;
f flat rate; otherwise, the top (marginal) PIT rate is given.
SST Social Security Tax. Figures for SST are subject to some uncertainty as countries differ widely in whether there is one unified or multiple contributions (pension, unemployment, disability, etc.) and how these are levied;
r regressive;
* these low rates were adopted in 2001; however, after IMF objections, PIT was re-increased;
1 tax rates of 1996;
2 data for 2004: new Georgian Tax Code as of January 2005;
3 the latest tax rate changes in Tajikistan came into force from January 2005;
4 new tax code in force since November 2004;
ii to be raised to 15 per cent from 2007;
j to be lowered to 17 per cent in 2005 and to 15 per cent in 2006;
iii 34 per cent for pensions, 2.9 social security, 1.9 unemployment; 0.86–13.8 accident insurance; the tax base is capped at around 350 EURO/month;
k only distributed profits (dividends) are taxed. Both the tax on dividends and the personal income tax are to be gradually reduced to 20 per cent by 2007.

Sources: Okno Group, East-West Letter, vol. 1, no. 3, summer 1992 (data for 1992); Schaffer and Turley (2001) (data for 1997); DFK International, Worldwide Tax Overview (for 2004); IMF country reports (various) (for 2001 and 2004).

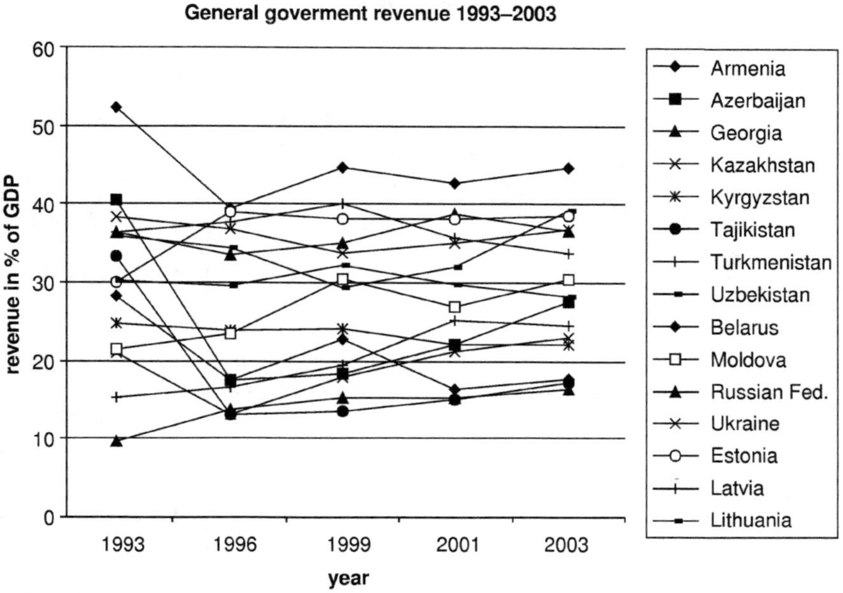

Graph 5.2: Government revenue in post-Soviet countries, 1993–2003

Sources: EBRD, Transition Report, various years

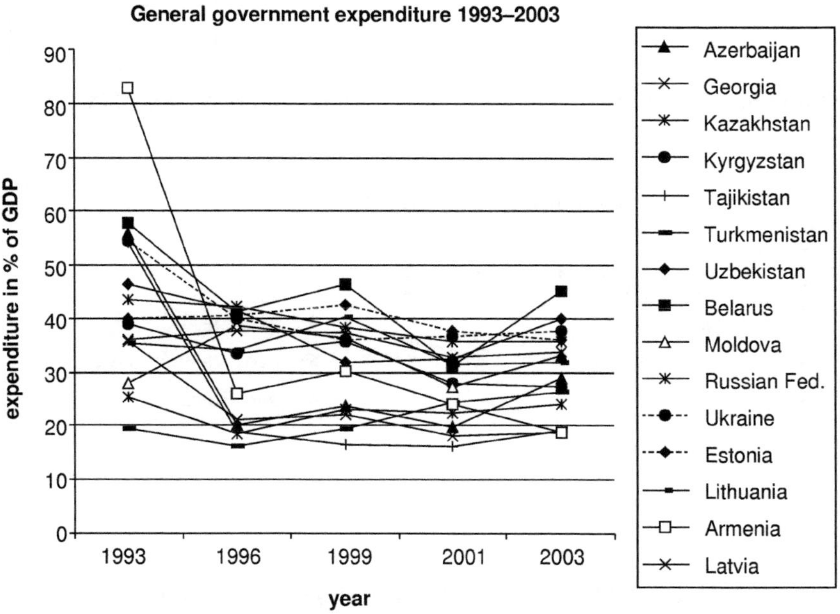

Graph 5.3: Government expenditure in post-Soviet countries 1993–2003

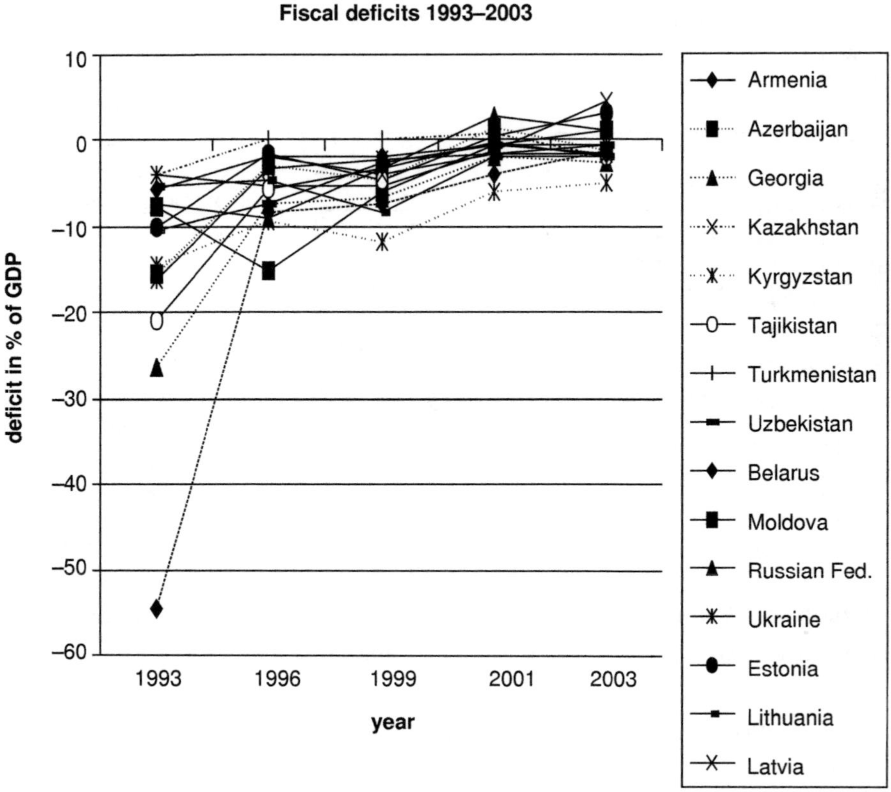

Graph 5.4: Government deficits in post-Soviet countries, 1993–2003

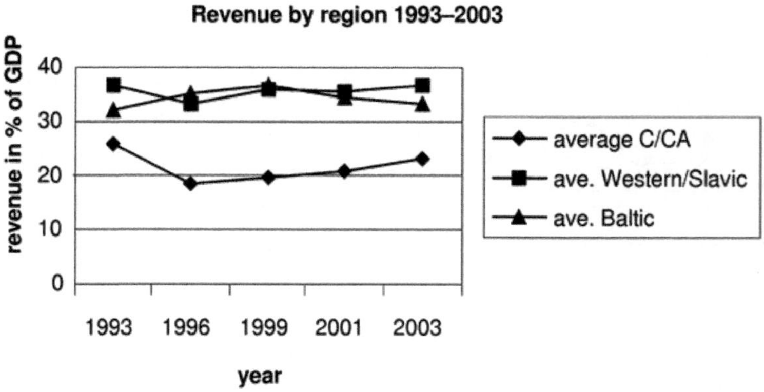

Graph 5.5: Government revenue by region, 1993–2003

Sources: EBRD, Transition Report, various years

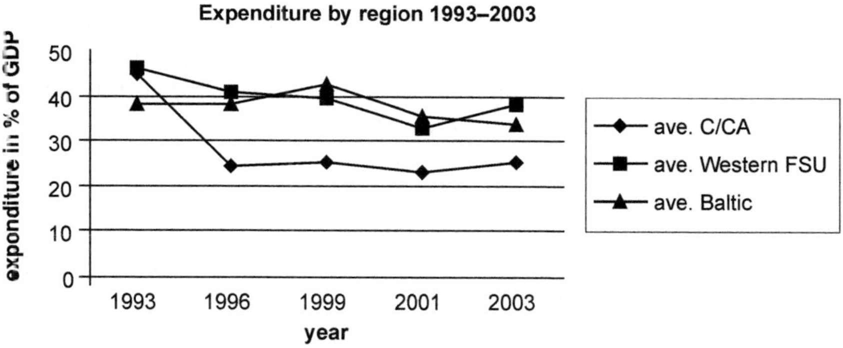

Graph 5.6: Government expenditure by region, 1993–2003

Sources: EBRD, Transition Report, various years

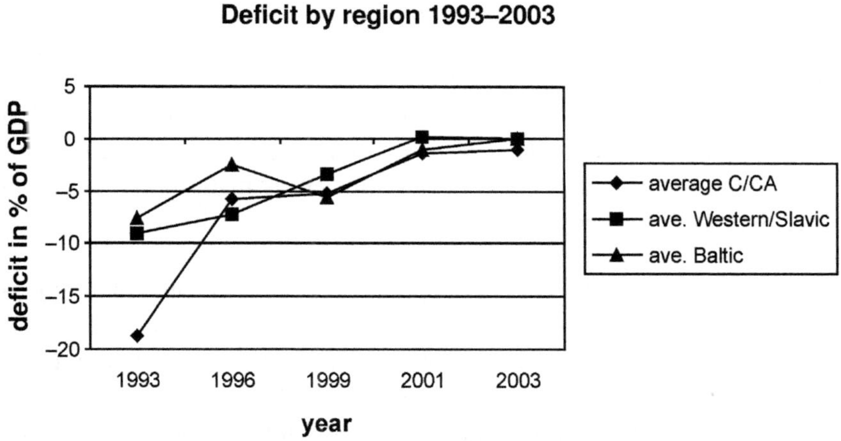

Graph 5.7: Government deficit by region, 1993–2003

Sources: EBRD, Transition Report, various years

In the Baltic states, flat income taxes were introduced, but at high rates (26 to 33) implying high taxation of labor, while profit taxes were lowered most radically in order to attract foreign direct investment (FDI). In Russia and other CIS countries in contrast, flat income taxes were later introduced at low rates (around 13 per cent), since the state was not able to tax higher incomes at progressive rates; while profit taxes were also reduced but less and later than in the Baltic states. Overall, and especially at the formal level, therefore, there was a clear departure from the past with regard to rules about taxation.

Informally, certain practices such as granting enterprises tax privileges—i.e., variable tax treatment—lingered as will be discussed especially in the chapters on Ukraine and Russia; and personal income taxation which had not existed in Soviet times proved difficult to introduce effectively.

Results of extraction (i.e., the percentage of revenues collected relative to GDP) differed vastly especially in the beginning (Graph 5.2). The considerable variation regarding deficits (see Graph 5.4) also indicates that governments had very different capacities to deal with the shock of independence and the disintegration of the Soviet Union. Expenditures far exceeded available revenues especially in Armenia, Georgia, and Tajikistan which were affected by armed conflicts. Over time, extractive capacity recovered at least to some extent across the region, including those post-Soviet countries with weaker states. However, considerable differentiation remained, primarily between countries at the lower and at the higher levels of per capita income; but also between countries at similar per capita income levels (for example, between Moldova and Georgia and Armenia; or between Belarus and Russia) (see Appendix, Table I.2.1 and Graph I.1.1).

Thus, both with regard to rules and with regard to results, legacies had an indirect rather than a direct and easily predictable impact. Furthermore, both the development of rules and of results was affected by institutional deterioration rather than exclusively by legacies.

2) Fiscal size, fiscal deficits, and international integration. In general, the fiscal size of post-Soviet states decreased considerably—with the partial exception of Belarus, which will be explored in Chapter 9. The initial drop in revenues is particularly stark when we take into account that the figures measure shares in GDP—while GDP itself sharply contracted. In absolute terms, therefore, government was reduced drastically in most countries.[39] At first glance, this may appear as a confirmation of the hypothesis that international integration and the peripheral status of post-Soviet countries forced a downward revision in the size of the state. However, this is not borne out when we take a closer look. Firstly, between the mid-1990s and 2003, that is, as international integration in terms of trade and FDI intensified, a new increase in the size of the state took place. Secondly, those countries which were economically most integrated in the global economy, i.e., the Baltic states, had *larger* rather than *smaller* states in terms of fiscal size.[40] Furthermore, in those countries in which revenue collection remained comparatively lowest (Tajikistan, Georgia, and Armenia), this was strongly related to domestic factors, including internal conflict, rather than to international and 'globalization' pressures.

At the same time, it is interesting to observe that very different economic systems produced similar aggregate fiscal results. Thus, Estonia—the economically most liberal post-Soviet country, and Belarus—which has a neo-Soviet system with an owner rather than a tax state, were the two countries with the largest fiscal size and the smallest deficits.

Still, there is one effect which appears related to the international realm: in all post-Soviet countries, fiscal deficits became much smaller towards the end of the decade with a number of countries even registering surpluses (see Graph 5.4 above). To some extent this was driven by the strong economic upturn since 2000 which generated higher than expected revenues and helped to reduce deficits. However, declining deficits were also a reaction to the debt-shock of the mid-1990s. Starting from a virtually debt-free situation in 1992, several post-Soviet states rapidly accumulated external debt which reached frightening proportions of shrinking GDPs. By 2001, the ratio of debt to GDP reached over 100 per cent in Kyrgyzstan and in Tajikistan, over 90 per cent in Moldova, and around 60 per cent in Armenia and Georgia.[41] As a result, debt service became a drain on budgets. In reaction to this trend, CIS countries reduced their deficits. At the same time, resource-rich CIS countries began to profit from rising energy prices in the 2000s which some used to run budget surpluses and to rapidly reduce their debt (see Chapter 11 on Russia; and Appendix, Table I.2.3, and Graph II.1.1).

Thus, while international factors do not appear to be a factor forcing convergence in fiscal size among CIS countries, they have played some role in the convergence towards much smaller deficits across the CIS region.

Two additional observations are the following—again pointing to the importance of the reaction to institutional deterioration:

3) Discrepancies between formal rules and results. Rules and results varied hugely particularly at the beginning of the decade. Thus, while tax rules were relatively similar in 1997, results (revenues) varied particularly strongly up to that time. By 2001, the gap between formal tax rules and revenue results had decreased somewhat as rules were revised downward while revenues stabilized in most countries to some extent (see Table 5.1 and Graph 5.2). This trend continued in the 2000s, with further downward revisions of formal rules and rising or stabilizing revenues—while service provision continued to suffer particularly in those states with the lowest revenue to GDP ratios (Tajikistan, Georgia).

4) Downward adjustment of rules. The reduction in discrepancies between formal and informal rules was achieved through a downward revision of rules.

The state had to adjust its demands on citizens to its capacity to actually implement taxation. Formal-informal discrepancies resulted inter alia from post-Soviet power relations, in which the state was especially unable to tax well-connected businesses, and wealthy individuals (see also Chapter 7 on Ukraine). The downward adjustment of rules can be a viable pathway for weak states to begin stabilizing their formal systems and for re-building capacity after a period of 'de-institutionalization' in which formal rules lost much of their credibility. Several CIS countries successfully increased anew their revenue extraction after the downward revisions.[42]

Regional diffusion of reforms also played a role in this regard: several countries followed reform steps taken by others—particularly the Russian tax reform of 1999-2000, discussed in detail in Chapter 11. Thus, between 2001 and 2005, both Ukraine and Tajikistan adopted a personal income tax similar to the Russian model. During the same period, a number of countries revised their profit tax rate downwards to the rate of 24 per cent, a rate which was first introduced in Russia.

Finally, the distribution of revenue decline across countries suggests that the level of development played a significant role. As Graphs 5.2 and 5.5 show, revenue levels generally fell steeper and remained lower in poorer CIS countries than in richer ones. The following section will therefore explore the relative importance of the level of development and how this relates to the importance of political consolidation.

5.4. Exploring some quantitative relationships: level of development and political consolidation

This section explores the effects of the level of development on the one hand and of regime transition and resulting political consolidation on the other hand, based on a range of indicators which are related to state capacity (proportion of revenue to GDP, size of fiscal deficits, levels of perceived corruption, and the overall development of the economy).

5.4.1. FISCAL SIZE

A proxy for the level of development at the outset of transition is the level of GDP in 1985 for each of the Soviet republics. 1985 was the year before the 'noise' of *perestroika* and dissolution set in, so it serves well as an indicator for the level of development that the republics had achieved by the end of the Soviet period. It does not reflect, however, the extent of the development which occurred primarily during the Soviet period or had longer historical roots. As discussed in Chapter 4, poorer countries, which also tend to be more rural, would be expected to be able to extract smaller shares of resources from the economy.[43] The following three graphs explore the relationship between the 1985 level of GDP per capita and the fiscal size of post-Soviet countries in the mid-1990s (Graph 5.8b without the outliers of Georgia and Uzbekistan), and of the relationship between the per capita incomes and the deficit levels which emerged in the mid-1990s.

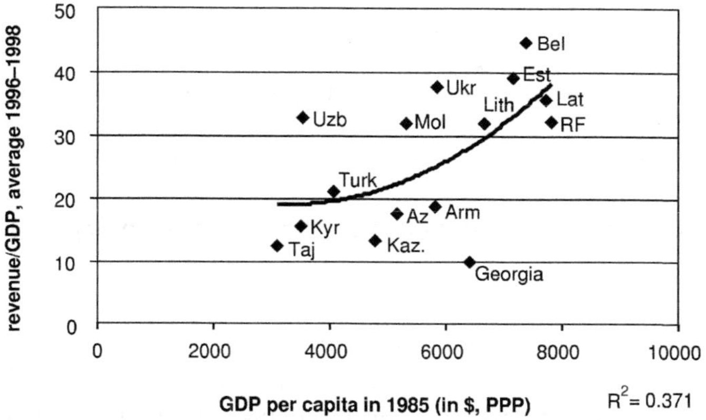

Graph 5.8a: Soviet level of development and fiscal size during transition

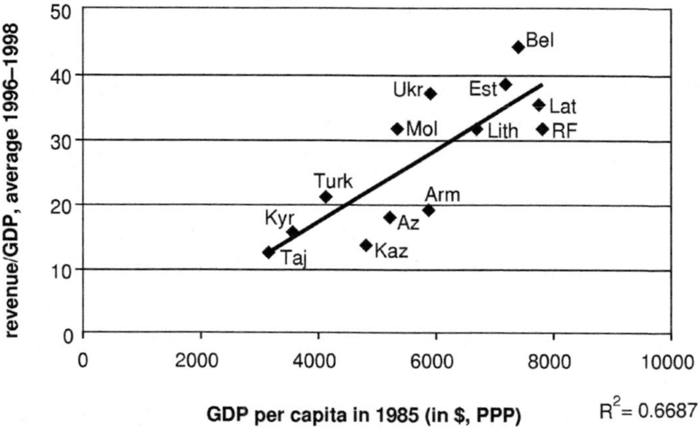

Graph 5.8b: Soviet level of development and fiscal size without outliers

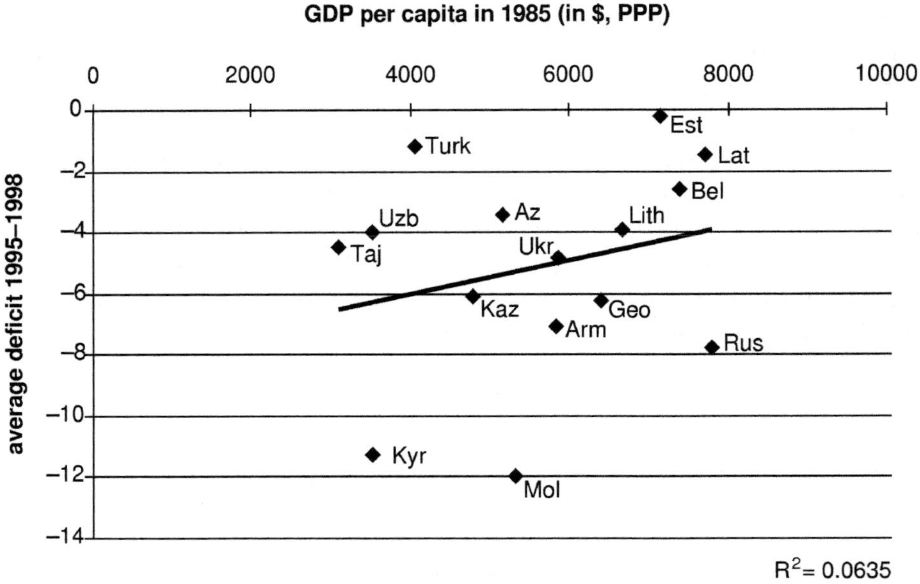

Graph 5.9: Soviet level of development and fiscal deficits during transition

Three observations result from these graphs:

As Graph 5.9 shows, there is no clear relationship between fiscal deficits during transition and the level of development—the points are scattered across the diagram. Thus, from the per capita income of a republic in 1985 one could not have predicted how this country would fare in terms of keeping the fiscal deficit within limits during the period of economic stress.

According to Graphs 5.8 a and b, there appears to be a relationship between the level of development achieved in the late Soviet period and fiscal size of a state (the ratio of revenue to GDP). This relationship becomes stronger when we leave two outliers (Georgia and Uzbekistan) out of the analysis (Graph 5.8b). The relationship is also observable for data from the early 2000s (Graph 5.10).

However, compared to the relationship for the earlier period the fit decreases (as reflected in the lower R2). Thus, while poorer post-Soviet states tend to have a smaller fiscal size than richer ones, this relationship is rather loose and accounts for only part of the story. Looking beyond the post-Soviet region, the less developed CIS countries still have a larger fiscal size than countries with similar per capita income levels, for example in Latin America.[44] Regarding the relationship between regime type and revenues, the distribution of cases contradicts the proposition put forth by Maravall that democracies tend to have higher revenues than authoritarian regimes.[45] Thus, both Uzbekistan and Belarus are in the high revenue-group together with the Baltic democracies, and several hybrid regimes from the Western FSU region (see Graphs 5.8a and 5.10).

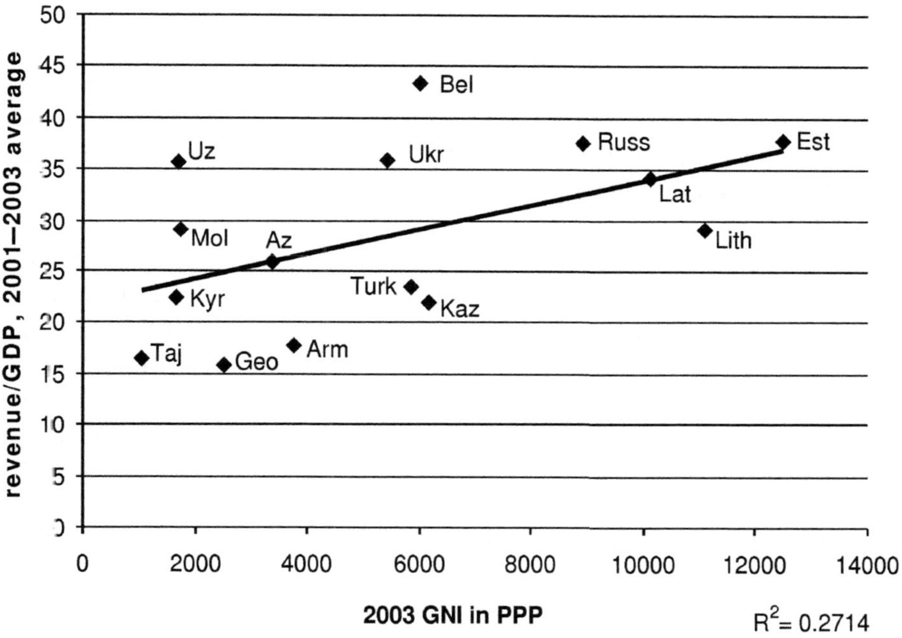

Graph 5.10: Levels of development and share of revenue to GDP, early 2000s

Furthermore, the graphs point to two interesting outliers: Georgia and Uzbekistan. Georgia has a (far) smaller fiscal size than expected given its 1985 level of per capita income, while in Uzbekistan the fiscal size is considerably larger. However, these outliers are in line with the second variable we are exploring, political consolidation. Thus, Georgia has been plagued by intense political contestation throughout the independence period.[46] Uzbekistan, in contrast, is a case of authoritarian consolidation. When we look at the economic side in greater detail, the high proportion of revenue to GDP in Uzbekistan is even more unexpected. The agricultural sector accounts for around 27 per cent of its GDP throughout the independence period—one of the largest in the post-Soviet region; and agriculture tends to be more difficult to tax than industry.[47] Therefore, Uzbekistan's high level of revenue extraction clearly contradicts economic predictions of fiscal size.

5.4.2. DEFICITS, ECONOMIC RESULTS, AND CORRUPTION

While the level of development appears as a relevant but 'imperfect' explanatory factor for fiscal size, it does not account very much for the degree of fiscal discipline during transition as Graph 5.9 indicated. This section therefore examines whether political consolidation—proposed in Chapter 4 as a key factor in the state-building process—can account for this aspect of fiscal development across the post-Soviet region.

As a proxy for regime consolidation, I use the classifications from Freedom House. If a country is classified as either a consolidated democracy or a consolidated autocracy, there is a clear allocation of power—around rules in the first case, around a leader or a leadership group in the second.[48] Those countries rated as lying in the middle of the spectrum, in contrast, are more likely to be affected by fragmentation and contestation as proposed in Chapter 4. Countries may also shift over time, as will be discussed in the case studies on Ukraine and Russia.

In addition, I consider possible correlations between political consolidation and two further indicators: the levels of corruption, and the depth of economic crisis (i.e. the drop in GDP) during transition. As laid out in Chapter 2, section 2, the prevalence of corruption can be taken as an indicator reflecting the degree to which the state is a source of problems. The second relationship is explored based on the assumption that—if political consolidation matters—then there should be a link between political consolidation, the capacity of institutions, and economic outcomes.

Graph 5.11 shows a rather close relationship between regime consolidation and fiscal discipline during early transition: those countries which Freedom House rated either as consolidated democracies or as consolidated autocracies in 1996 experienced comparatively lower deficits in the mid-1990s than countries with intermediary regimes.[49]

While this relationship between the political regime and deficit levels is relevant in the mid-1990s,[50] it disappears over time—due to the general reduction in deficit levels as discussed in section 3.

A further relationship to explore is the scale of GDP loss at the end of the transition crisis, and the respective linkages with regime consolidation and

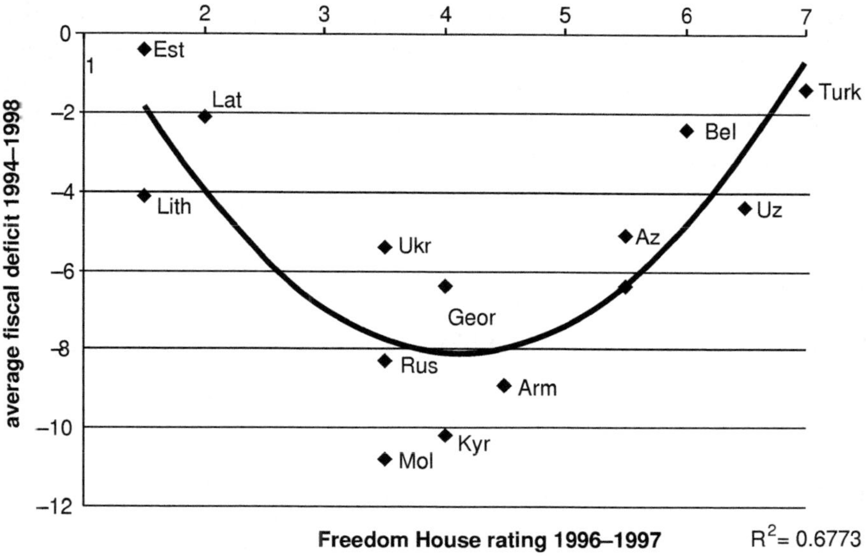

Graph 5.11: Relationship between political regime and fiscal deficits during transition

(FH ratings run from 1=perfectly democratic to 7=fully authoritarian)

Sources: Freedom House and EBRD Transition Report (2002).

with the level of GDP before the onset of transition. As Popov and others have pointed out, the loss of GDP in the post-Soviet countries is the deepest peacetime economic crisis recorded in modern history - deeper than during the great depression.[51] On the one hand, one might assume that the poorest countries would have lost out the most, since they were most dependent on intra-USSR subsidies prior to transition. On the other hand, there could be a relationship between regime consolidation, the strength of state capacity, and the scale of the loss of GDP. In contrast to standard neo-institutional assumptions such a linkage would assume that institutional capacity matters more than the type of institutions (i.e. whether they conform to a "market economy").

Graphs 5.12 and 5.13 indicate the following: rather surprisingly, there is no relationship between per capita incomes in 1985 and the scale of GDP loss by 2000. There is, however, a relationship between regime type and the level of GDP in 1999 relative to 1989. Thus, on the one hand, Uzbekistan and Turkmenistan have the highest levels of GDP relative to their levels in 1989 among all post-Soviet countries. The Western CIS, and in particular Ukraine and

Moldova, in contrast, are among the biggest losers of transition. Finally, the Baltic states initially saw rather sharp drops in levels of GDP, but then experienced a recovery already from 1993-94 onwards. Thus, in the second phase of state-building—the mid to late 1990s—they had already recovered GDP levels to some extent (see also Appendix, Table I.1.1).

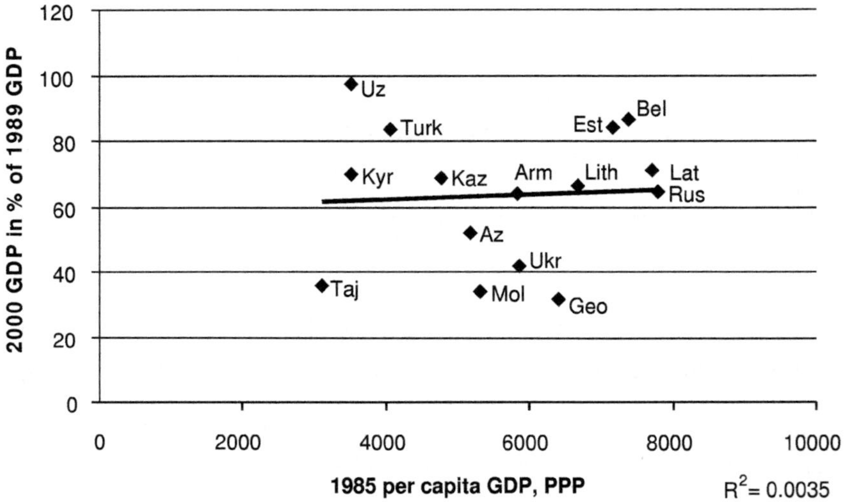

Graph 5.12: 1985 level of development and 2000 GDP level

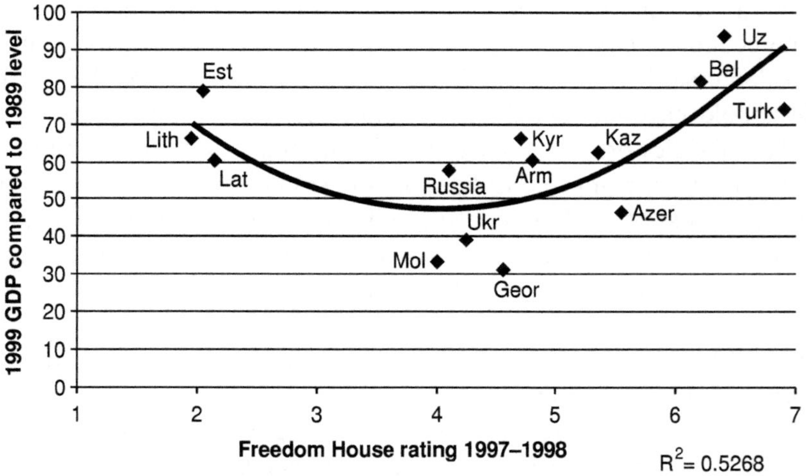

Graph 5.13: Regime and GDP level in 1999 (1989=100)

Sources: UNECE and Freedom House

Furthermore the relationship between regime consolidation and the level of GDP relative to 1989 remained strong or grew even stronger over time, especially when we use the electoral process rather than the overall democracy score as the regime indicator.[52]

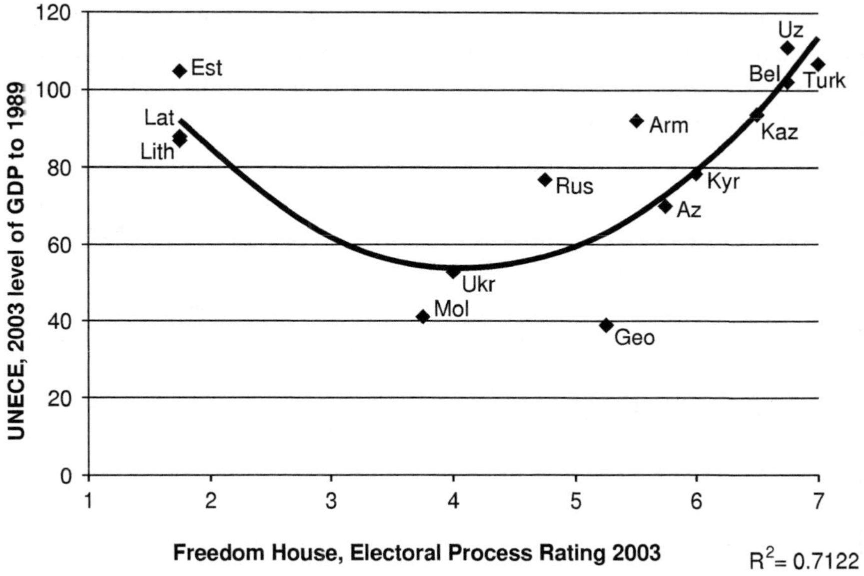

Graph 5.14: Electoral process and GDP level in 2003 (1989=100)

Sources: UNECE and Freedom House

The presence of relatively robust economies in consolidated autocracies cum non-reformed economies is particularly striking if we consider standard assumptions about the inefficiencies of communist-type institutional systems.[53] According to these assumptions, reforming countries should show considerably higher rates of growth than those sticking to the old system. However, countries with consolidated authoritarian regimes which retained modified versions of the Soviet institutional order maintained relatively high levels of GDP.[54] This may be associated with the assumption proposed in Chapter 3 that state formation without transformation is considerably less costly in the short and medium-term than state formation combined with transformation. Furthermore, as Graph 5.14 indicates, the authoritarian-cum-non-reformed countries maintained their position even when strong growth returned to the CIS region from 1999–2000 onwards.

The following two graphs look at the relationship between perceived corruption and the level of development on the one hand, and of political consolidation on the other hand. As discussed in Chapter 2, corruption can be regarded as a proxy measure for the state as a source of problems. A lower level of development is widely regarded as associated with higher levels of corruption—although the causal relationship is not entirely clear, and although there appears to be a somewhat different pattern, for example, in African and in Asian countries.[55] The relationship between regime consolidation and levels of corruption is less frequently thematized.

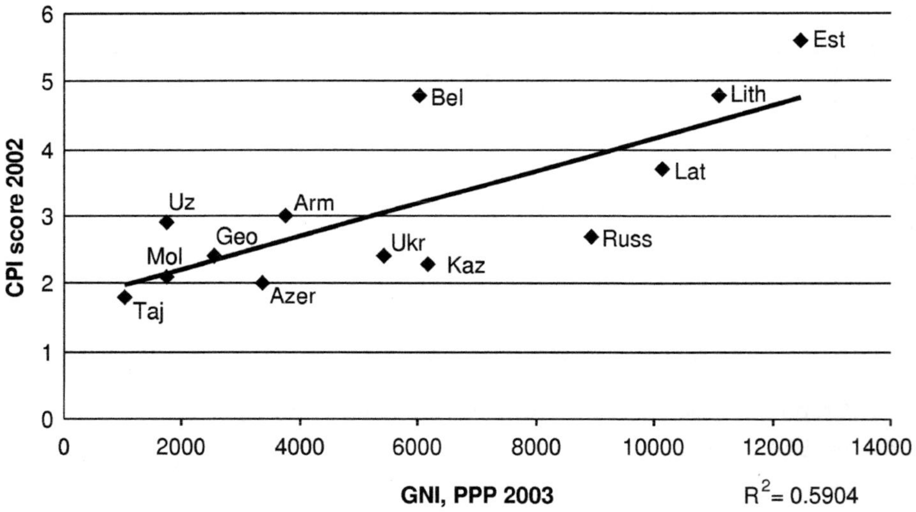

Graph 5.15: Relationship between level of development and perceived corruption
(CPI scores range from 10=no corruption; 0=absolute corruption)

Sources: World Development Indicators; Transparency International

The two graphs show that both relationships are strong—between the level of development and perceived corruption as well as between the regime type and corruption—with the latter being slightly stronger. This indicates that both the level of development and political consolidation matter for the degree to which the state became dysfunctional in the post-Soviet period.

Interestingly, a different survey, the BEEPS—conducted both in 1999 and 2002—suggests that businesses both in Belarus and Uzbekistan find the state to be less of a problem than in many other CIS countries. "A consistent finding in both the 1999 and 2002 BEEPS is the unexpectedly favorable perceptions of the business environment in Belarus and Uzbekistan, particularly given the limited extent of market-oriented reforms in these countries, including liberalization of markets and trade."[56]

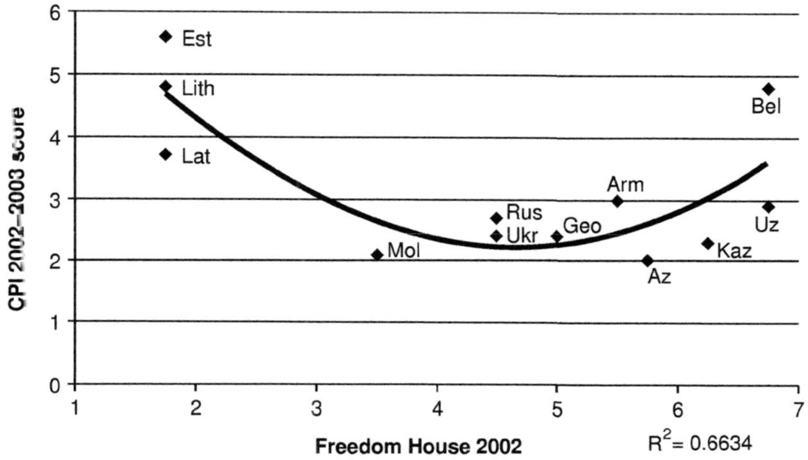

Graph 5.16: Relationship between regime and perceived corruption

Sources: Freedom House and Transparency International

As this observation and the correlations explored here reflect, the consolidated authoritarian systems diverge from the expectation that the 'worst' type of political system would also produce the 'worst' institutions and the worst economic outcomes. However, most recent CPI ratings suggest that the problem of corruption is increasing in the *dictaduras* of the former Soviet Union—Turkmenistan, Uzbekistan, and Belarus. As suggested in Chapter 4, while having done relatively well during the first post-Soviet decade, these personal dictatorships are likely to come under increasing strain, both due to domestic discontent and due to the difficulty of preserving communist-type institutions in a regional neighborhood of 'wild' capitalism.

5.4.3. REGIME TYPE AND SPENDING ON PUBLIC SERVICES

While this study is about the causes and pathways of state-building rather than on what states do, it is interesting to explore the link between the political regime and state activity in some more detail.[57] As pointed out above, among post-Soviet countries, those with authoritarian regimes do not have smaller fiscal sizes than democratic regimes as Maravall proposes; on the contrary, consolidated authoritarian regimes are associated with fiscal sizes that exceed expectations based on their level of development. This raises the question to what extent different regimes engage in spending on 'good' public goods, such as education and health (in contrast to public goods such as external and internal security). Graph 5.17 explores what share of GDP different post-Soviet countries spent on health and education on average in 1996 to 1998.

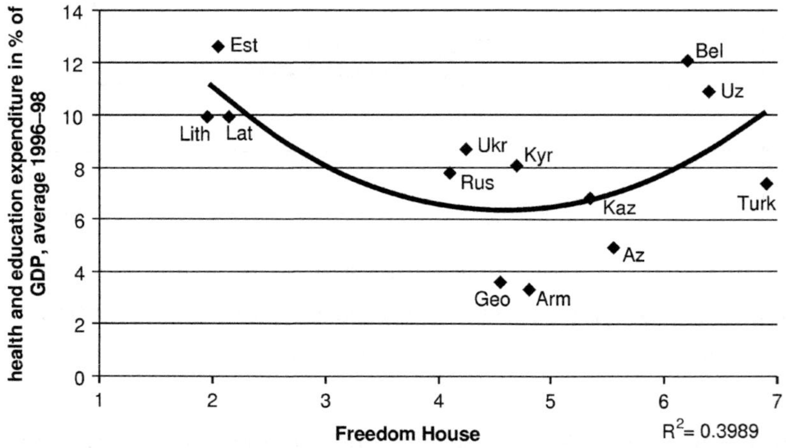

Graph 5.17: Regime consolidation and spending on education and health
Sources: Freedom House, World Development Report

The graph shows that consolidated regimes of both the democratic and authoritarian variant tended to spend a larger share of GDP on education and health than unconsolidated regimes.[58] However, the relationship is not very strong, given that most post-Soviet countries pursue relatively high public spending on education, due to the high social value attached to it—this is also reflected in substantial private spending for higher education. High levels of extraction are found in countries with authoritarian regimes, especially Belarus and Uzbekistan, providing the necessary funds. Importantly, there are also sharp differences within the group of consolidated autocracies: the Belarusian regime in particular derives its legitimacy from maintaining a Soviet-style welfare state; while Turkmenistan in contrast began to reduce educational opportunities as a deliberate policy for exercising control.[59]

5.5. Summary

The chapter provides an overview of the Soviet fiscal system, its disintegration, and fiscal developments in the 15 successor states of the Soviet Union. Section 1 outlined the main features of the Soviet fiscal system stressing its fundamentally different nature from a capitalist 'tax state.' Section 2 sketched the period of disintegration and institutional deterioration during the break-up of the Soviet Union, and the resulting fiscal crisis.

Section 3 looked at fiscal rules and results in terms of revenues, expenditures, and deficits, assessing two potential factors of convergence: (institutional) legacies and international influences. Section 4 explored the relative importance of the level of development versus that of political consolidation for several variables reflecting various elements of state capacity (the level of revenues, fiscal deficit, contraction/growth of GDP during transition, corruption, and spending on public services).

The description and data presented in sections 1 to 3 show that few direct legacies remained in the field of taxation from the Soviet to the post-Soviet period. From the start, the post-Soviet countries had substantially varying capacities to extract revenue. The common trend across the region has been a downward revision of tax rates and revenue levels over time, which appears as a reaction to the combined economic and 'stateness' crisis of the late Soviet and early post-Soviet period. In this sense, institutional deterioration, and the requirements of a changing economy shaped the current institutional system as much as or more than institutional legacies.

Looking at international economic integration, we do not find support for the assumption that being peripheral in the global economy has forced post-Soviet states to adopt a small fiscal size. While all states reduced their fiscal size during transition, the countries most integrated internationally are among those which maintained the largest fiscal size. Furthermore, since the mid-1990s the fiscal size increased again especially in those countries where contraction was initially the strongest (Georgia, Tajikistan, etc.)—even though international integration increased rather than decreased with time. All of this suggests that domestic and regional rather than 'global' international factors affected post-Soviet states most strongly.

While international factors had little impact on the fiscal size, they did play a role with regard to fiscal deficits. As analyzed in sections 3 and 4, the initial level of deficits was closely linked to the challenges of political transition. However, subsequently deficits sharply decreased across the region. The rapid rise in debt levels in the 1990s, and the 1998 financial crisis in Russia meant that countries either could no longer borrow abroad or became much more cautious. At the same time, in the early 2000s fiscal discipline was facilitated by strong post-depression growth; while sharply rising energy prices even allowed some resource-rich countries to accumulate substantial surpluses. In this sense, international opportunities and constraints had an impact on how much post-Soviet countries could overspend to finance expenditures during different phases of the transition process.[60]

In section 4, I looked at various aspects of state capacity and their relationship with the level of development on the one hand and with political consolidation on the other. In the mid-1990s, the fiscal size of post-Soviet states was rather closely associated with the level of development achieved during the late Soviet period, but this link became weaker by the early 2000s. Both for the early and for the later time period, political factors appear to drive several of the outliers that have either unusually low revenues (Georgia) or unusually high revenues (Uzbekistan and Belarus) relative to their level of development. Particularly in the second time period, there seems to be also a 'regional' driver of differentiation, with all the Western CIS countries being above the trend-line, and all the countries of Central Asia and the Caucasus below (with the exception of Uzbekistan) (see Graph 5.10).

The degree of political consolidation appears to be particularly important with regard to fiscal discipline during the mid-1990s (Graph 5.11), as well as with regard to two other dimensions: the level of GDP, and the level of perceived corruption. The effect of political consolidation on economic outcomes is particularly striking: those countries which combined a consolidated authoritarian regime with the preservation of the old institutional structure on the one hand and those which consolidated democratic regimes and undertook full reforms on the other hand, did relatively better than all others. Looking at the raw figures over time (see Appendix, Table I.1.1), we see that the first group appeared to have avoided the cost of institutional change. The second group incurred a higher initial loss of GDP, but began to recover relatively early, while the countries in the middle incurred far higher costs than benefits during the first 15 years of independence.[61] Perceived corruption, treated as a proxy for the degree to which the state is a source of problems, appears to be driven both by the level of development and by the degree of political consolidation (Graphs 5.15 and 5.16).

From this analysis, two important implications for the overall argument of this study emerge: one, domestic political factors appear to play a crucial role with regard to the development of state capacity in post-Soviet countries. Structural and institutional variables such as legacies, international economic integration, and the level of economic development are important, but they do not by themselves determine the development of state capacity.

The further chapters cover four cases which share key structural preconditions, especially with regard to the initial level of development, but due to their political configurations have followed four different trajectories as spelled out in Chapter 4. Ukraine, covered in greatest depth, has followed the path of a hybrid regime, with a tendency towards eventually greater democratization. Belarus has followed a path of political consolidation along autocratic lines. Lithuania, in contrast, has followed the 'Baltic' route of democratic consolidation and EU integration. Russia, finally, is another hybrid case, but—different from Ukraine—one which has veered towards a more authoritarian system over time. For each of these countries, their political configuration and its evolution is traced over time from 1992 to 2005 and is related to the development of their fiscal systems, and its implications for overall state capacity.

Notes

1 Schumpeter (1991).
2 Shearer (1996), 238: "Their aim was to create mechanisms that would allow the state to mobilize the maximum amount of resources from the population and the economy for industrial modernization. *Zagotovka sredstv naseleniia* (procuring the means of the population), the term Stalinist officials used [...], reflected the extractive character of the state's policies."
3 Andrle (1994), 158.
4 Sinelnikov and Reznikov (1995), 3.
5 Newcity (1986), 9, 30–32.
6 The control of the planning system was often flawed in practice; nonetheless, the state had power over allocation of funds well beyond that of states in market-based economies.
7 Hutchings (1983), 16, 95–96; Nove (1986), 235–8; Cheasty and Davis (1996), 10.
8 See White, Gardner, and Schöpflin (1987), 286–295; Kakwani (1995), 28; Connor (1997), 21–22.
9 Tanzi (March 1993), 27.
10 UNECE (2000, no. 1), 60.
11 Nove (1986), 251; Sinelnikov and Reznikov (1995), 15.
12 Tanzi (1993), 16.
13 Wittkowsky (1998), 39–44.
14 Shlapentokh (1998). "There were no manifestations of mass discontent in the 1970s and early 1980s. Most Soviet people, while critical of many aspects of their society, considered their life 'normal' and were essentially satisfied with it." (p. 30).
15 See Gibson (1996), 959.
16 Brunner (1975).

17 Simis (1982), 57.
18 Simis (1982), 46.
19 Shelley (1996); Solnick (1998), 3–4.
20 Simis (1982), 22–43, esp. 35.
21 Shelley (1996); Srivastava (1999).
22 Christian (1982), 75.
23 See also Huntington (1968), and Theda Skocpol, *States and Social Revolutions*, Cambridge: Cambridge University Press, 1979.
24 Bunce (1999a).
25 Willerton (1992). Shearer describes the development of the early Soviet administration as a bureaucracy operating not rationally but based on the logic of military command. Shearer (1996), 40–42, 235–240.
26 Srivastava (1999).
27 See Roman Zyla, in D'Anieri, Kravchuk, Kuzio (1999), 246; Hill (1990), 121; Jowitt (1992), 224–225; Shlapentokh (1989).
28 Sinelnikov and Reznikov (1995), 4–7.
29 Sinelnikov and Reznikov (1995), 6; Vavilov and V. Vyugin (1991).
30 Stroev, Bliakhman, and Krotov (1999), 293.
31 Sinelnikov and Reznikov (1995), 11; Nagy (2000), 65.
32 Srivastava (1999).
33 The hegemonic position of the CPSU was abolished in March 1990 when Article 6 of the 1977 constitution was changed.
34 Srivastava (1999), 81.
35 Solnick (1998), 7.
36 Srivastava (1999), 83.
37 Kuzio (2000), 171.
38 General government revenues refer to national and local budgets plus extra-budgetary funds (such as pension funds). However, the data provided by different organizations (national governments, IMF, EBRD) differ considerably; and are often revised in later editions from the same source. Therefore, data should be regarded as indicating approximate results and trends, especially for the early 1990s. For a summary of taxation developments covering a number of CIS countries up to 2004, see http://www.pwcglobal.com/hu/mag/main/home/CEE_CIS_2004.pdf [accessed: August 11, 2005].
39 See also Cheasty and Davis (1996).
40 Most post-Soviet countries have rather high ratios of trade turnover to GDP; see EBRD (2001).
41 Helbling, Mody, and Sahay (2004).
42 This is in line with Leitzel's ideas around rule evasion and the adjustment of formal rules. See Leitzel (2003).
43 Ardant (1975); Burgess and Stern (1993).
44 In 2000, Moldova and Bolivia, and the Russian Federation and Mexico had similar levels of per capita GDP; however, total revenue levels for Moldova and Russia were 10 per cent or more above revenue levels in comparable Latin American countries.
45 See Maravall (1997), 28.
46 See Wheatley (2003).
47 Data from EBRD (2001).

48 The measures of Freedom House are an imperfect proxy since FH's focus is on democratic freedom more than on power consolidation. This is most problematic for Tajikistan, which FH rated as a consolidated authoritarian regime in the mid-1990s despite civil war from 1992 to 1997. Tajikistan is therefore excluded from the analysis.

49 Bunce (1999b), 786 finds a similar relationship. See also Chapter 1, section 3.

50 Results are very similar when using alternative measures for the political regime, such as the World Bank's governance indicators (indicator 1, voice and accountability) available at http://www.worldbank.org/wbi/governance/govdata/.

51 Popov (2004), 96–98.

52 Freedom House has used various differentiations of its indicators over time. The 2003 democratization score is broken down as follows: Democratization Score (DEM) = average of Electoral Process (EP), Civil Society (CS), Independent Media (IM), and Governance (GOV) ratings.

53 See, for example, Leitzel (1995).

54 On Belarus, see Chapter 9. On Uzbekistan, see Zettelmeyer (1999).

55 Li, Xu, and Zou (2000); and Bardhan (1997).

56 EBRD, *Transition Report* (2002), 25.

57 See Maravall (1997), 24–25 who argues that: "As the index of democracy rises, so too does public expenditure on social welfare and education."

58 Moldova is excluded from the graph since it is a strong outlier—despite being a country with an unconsolidated regime it spends a high share of GDP on health and education (13 per cent).

59 *Eurasianet*, "Turkmenistan's Education System in Downward Spiral," May 5, 2004.

60 See also Helbling et al. (2004).

61 This leaves the question whether the dominant factor is regime consolidation or the degree of economic reforms. However, the two are closely aligned—there is no non-authoritarian regime which preserved the Soviet economic system, and there is no fully democratic case which did not undertake all-out reform. Looking at the dynamic of GDP loss to GDP recovery gives some further indication as discussed.

CHAPTER 6.

UKRAINE—FROM SOVIET BREAKDOWN TO DISORDERED INDEPENDENCE

One of the most remarkable features of post-Soviet developments in Ukraine has been their changing nature—deep decline followed by rebuilding and recovery, albeit still beset by distortions and deep-seated problems. In the early 1990s, the role of the state went so far out of kilter that hyperinflation emerged; while the economy fell into steep decline. By the early 2000s, the budget was back into balance, the currency had stabilized, and the economy was growing. The state stabilized, but many problems remained, including distortions which had been created during the Kuchma era.

Politically, Ukraine shifted from a regime in transition in the early 1990s, to a hybrid regime with growing concentration of power in the hands of the president in the late 1990s, and then made a renewed shift towards a democratic regime in late 2004, which initially, however, remained unconsolidated. The constitutional distribution of power between the president and parliament remained contested for the entire period.

For Ukraine's state capacity, as reflected in the fiscal sphere, this had a number of implications. On the one hand, once the initial period of crisis had passed, the state remained at a relatively safe distance from the brink of collapse. The potential risk of a break-up of Ukraine into an eastern and western part, or the lesser risk of a secession of the Crimean peninsula were at times politically exploited, but never reached crisis point. Revenue collection remained above 30 per cent of GDP throughout independence, which is substantial by comparison with other middle income and post-Soviet countries. On the other hand, continuous political contestation reduced the decision-making capacity within the state, while the practices of maintaining power in a hybrid regime fostered a number of dysfunctional aspects of the state; and the control and auditing system remained weak. Corruption, which especially affects the interface between the state and society, flourished in tax collection as well as in service delivery.

In Ukraine—similar to Russia—strong 'opaque' oligarchic interests emerged out of the disorder of transition. These interests had close links to government and engaged in state capture using their access to the state to derive economic rents. However, these 'opaque' and oligarchic networks were not unified, and relied on various *ad hoc* alliances; and their influence on the state did not shut out other interests altogether. Political parties—as a potentially balancing force—remained weak in Ukraine. To some degree, there was a self-interest in building the Ukrainian state among political leaders and the bureaucracy. Importantly, a significant and growing opposition appeared, and mass demonstrations eventually led to a change in government in late 2004. However, despite its own declared intentions, the opposition still proved less capable at fundamentally re-shaping the state, at least in the short term.

These are the broad outlines. This and the following two chapters trace developments in Ukraine from 1991 to 2005, looking at how political factors drove the development of institutions in this newly independent state. Chapter 6 covers developments from the struggle for independence to 1995, followed by Chapter 7 covering the period from 1996 to 2000. Chapter 8 reflects the period from 2001 to 2005, reaching into the period of new politics and renewed attempts of transforming the state in Ukraine.

The period from 1990–1991 to 1995 was primarily one of institutional deterioration and general disorientation. Ukraine suffered economically from the breakdown of the Soviet Union. The Communist Party was dissolved; but no strong new parties emerged. Instead, the political scene was dominated by various 'networks' which included former members of the CPU but without uniting them in an official organization. In the face of these trends, national unity was preserved and some—even if highly imperfect—foundations for the new state were laid. The transformation of the state, the changing of its role in the economy and in society, was begun, but remained in disarray and without any clear orientation.

Looking at developments in the fiscal sphere, state capacities weakened in terms of decision-making, implementation, and control. At the same time, the state continued to extract rather heavily from those parts of the economy still under its control (as privatization proceeded more slowly than in Russia).

Political fragmentation combined with a lack of orientation regarding the state-society model to follow. There was neither *de facto* nor *de jure* a well specified system of decision-making while the design of a new constitution dragged on, and contradictory decisions by disparate actors proliferated. The wide swings in economic policies from government to government indicate a lack of agreement over the basic directions to take. Legacies were most immediately present during this early period of state-building and provided some default-options in the operation of institutions. International factors mattered relatively less during this period since programs with international financial institutions were not in place, foreign debt did not yet pose a problem, and trade and financial integration with the non-CIS world occurred only gradually.

6.1. From Soviet republic to independent Ukraine

The Ukrainian SSR which moved towards independence in 1990–91 had been one of the most conservative republics in the late Soviet period.[1] The Ukrainian political leadership remained cautious in its support both for economic and political liberalization. However, over the course of the year 1990 as the Soviet Union began to seriously unravel, sovereignty and eventually independence became official policy goals. While the opposition gained influence during this period of independence, it remained in a minority, while parts of the old *nomenklatura* class transformed themselves into the new ruling class of independent Ukraine.

In March 1990, a new republican parliament was elected on a semi-competitive basis. Candidates from the opposition 'Democratic Bloc' won about a quarter of the seats, still leaving conservative and reformist members of the Communist Party with a comfortable majority.[2]

Throughout 1991, various declarations were issued, seeking to establish republican control over the economy and the state apparatus. A final tipping point came in August 1991: after it became clear that the putsch in Moscow against Gorbachev would fail, the Ukrainian leadership decided to embrace full independence. The Communist Party of Ukraine (CPU)—at that time an organization of 3.5 million members and controlling the commanding heights of the Ukrainian economy and polity—was outlawed on the initiative of Leonid Kravchuk, former secretary of ideology of the party and head of the presidium of the Ukrainian Supreme Soviet (*Verkhovna Rada*). Given that the position of old elites remained strong, the dissolution of the CPU may seem surprising, but apparently its most powerful members (correctly) assumed that they were well-enough positioned to dominate the emerging new system without the old party structure.[3]

In mid-1991, the office of a Ukrainian president was created, and in late 1991 the first presidential elections took place. Vyacheslav Chornovil the candidate of *Rukh*, the main opposition movement based in Western Ukraine, received 23 per cent of the vote, while the national communist, Leonid Kravchuk, won with a 62 per cent majority.

Both elites and various groups of the population held economic expectations related to independence. For elites, independence promised control over the republic's enterprises. Funds from the unraveling communist party provided the starting capital for industrialists and party members to establish new enterprises and the first commercial banks in Ukraine.[4] Broad popular support for independence was based on expectations that Ukraine would be better off outside the USSR.[5] According to Wilson, many Ukrainians believed that:

> Ukraine [...] suffered a net outflow of national income due to over-taxation, under-investment and the underpricing of key Ukrainian products, especially agricultural goods, iron, steel, and coal. [...] independence would allow Ukraine to gain control over its export surpluses, escape the fiscal and monetary chaos of the last days of the USSR, and free itself from discriminatory tax and investment policies.[6]

This economic consensus also included the miners in Eastern Ukraine who were a well-organized and vocal group at this point: they expected that independent Ukraine would invest more in the Donbas mines and steel industry than the federal USSR government, which in the 1980s had shifted investments to Siberia and other parts of the federation.[7]

The new Ukrainian state proved unable to meet these economic expectations—at least of the broader groups of the population. On the one hand, in the face of deepening economic crisis, the policies of trying to meet economic expectations—providing subsidies and expanding social welfare provisions—tended to worsen rather than improve the situation. On the other hand, moreover, in a situation of weakening institutions the self-interests of elites increasingly won out over those of the wider population, allocating wealth and resources to a small circle, at the expense of the public at large.

6.2. The great depression: economic crisis after independence

At the outset of independence, the economic prospects for Ukraine were judged rather optimistically not only within the country, but also by foreign experts.[3] However, from 1992 onwards, the economic situation deteriorated severely. In the course of the 1990s, the economic crisis turned out to be far deeper and longer than expected by anyone.

The macro-economic data on Ukraine for 1992 to 1994 reflect a nightmarish fall into economic depression: GDP fell by 9.9 per cent in 1992, by 14.2 per cent in 1993, and by 23 per cent in 1994. By 1995, the official GDP was only about half of what it had been at the start of 1992. Inflation spiraled to about 1,200 per cent in 1992, almost 5,000 per cent in 1993, and about 900 per cent in 1994. It wiped out the savings of the population and rapidly eroded the purchasing power of wages, pensions, and other monetary income.[9] Industrial output fell by about half between 1990 and 1994.[10]

This deep recession was brought about by a mixture of factors which included both external shocks (primarily the dissolution of the USSR), and inadequate policy responses.[11] In comparative perspective, the 'best-performing' FSU countries lost between 20 and 35 of their GDP as recorded in 1989 before turning around; in Ukraine, the loss in recorded GDP bottomed out only after the annual GDP had fallen to less than half its 1989 levels (see appendix, Table I.1.1). As argued in Chapter 5, it appears that the economic crisis in Ukraine became especially severe and long, due to the unconsolidated political situation, and the rather unconstrained influence of 'opaque' groups which this gave rise to.

Table 6.1: Macroeconomic indicators, 1991–1995

	1991	1992	1993	1994	1995
GDP % change	–10.6	–9.7	–14.2	–22.9	–12.2
inflation*	91	1210	4735	891.0	377.0

There is considerable divergence regarding data on post-Soviet countries. Inflation figures quoted by the IMF (International Financial Statistics) and UNECE (United Nations Economic Commission on Europe) are by and large the same as those given by the EBRD

* annual average change of the CPI.

Sources: EBRD, Transition Report (2002)

Policy makers in any country would be hard-pressed by such economic shocks and the resulting crisis. For established capitalist democracies the assumption is that their well-established institutional structures help them to cope with such shocks since they provide a framework for action.[12] However, Ukraine was hit by the economic downturn at a time of institutional weakness and reorientation.

The Ukrainian leadership lacked a clear vision of what socio-economic model to strive for. On the one hand, leading politicians sought reforms, on the other hand, they rejected the 'shock therapy' initiated by the liberal elite in Russia.[13] The first president after independence, Leonid Kravchuk, expressed this uncertainty over economic policy in January 1993: "If I completely knew what to do, I would tell the government, the local representatives and the organizers of the economy about it."[14]

At the same time, the leadership failed to keep the spreading arbitrage and corruption in check. During this early independence period, a well-connected individual could relatively easily use their position to make illicit—but not necessarily illegal—profits, for example, by using their access to raw materials traded below world market prices among the former Soviet countries and selling them to the West; or by access to government secured loans.[15]

6.3. The challenge of nation-building

The immediate post-independence years were the ones during which Ukraine experienced the greatest threat concerning its territorial integrity. The risk passed without ever becoming acute in Ukraine, but a number of other post-Soviet countries, including neighboring Moldova and Georgia experienced civil wars and secessionist attempts during this period which further weakened their respective states.[16]

It is rather contested how significant and acute the threat to Ukraine's territorial integrity was in the early 1990s and whether such a scenario might have involved 'ethnic' conflict.[17] In the early 1990s, disappointment with the 'results' of independence—especially the sudden loss of savings and income due to hyperinflation—ran high among all Ukrainians, but particularly in Eastern Ukraine, where the symbolic benefits of independence carried less weight.[18] Furthermore, the Ukrainization policies promoted by some politicians from Western Ukraine put off many Eastern Ukrainians.

Due to historical legacies and the economic realities born out of them, there were real differences in interests. Highly urbanized and industrialized Eastern Ukraine had strong economic links with Russia; while in the more rural Western Ukraine old links with Central Europe were still a powerful memory—even though historically, relations with Poland had also been strained.

However, the dividing lines were not very clear. According to the 1989 census, 72 per cent of the population was classified as 'Ukrainians' and 22 per cent as 'Russians'. At the same time, a significant number of Ukrainians living in Eastern Ukraine actually used Russian rather than Ukrainian as their everyday language ('Russophone' Ukrainians). Furthermore, regional differences in Ukraine involve more than a simple East-West division: there are also the rural central regions which have neither a strong Western nor Eastern identity, and to the south is Crimea which has its own particularities, such as the presence of Tatars as an ethnic minority, who had been deported during the Stalinist period and in the 1990s returned to Crimea from other parts of the former Soviet Union.

Most importantly, Ukraine's political structures as well as its economy were to a good part influenced or even dominated by Eastern Ukraine—during the times as a Soviet republic as well as after independence. The first president of independent Ukraine, Leonid Kravchuk, had won the elections particularly in Eastern and Central Ukraine. With the rise of Leonid Kuchma, first as prime minister in 1992–1993 and then as president from 1994 onwards, a politician with deep roots in Eastern Ukrainian industry became the national leader. Between 1994 and 2004, representatives from eastern Ukraine dominated the political life of the country tying the East firmly to Ukrainian national politics. The change from Kuchma to Yushchenko in the winter of 2004–2005 was accompanied by a resurfacing of regional issues; but threats of secession were more part of the political maneuverings rather than based on substance.

In summary, in contrast to both Belarus and Lithuania, Ukraine's state-building process *was* burdened by a potential territorial problem. However, in contrast to Russia, no actual secessionist conflict erupted; and the likelihood of such a development ultimately decreased over time as Ukraine became established as a state.

6.4. Struggles for power and institutional weakness

After a brief period of unity following the attaining of independence, the first years of Ukrainian statehood were marked by struggles for power between different groups and sets of office-holders, set off by the dissolution of the previous power structures.[19] During this early independence period the political regime in Ukraine can best be characterized as a regime in transition and possibly an 'inchoate' democracy. Members of the Ukrainian opposition had gained a share in the parliament in 1990 and came to play a real role in politics, but without achieving a full change in power as happened in the Baltic states.[20] The 1994 presidential elections were relatively free and fair, and resulted in the succession of Leonid Kravchuk by Leonid Kuchma.

The constitutional set-up of political institutions remained contested in Ukraine, and a new constitution failed to be adopted within this first period of independence. This initial challenge had its roots in the diverging visions about the new Ukrainian state, combined with an unclear institutional situation created in 1991. Adherents of socialist ideas still made up a considerable share of parliament; countered by an opposition movement most concerned with national symbols and linguistic Ukrainization; while many members of the upper echelons of the previous system were interested in the division of spoils from economic reforms while grappling with economic crisis. The parliament, dominated by left-wing deputies, and the president, leaning towards independent nationhood and at least limited reforms, were locked into a competition about who held greater control at central as well as regional and local levels.

The absence of clear institutional rules resulted in constant tensions between the president and parliament, which frequently led to a blockage of decision-making throughout the 1990s, including long delays in adopting annual budgets, as well as agreeing on the numerous and fundamental reforms which were necessary to transform the legal and institutional framework. Decision-making was further complicated by a dual executive composed of a president and a prime minister both of whom sought to dominate policy making.[21] For example, in 1993 president Kravchuk and his then prime minister Kuchma both sought to control the cabinet—weakening decision-making at a moment of deep and acute economic crisis.[22]

The problem of inter-institutional tensions also delayed the adoption of a new constitution and hence agreement on the fundamental rules of the game. Initial drafts of a new constitution in 1992 and 1993 proposed a mixed presidential-parliamentary system, but did not find sufficient support on either side.[23] Without a new constitution, the powers and responsibilities of the branches of government remained unclear and open to *ad hoc* tests of strength; and they lacked the formal coordination, one essential feature of Tilly's definition of a state (see Chapter 1).

In many areas, the lack of unity and direction from the top led to institutional evolution by muddling through, which involved a high degree of continuity—but without continued unity and coherence. Members of the former *nomenklatura* remained by and large in key positions; but they were no longer part of a centrally coordinated system. A number of existing institutions were either renamed and superficially re-modeled or simply remained as before: for example, the KGB was renamed the Security Service of Ukraine (SBU). The former deputy head, Yevgen Marchuk, was appointed as its new leader, and most of the previous staff continued in their positions.[24] The former central planning institution *Derzhplan* was re-modeled into the Ministry of Economy.[25] The new tax administration developed out of the financial departments which had been operating as agencies of the Ministry of Finance in every rayon during Soviet times.[26] Some observers concluded from this continuity that there was virtually no change. According to Checkel,

> [t]o describe developments in Ukraine over the past 8 years as a process of institutional change would be misleading; it is better to talk of the institutional inheritance bequeathed to the country by the USSR.[27]

In a comparative perspective, continuity in Ukraine was relative: certainly more pronounced than in the Baltic states but less so than in Belarus. In particular, while many members of the old elite stayed in place, this elite was no longer unified but rather split into various groups; and although the institutions themselves initially saw little change, the political core guiding them had taken on a different character.

6.4.1. INTERMEDIARY ORGANIZATIONS AND OPAQUE GROUPS DURING EARLY INDEPENDENCE

In Chapter 4, I introduced the notion that the weight of 'visible' intermediary and interest groups relative to 'opaque' groups was a potentially important factor in the state-building process. The strength of various groups has an impact both on the effectiveness and stability of the state and on the kind of state that emerges—i.e. whether it serves narrow circles, or wider groups of the population. Political parties are the key intermediary organizations in a democracy; they are important for aggregating and channeling interests in a 'visible' manner.[28] However, after some promising beginnings, the development of programmatically based political parties remained stymied in Ukraine.

In the early period of Ukrainian independence there were two origins of party formation: one was the opposition movement *Rukh* which was regionally based in Western Ukraine; the other was the Communist Party of Ukraine (CPU), from which a spectrum of successor parties developed—from one extreme to the other. A crucial problem was the high degree of party fragmentation and even absence of formal parties, as key politicians preferred to rely on informal networks.

After winning a share of parliamentary seats in 1990, politicians from *Rukh* and other opposition groups joined initial governments under Kravchuk. However, once independence was achieved in 1991, *Rukh* began to splinter and decline rather than increase in strength and political relevance.[29] In contrast to Lithuania, where *Sajudis* formed the first post-independence government, the Ukrainian opposition could not dislodge the former *nomenklatura* from power; however, it remained a political force and eventually—over a decade later—was successful in late 2004.

After the Communist Party was outlawed in August 1991, a number of branches grew out of the 'felled tree' of the CPU. On the left, these included the Socialist Party of Ukraine, founded by Oleksandr Moroz which attracted former middle-layer functionaries.[30] This party was to become one of the few rather stable parties in Ukraine, with a significant but limited impact on political developments. On the far left, a Communist Party was re-founded in 1993 in Donetsk, becoming the most orthodox left-wing party in Ukraine with a strong appeal among the older generation and those voters favoring some form of union with Russia.

The former leadership of the CPU, in contrast, did not form a new party but rather relied on an informal network which came widely to be called the 'party of power' (*partia vlada*). This 'party of power' was centered around the first president, Leonid Kravchuk. Although informal, the 'party of power' was widely recognized to exist, representing the higher levels of the former state apparatus, the media and the economy, but without pursuing any particular program.[31] Furthermore, being informal and lacking any unifying programmatic orientation, the 'party of power' was far from stable and itself disintegrated over time—not least due to the various struggles over economic resources.

The more 'reformist' elements of the former CPU rather loosely united in a parliamentary group called New Ukraine, which was closely linked to the emerging organization of enterprise directors, the Ukrainian Union of Industrialists and Entrepreneurs (UUIE; see below). Using this network, Leonid Kuchma formed an Inter-Regional Bloc of Reforms in early 1994 to serve as his base for the presidential elections.[32]

In contrast to the fragmented party system, broader socio-economic organizations continued to exist in Ukraine as direct holdovers from the Soviet period. The largest trade union was the Federation of Ukrainian Trade Unions (FPU), a successor to the former state-sponsored trade union organization which remained closely intertwined with the state. In 1995 the FPU still comprised more than 95 per cent of the unionized workforce,[33] but in spite of its size, the FPU was weak in a situation of economic crisis. For example, the first national collective agreement concluded in May 1993 stipulated that the state would consult unions on price increases and corresponding wage indexation. However, as inflation spiraled throughout the year, the government simply abandoned consultation (see also Chapter 7, Graph 7.1 showing the low level of trust in trade unions).[34]

Some independent unions had emerged in the late *perestroika* period particularly around the mining sector in Eastern Ukraine, the most important of which was the Independent Miners Union of Ukraine (NPGU). However, many of the Eastern Ukrainian coal mines were no longer profitable, and as a consequence the power of the miners who were locked into a declining industry eventually waned after two waves of large-scale strikes in 1993 and in 1996.

One of the most durable and important interest associations to emerge after independence was the UUIE formed in February 1992.[35] The organization quickly acquired political clout, having also a number of representatives in parliament. Furthermore, Leonid Kuchma was elected as president of the UUIE in December 1993 and launched his presidential campaign using the UUIE as his institutional base in 1994.[36]

Officially, the UUIE declared itself to be pro-reform and in favor of privatization and liberalization. However, given its membership, representatives of the UUIE favored certain types of reform such as 'nomenklatura privatization' over others.[37] On fiscal and budgetary matters, the UUIE was a lobby for more credits to state enterprises; but, at least since 1994, it also demanded lower taxes to stimulate the economy.

Overall, 'visible' groups remained relatively weak during this early period of independence—including a weakening of the social movements which had played an important role during the final years of the Soviet Union (*Rukh*, NPGU). The most important political 'party' of the time—the 'party of power' was itself a rather obscure structure without an official organization or program. The large socio-economic groups which continued to exist generally tried to defend the status quo rather than embracing the move to a different kind of society and economy—tending to add to the paralysis in the face of economic crisis.

6.4.2. OPAQUE GROUPS: THE RISE OF THE 'ROVING BANDITS'

With regard to 'opaque' groups there was a considerable degree of continuity with the Soviet era. The most important 'opaque' groups which arose in independent Ukraine were related to economic interests in the Eastern

Ukrainian industrial centers, Donetsk and Dnipropetrovsk, and as in previous periods, they were closely intertwined with the ruling class of the state.[38] Already in the Soviet Union of the 1970s, this Eastern Ukrainian region had spawned influential networks around Leonid Brezhnev, and around the long-term first secretary of the Ukrainian SSR, Shcherbytsky.[39] Moreover, important parts of the post-independence 'party of power' came from Eastern Ukraine.

In general, 'opaque' groups in Ukraine from the beginning tended to straddle the spheres of business and politics since opportunities for the 'primary accumulation' of wealth generally hinged on various forms of access to the state. Because large parts of the economy were still state-owned, managers of large enterprises remained formally as well as informally connected to central ministries.[40] Furthermore, as elsewhere in the former Soviet Union, funds of the Ukrainian branch of the Communist Party and of the communist youth organization *komsomol* were an important source of 'seed capital' for those budding entrepreneurs who had the right connections to access and profitably invest the funds.[41]

The rising 'opaque' groups included individuals and networks previously belonging to the Soviet economic or administrative establishment as well as 'upstarts' who gained economic wealth through deals in the early 1990s when state regulation was both at its weakest and most confused. These deals, which allowed the illicit and semi-illegal acquisition of wealth, took forms such as the access to subsidized credits and goods, access to import and export licenses, and access to state assets. Havrylyshyn and others have stressed that access to (subsidized) credits was a primary form of rent-seeking during the first period of independence which contributed to overstretching the budget and to hyperinflation in 1993.[42]

The export of goods without (fully) transferring the receipts to the state, was mostly done in the form of raw materials deals. Raw materials such as oil, coal or gas could be bought at low administrative prices in Ukraine (often after having been imported from Russia or Turkmenistan) and sold abroad at world market prices.[43] This was particularly profitable as long as Ukraine maintained a combination of price and export controls—for those individuals who were able to obtain the required licenses. Several of Ukraine's later oligarchs are assumed to have accumulated their initial wealth in this way—including Oleksandr Volkov, Pavlo Lazarenko, Yulia Tymoshenko, Ihor Bakai, and Hryhorii Surkis.[44] Through these deals, the state lost twice: it lost assets and—in particular with regard to oil and gas—it incurred debt vis-à-vis Russia and Turkmenistan. Privatization—which proceeded more slowly in

Ukraine than in Russia—was another way for those who managed to acquire profitable assets at a favorable price to enrich themselves.

While 'opaque' networks had been prominent in Eastern Ukraine at least since the 1970s, the possibilities for personal enrichment vastly increased with the deterioration of the old system. Furthermore, the lowering of institutional constraints on actors (see also Graphs 4.1 and 4.2 in Chapter 4) came after decades of a very oppressive institutional corset. Thus, as institutions suddenly became weak, the scale of potential redistribution of wealth was very large, giving potential 'opaque' groups vast new possibilities and incentives. This process involved considerable violence, especially in its early stages. In 1995, Akhat Bragin, a mafia-business boss, and owner of the Shaktar football club in Dontesk was killed by a bomb. In late 1996, the former oblast governor, Yevhen Shcherban, who also was a former business partner of Bragin, was shot dead at the Donetsk airport.[45]

As Zimmer, Wilson, and others have pointed out, on the one hand Ukraine's 'opaque' groups were not at all unified, and in particular there were intense rivalries between those based in Donetsk and those based in Dnipropetrovsk (as well as within these networks).[46] On the other hand, 'opaque' groups were closely intertwined with the power-holders of the day, first president Kravchuk and after 1994 president Kuchma. They illicitly acquired a large share of economic assets and became politically powerful, but without any one group controlling the political and economic game.

6.4.3. THE 1994 PARLIAMENTARY AND PRESIDENTIAL ELECTIONS

While the seeds of a potential Ukrainian party system were discernible in 1990, these seeds did not germinate. In terms of membership parties remained small, with the largest having some ten thousand members out of a population of 49 million. With the partial exception of the Socialists and Communists who opposed market-oriented reforms, parties largely lacked a program on economic policies and on how to reshape the role of the state in society. Thus, there was clearly a lack of 'visible' and moreover of 'encompassing' groups which could have articulated and represented broader interests and translated them into policies.

For the 1994 parliamentary elections, 'anti-party' electoral rules were adopted as was favored by members of the 'party of power' running as independents. These rules encouraged workers' collectives and informal groups of voters to nominate candidates, while complex requirements were applied to the process of nomination by parties.[47] More than two-thirds of the candidates ran as 'independents.' As a result of complicated election rules combined with a rather low turnout, 112 seats out of 450 could not be filled in the first two rounds, with many remaining vacant for almost two years.[48] The main winners of the election were left-wing parties as well as independents who aligned themselves either with the left or with factions related to the informal 'party of power.'[49]

Given this situation, and that party and faction formation remained in a state of flux, the factional composition of parliament changed fundamentally between 1994 and the next parliamentary elections of 1998. As it became highly fragmented and 'fluid' in terms of factional membership, parliament lost much of its capacity to aggregate interests. Furthermore, the 'messy' elections weakened parliament and facilitated the substantial strengthening of the role of the president from 1994 onwards.

The parliamentary elections were followed by presidential elections in July 1994. These were widely regarded as an indicator that Ukraine had passed an important test of democratic transition, since power passed from Leonid Kravchuk to Leonid Kuchma. The fact that only one of seven candidates was a member of any party (Oleksandr Moroz, leader of the Socialist Party), however, confirmed the low importance of parties at this point.

The results of the two rounds of voting are summarized in the table below. Regional patterns were reversed in comparison to 1991: Western Ukrainians overwhelmingly supported Kravchuk (whom they had opposed in 1991), while Eastern and Southern Ukrainians predominately voted for Kuchma.[50] Kravchuk advocated a further distancing from Russia, while Kuchma proposed a closer integration with Russia combined with economic reforms.

Table 6.2: Results of the 1994 presidential elections

	1st round	2nd round
Leonid Kravchuk	37.70	45.10
Leonid Kuchma	31.30	52.10
Oleksandr Moroz	13.00	
Volodymyr Lanovy	9.32	
Valerii Babych	2.39	
Ivan Plyushch	1.29	
Petro Talanchuk	0.54	

Source: Birch (2000), 96.

Kuchma was a candidate from industrial Eastern Ukraine who was viewed as competent in the economic sphere.[51] Shortly after being elected, Kuchma announced an economic reform program which was endorsed by parliament after some protracted discussion.[52] The program stipulated that privatization and price liberalization should be sped up. Moreover, fiscal reform was declared as one of the top priorities. The heavy tax burden was to be reduced, while the budget deficit was to be limited to 8 per cent of GDP in 1995 and to 4 per cent by 1997.[53] Thus, similar to Russia (see Chapter 11), the debate about fundamental tax reform began at this point in time, and the general aims of reform were rather clear early on (a reduction of rates and a broadening of the tax base).[54] However, in both countries, it took years for this reform to come to fruition—and in Ukraine this process was even longer and more piecemeal than in its eastern neighbor.

6.4.4. TRUST AND EXPECTATIONS

Given the recent achievement of independence, one might have expected relatively strong initial belief and trust in the new leadership. However, this was not the case in Ukraine. Comparing Ukraine, Russia, and Lithuania, we find extremely low levels of trust in the state, its institutions and representatives in the former two cases, while in Lithuania citizens initially had markedly more trust, even if the balance of trust versus distrust was still in the negative for most institutions (questions 1, and 2 below).

While public opinion polls by themselves do not reveal *why* certain opinions are widespread, there are a number of possible reasons: firstly, the recent communist history had probably instilled a general distrust of the state and the political leadership in all former Soviet citizens; and secondly, the emerging oligarchic structures may have served to erode any trust also in the old/new leadership—and did so more strongly in Ukraine and Russia than in Lithuania (see also Chapter 10). Furthermore, a large majority thought that law and order had deteriorated (question 4 below).

The low trust in the state coincided with a relatively high continuity with regard to the preferred socio-economic order—which we might broadly label as socialist. Many Ukrainians thought that the state should continue to own key means of production, and that it should also be responsible for providing housing and work for everyone. Furthermore, from different opinion polls over time—although these are not fully comparable—it appears that between 1992 and 1994 Ukrainians lost rather than gained faith in a market economy.

In a sense, these opinion polls, although they are just snapshots, provide a picture of a deeply troubled and uncertain society. Ukrainians were uncertain about the solutions to the grave economic crisis of the country and had no political leader or organization to turn to since trust was generally low with regard to all political parties.

Table 6.3: Public trust in leadership, 1992

1) Would you say that you trust the political leadership of this country to do what is right almost always, most of the time, only some of the time, or almost never?

	Ukraine	Russia	Lithuania
Almost always	2.4	2.0	2.6
Most of the time	15.6	17.0	24.6
Sometimes	56.9	56.3	53.8
Never	19.1	16.2	11.8
DK/no answer	5.8	8.4	7.2

2) How often do you think that politicians get away with doing certain things that the average citizen would be penalized for?

	Ukraine	Russia	Lithuania
Very often	58.3	72.6	22.4
Sometimes	15.9	16.1	47
Rarely	9.8	4.1	16.4
Never	3.6	1.4	2.0
DK/no answer	12.4	5.6	12.2

3) In your view, how many people fail to contribute their fair share in keeping our country strong and prosperous?

	Ukraine	Russia	Lithuania
Many	31.7	48.6	19.6
Some	29.7	26.8	39.4
Not very many	32.6	17.6	36.0
DK/no answer	5.8	6.9	5.0

4) In your view, has law and order [*pravoporiadok*] in the country strengthened, stayed the same or become weaker over the past year?

	Ukraine	Russia	Lithuania
Strengthened	1.8	0.8	16.2
Stayed the same	18.9	12.6	37.2
Weakened	76.8	84.7	40.6
DK/no answer	2.4	1.8	6.0

5) If the Russian [Ukrainian] [Lithuanian] government requires more revenue to meet its new responsibilities (in connection with an increase in its powers), are you willing to pay higher taxes or new fees for services provided?

	Ukraine	Russia	Lithuania
Yes	10.8	16.9	18.2
No	70.3	61.7	61.8
Undecided	11.0	12.0	14.8
DK/no answer	7.9	9.2	5.2

Source: Miller, Reisinger, and Hesli (1992).

Table 6.4: Expectations concerning the state, 1992

6) Speaking only of Russia [Ukraine] [Lithuania], what type of property would be best?

	Ukraine	Russia	Lithuania
Private	37.1	37.2	54.2
Collective	15.6	11.9	8.6
State	13.2	13.8	6.8
A combination of private & social	27.5	32.1	25.6
DK/no answer	6.4	4.8	4.8

7) Should government guarantee work and a high standard of living or should rather everyone look after himself? (on a scale from 1 to 5)

	Ukraine	Russia	Lithuania
1 full government guarantee	22.1	19.4	22
2	14.5	14.4	12.4
3	24.0	28.8	30.2
4	14.7	16.3	17.8
5 each person for himself	18.5	16.4	16
DK/no answer	6.1	4.5	1.6

Source: Miller, Reisinger, and Hesli (1992).

Table 6.5: Ukraine: Expectations of the state, December 1994

In your opinion, should Ukraine continue the process of reducing the state's role in running the economy, or should we return to a system where the state controls much of the economy?

	All	Men	Women	Men >45	Women >45
Reduce the state's role	30.9	50	26	33	18
Return to mostly state control	45.6	34	56	40	50
Don't know/no response	23.5	16	19	26	32

Source: www.ifes-ukraine.org/english/Surveys/December.1994

Table 6.6: Levels of trust in public institutions, Ukraine, February–March 1994

	Absolute	Somewhat	A little	None	Hard to Say
Government	2	6	26	59	7
President Kravchuk	4	8	24	58	6
Political parties	2	6	20	46	26
Army	20	27	22	20	11
Directors of SOEs	4	11	27	38	20
Private entrepreneurs	3	10	21	49	17

Source: Kubicek (2000), 46.

6.4.5. EXTERNAL LINKS AT A LOW EBB

International factors—both direct and 'diffuse' (such as international financial markets)—had the least influence on the process of state-building during this early period, except for the break-up of the Soviet Union itself. Russia was weakened, while ties with the West were still in their infancy. Ukraine distanced itself from Russia and only partially joined the CIS.[55] While it joined the IMF and the World Bank in September 1992, Ukraine received the first loans only from late 1994. Even later came the Partnership and Cooperation Agreement with the EU, which was signed in June 1994 and came into force in 1998.[56] The main aim of US foreign policy vis-à-vis Ukraine during this period was to ensure its independence from Russia, and at the same time that all nuclear arms would be transferred to Ukraine's eastern neighbor.[57]

In terms of trade and foreign investment, Ukraine initially was only weakly integrated with the non-CIS world. Although the share of trade to GDP was high, most trade was still conducted within the CIS. Exports to the non-CIS world reached $5 billion in 1994.[58] Inflows of foreign direct investment remained small. Since Russia had assumed the USSR's external obligations, foreign debt was minimal in 1992 ($0.5 billion) but increased to more than $8 billion by 1995. In 1994, debt service began to 'bite' for the first time, rising from the equivalent of around 1 per cent to more than 10 per cent of annual exports.[59]

Overall therefore, international factors did not have a decisive effect on state-building in Ukraine during this initial phase of independence. If anything, one might say that Ukraine was left to its own devices, with no external actors taking an active interest in supporting its internal state-building process.[60]

6.5. A fiscal system in crisis

In the immediate post-independence period, the Ukrainian fiscal system was in utter disarray as a result of economic crisis as well as the relative weakness of state capacity—of taking decisions and implementing policies. Experience in the executive was limited, since previously key budget (and physical) planning had been carried out in Moscow rather than Kyiv. At the same time, there was little experience with the relationship and interaction with a 'real' parliament, which suddenly had a say in fiscal matters.

6.5.1. BUDGETING: BULGING DEFICITS AND 'HAND-STEERED' EXECUTION

Although the Ukrainian fiscal year starts in January, budgets were adopted in June 1992, in April 1993 and in February 1994 respectively.[61] Moreover, policy makers were unable to cope with the effects of the sharp drop in GDP on the budget. They claimed to be preserving fiscal stability, planning annual deficits in the range of 2 to 6 per cent of GDP,[62] but these were based on expectations of a growing rather than a rapidly shrinking economy, as well as very high rates of extraction.

By the time parliament adopted the 1992 budget in mid-year, it was clear that the economy was in recession, but still the adopted budget plan was based on the assumption of modest growth.[63] The budget adopted in April 1993 proposed to increase the revenue by 22 per cent of GDP compared to the previous year.[64] Unachievable targets meant that budgets plans and deficit goals were of a rather declaratory character, not a real basis for government action and budget implementation inevitably deviated considerably from these plans.

Policy makers in parliament, which held considerable power in fiscal matters during this period, were more guided by ideas ranging from socialism to nationalism than by the need to make realistic budget plans.[65] As Ihor Shpak pointed out, initial budgets as submitted to parliament were composed of just a few pages, containing only highly aggregate numbers; which promoted a politicized rather than factual discussion of the government's plan.[66] Budget debates developed into intense policy battles between the legislative and the executive, with the government (under the prime minister) uncomfortably placed between parliament and the president.[67]

A particular feature during this period was the strong dependence of the Central Bank of Ukraine (NBU) on parliament.[68] Parliament could direct the

NBU (via the Ministry of Finance) to grant "non-budgetary allocations" to specific sectors—which had been part of the Soviet budgeting practice.[69] These were government-guaranteed long or short-term credits at artificially low interest rates. In late 1992, a round of NBU credits were extended to the agricultural, fuel, and mining sectors.[70] The total fiscal deficit (including such directed credits) for 1992 amounted to over 20 per cent of GDP.[71]

State expenditures as a share of GDP reached very high levels from 1992 to 1994, and only thereafter started to decline (see Appendix, Table I.2.2). The categories on which relative spending grew the most during this period were spending on the economy and on social protection.[72] The latter involved the creation of what a United Nations report has called "one of the most elaborate social security systems in the world."[73] An important motivation was to win support for the newly independent state. However, a number of the ambitious social programs adopted were not financed even in their early days. Also, the real social situation degenerated as savings were wiped out and incomes were sharply lowered by hyperinflation. As Vice-Prime Minister Viktor Pynzenyk remarked in late 1992: "In raising the amount of alleged social guarantees, we are merely blowing soap bubbles and showering people with pieces of paper that are backed with nothing."[74]

In late 1992 and early 1993, the government, under prime minister Leonid Kuchma (who had taken over from the ousted Vitold Fokin), tried to introduce some fiscal discipline by partially liberalizing prices and by canceling the indexation of wages.[75] Together with Viktor Pynzenyk, who was responsible for economic policy and an advocate of reforms, he forced a lowering of the *de facto* deficit by way of *ad hoc* cash management, i.e. daily high-level decision-making about expenditures and essentially "by withholding payments on all but the most immediate bills."[76]

This 'hand steering' (*ruchne upravlinn'a*) of expenditures, as it was called in Ukraine and practiced throughout the early 1990s, resulted in high transaction costs for the entire state spending apparatus. According to Oksana Serdyuk of the Ministry of Finance, the ministry filled each morning with representatives from spending agencies trying to obtain funds, thus burdening both the Ministry of Finance and spending agencies with permanent negotiations and extremely high transaction costs.[77] This kind of cash rationing imposed the highest possible uncertainty on spending units, and also meant that spending priorities were considerably shifted compared to what had been originally adopted in the budget.[78]

Moreover, because there was no integration of policy making across different branches of power, this *ad hoc* control over spending was repeatedly undermined. During the sowing season of 1993, parliament again granted preferential credits to agriculture; while in May 1993, parliament raised wages, pensions, allowances, and social payments. After Kuchma resigned as prime minister in September 1993, the policy pendulum swung back: the interim government under Yukhym Zviahylskyi attempted a return to a planned economic system with direct price controls and state orders, as well as ordering further subsidies to enterprises. However, in contrast to neighboring Belarus, in Ukraine the attempt to restore a Soviet-style system failed, both because there was no sufficient agreement to do so, and because power was too dispersed for Zviahylskyi to enforce his program. The weak fiscal policies contributed to the disastrously high inflation, and a further steep drop in real incomes.[79]

In 1994, the budget deficit again spiraled out of control, reaching about 20 per cent of GDP by mid-year, before being reined in once the parliamentary and presidential elections had passed.[80] In the fall, Kuchma, now newly elected as president, gave a devastating speech about the state of the economy and of public finances in particular, pointing to the untenably large share of GDP taken by the state, the deficit which absorbed nearly all resources of credit, and the general crisis of public finances with its immensely negative effects on the population. Furthermore, he promised far-reaching budget and tax reforms as top priorities of his government:

> Overcoming the financial crisis is possible only on the basis of a deep structural reform of the entire financial system in the country. [...] The determining factor in the wide range of problems concerning the reform of the financial system is radical restructuring of the taxation system towards its deep liberalization, reduction of tax pressure and formation of an effective economic mechanism to stimulate production and enterprise.[81]

Kuchma's resolve to address the fiscal crisis was also driven by his desire to achieve a program with the IMF—which demanded austerity measures both with regard to government spending and to monetary emissions.

For the financing of its initial large fiscal deficits, the government relied on debt financing and on seignorage (government "revenue" from printing money). Households had seen their savings wiped out in 1992, and current incomes continued to be devalued at an alarming speed in 1993 when inflation rose to almost 5000 per cent.[82] Compared to other post-Soviet countries at the time, the Ukrainian government was among those opening the floodgates of inflation the widest. Other countries with extremely high inflation included Georgia (peak in 1994 at 15,600 per cent), Armenia (peak in 1994 at 5,000 per cent), and Turkmenistan (peak in 1993 at 3,100 per cent).[83] In the Baltic states, in contrast, inflation reached a maximum of 1000 per cent annually already in 1992, and was quickly reduced thereafter. Even in Russia, inflation remained considerably more limited than in Ukraine.

A second instrument of financing large deficits was to incur domestic and foreign debt. From 1992 to 1994, Ukraine incurred about US $5.6 billion in foreign debt (reaching more than 20 per cent of GDP).[84] Such a debt to national economy ratio was still low by international comparison; however, the increase in debt was rapid, as was the increase in annual debt service due. Moreover, the debt incurred was used to cover current expenditures rather than to finance public investment. While debt service was negligible in 1992, it already reached more than US $1 billion in 1995.

6.5.2. THE REVENUE SIDE: TRYING TO BUILD A FINANCIAL BASIS OF THE STATE

On the revenue side, early post-independence was marked by indecision, mutual blocking between different branches of the state apparatus, and numerous policy changes lacking orientation. Policy makers undertook a number of changes in the tax system with the goal of creating a financial base for the new state. Some of these had been already planned during the final phase of the Soviet Union (e.g., replacing turnover taxes by a VAT), others were *ad hoc* measures, and some were based on planned-economy ideas, such as the adoption of extremely high tax rates for trading and banking activities.[85] The institutional structure of law-making itself was in its initial phase: only in 1994 was a proper committee for banking and finance of the *Verkhovna Rada* created which could bring expertise into the law-making process on the side of parliament.[86]

The first basic laws on the tax system, adopted in the winter of 1991–1992 and revised in February 1994, provided only a rudimentary legal basis, while actual tax rates and the tax base were subject to constant revisions. According to Dabrowski, "The specific feature of the Ukraine's tax system is its instability. It has become the object of permanent political struggle and lobbying both in the Parliament and in Government."[87] As competencies between the executive(s) and the legislature remained contested, it was not clear which body would have the power to decide on rates and tax bases. Tax rates on personal income were changed several times: the marginal rate was temporarily raised to 90 per cent (!) in 1993, but lowered again to 50 per cent in 1994. The list of exempted goods for VAT changed repeatedly. Rates and the base of enterprise taxation were subject to continuous debate. As a result, formal rules remained fluid and often un-respected: it was estimated that in 1992 only 30 to 50 per cent of taxes formally due were actually paid.[88] At the same time, high formal tax rates and the definition of the tax base (such as gross income rather than profit; high social security payments) could be crippling to enterprises which actually paid all levies due.[89]

Table 6.7: Tax rates and bases in 1992

	Rate	Base	Major changes
VAT	28%	sale of goods and services, numerous exemptions	lowered to 20%, Jan. 1993, re-increased to 28% April 1993, exemptions added
Enterprise Profit Tax	18%	gross income (profit plus wage fund)	debate to change to 30% tax on profit (instead of gross income) in 1993; eventually change in 1995 to 22% on gross profit
Personal Income Tax	10 to 50%	multiple of the minimum wage, highest tax bracket reached at equivalent of 100 to 150 US $	maximum tax rate increased to 60% in June and 90% in December 1993; lowered again to 50% in Sept. 1994
Excise Taxes	10 to 85%	sale of special goods (such as cigarettes, jewelry)	revision of list of goods and rates in February 1994 (from 10 to 300%)
Contributions to off-budget funds:			
– social sec. and pensions	37%	wage fund	
– Chernobyl fund	12%	wage fund	
– employment fund	3%	wage fund	
– infrastructure (road fund)	0.4 to 0.8%	of total turnover	

Sources: Dabrowski (1996), 6–7; Clement, Knogler, Sekarev, Lunina (1993), 70–71.

A Ukrainian tax service was created by two legal acts in 1990 as an arm of the Ministry of Finance: the Resolution of the Council of Ministers of the USSR "On the creation of state tax service within the State tax inspection of the Finance Ministry of USSR and state tax inspections in regions, districts, cities and districts in cities" dating from April 15, 1990 and the Law of Ukraine "On the state tax service in Ukraine" adopted on December 4, 1990.

Initial—even if cautious—liberalization in Ukraine brought about an expansion of the shadow economy, thus limiting the state's capacity to tax.[90] This resulted from the combination of increased freedom (i.e., the lowering of various controls) combined with attempts to maintain a wide variety of formal rules which the state was too weak to enforce. Thießen estimates that the shadow (i.e., untaxed) economy may have grown to as much as 90 per cent of GDP, Schneider and Enste put it at around 50 per cent for the early 1990s.[91] While the shadow economy expanded rapidly in both Ukraine and Russia in the early 1990s, in Lithuania it expanded by less and probably started to decline from 1994 onwards.

6.6. The first steps of state-building

In summary, decision-making as well as implementation capacity was weak during this first period of independence. Decisions involving several 'players' were frequently blocked due to disagreement between different participants in the decision-making process, as reflected in the late adoption of budgets. At the same time, decisions by individual 'players' and mostly regarding specific issues rather than more aggregate policies tended to proliferate. Furthermore, decisions and the rules created through them often were not regarded as binding by the different parts of the state. Thus, mutually contradictory decisions were taken, which introduced a high level of instability. Integration of and coordination among different parts of the state were lacking.[92]

Implementation capacity, as reflected in budget execution, and also in the collection of taxes, was likewise relatively weak, although it was less weakened than decision-making. To some extent, implementation capacity was hampered by decision-making chaos: contradictory and changing demands from above made it difficult to implement policies. Budget execution suffered from highly unrealistic budget plans. Making realistic budgets is very difficult in a situation of economic crisis, including high inflation and high levels of uncertainty about revenue;[93] and not only Ukrainian policy makers, but also Western advisors and analysts had expectations about the economic development of the newly independent states which were proven wrong in reality. However, the lack of clarity over institutional roles and competencies both with regard to decisions and with regard to implementation worsened both budget formulation and budget execution.

Nonetheless, the Ukrainian state maintained a basic capacity to extract revenue during this early period of independence and throughout the deep economic recession; while this capacity almost collapsed in some other newly independent states, especially in Georgia (as discussed in Chapter 5; see also Appendix, Table I.2.1). However, while extraction continued, the system started with deep flaws, since the administration had to make unrealistic demands and to impose constantly changing rules on taxpayers; while at the same time it was unprepared for taxing a budding private economy with many smaller enterprises.

In terms of its scope and size, the Ukrainian state was not significantly reduced during these first years in the sense that the share of the revenue of the GDP continued to grow, but mainly because the (official) GDP was shrinking so fast. As the expansion of social security and subsidies show, the basic policy intention was to maintain a large role of the state. However, while maintaining its claim to a wide scope, the state had become porous. Financially, a considerable share of programs formulated by decision-makers went unfunded.[94] Moreover, the horizontal and hierarchical integration of the state was frayed. Thus, several sources of rule making competed with each other, both in the issuing of legal rules and in bringing crucial institutions (such as the SPF, NBU) under their control. Faced with contradictory rules, lower levels of the administration failed to implement orders from above. Thus, in terms of keeping the state-as-a-problem in check, Ukraine moved towards having increasing problems.

Notes

1 Wittkowsky (1998), 45.

2 There was some overlap, as a number of opposition candidates were still members of the CPU. Birch (2000), 63; Nahaylo (1999), 257.

3 Kuzio (2000), 185–188.

4 Kuzio (2000), 187.

5 Kuzio (2000), 39-41; Wittkowsky (1998), 61; Birch (2000), 75.

6 Wilson (1997), 169.

7 Wittkowsky (1998).

8 A Deutsche Bank report from 1991 ranked Ukraine's economic prospects higher than those of the Baltic states or Russia. See Marko Bojcun, *Ukraine in the World Economy*, http://www.unl.ac.uk/ukrainecentre/WSS/ws-10.html [accessed: September 14, 2002].

9 By 1993, real wages had fallen to about a third of their 1990 level. See UEPLAC (September 2000), 28.

10 See UEPLAC, *Ukrainian Economic Trends*; UNECE (2000), statistical annex, Table B.4.
11 On the first years of economic transition in Ukraine, see Havrylyshyn, Miller and Perraudin, (1994); Sekarev (1995); Banaian (1999); Ishaq (1997); Shen (1996); Hinton (2000).
12 See Elster (1989), 147–158.
13 Nahaylo (1999), 439–440.
14 Lytvyn (1997), 275.
15 Wittkowsky (1998), 102–103; scams included selling oil and gas which had been bought cheaply from Russia to the West, as well as lending practices of *Ukreximbank*, where many government secured loans were not repaid.
16 Way (2003).
17 Wilson (1997).
18 Wittkowsky (1998), 106–09.
19 See Wolczuk (2001a), Chapters 3–5.
20 Alexei Sekarev, "Ukraine's Policy Structure," *RFE/RL research report*, August 14, 1992, 60.
21 Protsyk (2003).
22 Lytvyn (1997), 284; Nahaylo (1999), 451.
23 Nahaylo (1999), 437–438.
24 Kuzio (2000), 188.
25 '*Derzhplan*' is the Ukrainian equivalent to the Russian '*Gosplan,*' i.e. the state committee for planning charged with developing the USSR's and the republics' five-year-plans. Wittkowsky (1998), 84.
26 Interview with Viktor Chepenko, Tax Policy Analyst, former employee of the STA, Kyiv, November 1, 2000.
27 Checkel (1999), 18.
28 See Elster, Offe, and Preuss (1998), 109–155.
29 Haran (2000), 8; Wittkowsky (1998), 51.
Wittkowsky (1998), 51.
30 Kubicek (2000), 42; Wittkowsky (1998), 95.
31 Dyczok (2000), 57; Birch (2000); 94. Kuzio (1998), 36.
32 However, membership meant little, since it was not cancelled even when members stopped paying their dues, or became pensioners.
33 Kubicek (2000), 46.
34 See www.uspp.org.ua (accessed: November 13, 2002); Kubicek (1997), 113–114.
35 Wittkowsky (1998), 88; Kubicek (2000), 90.
36 Kubicek (2000), 124.
37 See Inna Pidluska, *Political Elites in Ukraine*, UCIPR, undated manuscript.
38 Nahaylo (1999), 499.
39 On the early privatization process in Ukraine, see Shen (1996), 110–117; Pleines and Sobko (1997), 439.
40 Wilson (2005b), 32–33.
41 Havrylyshyn (2000), 49–50.
42 For example, the company *Ukrneftechim*, procured 32 million tons of oil from Russia in 1992 at Russian domestic prices. A quarter of this was illegally re-exported or domestically resold at world-market prices. See Wittkowsky (1998), 102.
43 Incidentally, none of these later 'oligarchs' came from a high nomenklatura position. Lazarenko had been head of the agricultural division of the Dnipropetrovsk oblast organi-

zation of the KPU. Bakai had been a football trainer in Prikarpatia oblast and from 1989 to 1991 managed a wood-processing plant in Yakutia. Surkis had been a housing-construction engineer. See Roth (2001), 251.

44 Wilson (2005b), 10.

45 Zimmer (2003); Wilson (2005b).

46 Birch (2000), 82.

47 Birch (2000), 83. A candidate had to achieve above 50% of the vote in the run-off. However, voters could cast negative votes against both candidates.

48 See D'Anieri, Kravchuk, and Kuzio (1999), 156–7.

49 In the next presidential elections in 1999 there was again a regional shift: Kuchma was overwhelmingly supported in Western Ukraine, while his communist challenger Symonenko did well in the East.

50 Birch (2000), 95.

51 Shen (1996), 56.

52 D'Anieri, Kravchuk, and Kuzio (1999), 195.

53 "Ukraine changes tax laws," *Nachrichten für den Aussenhandel* [News for External Trade] (NfA), January 4, 1995.

54 Nahaylo (1999), 446. Ukraine is a signatory to the founding treaty of December 8, 1991. However, Ukraine did not sign the Collective Security Treaty (1992) and did not become a member of the Inter-Parliamentary Assembly of the CIS.

55 An interim agreement entered into force on February 1, 1996.

56 See Nahaylo (1999), 440–441.

57 See UNECE, *Economic Survey of Europe 2002*, no. 2, Table B.11.

58 EBRD, *Transition Report Update*, April 1999, 72; *Transition Report* (2000), 225.

59 Vira Nanivska, director, ICPS, interview, Kyiv, November 30, 2000, and April 19, 2002.

60 Ukrainian budget laws can be found at http://www.rada.kiev.ua/laws/pravo/new/cgi-bin/search.cgi (website of the *Verkhovna Rada*).

61 "Zvyahilskyy at press conference comments on economic policy and Crimea," UNIAN news agency, Kyiv, May 5, 1994.

62 The year ended with a fall in GDP of 9.9 per cent. Clement, Slama (1992), 65–66.

63 Banaian (1999), 44.

64 Dabrowski et al. (2000), 125–131. See, for example, *Plan of the Economic and Social Development of Ukraine for the year 1994*, edict (postanova) of the VR, No. 3886-XII.

65 Interview, Ihor Shpak, head, Fiscal Analysis Office of the *Verkhovna Rada,* Kyiv, September 26, 2000. See also the budget documents of those years: Закон від 25.12.1990 № 579-XII, Про Республіканський бюджет Української РСР на 1991 рік, [Law on the Republican budget of the Ukrainian Socialist Republic for the year 1991]; Закон від 18.06.1992 № 2477-XII Про Державний бюджет України на 1992 рік [Law on the Ukrainian state budget for the year 1992], Закон від 09.04.1993 № 3091-XII Про Державний бюджет України на 1993 рік [Law on the Ukrainian state budget for the year 1993], Закон від 01.02.1994 № 3898-XII Про Державний бюджет України на 1994 рік [Law on the Ukrainian state budget for the year 1994].

66 "The budget forces Ukraine to tighten the belt," *Izvestiya*, Sept. 16, 1992.

67 Robert Kravchuk, *Who Paid the Inflation Tax* (1997), www.huri.harvard.edu/workpaper/kravchuk/inflation.html [accessed: August 31, 2002]. On December 30, 1996 a new law granting the Central Bank more independence was adopted by parliament. EIU, 1st quarter 1997, 24.

68 In 1997 the NBU was ranked among the least autonomous among post-Soviet Central Banks. Tonny Lybek, "Central Bank Autonomy, and Inflation and Output Performance in the Baltic States, Russia, and Other Countries of the Former Soviet Union, 1995–1997," *IMF Working Paper*, January 1999, Appendix III.
69 Banaian (1999), 44.
70 See Legeida (2000).
71 Data on the total (consolidated) budget, and on revenue and expenditure categories for this early period differ substantially from source to source (such as UEPLAC, IBRD, IMF, Ukrainian Ministry of Finance); but this broad trend is reflected by all of them.
72 Dyczok (2000), 94.
73 Interview with Larisa Leshchenko, Economist, World Bank office, Kyiv, November 8, 2000; the quote is from Chandler (1996), 200.
74 Various forms of wage controls, indexation, and an excess wage tax had been adopted in quick succession since fall 1991. Banaian (1999), 20.
75 Banaian (1999), 44.
76 Interview with Oksana Serdyuk, Deputy Chief of State Revenue Forecasting Division, April 19, 2002.
77 Vakhnenko (1999), 69. According to Cheasty and Davis: "the Ukrainian cash rationing system allows for more discretion [...], by having high-ranking officials choose among payments on a day-to-day basis, [...]." Cheasty and Davis (1996), 20.
78 Pynzenyk (2000), 81; see also Wittkowsky (1998), 90.
79 The Russian press remarked ironically that Ukraine had reached world leadership in its deficit levels by October 1994. "Economic Situation in Ukraine is Worsening," *ITAR-TASS*, October 11, 1994.
80 "Kuchma presents keynote speech to parliament on economic reform," *BBC Summary of World Broadcasts*, October 13, 1994.
81 Kravchuk (1997).
82 Annual average. See EBRD, *Transition Report* (2002), 60, Table A.3.3.
83 EBRD, *Transition Report* (2002), 213. See also Appendix Table II.1.1.
84 See Clement and Slama (1992), 67.
85 Interview with Victor Suslov, head of the committee on banking and finance 1994 to 1997, Kyiv, November 3, 2000.
86 Marek Dabrowski, Marcin Luczynski, and Malgorzata Markiewicz, *Ukraine's Fiscal Policy in 1991–96*, draft, The Center for Social and Economic Research (CASE), Warsaw (1996), 9.
87 Clement, Knogler and Sekarev (1993), 82.
88 "Ukraine: inflation, taxes suffocate firms at birth," *Washington Times*, June 20, 1994.
89 The 'shadow economy' ranges from non-registered activities by regular firms in order to avoid taxation, to the trade in illegal goods (drugs, weapons, etc.).
90 The estimates are based on various calculations; and tend to differ rather widely. The share of the shadow economy in OECD countries ranges between 10 and 20 per cent of GDP. See Schneider (2002).
91 Thus contradicting parts of Tilly's definition of a state (see Chapter 1, 1).
92 Wildavsky (1975).
93 There are two ways of non-funding: some programs were adopted but did not received funding in the budget plans. Other programs received funding in the budget plan but then were un-funded (or saw their funding cut) as revenue fell short during the fiscal year.

CHAPTER 7.
A NEW TRAJECTORY TAKING SHAPE

While the first years of Ukrainian independence were marked by weakened state structures, during the second half of the 1990s some important steps towards rebuilding occurred. However, the institutional structure that was being re-created had serious flaws. In the fiscal sphere incremental improvements occurred but fundamental reform continued to fail while political abuses of the tax administration flourished. Key driving forces behind this path of institutional development were the president and the oligarchic groups which had developed in Ukraine.

Economically, deep depression continued until 2000, when the Ukrainian economy grew for the first time after a decade of decline. Politically, Ukraine came to be regarded as a "competitive authoritarian" regime with uncertain prospects for further transition to democracy.[1] A series of political events marked the period: in 1996 a new constitution was adopted; followed in 1998 by the second parliamentary elections and in 1999 by the third presidential elections. Kuchma was re-elected as president and in late 1999 appointed the Central Bank governor, Viktor Yushchenko, as prime minister.

In retrospect, 2000 appears as a watershed, not only economically but also politically: in the spring, Kuchma forced, and won, a referendum on the strengthening of presidential power. However, the envisaged changes were not implemented. In the fall, the president became embroiled in a scandal over the murder of an investigative journalist and leaked audio-tapes from the presidential office (see Chapter 8, section 1). From then onwards, the Kuchma 'era' entered a decline, challenged both from 'within' and by demonstrators on the streets.

Decision-making and implementation capacity recovered in the course of the late 1990s, but were affected by the distortions and 'defensive' actions of a hybrid regime. In 1997, a bold attempt at 'big leap' reform of public finances failed. Still, incremental improvements of the fiscal system proceeded. In this process of developing capacity, however, the tax administration developed into a veritable 'state within the state' and became widely used to oppress political opponents. Various forms of corruption and state capture flourished, with an expanding list of tax privileges. In such a situation, control was largely 'defensive' and focused on maintaining power rather than on developing a well-run state. Consequently, accountability to the electorate remained weak, although at least the institutional foundations for it were laid with the setting up of the Accounting Chamber and the development of specialized parliamentary committees.

7.1. Economic stabilization and virtualization

The economy continued to shrink throughout the late 1990s and Ukraine came to be regarded as one of the worst transition performers, losing almost 60 per cent of its pre-1990 GDP and one of the last countries to register growth.

Table 7.1: GDP growth in selected post-Soviet countries 1995–2000

	1995	1996	1997	1998	1999	2000
Ukraine	*–12.2*	*–10.0*	*–3.2*	*–1.9*	*–0.2*	*5.9*
Russia	–4.1	–3.5	0.8	–4.6	5.4	8.3
Lithuania	3.3	4.7	6.1	4.0	–3.9	3.8
Belarus	–10.4	2.8	10.4	8.0	3.4	5.8
Kazakhstan	–8.2	0.5	2.0	–2.5	2.7	9.8
Azerbaijan	–11.8	1.3	5.8	10.1	7.4	11.1

Source: EBRD (2001)

Inflation was brought under control from 1995 onwards, which allowed the introduction of a new permanent currency, the *hryvnia*, under the guidance of Viktor Yushchenko as Governor of the Central Bank in September 1996. However, this stabilization came at a high price, as it was accomplished by means of a rapid contraction of the budget deficit—and a shifting of the deficit onto the population by the non-payment of wages and pensions (see below).

While the economy was less in a free fall than it had been during the early years of independence, it was beset by problems of shadowization and virtualization which peaked during this second phase of Ukrainian state-building.[2] Tight monetary policy combined with a post-Soviet regulatory jungle but weak enforcement capacity meant that a large share of business transactions took place outside the legal framework—and furthered the frequent use of barter, i.e. non-cash payments, even to pay for tax and budgetary obligations.

The Russian crisis of 1998 had some immediate negative economic effects, but eventually became an economic stimulus. Because the *ruble* depreciated more than the *hryvnia*, Ukrainian exports to Russia shrank initially.[3] Also, Ukraine's rapidly accumulated debt could not be rolled-over and needed to be restructured. After some months, however, the devaluation stimulated production for the domestic market (as imports had become more expensive) and made Ukrainian exports more competitive.

Overall, the late 1990s were a period of hardship for people, before the recovery beginning in 2000 brought some relief. A small group of early entrepreneurs grew wealthy, but the majority of people suffered. In the late 1990s, pension and wage arrears in the public sector grew rapidly. Even when people were paid, pensions and wages were meager, and regular pensions remained below the subsistence minimum. The average annual income per capita fell below $1000—and in 1999 dipped below the per capita income of Albania, that is, it fell to the level of the poorest transition countries.[4]

7.2. The bid for presidential consolidation

Immediately after being elected as president in July 1994, Kuchma set about to consolidate power in his own hands. In August, he issued a decree (*ukaz*) which subjugated the chairmen of local and regional councils (*radas*) directly to the president. This contradicted his electoral promises of decentralization and instead served to extend so-called 'presidential verticals' into the regions.

In late 1994, the president proposed to replace the outdated 1978 constitution by a temporary 'Law on Power' while the drafting of a new constitution continued; which parliament grudgingly accepted. A new constitution was finally agreed upon and adopted in 1996.[5] It was a rather inconclusive compromise with a government "responsible to the President of Ukraine and [...] under the control of and accountable to the *Verkhovna Rada*" (Art. 113). The president gained rather extensive rights of appointment, and received substantial powers to dissolve parliament (Art. 106), while the requirements for parliament to dismiss the president were defined rather stringently (Art. 111).

Furthermore, the constitution reflected both nationalist and socialist ideas present in the *Rada* at the time: "[t]he state promotes the consolidation and development of the Ukrainian nation," but also: "citizens in need of social protection are provided with housing by the State and bodies of local self-government, free of charge or at a price affordable for them, in accordance with the law." (Art. 47).

From the adoption of the constitution in 1996 until late 2000, president Kuchma continued with his drive to strengthen the powers of his office. He built up a presidential administration which came to parallel many functions of the Cabinet of Ministers and later posed serious problems for institutional reform.[6] A further key institution in the presidential power structure was the Council for National Security and Defense which formally supervised the so-called power ministries, but *de facto* wielded even wider ranging powers.[7]

In addition, Kuchma used his power to promulgate legal acts extensively, doubling the annual number of presidential decrees and orders compared to the Kravchuk years. Between 1996 and 1999, he issued almost 2000 legal acts (decrees and orders) per year (see Appendix, Table II.6.1).[8] The final part of the constitution awarded the president the right to issue decrees in the field of economic policy making for a period of three years.[9]

The president based his power on the industrial elites or 'oligarchic clans' from Eastern Ukraine. The absence of a real party system, i.e. of stable 'visible groups,' and especially of a pro-presidential party as a power-base, added to the relative importance of these 'clans.' A number of the members of Kuchma's administration were recruited from the large industrial centers of Eastern Ukraine and particularly from his own regional base, Dnipropetrovsk.[10] These region-based networks were dubbed 'clans' in the Ukrainian media and among political observers: the 'Dnipropetrovsk-clan,' the 'Donetsk-clan' and the smaller 'Kharkiv-clan.'[11] These clans were not internally coherent: Pavlo Lazarenko whom Kuchma appointed as prime minister and Lazarenko's ally Yulia Tymoshenko were representatives of the Dnipropetrovsk clan who eventually went into opposition to the president. In Donetsk, a number of high-level killings took place in 1995 and 1996 among the business elite, indicating that several 'roving bandits' were competing for the territory.[12]

The expansion of 'opaque' networks into the political sphere was not limited to the presidential sphere, but also included parliament. From the mid to late 1990s the new Ukrainian business elite increasingly entered politics by being elected to parliament. The result was not a replacement of elites, but a combination of recycled old elites (members of state and party structures in Soviet times), and rising new *biznismeny*.

7.3. State-society relations—the rise of political-business groups and weak democratic accountability

State-society relations during this period were marked by the ascendancy of political-business groups, and by disregard for democratic accountability. With regard to political parties, the two trends of a high flux in membership and in the affiliation of deputies, and the rise of parties based on business interests continued. Some of these business-based parties gained political influence without ever winning a single vote: *after* the 1998 parliamentary elections, a number of parties developed in parliament by attracting deputies elected as independents or on the ticket of other parties to newly formed factions. Another form of disregard for accountability was the increased use of '*adminresurs*'—administrative resources to manipulate the outcome in favor of the incumbent during the 1999 presidential elections. Citizens reacted to these political manipulations with very low levels of trust in state institutions.

7.3.1. TRADE UNIONS AND CAPITALISTS' UNIONS

Among the socio-economic intermediary organizations, it was the association of large businesses, the UUIE, which continued to gain political influence, while trade unions—both old and new—lost political clout.[13] When the government sought to reign in inflation in 1996, wage arrears grew rapidly (see section 5.5), triggering a strike-wave in industrial eastern Ukraine involving miners from dozens of mines in the region.[14] While winning some concessions from the government, the strikes ultimately failed, reducing the influence of the miners and their unions.

Social pacts and agreements on wages continued to be concluded between the government and the unions—however, the government regularly broke its promises when revenue fell short. Given the ineffectiveness of the unions as well as a gradual shift in employment towards the private sector, formal union membership declined.[15]

The UUIE in contrast, representing the owners and managers of Ukraine's large enterprises, gained political clout, not least due to its close ties with Kuchma, who had been head of the UUIE when running for president in 1994.[16] Through its combination of close relations with the president and with parliamentary deputies, the UUIE was able to lobby for legislation, such as a law on financial-industrial groups which, following the Russian model, was aimed at creating close ties between banks and large enterprises.[17]

7.3.2. THE ZENITH OF THE POLITICO-BUSINESS GROUPS

Several new parties were founded in the late 1990s, a few of which became more durable. In early 1996, members of the amorphous 'party of power' founded the People's Democratic Party (NDP). This new creation was backed by the president, although he did not become a formal member. Soon afterwards, however, a Social Democratic Party (united—SDPU (o)—split from the NDP, reflecting the diversity of interests within the 'party of power.' The co-founders of the SDPU were former prime minister and head of the security services, Yevhen Marchuk, and former president Leonid Kravchuk. The SDPU was a party of powerful business interests in Ukraine—having little to do with the party's label as social-democrats. Another competing 'center' party, *Hromada*, was created by Pavlo Lazarenko, prime minister in 1996 and 1997, who represented a branch of the Dnipropetrovsk regional 'clans.' Generally, as D'Anieri observed, 'centrist parties' remained fronts for interest politics rather than real centrist parties seeking broad electoral appeal.[18]

A more programmatic party advocating economic reforms, 'Reform and Order' (*Reformy i Paryadok*), was founded in October 1997 by Viktor Pynzenyk and other reform-oriented politicians.[19] On the left, the formation of new parties also continued—amid suspicions that the administration was creating some new parties in order to split the left vote, in particular 'Working Ukraine' (*Trudova Ukraina*), and a new Agrarian party (*Ahrarna Partiia Ukraini*).[20]

The late 1990s were the zenith of president Kuchma's quest for power, and of unfettered opportunities for Ukraine's oligarchic class. Opaque groups controlled several important political parties (the SDPU, Hromada, and others); and at the same time siphoned money from public assets and moved them abroad with relative impunity.[21] Businesses controlled by oligarchic groups enjoyed generous tax privileges.

Then the situation began to shift: the Yushchenko-Tymoshenko government which was in place between late 1999 and early 2001 brought some of the most irregular practices in the energy sector under control, and reduced the range of tax privileges. Nonetheless, oligarchic groups experienced another surge in economic opportunities as the president became weakened. In the run-up to the 2004 presidential elections, major assets were privatized, a number of which were sold at manipulated prices to those with the right connections.[22] By the early 2000s, several Ukrainian businessmen were assessed to own upwards of $1 billion in assets.[23] At the same time, the average monthly wage in Ukraine stood at UAH 230, or less than $45.[24]

7.3.3. TRUST AND EXPECTATIONS

The trust of Ukrainians in their public institutions and organizations became extraordinarily low—even in comparison to other Eastern European countries—across all governmental institutions (parties, courts, police, civil servants, government, parliament, president, and prime minister).[25] Parliament was one of the least trusted public institutions, which is dramatic given its centrality as a democratic institution.

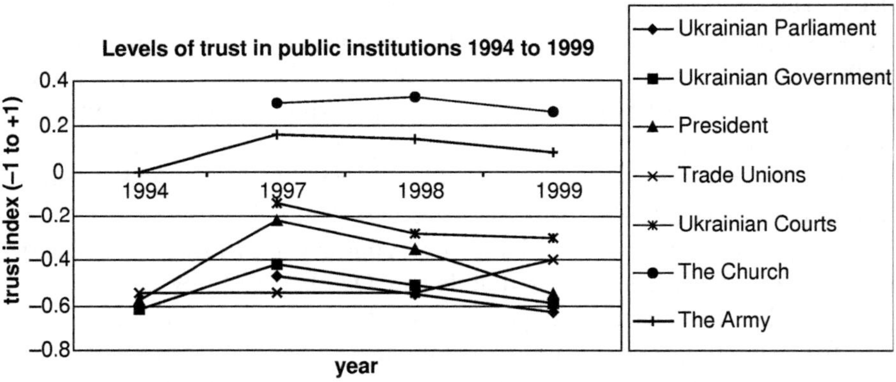

Graph 7.1: Levels of trust in public institutions, 1994–1999

The reasons for the low level of trust in public institutions appear to be a combination of the extremely bad economic situation with its severe effects on households, the inefficacy of public institutions in dealing with the economic crisis,[26] and the feeling that corruption had increased substantially as compared with communist times.

While Ukrainians further lost trust in their public institutions in the mid- to late 1990s, they continued to expect the state to play a strong role in the economy and as a welfare provider.

The seeming paradox between low trust in state institutions and low trust in the private sector may be explained by the fact that private business was even more distrusted than the state. In particular, privatization was viewed as having led to 'mafia rule' rather than a market economy. Thus, the "mafia, criminal world, [and] representatives of the shadow economy" were rated as the most powerful groups in Ukraine—far ahead of the presidential administration, parliament, or the IMF.[27]

Table 7.2: State responsibility for social welfare and industry

	These should be mainly done by the state, rather than left mainly to private businesses and the market-economy			
	health-care	jobs	housing	setting prices for basic goods
Russia	93	89	75	93
Ukraine	88	89	90	88
Czech Republic	81	56	69	73
Slovakia	97	77	85	91
Hungary	94	84	85	78

	These should be run mainly by the state, rather than mainly by private businesses			
	farming	car factories	computer manuf.	newspapers
Russia	60	79	68	79
Ukraine	43	73	71	72
Czech Republic	53	39	27	34
Slovakia	72	44	32	57
Hungary	44	55	55	46

Source: Miller, White, and Heywood (1998), 114, 112.

As a result of distrust in the market and in semi-democratic political institutions, Ukrainians voiced preferences for authoritarian alternatives: a 1998 survey found that among the sample cases (which included Belarus but not Russia) Ukrainians were the strongest supporters of alternatives to democracy, either in the form of communist rule or rule by a strong leader.[28] It is quite remarkable therefore that Ukraine was the site of broad pro-democracy protests just a few years later, and in contrast to the more authoritarian pathways in Belarus and Russia.

Despite their deep distrust of political institutions, Ukrainians attempted to exercise political accountability. 71 per cent of the electorate turned out for the parliamentary vote in 1998—and only a small share voted for parties that had been created top-down. Electoral accountability, however, was undermined by fluidity in faction membership as many MPs did not remain with the party on the ticket of which they had been elected.

7.3.4. THE 1998 PARLIAMENTARY ELECTIONS

From 1994 to 1998, the parliament had been dominated by a relatively strong left wing holding about 140 out of 450 seats, and various center factions, which by 'acquiring' deputies grew to over 180 members in late 1997 (see Appendix, Table III.1.). In the 1998 parliamentary elections, the role of the state and the continuing economic crisis were key election issues; in addition, opposition parties attacked the corruption of the state apparatus. The re-founded orthodox Communist Party called for a restoration of state control over the economy; while the Socialist/Rural bloc advocated state control over the banking system and over "strategic markets." In the center of the party spectrum, the NDP tried to convince voters that the state apparatus—which it represented—was "not a monster" and that privatization could bring prosperity for many rather than only for few; also, it promised to tax the rich to support the needy, while at the same time calling for a "stimulating" rather than "oppressive" tax system. *Rukh* advocated privatization free from *mafia* and other corrupt interests as well as a "stable, simple, and stimulating" tax system; and continued to combine its national message with the goal to 'return to Europe.'[29] All parties promised to pay off wage and pension arrears, to raise living standards and to overcome the problem of unemployment.[30]

In the elections, the communists became by far the strongest single party winning 24.7 per cent of the popular vote. They were followed by the other 'real' parties, *Rukh* with 9.4 per cent, and the Socialist/Rural bloc with 8.6 per cent. Four center parties (NDP, *Hromada*, SDPU, and the Greens) and the Progressive Socialists just cleared the 4 per cent hurdle.[31] In spite of being the government-favored party with privileged media access and financing, the NDP did poorly (for the election results, see Appendix Table III.2).

After the elections, the NDP set out to 'collect' independent deputies in its faction. Starting with an original faction of only 29 deputies, it managed to add 64 more in the coming months. This still failed to produce longer-term stability and strength, however, as key members of the NDP split away, eroding its significance.[32] A particular feature of the Ukrainian parliament at the time was that deputies saw themselves primarily as members of 'factions' rather than parties, i.e. of temporary alliances of MPs.[33] The fluid nature of factions further reinforced personalization rather than interest aggregation in Ukrainian politics.[34] Between 1998 and 2001, 528 instances of faction-changing took place among the Rada's 450 deputies.[35]

7.3.5. THE 1999 PRESIDENTIAL ELECTIONS

The third presidential elections took place in October and November 1999. The left-wing and the national democratic opposition each fielded multiple candidates against Kuchma.[36] The main left-wing candidates were the Communist Petro Symonenko, and the Socialist Oleksandr Moroz.

The elections showed a regression in terms of democratic rules. Most of the media with national coverage were either state-controlled or controlled by various oligarchic groups close to the President.[37] Media critical of the president or simply more neutral in their coverage—such as STB, the TV channel—were put under pressure by the tax administration and the fire inspectorate.[38] This formed part of the widespread use of 'administrative resources', i.e., using the administrative apparatus of the state to maintain political control and influence election.[39] Complaints of pressure by officials were widespread among the population.[40]

Table 7.3: Results of the presidential elections, 1999, first and second rounds

Candidate	Party or bloc	Result (%) first round [second round]
Leonid Kuchma	Zlahoda	36.49 [56.18]
Petro Symonenko	Communist	22.40 [37.49]
Oleksandr Moroz	Socialist	11.29
Natalia Vitrenko	Progressive Socialist	10.97
Yevhen Marchuk	Social Democratic Union	8.13
Yurii Kostenko	Rukh	2.17
Hennadii Udovenko	Rukh	1.22
Vasyl Onopenko	Social Democratic	0.47
others (5 candidates)		1.27

Note: several of the parties/blocs listed were not very serious entities. Thus, Zlahoda was created as a political movement to support the incumbent, but he did not become a member; likewise, the Social Democratic Union was created for the presidential elections only.

Source: Taras Kuzio, *Ukraine after the elections* (undated manuscript), 13–14.

Using such 'administrative resources,' the regime avoided large-scale infringements on the rules of the vote itself.[41] Moreover, Kuchma ran against his preferred candidate, the communist Symonenko in the second round. Against Symonenko, who advocated a return to a Soviet-style system, a majority of voters probably supported Kuchma as the lesser of two evils.[42] Notably, in contrast to 1994, this time Kuchma was overwhelmingly supported in Western Ukraine (where rejection of the communist alternative was stronger), while Symonenko won in a number of oblasts in Eastern and Central Ukraine.[43]

7.3.6. YUSHCHENKO AS PRIME MINISTER

In the months following the elections, important political changes took place. In mid-December, the president reduced the number of cabinet members from 89 to a still sizeable 46, which had long been advocated by IFIs.[44] Then, after parliament voted against the re-appointment of Valerii Pustovoitenko as prime minister, the Central Bank governor Viktor Yushchenko was chosen for the post. As one of the central figures in the new cabinet, Yushchenko drew Yulia Tymoshenko from her post as head of the parliamentary budget committee to become deputy prime minister responsible for the energy sector.

After the formation of the new government, pro-presidential factions sought to take over power in the legislative. Up to then, left-wing factions had occupied key positions, including those of the speaker and his deputy, as well as the leadership of important parliamentary committees. After several weeks of struggle, the pro-presidential forces won out, taking over the positions of speaker (Ivan Plyushch, NDP) and deputy speaker (Viktor Medvedchuk, SDPU), as well as other committees, and forming a so-called 'presidential majority.'

The president still perceived parliament as an obstacle to his consolidation of power, however. Hence, Kuchma initiated a referendum in April 2000 intended to dilute the powers of the legislative branch and to increase presidential powers.[45] The outcome marked a victory for the president: all four questions—on the presidential powers to dissolve parliament, of reducing deputies' immunity, on reducing the size of parliament, and on creating a second chamber—were supported by over 80 per cent of voters.[46]

However, in one of the many unexpected twists of Ukrainian politics, this impressive showing proved far less decisive than it appeared at first sight. The referendum had been a peak in the president's influence; in the coming months, the results of the referendum were not implemented, and at the end of 2000, Kuchma's position was seriously weakened when he became embroiled in a major scandal (see Chapter 8, section 1 below).

The government led by Viktor Yushchenko remained in a tenuous position throughout 2000, but managed to achieve some important improvements in the functioning of the fiscal system (see below). The parliamentary 'majority' became increasingly split between those supportive of the government and those closer to the president. Still, legislative activity was high: in 2000, 297 laws were passed—the most in any year since independence (see Appendix, Table II.6).[47] Furthermore, the government improved revenue collection and hence was able to reduce the wage and pension arrears which had accumulated since 1996—laying part of the foundations of Yushchenko's and Tymoshenko's popularity.

Table 7.4: Prime ministers and ministers of finance, 1994–2001

Prime ministers	06/1994–03/1995	Vitalii Masol
	03/1995–05/1996	Yevhen Marchuk (03/95–06/95 acting)
	05/1996–07/1997	Pavlo Lazarenko
	07/1997–12/1999	Valerii Pustovoitenko
	12/1999–04/2001	Viktor Yushchenko
Ministers of finance	07/1994–06/1996	Petro Hermanchuk
	06/1996–02/1997	Valentin Koronevskii
	02/1997–12/2001	Ihor Mityukov

7.4. External factors

External influences on the state-building process increased somewhat during the second half of the 1990s, but without becoming dominant relative to domestic factors. Importantly, there was still a lack of serious engagement with and by the EU.

Ukraine's economy is trade-intensive with imports and exports amounting to around 70 to 80 per cent of GDP. [48] In the second half of the 1990s, trade shifted gradually towards Central Eastern Europe and the European Union, although Russia and the CIS remained the largest trade partners. Foreign direct investment remained relatively small in Ukraine in the late 1990s, as in other non-resource-rich CIS countries.[49] This generally reflected the poor investment climate—despite some tax breaks for enterprises with foreign investment (which were primarily used by Ukrainians re-importing capital).

Ukraine only began to be rated by international agencies in the late 1990s and started in the worst possible category.[50] In 1997, just before the first ratings were issued, the government borrowed heavily in international credit markets—at unsustainably high interest rates. The 1998 Russian financial crisis then closed off international credit markets for some time. As a result, Ukraine's debt peaked in 1999 at around 50 per cent of GDP and afterwards diminished due to slower borrowing and a growing GDP. While external credit ratings are important for countries already deeply engaged in international credit markets (where a drop in ratings can cause sudden outflows), this was not yet the case in the late 1990s in Ukraine.

The international financial institutions, primarily the IMF and the World Bank, were the most direct and visible external influence. As will be described in the sections on fiscal developments below, they sought to influence fiscal policies and the restructuring of the public sector more broadly. While in the short term, some demands were fulfilled, by and large the impact of IFIs on Ukraine's state-building process remained limited.

In 1997, promises of a major IMF loan failed to entice parliament to adopt a major package of tax and expenditure reforms (see section 5.2 below).[51] In the wake of the Russian financial crisis in 1998, the IMF demanded a sharp reduction in expenditures. After the newly elected parliament refused, the president ordered the cut by decree; and finally the loan was approved in September. Still, Ukraine repeatedly did not follow the agreed conditions—at the price of receiving only about half of the agreed-upon loan.

Furthermore, a number of programs by international donors, such as the attempt by the World Bank to reform the coal mining sector in Ukraine, failed.[52] Given the industrial power structures in Ukraine, it was clearly not easy to exercise external leverage.[53] The IMF and the World Bank nonetheless played a role at the margins: their conditionality and advice shaped some reforms in the public sector, including the importation of some institutional models, such the treasury system which the IMF promoted across the former Soviet Union.

In a broader sense, Ukraine's state-building was influenced by its situation between Russia and the expanding European Union. Ukraine remained excluded from EU considerations of eastward enlargement in the 1990s. Close economic links with Russia continued, but Ukraine was large and important enough to keep a distance politically. The US had a geopolitical interest in terms of ensuring Ukraine's permanent independence from Russia and hence provided economic as well as political support, but its financial support was limited (see also Chapter 8). Overall, therefore, Ukrainian state-building continued to be primarily driven by domestic factors, but external factors began to play a more significant role at this stage.

7.5. Stabilizing the fiscal system

During the late 1990s, the fiscal system was marked by incremental improvements and the strengthening of capacity on the one hand, but by the failure of fundamental reform and deliberate distortions on the other hand. Attempts at fundamental reform failed in 1997, and again in 2000–2001, even though by then a so-called 'pro-presidential majority' existed in parliament.

Budget spending continued to be marked by considerable diversion between budgets as planned and as executed; and a mixture of formal and informal practices of hand-steering and *ad hoc* cuts in the budget remained in use. This was especially acute in 1998, when the Russian crisis caused unexpected shortfalls in revenue, while parliament refused to vote for major spending cuts.

The economic virtualization (mentioned in section 1) also extended into the fiscal sphere: tax and expenditure arrears mounted, and the government collected a considerable share of its revenue in non-cash form, creating a highly intransparent system. Expenditure arrears inflicted serious difficulties especially for pensioners who depended on the state for their livelihood. At the same time, efforts at (re-)strengthening the state involved the development of considerable distortions in particular with regard to the tax administration—which evolved into a "state within the state."[54] Given a messy and unreformed tax system, formal rules were routinely broken—which opened the possibility of selective enforcement for the executive.

The 1999 to 2001 Yushchenko-Tymoshenko government achieved major improvements in the operation of the revenue and expenditure system by reducing non-monetary payments and arrears. However, such reforms proved unpopular with Ukraine's elites, and in April 2001 the Yushchenko government was ousted from power by a "red-grey" coalition between supporters of the president-led oligarchy and the communists.

7.5.1. THE TAX SYSTEM IN URGENT NEED OF REFORM

Throughout the 1990s, there was deep disagreement about the role of the state in Ukraine. Extraction remained rather high but declined especially between 1994 and 1996 and in 1999, bringing government revenue from over 40 per cent in the early 1990s to around 33.5 per cent of GDP by 2000 (see Appendix Table I.2.1). Moreover, the complex and unstable tax system was detrimental to investment and economic recovery. The unholy alliance between an executive interested in possibilities for selective enforcement, oligarchs interested in a system with privileges rather than a level playing field, and a Communist Party opposed to a market economy upheld this situation.

Since independence, Ukraine had relied on five major types of taxes: value-added-tax (VAT), personal income tax (PIT), enterprise profit tax (EPT or:

company income tax, CIT), excise taxes, and deductions to social funds ('payroll tax'). In addition, the state collected contributions to a number of special funds (Chernobyl fund, road fund, etc.). As reflected in table 7.5, the respective shares of taxes in total revenue changed over time, as VAT and EPT collections declined.

Table 7.5: Share of different taxes in total revenue

	1992	1993	1994	1995	1996	1997	1998	1999	2000
EPT	16.5	25.3	26.9	23.7	18.1	15.3	16.8	15.1	12.8
VAT	28.7	29.8	24.4	22.2	21.0	20.5	19.1	19.2	14.6
Excise tax	3.7	4.5	3.3	2.0	2.1	3.1	3.3	4.1	3.5
PIT	8.2	5	6.3	7.7	8.8	9.0	9.5	10.0	9.9
Pension fund	28.0	14.8	17.3	20.4	23.1	26.4	24.6	25.9	25.2
Chernobyl fund	7.3	4.5	4.5	5.0	4.9	4.7	3.8	0.5	0.2

Figures do not add up to 100% since not all revenue sources are covered—smaller taxes, revenues from privatization, etc.

Source: UEPLAC, Dec. 2000, 50.

Major problems with the tax system in the 1990s were its instability, and, especially towards the late 1990s, proliferating exemptions and other tax avoidance schemes, which narrowed the tax base and made the tax system increasingly unfair. Moreover, these practices drained resources from the budget, and hence meant that the state reneged on many of its obligations exposing society to additional hardship during the transition.

7.5.1.1. INDIRECT AND DIRECT TAXES IN A 'VIRTUAL' ECONOMY

The value added tax (VAT) had been the main indirect tax since independence. However, the VAT is a relatively complex tax to administer and implement effectively, particularly in an increasingly 'virtual' economy, and in a situation of a captured state.[55] The VAT in Ukraine was subject to constant changes throughout the 1990s concerning rates, the tax base, and exemptions. In 1999, Serhyi Teriokhin, head of the tax and customs subcommittee of the *Verkhovna Rada*, estimated that "since independence, Ukraine [...] has revised its value added tax rules more than 200 times."[56]

The VAT rate was lowered from a very high level of 28 to 20 per cent in 1995, which led to a one-off drop in revenue from it.[57] Due to proliferating exemptions (see below) its importance continued to decline further thereafter.

Regarding direct taxes, taxing enterprises had been the major source of budget revenue under the Soviet system. The enterprise profit tax (EPT) continued to be an important source of revenue in Ukraine—although collections fell even faster than those from the VAT since 1995.[58] Exemptions from the EPT were justified as "the best way to promote production or consumption." As part of the socialist legacy, production of 'material values' was considered superior to any trading activities profits; therefore profits from the latter were more highly taxed (at 45 per cent rather than the standard 30 per cent rate).

In 1997, a new enterprise profit tax law was adopted as part of what remained from Pynzenyk's *Economic Growth* package.[59] Furthermore, in 1998, various simplified tax schemes were introduced for small enterprises to reduce their costs of compliance (bookkeeping, etc.).[60] While beneficial in principle, these schemes resulted in new forms of tax avoidance (large firms splitting up into small units). Furthermore, starting in 1998–1999, a number of Ukrainian regions rapidly set up Free Economic Zones—creating another source of distortions in the tax system.[61]

The taxation of personal income was new to citizens (see Chapter 5), and the system immediately put a high burden on them. Because tax brackets were not sufficiently indexed against inflation, incomes of between $200 and $500 were already subject to the maximum 40 per cent rate (see Table 7.6), and even incomes below the official poverty line (118.3 UAH or $24 in 1999) came to be taxed at a rate of 10 to 15 percent.[62] At the same time, truly high incomes often were not taxed. In 1999, only 40 Ukrainians declared incomes above $250,000, while in that year alone 6000 luxury cars were imported into the country.[63]

Overall, labor was rather heavily taxed, due to a combination of high income tax rates even for moderate salaries and high payroll taxes (social security contributions), which until 1997 amounted to 52 per cent of wages (subsequently reduced to 37.5 per cent of wages).[64] As a result, firms had a strong incentive to pay a share of wages 'under the table' and employees largely welcomed this practice.[65]

Like other taxes, sub-national taxes and levies varied considerably; but their yield was rather insignificant.[66] An important potential revenue source, property taxes, remained untapped in Ukraine, because private property did not receive full legal recognition for a number of years and, moreover, because those who would have had to pay it wielded increasing influence in parliament.[67]

Table 7.6: Income tax rates (since 1996)

Taxable income in UAH	In US-Dollar Q4	Tax rate in %
< 17	< 3.5	0
17–85	3.5–17.3	10
86–170	17.4–34.7	15
171–1020	34.7–208.2	20
1021–1700	208.2–346.9	30
> 1700	> 347	40

Source: UEPLAC (December 1999), 39.

7.5.2. TAXES NOT PAID: EVASION, ARREARS, WRITE-OFFS, AND EXEMPTIONS

Two broad types of non-payment of taxes may be distinguished: evasion—which is intentional as well as illegal, and avoidance which may involve using (or lobbying for) exemptions.[68] Furthermore, in Ukraine, arrears and eventual write-offs were an important mechanism for the non-payment of taxes.

Evasion or abuse of the VAT was particularly widespread—and the lines between private abuse and political stealing were fluid, as became apparent in the aftermath of the 'Orange Revolution' (see Chapter 8).[69] In particular, illegal claims for VAT refunds by exporters were a widespread problem, as the State Tax Administration (STA) lacked the capacity to check all refund-claimants.[70] Vertical chains of companies were set up for short periods of time with one member firm engaging in exports. The up-stream firm would disappear before paying the VAT, and the down-stream, exporting firm would claim a refund of VAT allegedly paid to the disappeared firm.[71] In order to combat this practice, in 1999 the STA began to slow down VAT refunds—hurting all those with justified refund claims. Furthermore, a slow and inefficient court system made it difficult to sort out legal and illegal claims. As will be discussed in Chapter 8, in 2004, the pro-presidential political forces then used the highly intransparent system to siphon money out to pay for the costly election campaign.

Mounting tax arrears were a further element of the economic and fiscal 'virtualization' and contributed to intransparency and distortions (see Table 7.7). The massive explosion of tax arrears in 1998 resulted from the acute economic crisis of that year which caused a further drop in production. In industry, especially the fuel and energy industries, in machine-building, and in the food industry tax arrears rose more than seven-fold.[72]

Table 7.7: Tax arrears in millions of Hryvnia (end of period)

	1994	1995	1996	1997	1998	1999	2000 Q2
End-period stock	na	na	2946	4972	13876	10202	12478
State Tax Admin	52	544	1365	2342	10302	8930	11151
– VAT	30	221	575	920	4070	5565	6639
– Excises	2	22	35	63	509	534	677
– EPT	17	164	318	335	1508	2424	3256
– P T	–	–	3	7	35	30	37
– Other	3	137	434	1017	4180	376	543
Arrears in % of GDP	0.4	1	1.7	2.5	10	7	6.9

Sources: IMF, World Bank

As tax arrears coincided with budget arrears (i.e. the state not paying for its goods, energy consumption, etc.),[73] mutual debt write-offs and tax amnesties were increasingly used to solve this situation, especially at local and regional levels.[74] These practices largely took place outside a legal framework, while attempts to outlaw them were ineffective.[75]

Table 7.8: Payment arrears 1996–2000, in millions of Hryvnia

	1996	1997	1998	1999	2000 Q2
Total Arrears (stock)	5902	2614	4339	7979	8785
Social Arrears	2982	2614	4339	3089	2363
– wages	1231	1278	1679	1045	878
– pensions	1255	869	2013	1255	759
Energy Arrears*	967	–	–	3643	5297
Water supply and sewage	0	0	0	737	1125

Source: IMF (2000)

Apart from such mutual settlements, different branches of power granted various tax write-offs. In 1997, 5.4 billion UAH in tax debts were written off through a law adopted by the *Rada*.[76] In June 1998, the president issued a decree freeing agricultural enterprises and sugar mills from all fines and sanctions connected to overdue tax payments, and ordered a restructuring of their tax debt. In March 1998, the Cabinet of Ministers approved a list of enterprises from the military-industrial complex for which land tax payments for 1997 were to be written off.

In general, tax exemptions proliferated due to the combination of institutional fragmentation and state capture. In 1999, the list of tax exemptions in Ukraine consisted of about 200 items—many of which applied to individual enterprises.[77] In Lithuania, in contrast, such an individualized practice of tax exemptions had never been practiced according to Dzintra Sakevičienė of the Lithuanian Ministry of Finance.[78]

The Ukrainian tax administration claimed that revenue losses from privileges reached 200 per cent (!) of collected tax revenue in 1998 and 1999.[79] The highest share of revenue lost due to privileges was registered in the three richest oblasts (Dnipropetrovsk, Kyiv, and Donetsk). Many exemptions were company-specific: in 1998, for example, 105,200 legal entities enjoyed some kind of tax privileges equaling 20.9 billion UAH (or more than 50 per cent of all revenue).[80] Exemptions from VAT, which had multiplied since 1993, accounted for more than half of the lost revenue.[81] Furthermore, in the late 1990s, more and more Free Economic Zones were set up in which exemptions from VAT as well as EPT applied.[82]

In 1997, deputy-prime minister Pynzenyk attempted to cut back on these privileges (see also section 5.2 below).[83] However, a law passed on April 3, 1997 was quickly overturned and the exemptions were reinstated after consultations with "top executives from some of Ukraine's largest companies" in October of that year.[84]

Given the deep economic crisis of the Ukrainian economy at the time, it would have been impossible to collect all statutory taxes; but there was a real loss of revenue, and moreover, proliferating tax privileges created a highly intransparent and unfair tax system. The buying of legislation—one of the key features of "state capture"—became particularly widespread because of the fragmentation of the Ukrainian government machinery. A World Bank report commented on cabinet decision-making structures:

> As opposed to most countries, Cabinet decisions in Ukraine were made primarily by getting all Ministers to sign a draft resolution separately. Policy coherence had been almost completely eliminated [...] [The] requirement [issued in 2000] to take decisions on the basis of votes taken at a Cabinet meeting had dramatic impact on the policy process [... since it] decreased opportunities to come to secret private side deals.[85]

Furthermore, those seeking privileges benefited from the fact that in Ukraine multiple bodies created competing legal rules. The president only lost his power to directly issue economic policy decrees three years after the adoption of the constitution, in June 1999. In parliament, the degree of fragmentation and "state capture" was promoted by the combination of strong left-wing parties, which were opposed to most market-oriented reforms, and the political power of oligarchic networks—which moreover, could buy votes from the left wing when necessary.[86]

7.5.3. THE FAILURE OF 'BIG LEAP' REFORM

In 1996, deputy-prime minister Viktor Pynzenyk proposed a major reform of the Ukrainian fiscal system.[87] He had ample support from foreign advisors—including the Harvard Institute of International Development, the German Advisory Group, and the IMF.[88] He proposed a 'big leap' reform—which included significant reductions in tax and payroll obligations; and concomitantly reductions of non-priority spending and spending on the national economy. The pension system was to be radically reformed and cash privatization also to be accelerated to help finance the reform.[89]

However, by early 1997 it became clear that the package would not go through parliament and Pynzenyk was tendering his resignation. The failure of this ambitious reform was initially widely blamed on the left-leaning parliament, but this was a deliberate simplification. While designing an ambitious technical reform plan with the assistance of foreign advisors, Pynzenyk had failed to invest in finding political allies. Potential reform supporters in parliament felt left out, as attempts at consultation and consensus-building had been late and botched.[90]

Moreover, the president and powerful oligarchic groups were not interested. Then Prime Minister Lazarenko had substantial business interests in Eastern Ukraine which enjoyed generous tax exemptions; and he allegedly also benefited from the bribes which other enterprises paid to receive exemptions.[91] The president had begun to strengthen the tax administration after the adoption of the constitution in 1996 (see section 5.6 below), and apparently found a complex tax system combined with a tax administration accountable to himself a convenient instrument of exercising control and dispensing favors.

Eventually, parliament only adopted some partial reforms in April 1997. Procedures for VAT reimbursements to exporters were streamlined.[92] The definition of profits and costs to calculate profit tax obligations, as well as the rules for depreciation and deductions were improved. Some tax privileges were cancelled, but most of these were soon re-instated. The envisaged sweeping reform of the pension system and of the banking sector failed altogether; and the tax burden on labor remained high, despite a limited reduction in payroll taxes—

keeping wages in the shadow. Parliament refused to adopt a property tax which would have provided an important revenue base for local governments; but would have hurt the interests of Ukraine's budding capitalist class.

7.5.4. THE CONTINUING QUEST FOR A TAX CODE

The issue of a tax code remained on the political agenda. In 2000, under the Yushchenko government, the next serious attempt to pass a tax code again failed. After being adopted in a first reading in July, more than 5000 amendments were suggested by deputies, essentially stalling the final adoption of the code.[93] The Kinakh government, put in place after the ouster of Yushchenko in April 2001, tried to revive the code. Viktor Medvedchuk, leader of the SDPU and deputy speaker of parliament, styled himself as a key advocate of the reform. However, as the head of the committee on finance and banking, Valerii Aloshyn, commented: "To adopt the Tax Code in parliament we need to form a majority, which agrees simultaneously to lower the tax burden and to cut tax privileges. I'm convinced that such a majority does not exist in the hall of the *Verkhovna Rada*."[94]

As a result, even this alliance between a technocrat (Kinakh) and part of the oligarchic forces (around Medvedchuk) failed to achieve a breakthrough in tax reform. Instead, in mid-December 2001 Viktor Medvedchuk was ousted by a right-left alliance from his post as deputy speaker in revenge for earlier political and policy actions. Thus, the climate of constant political fragmentation, shifts and turns yet again prevented a more fundamental reform in Ukraine.

The need to use the tax administration according to a 'defensive logic' to oppress political opponents was an important reason against adopting a more transparent tax system—since the existing system ensured that almost any entrepreneur broke formal rules in one way or another, which allowed the state to engage in selective enforcement (see section 5.6 below).[95]

7.5.5. STEPS TOWARDS REGULARIZING THE BUDGETING PROCESS: THE BUDGET CODE OF 1995

In contrast to the tax system, the budget system was reformed in two stages in 1995 and 2001. The first more regularized budget system was introduced by the Law "On the Budget System of Ukraine" adopted in August 1995, replacing the initial law from 1990 "On the Budget System of the Ukrainian SSR."[96] The 1995 code provided improved definitions of the rights and responsibilities of different participants in the budget process. A balanced budget was formulated as a general goal, while parliament received the explicit right to establish a deficit ceiling and to determine the sources from which to cover it.[97]

However, ongoing legal changes such as the adoption of a new budget classification system in 1996 had to be incorporated into the budget system law; and new budgetary institutions such as a state treasury and an external audit institution were set up in the second half of the 1990s. As a result, debates on a new and more permanent budget code continued.[98]

Budget cycles consist of four broad phases: the forecasting and drafting phase, the approval phase, the execution or implementation phase, and auditing.[99] All of these phases suffered from serious shortcomings, which the 1995 code could only partially alleviate. At the start, both the president and parliament had a right to issue general budget guidelines (a presidential decree and parliament's budget resolution).[100] Macro-economic forecasting was to be done jointly by the Ministry of Economy with the Ministry of Finance, the National Bank and other agencies.[101] However, given the lack of institutional integration, this joint exercise was flawed, and forecasts of economic growth and inflation were often unrealistic until the late 1990s.[102]

Regarding budget preparation, submissions by spending agencies often far exceeded possible financing—at one point even exceeding total GDP by one-and-a-half times.[103] Wildavsky has described this "padding", i.e., submitting unrealistically high requests in the expectation of cuts as typical for poorer, less stable countries.[104] While in Ukraine, this practice became extreme, in Lithuania, in contrast, such practices remained within well-manageable proportions.[105]

Parliamentary approval of the budget took place through a process of three readings. Given that many spending requests found support in the Rada, the budget was usually revised upwards during the negotiation period. Thus, the parliament contributed to unrealistically high expectations about available revenue and expenditure.

Once the budget was approved, the Ministry of Finance would draw up quarterly and monthly spending plans (*rospis*), according to which the budget was to be executed.[106] However, in reality, much more *ad hoc* forms of spending control—sequestration and 'hand management'—continued until the late 1990s; and consequently important shifts in expenditure allocations occurred during implementation.

The auditing phase remained weak at least until 1997. According to the budget system law, by May 1 the executive had to report on the execution of the previous year's budget to the parliament, which in turn would adopt and publish a resolution on it. However, this deadline usually shifted to much later in the year.[107] Moreover, before 1997 there was no external audit institution, which could have provided an independent report on the execution of the budget. Primary control over budget execution was exercised by an internal agency, the State Controlling and Revision Agency (DKRS - *Derzahvna Kon-*

Table 7.9: Budget implementation of different expenditure categories
(in % of planned expenditures)
(See also the distribution of expenditure shares, Appendix, Table II.4.1)

Type of expenditure	Percentage fulfilled (in % of budget adopted by parliament)		
	1996	**1997**	**1998**
Social protection of the population	60.3	82.9	82.4
Financing of the social-cultural sphere (including education and health protection)	62.5	73.1	59.5 –69.9 (edu.) –49.1 (health)
Science	68.0	79.1	58.0
Restructuring of coal-mining	73.4	91.4	100.0
National economy	71.9	69.6	83.4
Fund of the heating-energy complex	96.5		
National defence	88.9	118.1	79.1
Law protection agencies	82.8	91.9	82.2
Legislative, executive and judicial branch	88.9	91.3	83.2
– legislative	64.5	75.9	87.4
– executive	97.7	97.6	93.6
– judiciary	78.6	87.7	80.9
International activity	37.9	44.4	69.5
Reserve fonds on the CabMin	70.5	87.9	96.2
Spending on consequences of Chernobyl	84.9	69.5	54.5
Pension fund	99.1		69.3
Payments on external debt	73.9	82.3	93.0
Payments on internal debt	123.4	97.9	80.5
Transfers to local budgets	88.7	95.4	75.4
Total expenditures	**82.8**	**84.3**	**73.2**

Note: data does not add up with total expenditures as spending categories have different weights; only major spending categories are included; spending classification is approximate as major changes occurred in 1998.

Source: data of MinFin, State Treasury; data only refers to the central state budget.

troľno-revisiyna Sluzhba),[108] an institutional hold-over from Soviet times. It had a staff of about 14,000 in 1998 and a presence in all regions of Ukraine. The DKRS regularly revealed abuses of public funds; but most cases were not prosecuted and those responsible were rarely punished.[109]

As Bubovna and Way have pointed out, despite its numerous weaknesses, the Ukrainian budget system still achieved some goals, especially a significant redistribution across regions, channeling money from richer regions in the East to poorer ones in the West.[110] Also, social sectors, including education, health and social welfare, social transfers and pensions received half of all expenditures or more.[111] The fundamental problems were that on the one hand, elites could exploit the system in a number of ways, receiving assets and rents without having to pay full taxes in return, and on the other hand disagreement among various political groups held back the development of a stronger institutional system, and as a result played into the hands of elite state capture. The result was an expenditure system in which unrealistic promises were regularly made, but not matched with available funds. As reflected in Table 7.9, it was particularly in health and education as well as expenditure on the aftermath of Chernobyl which suffered from unpredictable cuts during budget execution.

7.5.6. BUDGETING IN THE LATE 1990S

In the mid- to late 1990s, annual budgeting processes were still very much marked by the *ad hoc* management of economic crisis on the one hand and by unsettled institutional roles on the other. Both the 1996 and the 1997 budgets were adopted late, with the latter becoming embroiled in the struggle over fundamental fiscal reform proposed by Pynzenyk. In 1996, the government had to juggle demands from striking miners in Eastern Ukraine to pay wages which had been delayed for months, and demands from the IMF who insisted on reducing the budget deficit.[112]

The 1998 budget was adopted on time, but then its execution was wrecked due to renewed economic crisis. In February, miners, teachers, and pensioners staged protests chanting ‘pay us, pay us’ as they marched from the government to the president’s building.[113] It was in this situation, that the 1998 parliamentary elections took place in which left—wing parties again scored well (see section 3.4 above). Shortly after the elections, the Ministry of Finance announced further across-the-board cuts for all state spending *by a third*, in order to meet the criteria for a new IMF loan. However, the newly formed parliament dominated by left-wing parties was unwilling to assume the responsibility for such sharp expenditure cuts.[114] In August 1998, after the full onset of the Russian crisis, the president revised the budget by decree;[115] which eventually led to the approval of the IMF loan. Given these cuts, budget execution was heavily 'hand steered' throughout the year.

In 1999, presidential elections were due in the fall. Contrary to what standard political economic assumptions would suggest, spending remained relatively tight. Parliament rather than the president called for higher expenditures. The parliament's budgetary committee, then headed by Yulia Tymoshenko, suggested that revenue could be significantly increased, allowing higher expenditures on social programs and wages. However, apparently, president Kuchma felt rather secure about his re-election, and did not perceive a strong necessity to seek greater revenue. This situation was very different in 2004 when spending was sharply increased ahead of a more seriously contested presidential election (see Chapter 8).[116]

However, as the presidential campaign unfolded in late 1999, several presidential candidates in parliament used the budget debates to lambaste current policies.[117] The size of the foreign debt and the cost of debt service for the first time became major election issues.[118] Natalia Vitrenko, candidate for the Progressive Socialists, and the communist candidate Petro Symonenko criticized Ukraine's dependence on international financial institutions and demanded that all relations with the IMF be cut off.

As new prime minister, Yushchenko sought to establish a more "civilized" budget process through closer cooperation with the parliament.[119] In a crucial move, he recruited Yulia Tymoshenko from her post as head of the budgetary committee to become vice prime minister for energy affairs in January 2000. One of Tymoshenko's close associates, Oleksandr Turchynov succeeded her as the committee head, thus creating good lines of communication between the government and the relevant committee.[120]

Budget fulfillment in 2000 was greatly eased compared to previous years, as economic growth turned out stronger than expected (see Table 7.1). This enabled the government to finally eliminate pension arrears by the fall of 2000 and to reduce wage arrears considerably.[121] Furthermore, the government managed to reschedule both private and official external debts, avoiding a default. While Ukraine's debt levels were not excessive, it continued to accumulate debt very quickly (from just 20 per cent of GDP in 1996 to 50 per cent in 1999) and had incurred some of its debt at high interest rates in 1997 and early 1998.[122]

Overall, the budget process had improved by the end of the decade; although this had come in fits and starts rather than as smooth progress. Furthermore, progress included formal changes, such as the 1995 budget code, as well as informal changes, especially better relations between the executive and the parliamentary budget committee. However, the formal system was still far from well-developed and continued to evolve, while the informal system was marked by continuous shifts and always uncertain political alliances.

7.5.7. BUILDING IMPERFECT INSTITUTIONS: THE TAX ADMINISTRATION AND THE AUDIT CHAMBER

The development of two institutions which epitomize the dual challenge of building a capable and a well-governed state are discussed here in some detail: the tax administration and the external audit institution. Tax administration is a key institution of any state, but had to undergo significant rebuilding in all transition countries due to the far-reaching changes in the economy. External audit institutions are much smaller and more specific than tax administrations. They are crucial for instituting effective checks and balances, as they provide independent, expert reports on the use of public funds—usually to the parliament and the public—and can issue recommendations. However, it is the task of the executive or parliament to follow up on these. In socialist states, there was no room for such independent audit bodies.[123] Rather, socialist states relied on extensive internal auditing structures with the party was the ultimate controller and arbiter, as described in chapter 5. More so than tax administrations—for which there is an intrinsic need in any state—external audit institutions as they were set up in the 1990s across Eastern Europe and the former Soviet Union are an institutional import based on Western models.

7.5.7.1. DEVELOPING THE UKRAINIAN TAX ADMINISTRATION

The Ukrainian tax administration well illustrates the two-sided character of the state: by some external observers, tax administrations in post-Soviet countries were perceived as too weak and, hence, as an explanatory factor for low revenue collection.[124] However, the full picture is more complex: initially, tax administration suffered from weakness and inexperience in taxing a market economy. As a result of the institution-building efforts of the executive, the Ukrainian tax administration then became a rather powerful organization, but at the same time also developed highly dysfunctional aspects, burdening the emerging private sector and becoming a tool to oppress political opponents.

The fundamental reorganization of the tax administration was launched by president Kuchma shortly after the adoption of a new constitution in mid-1996 with two decrees on the "Reform of tax policy" and the "Creation of a State Tax Administration." The STA became independent of the Ministry of Finance, obtained a 'Tax Militia' to pursue tax-evaders (the *Golovne upravlinnia podatkovoi militsii* – previously under the Ministry of Internal Affairs), and received additional funds and training facilities. The STA formally reported to the Cabinet, but *de facto* became controlled by the presidential administration.[125] In October 1996, Mykola Azarov, a close associate of President Kuchma, was appointed head of the STA.[126] Due to the tax administration's power to investigate and prosecute, Azarov became one of the most powerful figures in Ukraine over the coming years.

Between 1997 and 1999, the organization of the STA was streamlined and the number of local inspectorates was reduced, but the number of employees expanded significantly. Overall, the STA had a staff of 56,500 in late 2000.[127] Thus, it evolved into the largest single administrative organization of Ukraine.[128] A similar expansion occurred in Russia.

In reaction to its growing power, a very negative image of the STA developed as overly bureaucratic and a major cause for the bad business climate; as corrupt, and as a political tool used against independent media and enterprises which did not support the ruling elite. Representatives of small enterprises complained that the STA had developed into "a monster,"[129] filling the budget on the back of those who did not enjoy tax exemptions.[130] Tax legislation made matters worse by allowing the STA to impose high fines.[131] Frequent changes in tax rules increased the compliance costs for businesses. Newspapers and even TV shows regularly carried jokes and caricatures about the tax service.[132]

The STA was widely regarded as corrupt.[133] Johnson et al. report that a majority of Ukrainian firms had to make substantial under-the-table payments to tax inspectors, although the tax administration claimed that it was successfully combating corruption.[134]

Given the centrality of a well-functioning tax administration, IFIs not only advised on but also became directly involved in reforms of the tax administration. The IMF promoted the establishment of Large Taxpayer Units (LTUs) since the late 1990s, a standard IMF institutional device to cover a country's largest companies. The World Bank started a long-term project of STA modernization in the early 2000s which aimed at developing a modern, efficient tax administration.[135]

Despite these external efforts, the tax administration was not only plagued by corruption, but it was also heavily (ab)used for political purposes during the late 1990s. Such abuses appear characteristic for hybrid regimes, which are limited in using outright oppression (exercised by the police or the military) and hence seek to use more covert forms of pressure.[136] Also, since the power-holders in a hybrid regime face a risk of losing control, particularly during semi-free elections, they have a considerable need to use the levers of covert pressures at their disposal.[137] Its presence at all levels of the state (center, regions, local level) made the STA an extremely powerful potential instrument of political control.

The use of the tax administration against the media became widespread in the second half of the 1990s.[138] Tax inspections were used to block the accounts of critical newspapers and TV stations. In tandem with libel suits, inspections developed into a prime means of controlling the media—without resorting to any formal censorship.[139] Moreover, the STA became one of the crucial 'administrative resources' during elections.[140] In the course of the Ukrainian 'tape scandal' (see Chapter 8, section 1 below), conversations from the presidential office became public. In one of the passages the president instructs the head of the tax administration in the run-up to the 1999 presidential elections:

> The [tax] militia will have to work seriously [...] It's necessary for a tax worker to go to every collective farm head in every village and say: dear friend, you understand clearly how much material we have on you so that you could find yourself in jail tomorrow [...] And there is probably more than enough material on every collective farm head. Yes or no? Probably yes. That's why the militia [...] that is, the services [...] they all have to, that is, take to (the task) and have a serious talk with every collective farm head.[141]

Reacting to domestic and international criticism of its role in the 1999 presidential elections, the STA announced a hands-off policy during the 2002 parliamentary election not investigating any media during the campaign period. However, political abuse was shifted to the time after the election. A large number of MPs had run as independents, many of whom were business people. A considerable number of these independents eventually joined pro-presidential factions, thus increasing their share of seats considerably—despite the fact that the pro-presidential bloc had received only 11.8 per cent of the list vote on the proportional part of seats. The STA was rumored to have put pressure on independent deputies to 'motivate' their choice of joining pro-presidential factions.[142] In the fall of 2002, the *Kyiv Post* claimed:

> Under his [Azarov's] leadership, the STA has grown into a highly corrupt state within a state—one that is largely unaccountable to anyone but the president. Inadequate legislation and the absence of a strong, independent judiciary have enabled the STA to hijack the process of tax collection. In addition to collecting funds for the budget, the STA's mission has included taming recalcitrant businessmen and critical media organizations. Over the months since the parliamentary elections, the STA has been used as a blunt weapon in a series of assaults on businesses linked to deputies reluctant to join the pro-presidential 'majority.'[143]

In addition, the head of the STA, Mykola Azarov, became a powerful figure in Ukrainian politics. In early 2001, Azarov had assumed the leadership of a new 'oligarchic-bureaucratic' party, the Party of Regions, based primarily in the Donbas region. This party in turn became a central pillar of the pro-presidential electoral bloc "For a United Ukraine" in the spring 2002 parliamentary elections.[144] Such openly partisan and political action of the chief tax administrator was widely criticized in Ukraine.

Overall, the development of a tax administration was sufficiently successful to ensure a continued flow of revenue in the 1990s. However, there were deep flaws in the development of this institution which burdened the economic as well as the political development of Ukraine, and which re-enforced inequality between different groups. More broadly, the story of the STA reflects the fact that, except for the Baltics, post-Soviet countries failed to develop institutions which were capable as well as accountable.

7.5.7.2. EXTERNAL AUDIT: AN INEFFECTIVE INSTITUTIONAL IMPORT

The Accounting Chamber (*Rakhunkova Palata*; AC) is another, but somewhat different example of an initially flawed institutional development in the context of a hybrid regime. The initial establishment of the AC became deeply entangled in the negotiations over the constitutional division of power.[145] After the adoption of the 'Law on Power' in May 1995 (see section 2 above), parliament struggled to regain a stronger position. One potential instrument was the establishment of a powerful Accounting Chamber "equipped with extraordinary powers of oversight of the government programs and ministerial budgets."[146]

Parliament adopted a law on the Accounting Chamber in May 1996, giving the AC quite sweeping powers. The president vetoed the law; but his veto was overturned by parliament. President Kuchma then submitted the law to the Constitutional Court. The Court had likewise just been established and took one of its first decisions on the Accounting Chamber. In two decisions in July and December 1997, the Court significantly reduced the general control powers of the Accounting Chamber and in particular ruled that it could only oversee expenditures and not the revenue side of the budget.[147] It also struck down some of the very broad-ranging powers of the Chamber, such as the right to initiate legal proceedings and to freeze financial activities of an organization if it did not comply with the audit recommendations (Art. 26 and 33 of the law as initially adopted). In the toned-down version of the law which went into force in January 1998, the Chamber only received the right to transfer materials to law enforcement bodies if it detected corruption and other abuses.[148]

While the struggle over the legal base continued, parliament appointed a first chairman of the AC in December 1996. Valentyn Symonenko had been a regional Communist Party secretary in Odessa and a parliamentary deputy from 1990 onwards. The total initial professional staff of the AC was about 180. During its initial work, the AC faced resistance from executive organs which were unwilling to provide the required access to information, and it stood in competition to the DKRS, the internal control institution inherited from the Soviet period (see section 5.4 above).[149] The DKRS had a much larger staff and was well entrenched; while the AC was struggling to establish its role.

In its process of institutional development, furthermore, the AC suffered from rather poor leadership. Its chairman often focused strongly on accusations about particular abuses, even of minor importance. The Ministry of Finance in turn publicly criticized the AC as biased and questioned its professionalism.[150] Moreover, in contrast to the president who used the tax administration as a threat to economic actors, parliament had no collective interest in following up on the audit findings of the AC and the judiciary rarely pursued material submitted by the AC.

Overall, this imported institutional model did not put down roots and become effective in the Ukrainian context of the late 1990s. The creation of the AC added some supervision of the financial system of the state, but it failed to develop an institutional impact of limiting dysfunctional aspects of the state—and hence to fulfill the fundamental *raison d'être* of an external audit institution.

7.6. Shaping and distorting the new state

In the late 1990s, the new Ukrainian state began to acquire more shape: a new constitution was adopted, and a new institutional system began to crystallize. Politically, a hybrid regime emerged. Between 1994 and mid-2000, the president was in the ascendancy: he successively strengthened his position against parliament as well as against the regions, and after the referendum of April 2000, it looked as if the president was to acquire also greater constitutional powers. In contrast to Russia, however, the route towards further authoritarian consolidation was blocked by the relative strength of various 'opaque' and visible groups in Ukraine which proved to be impossible to subdue by a single center of power. The 'tape scandal' which erupted in late 2000 and which sparked the first larger scale protests eventually weakened the position of the president (see Chapter 8).

Based on this political situation, state capacity improved in fits and starts, but it also became geared towards the maintenance of power, which at the same time made it less oriented towards serving the general welfare. Opaque groups benefited enormously from the combination of continued institutional weakness and the presence of this 'defensive logic' in developing state capacity; while the vast majority of the population suffered as a result of the deep and long economic decline, with more than 30 per cent falling below the national poverty line in the late 1990s.[151]

A number of bigger and smaller decisions were taken in the state and the fiscal sphere: the constitution, the budget code of 1995, partial tax reforms in 1997, etc. However, the decisions made contained deep flaws. The constitution created a rather unworkable distribution of power, the adoption of regular budgets was still repeatedly delayed, and extensive tax privileges were not curtailed until 2000.

Ukraine still suffered from a dual blockade. Left-wing parties did not want reforms towards a market system and blocked decisions for this reason. The president and oligarchic groups preferred a muddled situation since it allowed the use of selective enforcement for the former, and brought competitive advantages and tremendous financial profits through privileges and special access for the latter. It was, however, this very unholy coalition of left-wing parties and oligarchic interests which brought down Yushchenko as prime minister in April 2001.

While the capacity of the state increased during this period, the quality of governance remained poor or even worsened. Budget implementation became somewhat more regularized, except in 1998, and the tax administration was clearly strengthened. However, serious distortions were built particularly into implementing revenue extraction, some of which were due to a deliberate effort by the political leadership to use the tax administration as an instrument for maintaining power. In 2000, a decisive reinforcement and reorientation of implementation capacity occurred when the state, in the aftermath of the 1998 crisis and under the leadership of Yulia Tymoshenko as minister for the Energy Sector, began to insist on cash payments of tax obligations. This brought tangible benefits for the people many of whom finally received the pensions and wages they were due.

New capacity for control was created, a treasury system and an Accounting Chamber, and set side by side other institutional structures—the DKRS—which were continued from the Soviet period. None of these systems fully functioned in the sense of ensuring that fiscal funds would flow as budgeted. Because the Accounting Chamber institutionally 'belonged' to parliament, the executive tended to oppose it, while few parliamentarians had a real commitment to exercising their rights of budgetary oversight.

This twisted and turned trajectory of developing new state capacity bears substantial responsibility for why Ukraine became one of the worst 'transition performers' by the late 1990s. The Ukrainian state did not collapse and was far from uniformly weak, but the way in which it was built was very costly for society and for the economy.

Eventually, after falling as low as 40 per cent of the level of GDP in 1989, the economy began to recover. At the same time, the power of the president began to wane; eventually resulting in a second political transition and a new attempt at transforming the state. This process will be traced from late 2000 until 2005 in the following chapter.

Notes

1 Levitsky and Way (2002).
2 Gaddy and Ickes (2002); Marin (2002).
3 UEPLAC, *Ukrainian Economic Trends*, March 1999, 68.
4 See World Development Report, Table 1.1 (2000 and 2001).
5 Wolczuk (2001a), 192 and 194–95. On the process of compromising on a constitution in Ukraine, see Wolczuk (2001b); and Wolczuk (2001a), as well as Vorndran (1997).
6 Wise and Brown (1999), 30. UCEPS, *National Security and Defense*, no. 5/2000, 12.
7 Ott (2002), 78.
8 These numbers of decrees reflect the wide-ranging powers to appoint and dismiss government personnel. See Protsyk (2005).
9 See Constitution of Ukraine, Chap. XV (Transitional Provisions), §4.

10 Nahaylo (1999), 499.

11 See Inna Pidluska, *Political Elites in Ukraine*, UCIPR, undated manuscript (about 2000). 'Clan' in the Ukrainian context does not refer to kinship but rather to patronage ties based on a common regional background and common experience in Eastern Ukrainian industries.

12 See Wittkowsky (1999), 166; "The Clan from Donetsk (part 1)," *RFE/RL Newsline*, November 26, 2002.

13 Kubicek (2000).

14 Kubicek (2000), 82–83.

15 Dauderstädt (1999).

16 Another prominent politician with close links to the UUIE is Anatolii Kinakh. Kinakh was vice-prime minister for industrial policy from 1995 to 1996, then was elected head of the UUIE in October 1996. In May 2001, Kinakh became prime minister.

17 D'Anieri, Kravchuk, and Kuzio (1999), 196.

18 D'Anieri, Kravchuk, and Kuzio (1999), 159.

19 "Party Focus: Reforms and Order," *Romyr Report* (Spring 2000).

20 This practice of creating "fake parties" has a long tradition in Eastern Slavic lands. See Wilson, "Virtual Politics," 2005. Wilson and Birch (1999), 1043.

21 Pavlo Lazarenko moved tens of millions of US $ to bank accounts in Switzerland and in the US. Ihor Bakai, the head of Oil and Gas of Ukraine (*Naftohaz Ukrainy;* from 1998 to 2000) bought several expensive assets abroad. Oleksandr Volkov moved *$15 millions* of unexplained funds through Belgian banks in the mid-1990s. See Wilson (2005b), 39–40, 46, 55. Lazarenko fled to the US in 1999 where he was subsequently tried and found guilty on money-laundering charges. See "Ukraine: Why Was Former Prime Minister Lazarenko Tried In The U.S.?" *RFE/RL Newsline*, June 8, 2004.

22 The most famous case was the sale of Ukraine's (and one of the world's) largest steel mill *Kryvorizhstal* to Viktor Pinchuk and Renat Akhmetov, respectively Kuchma's son-in-law and Eastern Ukraine's wealthiest oligarch for $800m. In 2005, *Kryvorizhstal* was re-privatized for six times this sum to an international bidder.

23 In 2004 this included Renat Akhmetov, Serhii Taruta, Viktor Pinchuk, and Ihor Kolomoiskyi. Wilson (2005b), 40–41.

24 Average monthly wage for 2000. See National Bank of Ukraine, http://www.bank.gov.ua/ENGL/Macro/pok_96_2000.htm [accessed: June 21, 2001]

25 *New Democracies Barometer V*, CSPP 1998.

26 71 per cent of Ukrainians were totally unsatisfied or rather unsatisfied with what the legislative and executive powers were doing in January 1997.

27 KIIS surveys, January and June 1997, November 1998.

28 *New Democracies Barometer V* (1998), 19.

29 Wilson and Birch (1999), 1043.

30 Collection of party programs for the 1998 elections, provided by UCIPR.

31 Wilson and Birch (1999), 1053, 1055.

32 For example, Anatoliy Matvienko, who headed the pro-presidential party NDP from 1996 to 1999; in 1999 Matvienko broke with the president and founded a small oppositional party, Sobor. Interview, Kyiv, October 10, 2000.

33 D'Anieri, Kravchuk, and Kuzio (1999), 154–155. When doing interviews in Ukraine in 2000 I was always advised to speak to members of factions rather than representatives of parties. See also Herron (2002) and Whitmore (2003).

34 See also Birch (2000), 102.

35 *Kyiv Post*, March 7, 2001.

36 Attempts to unite at least parts of the opposition failed. See: Katya Gorchinskaya, "Kaniv-4 Grouping Falls Apart," *Kyiv Post*, October 28, 1999.

37 There are four national TV stations: the state-owned UT1, Inter and 1+1 owned by oligarchs, and STB.

38 Freedom House, 2001 report on Ukraine, 397. See also OSCE/ODIHR, *Joint Preliminary Statement, Second Round*, November 15, 1999, 2.

39 Wilson (2005a), Chapter 4. After the first round of elections three governors of central Ukrainian oblasts (Kirovohrad, Poltava, and Vynnytsya) and eleven heads of rayon administrations not producing a sufficiently high vote for the incumbent resigned. See *RFE/RL Newsline*, November 4, 1999.

40 For example, villagers in the Sumy oblast complained about being threatened that a planned gas-pipeline to their village would not be built should they vote against the incumbent. Interview conducted as election observer in Sumy oblast, November 1999.

41 See OSCE, Final Report, Warsaw, March 7, 2000, http://www.osce.org/odihr [accessed: May 10, 2000].

42 Taras Kuzio, "A Dirty Election Campaign," *Ukraine List*, no. 60, October 25, 1999.

43 See *Ukraine List* no. 65, November 24, 1999 for second round election results.

44 *Stratfor.com*, December 15, 1999.

45 After the Ukrainian Constitutional Court had rejected two questions, four were eventually put to the voters. Sarah Whitmore, "Ukraine, the year in review 2000," *Central European Review*, at http://www.ce-review.org/00/43/roundup43ukraine.html [accessed: March 1, 2001].

46 The turnout was also high at around 80 per cent.

47 "New economic legislation 2000–2001," *ICPS Policy Studies*, no. 16 (2001).

48 By 1999 average custom's tariffs stood at 11 per cent. "Ukrainian Legislation Review", *Business Law Review*, March 27, 2001.

49 EBRD, *Transition Report* (2004), 45.

50 Standard and Poor's rated Ukraine for the first time in 2001; Moody's rated Ukraine since 1998.

51 The proposed IMF-conditionality largely resembled the Economic Growth '97 reform program suggested by Pynzenyk. See *Kyiv Post*, April 10, 1997: "Government faces another fiscal fight".

52 For a (quite critical) self-evaluation of the World Bank of its activities in Ukraine in the 1990s, see "Ukraine, Country Assistance Evaluation," World Bank, Operations Evaluation Department, November 8, 2000.

53 Also as some representatives of the World Bank acknowledged, programs had often not been sufficiently adjusted to the conditions of post-Soviet countries in the early 1990s. Interviews, Kyiv, October-November 2000, and Minsk, May 2002.

54 "Time to rein in the STA", *Kyiv Post*, April 18, 2002.

55 For its proper administration, the VAT requires a seamless chain of reporting to ensure that VAT obligations and refund claims can be assessed and administered smoothly. Interview with Jaroslav Romanchuk, economist, director of the Mises Center, Belarus, Minsk, May 1, 2002.

56 Teriokhin (2000), 151.

57 Polomski (1999), 15.

58 In Ukraine, Company Income Tax (CIT) is called Enterprise Profit Tax (EPT).

59 Ukraine Gateway Project; Luzik (1999), 36.

60 Thiessen (2001).

61 Olexander Baranovsky, "Problems of Forming Free Economic Zones in Ukraine," at www.ucipr.kiev.ua/ert/ert3308.html [accessed: March 29, 2001].

62 See: Mandibura (1999); also: Dabrowsky et al. (1996). "The living minimum - a system of double standards," *Zerkalo Nedeli*, February 2001.

63 "Money under the bonnet," *Business Central Europe*, September 2000.

64 Thiessen (1997), 400.

65 Mandibura (December 1999).

66 D'Anieri, Kuzio, and Krachuk (1999), 177.

67 Teriokhin (2000), 159-160. See *UCIPR Research Update*, June 21, 1999 ("Oligarchology"), 2. In contrast to Ukraine, Russia had introduced a property tax on legal entities in 1991. See http://www.garweb.ru/project/mns/en/law/garweb_law/10002520/10002520.htm [accessed: March 15, 2001], and "Russia's Self-Defeating Tax System," *Jamestown Monitor*, November 1, 1996.

68 Leitzel (2003), 13.

69 Interview with Viktor Chepenko, Tax Policy Analyst, Barents group and former employee of the STA, Kyiv, November 1, 2000.

70 See IMF (1999), 36. Exporters receive VAT reimbursements in most countries; while VAT has to be paid on imported goods which are consumed in that country.

71 Hansen and Nanivska (1999), 65.

72 EIU, *Ukraine, Country Report* (1st quarter 1999), 19; Remiga (1999), 42.

73 If a budgetary organization (such as a school, or a local public administration) owed an amount (for example, 100UAH) to a supplier (for example, an energy company, or a supplier of materials), and this supplier had tax liabilities, then these tax liabilities could be settled by writing off the debt owed by the budgetary organization. Bubnova and Way (1998); Ebrill and Havrylyshyn (1999), 6.

74 Ebrill and Havrylyshyn (1999), 6; Bubnova and Way (1998), 29.

75 Bubnova and Way (1998), 31. Also http://www.bisnis.doc.gov/bisnis/isa/010222ukenhl20.htm and http://www.state.gov/documents/organization/8239.pdf [accessed: June 12, 2003].

76 Remiga (1999), 42; Hansen and Nanivska (1999), 71. "On Writing Off and Restructuring Tax Arrears as of 31 March 1997;" law adopted by the VR on June 5, 1997.

77 Remiga (1999), 37.

78 Interview with Dzintra Sakevičienė, Deputy Director, Fiscal Policy Department, Ministry of Finance, Vilnius, July 31, 2001.

79 Yurhelevych and Downey (2000), 47.

80 EIU, *Ukraine Country Report*, (1st quarter 1999), 16.

81 Remiga (1999), 38; Yurhelevych and Downey (2000). IMF, *Staff Country Report no. 99/42* (1999), 38. "VAT exemption for agriculture prolonged," *EED*, July 25, 2000.

82 Oxana Remiga, "Budget Revenues," in: Gonciarz and Pynzenzk (1999), 40.

83 Thiessen (1997), 400.

84 "Parliament passes VAT law amendments," *Kyiv Post*, October 2, 1997.

85 See www.worldbank.org/wbi/publicfinance/publicresources/module1.pdf. These fragmented decision-making structures were also criticized by Volkhart Vincentz, Economist, German Advisory Group, interview, April 25, 2002.

86 According to Inna Pidluska, Communist Party members used to profit from vote buying as well. However, in an effort to increase party discipline and to expose corrupt practices, the Communists achieved open voting in parliament. This hurt the party by depriving it of financial resources. Inna Pidluska, Vice President, Ukrainian Center for Independent Political Research, Interview, Kyiv, October 19, 2000.

87 Viktor Mikhailovich Pynzenyk, a Moscow-trained economist from Western Ukraine, was a cabinet member almost continuously from 1992 to 1997 in various posts from Minister of the Economy to Vice-Prime Minister. See *Khto e khto v Ukraini* (2000), 370.

88 Interviews with Viktor Pynzenyk, December 11, 2000; with David Snelbecker, Harvard Institute for International Development - Ukraine, Kyiv, October 26, 2000; with Olya Onyshko, Kyiv, October 13, 2000; with Peter Luzik, Kyiv, October 16, 2000.

89 David Snelbecker, "1997 Program for Economic Growth in Ukraine" (memorandum), November 3, 1996. See also Roman Woronowycz: "Pynzenyk leads public relations campaign to push reforms," *Ukrainian Weekly*, December 15, 1996. Thiessen (1997), 400–401.

90 Interview with Viktor Suslov, Kyiv, November 3, 2000. Olya Onyshko, interview, Kyiv, October 13, 2000.

91 Lazarenko was later accused by Ukrainian authorities of having ordered the assassination of Yevhen Sherban, a member of the Dontesk clan. After seeking asylum in the US, he was tried there on charges of money-laundering and corruption. Lazarenko and his political and business ally Yulia Tymoshenko had close connections to United Energy Systems which benefited from generous tax exemptions for joint-ventures. *Ukrainian Weekly*, October 5, 1997.

92 Fiscal Analysis Office, *Budget and Fiscal Review*, 3rd Quarter 1998, 36.

93 Denis Yershakov, "Analysis of Draft Tax Code of Ukraine and Proposals for Improvement," UCIPR, Kyiv, November 24, 2001. Interview with Valeriy Alioshin, head of the committee for banking and finance, April 18, 2002.

94 Valerii Aloshyn, cited from "Sleep quietly, tax code," *Zerkalo Nedeli*, December 15–21, 2001.

95 D'Anieri (2005).

96 Dabrowski, Luczynski, and Markiewicz (2000), 119.

97 Article 21, 1995 budget law.

98 Law No. 327 "On the Structure of Budget Classification of Ukraine," Directive of the Ministry of Finance No. 265 of December 3, 1997. See Inna Lunina, "Budget Formulation: Strategy and Process," in: Gonciarz and Pynzenyk (eds.) (1999), 47.

99 These phases—particularly the forecasting and drafting phase—may be further subdivided.

100 Lunina (1999), 50.

101 Lunina (1999), 49.

102 Lunina (1999), 50. She stressed this point in an interview with the author on October 2, 2000.

103 Lunina (1999), 53. "Agenstvo Humanitarnykh Tekhnologii," *Sindrom Nalogovogo Kodeksa* [The Tax Code Syndrom], Kyiv 2000 (http://aht.org/economy/Codeks/Codeks.htm), 3–5. [accessed: April 5, 2001]

104 Wildavsky (1975), 162–163.

105 Interview, Andrius Želionis, Deputy Director, Budget Department in the Lithuanian Ministry of Finance, Vilnius, July 25, 2001.

106 Tatyana Vakhnenko, "Budget Execution and Expenditure Control," in: Gonciarz and Pynzenyk (eds.) (1999), 68.

107 UEPLAC, *Ukrainian Economic Trends* (October 1997), 3. *The Day* (*Den'*, English digest), November 2, 1999 "Budget Merry-Go-Round".

108 Vakhnenko (1999), 78. The DKRS is an organ derived from the Soviet system of financial control (the KRU - *Kontrolno-Revisionnoe Upravlenie*, in Russian.) The self-defined 'organizational history' can be found at: http://www.dkrs.gov.ua/www/wwwdkrs.nsf.

109 Vakhnenko (1999), 79.

110 Bubnova and Way (1998).

111 Chandler (1996). Spending on health, education, and social transfers including pensions amounted to 50.3% in 1994, to 61.8% in 1995, to 55.9% in 1996, and to 56% in 1997.

112 UEPLAC, *Ukrainian Economic Trends*, April 1996, 5: "These changes [to a monthly payments schedule] ... are aimed at encouraging the Ukrainian Government to better control the day-to-day financial situation in Ukraine."

113 "Empty treasury fills streets," *Kyiv Post*, February 20, 1998.

114 "Ukrainian parliament reluctant to debate budget cuts," *UNIAN News Agency*, July 21, 1998. EIU, *Ukraine Country Reports* (3rd quarter 1998).

115 Vakhnenko (1999), 70.

116 "*Verkhovna Rada* passes budget," *Ukrainian Weekly*, January 10, 1999. "President Kuchma Vetoes Law on Sharp Increase of Minimum Wages," *Ukraine Today*, December 14, 1998. 226 out of a total of 450 deputies voted for the budget.

117 "As expected, politics at top of agenda for *Verkhovna Rada,*" *Ukrainian Weekly*, Sept. 12, 1999.

118 "Ukrainian Communist Presidential Candidate Symonenko Addresses the Nation," *BBC Monitoring Service*, September 29, 1999.

119 "Ukrainian Prime Minister urges 'civilized' budget system," *BBC Monitor*, December 27, 1999.

120 See www.ukrweekly.com/Archive/2000/020001.shtml. Interview with Kateryna Mainziouk and Wayne Thirsk, Fiscal Analysis Office, Kyiv, April 16, 2002.

121 Fiscal Analysis Office, *Budget and Fiscal Review*, October 2000, 45; *Budget and Fiscal Review*, April 2001.

122 "Business outlook Ukraine: So bad it's good," *Business Eastern Europe*, March 9, 1998.

123 Some late socialist countries—China and Vietnam—have created audit institutions in the 1990s. However, these report primarily to the executive.

124 Tanzi (1998); Easter (2001).

125 Interview with Peter Luzik, Tax Reform Specialist, USAID, October 16, 2000.

126 See portrait of Azarov on the STA's webpage: www.sta.gov.ua/page.php3?azarov. Interview with Chepenko, November 1, 2000.

127 Declaration of the STA, No. 6696/6/33-0116/759, December 4, 2000. Before the streamlining, there were about 70,000 employees in the STA. Interview with Chepenko, November 1, 2000. The Russian Federation had a Tax Service with a staff of 200,000 in the late 1990s (see also Chapter 11). Gustafson (1999), 199.

128 *Bisnes*, March 6, 2000, 9. Second was the custom's administration with 18,200 employees. While in the US there was approximately one tax inspector for every 4000 inhabitants, in Russia and in Ukraine the ratio was closer to one to 1000 (while the contrast in terms of GDP is even starker).

129 Interview with Ksenija Lyapina, Kyiv, September 26, 2000.

130 Interview with Valentyna Mandryk, Kyiv, December 11, 2000.

131 *ICPS newsletter,* no. 39, October 25, 1999. "The people from the agency call a check 'successful' not when an enterprise honestly pays taxes, but when they succeed in imposing huge penalties. In fact, the requirements of tax legislation are so muddled and irrational that a tax inspector always has an excessive amount of power." Lyudmila Shapilova, http://www.usukraine.org/cpp/journal/as9901/investor.html [accessed: February 14, 2003].

132 See for example, *Den'*, November 22, 2000; *Bisnes*, October 16, 2000.

133 See www1.worldbank.org/beext/resources/documents/Ukraine.pdf. Yurhelevych and Downey (2000), 48. *Nations in Transit* (2001), 680.

134 Johnson et al. (2000). Communication of the Ukrainian Tax Administration to the author, December 4, 2000, doc. no. 6696/6/33-0116/759.

135 See World Bank, Ukraine: Tax Policy and Tax Administration, draft, March 28, 2003, 80. Interview with Svetlana Budagovskaya, Economist, World Bank, October 27, 2000. Interview with Craig Neil, Lead Expert, World Bank, January 2, 2005.

136 Levitsky and Way (2002).

137 See also Wilson (2005a), 84.

138 US Department of State, Ukraine Country Report on Human Rights Practices for 1998. "Three opposition newspapers were forced to cease operations because their accounts were frozen at various points during the year by the Tax Inspectorate: Pravda Ukrayiny; Polityka; and Vseukrayinskiye Vedomosti." www.state.gov/www/global/human_rights /1998_hrp_report/Ukraine.html [accessed: May 2, 2000].

139 Freedom House, *Nations in Transit* (1999–2000), 670.

140 These complaints against the STA were primarily raised with regard to the 1999 presidential elections; however, the STA had already been involved in investigating media outlets during the 1998 parliamentary elections. See www.osce.org/odihr/documents/reports /election_reports/ua/ukra1-2.pdf [accessed: December 5, 2002].

141 See www.pravda.com.ua/?10211-3-1, translation by Kyiv post staff, [accessed: January 2, 2005].

142 "Time to rein in the STA," *Kyiv Post*, April 18, 2002.

143 "The grim government," *Kyiv Post*, December 5, 2002.

144 "The chief 'tax man' of the country heads the party of regions," *Den'*, March 6, 2001.

145 See Vitalyi Melnychuk, *Monitoring Budget Fund Spending by Parliament: European Experience*, paper prepared for the East-West Institute (manuscript, no date).

146 Wise and Pigenko in: D. Anieri, Kravchuk, and Kuzio (1999), 25–55.

147 Charles Wise and Trevor Brown, *The Constitutional Court of Ukraine* at: http://www.spea.indiana.edu/pdp/analyses/National%20Government/Constitutional%20Court.htm [accessed: January 24, 2002]

148 Art. 29, Law No. 18/98, *Verkhovna Rada.* This is the standard in most countries.

149 Interview with Vitaliy Melnichuk, deputy head of the AC, November 7, 2000.

150 "Budget Merry-Go-Round" *Den'* November 2, 1999. The IMF advisor to the treasury in Ukraine, Janis Platais, remarked in the fall of 2000 also critically, that the AC came up with 'wild stories about the misuse of funds'. Interview, Kyiv, October 12, 2000.

151 World Development Indicators (2002).

CHAPTER 8.
THE SECOND TRANSITION IN UKRAINE

> Ukraine can be characterized, in 2001, as an enlightened autocracy.
>
> *(Hans van Zon, 2001)*

> Most observers agree that Ukraine has achieved some success in establishing and developing democratic norms and procedures.
>
> *(Pigenko, Wise and Brown, 2002)*

From late 2000 to the end of 2004 was a period of suspense in Ukrainian politics. From late 2000 onwards, Kuchma began to appear vulnerable and lost the momentum towards presidential and authoritarian consolidation of power. However, Yeltsin had been a vulnerable president during his second term in office and still had managed to hand over power to a chosen successor, and one who continued the path of presidential consolidation more vigorously. In Ukraine, the political future hung in a balance until a decisive shift took place during the presidential elections in late 2004. With the 'Orange Revolution' and Yushchenko taking over the presidency, a new political regime emerged and a new phase in Ukraine's state formation process began. However, this was by no means a smooth path.

The dysfunctional aspects of the state, and especially those dysfunctionalities deliberately created to maintain power had been a target for the opposition during its campaign. However, once the 'Orange Revolution' was won, reforming the state proved to be a considerable challenge. Creating a liberal but effective state was difficult given the enduring influence of opaque groups, and the way the state and its administration had been built during the Kuchma era. Moreover, internally, the new government could not agree on important aspects of how to transform the state, and it lacked coherence and hence was often indecisive in its approach. The democratic regime was not immediately consolidated, and the internal coherence of post-Orange governments was immediately tested by the specter of constitutional reform that had been agreed as a compromise with the outgoing Kuchma government.

8.1. From hybrid regime to unconsolidated democracy

In late 2000 the first larger scale demonstrations erupted in Kyiv in protest against the murder of an investigative journalist, but they eventually subsided without any definite impact. Four years later, the situation had changed decisively: in late 2004, millions of Ukrainians mobilized to oust Kuchma and his entourage from power after a flawed presidential election.

The early 2000s were generally marked by an economic upswing which eased fiscal pressures and facilitated some further advances in state capacity. However, the existing dysfunctionalities of the state—high levels of (tolerated) corruption on the one hand, and the abuse of state institutions for covert political oppression on the other hand—remained a persistent feature. Arguably, it was these aspects of the state and the political regime which created them, which motivated people to revolt in late 2004. While this 'second transition' was successful in ousting the Kuchma government, and moved Ukraine closer to a democratic regime, it did not result in rapid consolidation of the new regime. This in turn made it difficult to re-engineer the distorted state as it had emerged during the Kuchma era.

In mid-September 2000, the journalist Hryhorii Gongadze, editor of an online newspaper that specialized in exposing corrupt links between politicians and business interests had disappeared. His decapitated body was found in mid-November. About two weeks later, the prominent socialist politician Oleksandr Moroz published the first samples from audiotapes that had been made in the president's office by one of the security guards, Mykola Melnychenko.[1] The taped conversations indicated that the president may have been involved in Gongadze's disappearance;[2] also, they confirmed that Kuchma had called on the tax administration to exert pressure on businesses and the bureaucracy during the 1999 presidential election (see Chapter 7). Moreover, they corroborated widely-held suspicions about large-scale corruption at the highest level of Ukrainian politics.[3]

In reaction to this 'tape-scandal', a—albeit still limited—protest movement developed under the banner of 'Ukraine without Kuchma' began in fall 2000.[4] During the same period, president Kuchma and various oligarchic groups opposed the energy sector reforms pursued by Yulia Tymoshenko as deputy prime minister and in January 2001 brought criminal proceedings against her for the smuggling of gas, document forgery and tax evasion during her earlier tenure as head of United Energy Systems.[5] The president then used this pretext to dismiss Tymoshenko. This proved a tactical mistake: it triggered the further formation of the opposition as a "National Salvation Forum" involving a number of politicians particularly from *Rukh* and from the socialist party,[6] with Tymoshenko becoming a crucial opposition leader. Meanwhile, prime minister Yushchenko kept his distance from the protests—which by that time involved up to around 10,000 people.

In late April 2001, while the street protests were subsiding, Yushchenko was brought down as prime minister by an unholy coalition: left-wing critics of the government's market reforms united with oligarchic groups in parliament and passed a vote of no confidence. After being pushed out of office, Yushchenko stated that his government had been brought down because it did not pay "for political votes with *oblenergos* [regional energy distribution companies], other enterprises, customs or tax breaks."[7]

Yushchenko was replaced by Anatolii Kinakh, until then president of the UUIE.[8] Kinakh did not belong to any of Ukraine's oligarchic clans, but was rather an efficient administrator loyal to the president. However, he was more beholden to particular interest groups than his predecessor. During his first year in office he failed to bring tax reform to a successful conclusion as he had initially promised.

At the same time, the president sought to strengthen his control over the government by creating new secretary of state positions in Ukraine's ministries. While such posts exist in many countries to preserve administrative coherence over time, in the Ukrainian version, state secretaries were appointed and could be dismissed exclusively by the president, rather than being permanent civil servants; which made their creation an attempt to intensify presidential power over the state apparatus.[9]

8.1.1. THE 2002 PARLIAMENTARY ELECTIONS

By the summer of 2001, the campaign for the 2002 parliamentary elections began. In mid-July, Yushchenko announced the formation of an election bloc 'Our Ukraine', uniting the two *Rukhs* and *Reforms and Order* (see Chapter 7, section 3). This bloc remained separate from the National Salvation Forum (uniting a number of smaller parties) led by Yulia Tymoshenko, and eventually named the 'Bloc Yulia Tymoshenko.'[10] Yushchenko hesitated to join forces with this more radical opposition. Instead, he preferred to court politicians and parties which were 'centrist' but also close to the president, such as the Party of Regions and Labor Ukraine.[11] The remaining pro-presidential politicians and parties meanwhile united in an electoral bloc called "For a United Ukraine," chaired by the head of the presidential administration, Volodymyr Lytvyn.

After a rather dirty campaign, parliamentary elections took place in late March 2002. For the first time, the democratic rather than the left-wing opposition became the single strongest force in parliament. The left had lost some of its programmatic appeal as well as credibility with voters, given that left-wing parties had repeatedly supported pro-presidential forces in parliament—as in the ouster of the Yushchenko government.[12] Compared to the 1998 elections, both the communists and the socialists lost in the proportional vote, and even more heavily with regard to majoritarian seats. 'Our Ukraine' became the strongest electoral bloc with 23.4 per cent of the proportional vote; 7.1 per cent went to the Bloc Yulia Tymoshenko (for a breakdown of the election results see Table III.3, Appendix).

Oligarchic parties were less popular and did poorly in the proportional vote. However, their candidates won in a number of majoritarian districts. Moreover, in the aftermath of the election, oligarchic parties 'collected' deputies who had obtained seats as independents (see Graphs 8.1 to 8.3). To 'collect' these independents, as well as some deputies from other factions, the presidential apparatus used the tax administration to exert pressure. As a result, the ranks of pro-presidential/oligarchic factions in parliament swelled, but they remained separate and did not unite in one permanent faction which could have provided reliable support for policies pursued by the president.[13] Also, while the pro-presidential parties captured the key leadership positions in parliament (chairman and deputies) leadership of the parliamentary committees remained more evenly allocated among the parties.[14]

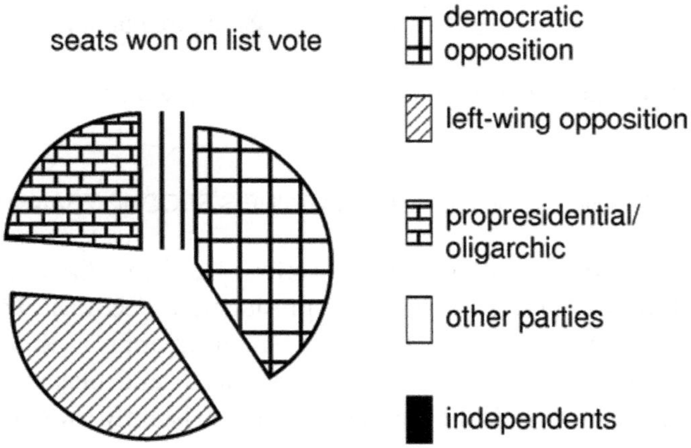

Graph 8.1: Share of seats according to list vote, March 2002

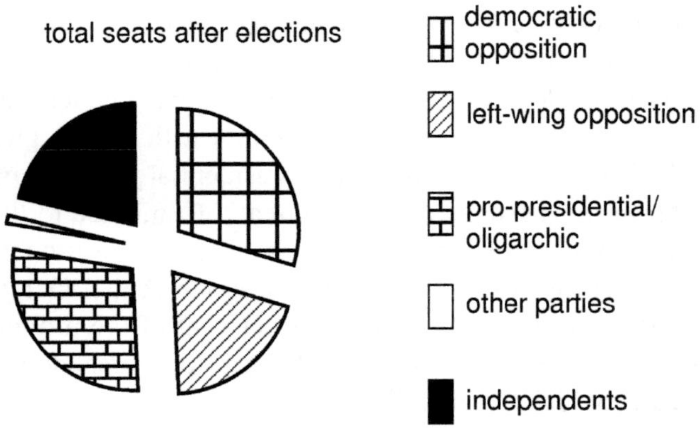

Graph 8.2: Share of seats according to list and majoritarian vote, March 2002

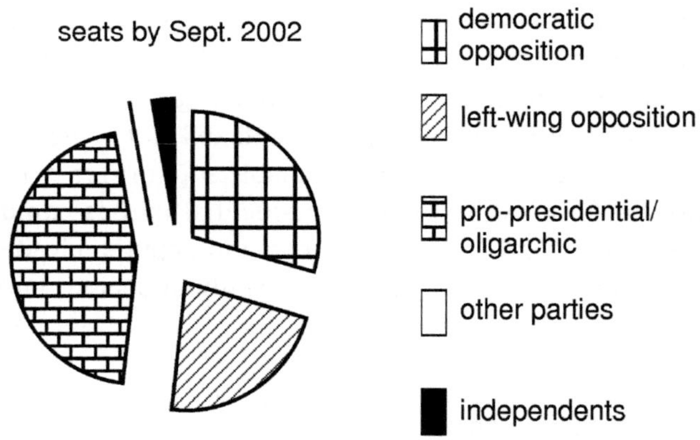

Graph 8.3: Share of seats after re-distribution of factions, fall 2002

8.1.2. THE ORANGE REVOLUTION—UKRAINE'S SECOND TRANSITION

Once the results of the parliamentary elections had been digested, political attention in Ukraine turned to the 2004 presidential elections. There were wide-spread expectations that the president would attempt a "Russian-style" hand-over of power; possibly to the SPDU politician and oligarch Medvedchuk. However, opinion polls during this period consistently showed that Viktor Yushchenko was by far the most popular politician in Ukraine—creating a serious risk in the case of reasonably free elections.

In a surprising *volte face* in August 2002, president Kuchma began to advocate a change to a 'parliamentary-presidential' system, i.e., shifting power from the presidential office to parliament and basing government on a parliamentary majority—a demand that had been voiced by the opposition for some time. The suggestion included having the future president elected by parliament rather than by popular vote—based on the calculation that this would make it easier to select a candidate backed by 'oligarchic' groups.[15]

In mid-November 2002, Kuchma replaced prime minister Kinakh with the Donetsk governor Viktor Yanukovych. Yanukovych was widely perceived as a representative of the Donetsk clan, and thus of a narrow group of interests, and as a hard-liner with little respect for the democratic rules of the game.[16] Mykola Azarov, the powerful head of the tax administration, was promoted to minister of finance and deputy prime minister. At the tax administration, Azarov was replaced by Yurii Kravchenko, another 'strongman' loyal to Kuchma who had been interior minister during the 'tape scandal' and had been forced to resign due to the protests. In June 2002, Kuchma had already appointed Viktor Medvedchuk, the leader of the oligarchic SDPU, as head of his presidential administration.[17] All of these were potential candidates of the pro-Kuchma camp in the presidential race. However, the president kept his options open. In late 2003, Kuchma master-minded a Constitutional Court ruling according to which he would be eligible to run for a third term in 2004, given that he had started his first term in 1994 before Ukraine's post-independence constitution was adopted.[18]

In 2003 and 2004, two attempts were made to push the constitutional changes through parliament, which would shift power towards the *Verkhovna Rada*. The democratic opposition at this stage voted against such a constitutional change (which it had earlier supported), given that it now had the stronger candidate for the 2004 presidential elections. While these two attempts were unsuccessful, eventually, constitutional changes along these lines were adopted during the "Orange Revolution" as a 'deal' between the old and the new regime.

In late 2003, parliament preliminarily adopted constitutional amendments which would reduce presidential powers and increase those of parliament and the prime minister. In trying to assemble 300 out of 450 votes necessary for the constitutional amendments, the pro-Kuchma camp made a deal with the socialists and the communists, offering them to change to a fully proportional electoral system (which would benefit the left but disadvantage most 'oligarchic' parties). These new electoral rules were successfully adopted in late March 2004. However, in April 2004 the *Verkhovna Rada* nonetheless failed to give the final passage to the constitutional changes due to defections from the pro-presidential parties.[19] A similar bill on constitutional reform was then re-introduced in June 2004, but again failed in the second vote in September, when the pro-Kuchma/Yanukovych coalition of factions in parliament disintegrated for good due to internal disagreements, involving political as well as business interests.[20]

As the presidential campaign unfolded in 2004, presidential forces used increasingly tough tactics against Yushchenko and his supporters. The tax administration was used to target businesses providing financial support to his campaign; campaign meetings were disrupted, particularly in Eastern Ukraine, and opposition newspapers were closed down. The opposition retaliated by calling Ukraine a "blackmail state" in the (Western) public forum.[21] Media coverage was heavily biased in favor of Yanukovych—whose popularity ratings did improve substantially as a result.[22] Russia's president Vladimir Putin openly supported Yanukovych's candidacy. On September 6, Yushchenko was severely poisoned.[23] Yushchenko survived but was heavily disfigured. He was able to return to the campaign after a few weeks—and apparently more determined than before in his opposition to the Kuchma regime.

The number of presidential candidates eventually reached 26. Apart from Yushchenko and Yanukovych, Oleksandr Moroz (socialists) and Petro Symonenko (communists) were the two most serious candidates—but either without a real chance to enter the second-round run-off. Amid wide-spread expectations in Ukraine and abroad that they would not be free and fair, the first round of presidential elections took place on October 31, 2004. Western election observers reported considerable fraud.[24] Initially, the Central Election Commission announced Yanukovych to have narrowly won, but then declared a slight lead for Yushchenko in the official results. The run-off was to be held on November 21.

The second round of voting took place under immense tension. On November 22, the Central Election Commission preliminarily indicated that Yanukovych had won by a small margin of 49.4 to 46.7 per cent. There were strong suspicions of fraud, as absentee ballots—allowing voters to vote outside their registered district—had been used on a massive scale. In Donetsk, reported voter turnout was improbably high (96.7 per cent of eligible voters). Exit polls by the Ukrainian Institute of Social Research as well as by the Razumkov Center showed Yushchenko ahead (by 52 to 44 per cent).[25] Western observers criticized the electoral process; while president Putin congratulated Yanukovych on winning the elections—despite the fact that the Central Election Commission had not yet declared the final result.[26]

Table 8.1: Presidential elections 2004, first round

	Results declared by the Central Election Commission, Nov. 1	Exit poll by Razumkov Center et al.	Exit poll by Ukrainian Institute of Social Research et al.
Viktor Yushchenko	39.90	44.40	39.3
Viktor Yanukovych	39.30	38.00	43.0
Oleksandr Moroz	5.77	5.62	6.3
Petro Symonenko	5.02	5.00	4.7
Natalia Vitrenko	1.54		

The opposition had well prepared for the event of fraudulent elections. Upon the announcement of the preliminary results, Yulia Tymoshenko called for a general strike. The day after the elections, around 100,000 people demonstrated in Kyiv, while the youth-movement *Pora* organized a tent-city on Kyiv's main street. Street protests lasted and grew in scale despite cold temperatures; with orange becoming the ubiquitous color of the protesters, giving the revolution its name. On November 26, Yushchenko suggested a re-run of the second round of elections as well as changes to the electoral law, particularly the banning of absentee ballots. The same day, Polish president Kwasniewski and the EU high representative on foreign affairs, Javier Solana, arrived in Kyiv to mediate. Meanwhile, up to 1 million protesters had assembled in Kyiv. A growing number of the members of Ukraine's elite defected from the pro-Yanukovych camp, and free debate spread on Ukraine's media. As was revealed later, a real threat of a violent reaction by the incumbent regime existed during this period, but was averted, not least due to careful planning and a built-up of contacts by the opposition within the security apparatus.

A decisive turn was the Supreme Court's decision on December 3 declaring the second round of the elections invalid and ordering a repeat vote. Despite this ruling, the presidential side still demanded constitutional changes which would decrease the powers of the president, in return for its deputies to agree to the changes in the electoral law which would curtail the use of absentee ballots. The Yushchenko camp was split over the issue, but eventually agreed to the deal. On December 8, parliament adopted changes to the electoral law and simultaneously amendments to the constitution (402 in favor, 21 against, and 19 abstentions)—scheduled to come into effect on September 1, 2005 or January 1, 2006 at the latest.[27]

In the repeat round held on December 26, Yushchenko received 52 per cent of the vote, against 44 for Yanukovych. While this was a resounding victory for Yushchenko, it also showed that a substantial share of the population was *not* in his favor, particularly in Southern and Eastern Ukraine (Donetsk, Luhansk).

After assuming office, Yushchenko appointed Yulia Tymoshenko as the new prime minister. She was endorsed in parliament by a large majority, including many deputies of oligarchic parties, such as the SDPU and the Party of Regions, who had masterminded her ouster four years earlier.[28] Her cabinet assembled older politicians who had served in previous cabinets (Anatolii Kinakh as first deputy prime minister, Viktor Pynzenyk as minister of finance, and Borys Tarasyuk as minister of foreign affairs), as well as younger politicians who had been allies in the opposition movement.

The change of the guard was accompanied by high-level suicides, which testified to the distortions the state had developed during the Kuchma era. The former minister of transport, Heorhii Kirpa committed suicide on December 27, apparently motivated by the misuse of funds from the transportation sector for financing Yanukovych's election campaign.[29] The second suicide was committed by former interior minister and head of the STA Yurii Kravchenko on March 4, just hours before he was due to be questioned in relationship to the Gongadze murder.[30]

While the new government sought to move from a hybrid to a democratic regime, consolidation remained elusive throughout 2005, not least due to the cuckoos' egg which the outgoing regime had laid in its nest, by forcing the issue of constitutional reform immediately onto the agenda.[31] Moreover, the 'electoral' honeymoon period of the new administration was short, with parliamentary elections due already in March 2006.

The new government's program "Towards the People" was approved by parliament in early February.[32] The program put the development of a state serving Ukraine's citizens at center stage, apart from addressing a broad list of policy issues, such as membership in the WTO (sought by late 2005) and a membership perspective for the European Union. Furthermore, it proposed a "new ideology of the budgetary process" aimed at providing a more just allocation of resources, providing health-care to all, as well as housing for the poor, and promised to create better regulation of the banking sector, to overcome corruption, and to provide better and more accessible public services.[33] Taxes were to be lowered and simplified, but at the same time to be enforced on a broad base.

From the start, there was considerable disagreement within the new government and in particular between Yulia Tymoshenko, the prime minister, on the one hand and Petro Poroshenko, the head of the National Security Council, on the other. Internal divisions were intensified by the prospect of the March 2006 parliamentary election and the fact that the Yushchenko/Tymoshenko government was formed on the basis of four rather diverse political parties (the Socialists; the People's Party headed by parliamentary speaker Volodymyr Lytvyn; Our Ukraine; and the Bloc Yulia Tymoshenko). Especially the socialists on the left and the People's Party on the right would not easily fit into an electoral bloc for the parliamentary elections. The socialists had opposed many market-oriented reforms during the transition, while the People's Party and its leader Volodymyr Lytvyn had been close to the Kuchma regime, in which Lytvyn had served as head of the presidential administration until 2002.

Moreover, the new government faced a number of difficult policy questions which provided ample basis for programmatic as well as personal disagreements. This included the thorny question of re-privatization, especially those that had been carried out during the last months of the outgoing government and which had clearly favored insiders, granting them control over several of Ukraine's largest enterprises, such as *Nikopol* (steel pipes) and *Kryvorizhstal* (steel) at steeply devalued prices. Another was the question of whether to continue the substantial pension and wage increases adopted by the outgoing government in its attempt to lure voters; and the question of whether Ukraine should switch to a fully cash-based system in its gas contracts with Russia.[34]

In early September 2005, amidst growing accusations of corruption among various government members Yushchenko dismissed Tymoshenko as prime minister. Two weeks later, Yurii Yekhanurov, an experienced politician who had served in the 2000 Yushchenko government, was approved by parliament as her successor. However, in order to secure the necessary votes for Yekhanurov's confirmation—and since Tymoshenko's supporters refused—Yushchenko concluded a deal with Yanukovych and his Party of Regions. They agreed to support Yekhanurov's confirmation in exchange for a law which would guarantee immunity to those who had been involved in the 2004 election fraud.

The constitutional changes demanded by the Kuchma camp during the 'Orange revolution' were eventually agreed upon to come into force in January 2006. The changes increased the constitutional weight of the prime minister and lowered that of the president. This only served to make the post-Orange coalition more tenuous, as it added significance to the March 2006 elections (as they would influence who could claim the role of future prime minister).

Table 8.2: Prime ministers and finance ministers, 2001–2005

Prime ministers	12/1999–04/2001 05/2001–11/2002 11/2002–12/2004 02/2005–09/2005 09/2005–	Viktor Yushchenko Anatolii Kinakh Viktor Yanukovych Yulia Tymoshenko Yurii Yekhanurov
Ministers of finance	02/1997–12/2001 01/2002–11/2002 11/2002–12/2004 02/2005–	Ihor Mityukov Ihor Yushko Mykola Azarov Viktor Pynzenyk

8.2. Economic recovery and socio-economic policies of the new government

The economic situation of Ukraine improved considerably in the early 2000s—as it did across the former Soviet Union. This long-awaited economic recovery from the deep transition recession was accelerated by the rise in energy prices that boosted the Russian economy which was still the economic motor of the region. High international demand for steel benefited Ukraine in particular. Strong growth across the region furthermore indicates that particular policies were less decisive; however, institutions had overall become more stable across the region as well. Strong growth of slightly over 12 per cent was reported for 2004; but growth then slowed markedly in 2005.[35]

In contrast to the 1999 presidential election, budget spending increased significantly during the 2004 election year, leading to a deficit of 4.4 per cent and a new increase of inflation to 9 per cent (see also section 5.4 below). Living standards improved as a result of the strong growth and the share of those living under the official poverty line fell from 30 per cent in 1999 to 19 per cent in 2003.[36]

Table 8.3: GDP growth in selected post-Soviet countries 2000–2005

	2000	2001	2002	2003	2004	2005
Ukraine	5.9	9.1	4.6	9.4	12.1	4.0
Russia	8.3	4.9	4.3	7.3	7.1	6.0
Lithuania	3.8	5.9	6.7	9.0	6.7	6.8
Belarus	5.8	4.1	4.7	6.7	11.0	8.0
Kazakhstan	9.8	13.2	9.5	9.2	9.4	9.0
Armenia	6.0	9.6	12.9	13.9	10.1	10.0

Source: EBRD, Transition Report (prognosis for 2005).

While the economic situation was broadly propitious, numerous risks for long-term development remained, including the concentration of ownership and the dependency on relatively few key industries, as well as potentially contested ownership structures. Thus, the new government faced a number of challenges in economic policy. It was intent on 're-designing' the state, including legal and administrative reform; and improving the relationship between the state and citizens.[37] This included a plan for territorial-administrative re-organization which deputy prime minister Roman Bezsmertnyi was charged with.

The new government was committed to a more social state—which Tymoshenko in particular had consistently advocated during her political career (see also Chapter 7, section 5). Thus, it confirmed the pension and wage increases introduced by the Kuchma administration in 2004 in an attempt to shore up support for Yanukovych.[38] Furthermore, as Tymoshenko had previously argued, the state was in fact able to increase revenue significantly by canceling a range of tax privileges and combating smuggling more effectively (see below). At the same time, some policies by the new prime minister were overly populist, such as her attempt to intervene in the market in an attempt to bring rising fuel prices down.[39] Furthermore, disagreement within the government coalition endangered ambitious policy projects such as a rapid joining of the WTO, as the loose 'Orange coalition' failed to support the necessary legislative changes.[40] Membership subsequently was not achieved in 2005.

While it was widely expected that there would be some re-privatization of enterprises sold below their value to 'insiders' by the previous government, investors and observers turned critical when the list of such enterprises was delayed several times, creating uncertainty.[41] Ultimately, various forces in government agreed to pursue limited re-privatization only, and the incoming Yekhanurov government announced that it would give preference to amicable out-of-court settlements rather than re-privatization in an effort to shore up Ukraine's international image.

The most positive steps of the new government were taken in the direction of increasing transparency in key areas of the public and private sector. In April, the government announced that in its gas imports from Russia it would switch from barter to monetized arrangements which would offer fewer opportunities for gas theft and corruption.[42] However, Russia retaliated by threatening to raise energy prices decisively, using Ukraine's dependency on gas imports to exert political pressure. Still, eventually an agreement for a cash-based system was reached.[43]

Thus, the economic policies of the government were faced by popular demands on the one hand (higher spending, reversal of some privatization), by a more difficult relationship with Russia, and by the need to attract investments and sustain growth on the other hand—and preferably keep all of this in balance at least up to the 2006 parliamentary elections.

8.3. The power of civil society and the continuing importance of opaque groups

The 'Orange revolution' of late 2004 was an impressive demonstration that an organized civil society had emerged in Ukraine. At the same time, this 'second transition' reduced but did not end the power of opaque groups in Ukraine.

Civil society in Ukraine had become increasingly diverse. A central group during the 2004 elections was the youth-group *Pora,* which was modeled on similar groups in Serbia and in Georgia.[44] Important NGO coalitions had grown out of election monitoring activities in earlier years.[45]

While the revolution had demonstrated the increased power of civil society, opaque groups continued to play an important role in the new era. The impact of the 'revolution' on their economic leverage was limited, and they continued to strengthen their links with politics. The acrimonious debates about re-privatization as well as the accusations of corruption within the first post-'Orange' government were closely linked to the relative power and influence of the oligarchic system in Ukraine. In the re-privatization of the major *Nikopol* steel pipe plant, Tymoshenko was accused of siding with one oligarchic group against another.[46]

President Yushchenko sought to turn the oligarchic groups into supporters of a modern state and economy by bringing several of them into his own political alliance, as well as by holding official meetings with well-known oligarchs.[47] In contrast to Putin, his declared aim was to turn the oligarchs into a national bourgeoisie which would support the state—by paying their taxes due, by engaging in big infrastructure projects, etc.—rather than to enforce a strict division between the business groups and politics.

The new opposition around Viktor Yanukovych and his Party of Regions continued to collaborate closely with oligarchic groups; and especially with Renat Akhmetov, Ukraine's wealthiest businessman.[48] Akhmetov and a number of managers of his company were entered on the Party of Region's election list. *Kryvorizhstal* and some other major assets had to be returned to the state for re-privatization, but many oligarchic owners were allowed to keep their assets on the condition of making some additional payments to the budget. However, some oligarchs who had made an earlier entry into the political scene lost some of their influence as their parties—especially the SDPU founded by Medvedchuk and Surkis—failed to garner any popular support.[49]

Overall, the 'Orange revolution' brought about a much greater organization and mobilization of society—even if it was quickly followed by disappointment about the new regime's achievements. At the same time, Ukraine's oligarchic groups were not dislodged, but their assets and political influence were only cut back to some extent—including a reduction in tax privileges, and greater pressure to pay taxes (see section 5.1 below).

8.4. External influences on the rise

Ukraine became further integrated into the international economic system during this period. Progress in the fiscal situation led to improved international credit ratings and better access to international financial markets.[50] Growth combined with low deficits helped to lower the external debt, and made Ukraine less dependent in its policy decisions on the IFIs (which *inter alia* opposed the large pension and wage increases). However, growth was *inter alia* driven by high prices for steel, Ukraine's main export product (see Graph 8.4), and hence it slowed down markedly when prices leveled off in 2005.

A lot was made of both Western and Russian influence in the context of Ukraine's contested elections. Ukraine possesses strategic value both for the US and for Russia. Both sides contributed financing to the 2004 presidential election campaign and to the organizations involved. The impact of this external financing is difficult to gauge, but should not be overestimated. The US was Ukraine's largest bilateral donor; and in 2003 and 2004, Ukraine received \$188.5m and \$143.5m respectively in total.[51] However, funding decreased as US policy priorities shifted to Central Asia since September 11, 2001. Allegedly, \$14m were made available immediately for supporting the electoral campaign.[52] Some additional money came from the Open Society Institute and similar sources. Given the total cost of the campaign (estimated at \$300m or more), and the resources at the disposal of the incumbent, these were not particularly large sums.[53] Furthermore, allegedly the Yanukovych campaign received substantial financial support from Russia—according to Aslund, half of its total funds.[54] Russian financing may have backfired, since many Ukrainians resented the very overt Russian attempt at influencing the election outcome.[55] Western financing and other assistance played a role, but primarily by helping an already growing opposition movement to develop organizational skills.

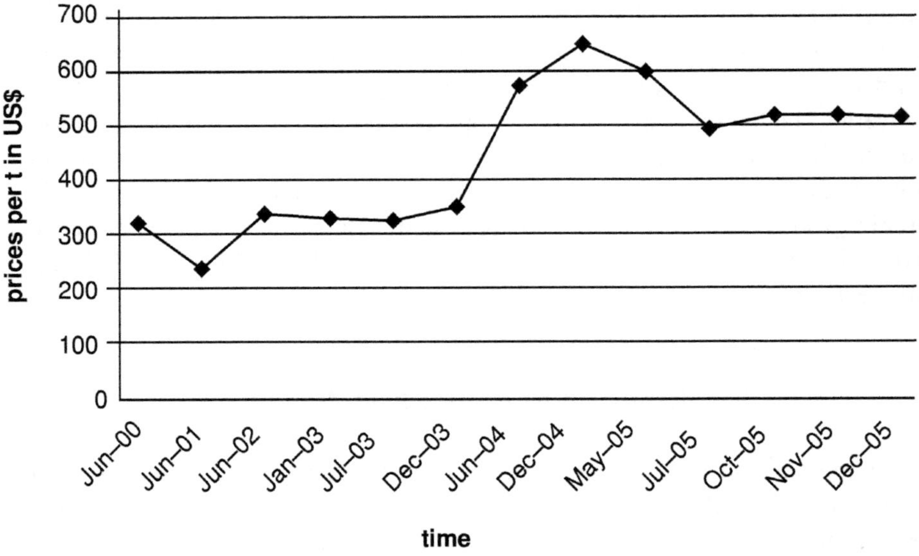

Graph 8.4: International steel prices, 2000–2005

Arguably, external influences became more important *after* the elections, but in a way which was driven by domestic choices. These were related to the commitment of the new government to lead Ukraine into Western clubs of variable exclusivity (WTO, NATO, and the EU) and its related hesitancy of joining a Single Economic Space with Russia, Kazakhstan, and Belarus. Furthermore, a renewed wave of Western economic policy advice was generated—apparently, however, with limited effect on the new government.[56]

Membership in the WTO and in the EU had been pursued already under the Kuchma regime, albeit rather superficially.[57] The new government declared membership in the EU as a strategic policy goal; and Oleh Rybachuk was appointed deputy prime minister for European Integration. However, while the EU expressed an interest in closer cooperation with Ukraine, EU representatives were still unwilling to grant Ukraine a membership perspective; not least due to the EU's own internal 'fatigue' at the time. In this sense, the interface between domestic politics and external influences played an important role; but it was still the absence of an integration offer rather than any active influence which was seen as most important.

WTO accession was a more immediate policy goal; and one which Russia and Ukraine were pursuing in parallel and to some degree in competition. Ultimately, neither Russia nor Ukraine achieved the goal of acceding in 2005, but both made considerable progress in the negotiations with crucial trading partners.[58]

Overall, as the result of domestic choices and changes, Ukraine's international economic integration increased—both via trade and by seeking membership in international clubs. External factors mattered more than previously, but still without being dominant relative to domestic factors, especially as long as an EU accession perspective remained absent. Ukraine was searching for options of international integration and this search was closely related to its process of state formation, and to the efforts at transforming the state after the 'Orange revolution.'

8.5. Fiscal developments: reforms and revelations

Further reforms in the fiscal area had been undertaken by the Kuchma government during its last years; although several fundamental problems—especially tax privileges and slow VAT refunds, and opportunities for abuse of the system—remained (deliberately) unaddressed. A number of factors motivated the changes that were undertaken: firstly, the regional trend towards lowering taxes (see Chapter 5) which Ukraine was under some pressure to follow. Secondly, 2004 was a decisive election year, making it attractive to phase tax cuts in just then.

The new government taking over in 2005 brought the size of loopholes in the fiscal system to light. These loopholes were both 'acute' and 'chronic': acutely, substantial funds were diverted from the budget in 2004 to finance the Kuchma/Yanukovych campaign; and chronically, well-known loopholes such as weak and corrupt customs control and Free Economic Zones had been permitted to exist. As a result of reducing several of these loopholes, the new government was able to generate substantially higher revenue in 2005 despite slowing growth.

8.5.1. TAXES: POLICY REFORM AND A POST-ORANGE BOOST

The partial tax reform which was adopted in late 2002 and 2003 had been developed by Mykola Azarov, the former head of the tax administration who turned Minister of Finance. It reduced rates in particular of direct taxes (personal income and profit taxes). For personal income, a 13 per cent flat rate—

similar to the Russian model—was chosen. This meant a decisive lowering of formal tax obligations for those earning more than the equivalent of around $300 per month, who had faced a marginal tax rate of 40 per cent before the reform. The profit tax rate was lowered from 30 to 25 per cent, and depreciation rates of fixed assets were increased, making it easier for businesses to subtract costs from their taxable profits. An intended reduction of the VAT rate from 20 to 17 per cent, however, failed twice due to a presidential veto in late 2003. Also, parliament still would not cancel most 'non-standard' tax privileges outright, but rather chose to suspend a number of tax privileges via the 2004 budget law.

An important motivation for adopting these tax reforms, which had been discussed for years, was the recognition among pro-Kuchma forces that by stimulating the economy and possibly boosting tax collection they could increase the chances of having a chosen successor elected.[59] The lowering of tax rates came into force on January 1, 2004 coinciding with strong economic growth.[60] Revenue from personal income taxation declined relative to GDP, but stayed nearly flat in nominal terms; while revenue from the Enterprise Profit Tax dropped slightly in percentage terms, but increased substantially in volume (see Table 8.3).

The administration of the value added tax, however, continued to be an area of particularly murky governance throughout the early 2000s. Due to VAT exemptions as well as large-scale evasion, VAT collections relative to GDP remained substantially lower in Ukraine than in Central and Eastern Europe and the Baltic states. In 2003, non-standard VAT exemptions were estimated to account for some UAH 8 billion in lost revenue according to the Ukrainian Ministry of Finance—more than 10 per cent of total tax revenue for that year.[61] In early 2004, Petro Poroshenko, then a prominent businessman in the Yushchenko camp, accused the government of paying out fictitious VAT refunds as a way to siphon money from the budget, an accusation which was substantiated by the new leadership of the STA in 2005 (see below).[62]

Upon taking office, new 'Orange' government sought to widen the tax base. It urgently needed more revenue to finance higher public sector wages and social security, and the first government under Tymoshenko had a clear idea of major loopholes. However, in her efforts to overhaul the rules of the game, Tymoshenko had less regard for the effects this would have on the perceived 'business climate.' In March 2005, along with voting on the revised 2005 budget, parliament adopted an end to most tax privileges and exemptions (in particular those pertaining to VAT), and decided to increase excise taxes.[63] Special economic zones and territories of priority development were eliminated.[64] While these steps were overdue and positive in principle, deputy prime minister Kinakh later argued that the abrupt abolition of these zones—in the middle of the tax year and in combination with the discussion about re-privatization—was a mistake *ad hoc* rule changes undermined the trust of potential foreign investors which the new government was hoping to attract.[65]

Tax revenue rose substantially in 2005, despite decelerating growth.[66] The reduction of tax privileges, and the incentive for enterprises to seek good standing with the new government led to a rise in VAT and profit tax receipts in particular, while rising wages boosted revenue from personal income taxation (see Table 8.3).[67] More business transactions were brought into the official economy.[68] Still, the new government continued to delay paying VAT refunds to exporters—despite promises to end this practice.[69]

Table 8.4: Revenue from main taxes 2002–2005

	2002	2003	2004	2005 (estimate)
In bn UAH				
EPT	9.4	13.2	16.2	20.0
VAT	13.5	12.6	16.7	28.0
PIT	10.8	13.5	13.2	17.1
SST	19.6	23.2	31.8	n.a.
In % of GDP				
EPT	4.3	5.0	4.7	4.8
VAT	6.0	4.7	4.9	6.7
PIT	4.8	5.1	3.8	4.1
SST	8.7	8.7	9.2	n.a.

Source: IER, Tax Revenue Outlook for Ukraine, no. 2, 2005. IMF Country Report 05/417.

Non-tax revenue also increased. The government started a major anti-smuggling campaign which led to rising customs revenue. Those re-privatizations which were eventually undertaken brought much higher prices. The largest re-privatization of the *Kryvorizhstal* steel mill generated a price six times higher than the one paid in 2004. As a result, revenue from privatization exceeded planned levels three times for the year.[70]

The debate about further tax reform heated up again in the second half of 2005—as one of the topics of the campaign for the March 2006 parliamentary elections. In early October, Yushchenko promised to prepare the outline of a new tax system, calling the 'unregulated' tax regime one of the greatest domestic policy challenges in Ukraine.[71] Public discussion also focused on continued problems with the VAT, the question of introducing property taxation, and renewed promises about lowering tax rates and widening the tax base. Minister for economic affairs, Arsenii Yatsenyuk, in contrast, proposed a moratorium on tax policy changes for 2006, and to halt the flow of continuous changes.[72] Thus, while fiscal developments were generally heading in a positive direction, the challenges of finding consensus and clear policy orientation remained present in Ukraine.

8.5.2. TAKING ON THE TAX ADMINISTRATION

Towards the end of the Kuchma-era, some attempts were made to improve the tax administration; including a major World Bank funded project to support the modernization of the STA. However, those incremental improvements which were achieved continued to be contradicted by the need to abuse the STA for political purposes.

Due to the need for a top-down control over the STA, no external oversight of the tax administration—by the Accounting Chamber or even by the internal audit body, the DKRS—had been put in place. The AC and the DKRS could audit administrative expenditures of the STA, but not its process of revenue collection and practices as such.[73] This reduced the pressure to reform dysfunctional practices such as delaying VAT refunds, and violating the rights of taxpayers.

Since the late 1990s, Ukrainian businesses had begun to defend themselves against unfair practices by the tax administration. In one case, a business, Terem Ltd. first sued the tax administration before a Ukrainian court for the confiscation of its property by Ukrainian tax police in 1999. Although the company won the case in 2003, the government failed to follow up with the compensation, citing a lack of budgetary funds. The company then sued before the European Court of Human Rights, where the Ukrainian state was found to be liable to pay out the compensation.[74]

As a consequence of these problems, the tax administration was seen as one of the key problematic state structures both by independent observers and by the Ukrainian opposition. Accordingly, Yushchenko's pre-election program included the abolition of the tax police (or tax militia) and overall reforms of the STA as one of its main elements.[75] Moreover, in August 2005, the government revealed that up to UAH 5 billion (or $1 billion) had been paid out in 2004 as value-added taxation rebates that were based on fictitious exports; and at least some of the money was used for the Yanukovych election campaign.[76]

An important change initiated by the new government was to move the tax administration (as well as the customs administration) back under the control of the Ministry of Finance from where it had been removed in 1996 (see Chapter 7, section 5.6 above). In March 2005, some weeks after forming the new government, Yushchenko appointed Oleksandr Kiryeyev as the new head of the tax administration. The promised abolition of the tax police did not take place in 2005; however, a reduction of its numbers from a staff of 15,000 to 7,000 was announced by Kiryeyev in late May 2005. After considerable criticism for failing to honor this important campaign pledge, Kiryeyev reiterated that the tax police would be abolished and replaced by a tax investigation service.[77] He also spoke out in favor of a wider overhaul of Ukraine's tax policy and administrative system.[78]

As part of the with changes in administrative personnel across government, a number of STA staff were dismissed.[79] However, this did not lead to an immediate decrease in corruption and may have even made it worse as the size of bribes and the treatment provided in return became more unstable.[80] Nonetheless, the STA did seem to become more serious about addressing corruption internally: 162 claims about corrupt tax administrators were submitted to the public prosecutor in 2005.[81]

On the one hand, the new government had ambitious expenditure plans which it needed to cover; and the tax police had developed into an important enforcement mechanism. On the other hand, the government also seemed unwilling to give up some of the practices of Ukraine's "hybrid regime." Thus, in summer 2005, the STA revived a tax investigation of a media holding company (Blitz-Inform).[82] Newspapers under control of the holding company had criticized members of the Yushchenko team. In another case, in August 2005, the tax police was deployed to raid the offices of one of Ukraine's main oligarchs, Renat Akhmetov.[83]

8.5.3. TAX AND BUDGET ARREARS

Tax arrears had been reduced in 2001 but essentially bounced back to earlier levels already in the following year (Table 8.5). Moreover, the reduction in 2001 was due to a major write-off of tax debt and accumulated fines, rather than being the result of actual payment of taxes.[84] Apparently, tax arrears accumulated both from loss-making as well as from profit-making enterprises. The tolerance of tax arrears and the repeat occurrence of bail-outs amounted to a form of indirect state-aid—which would become more difficult to sustain as Ukraine moved towards deeper international integration (aspiring to accede to the WTO, and the EU).

Table 8.5: Tax and pension fund arrears, 1998–2004

	1998	1999	2000	2001	2002	2003	2004
Arrears, stock as % of GDP (end of period)	13.5	8.0	6.2	3.3	*7.0*	*5.6*	*2.9*
In UAH mn	13,295	13,006	11,349	6,702	*15,421*	*14,993*	*9,981*

Note: Arrears including to the STA and to the pension fund. A part of the arrears are accumulated fines.

Source: IMF various Country Reports.

Table 8.6: Wage and pension arrears, 1999–2004

	1999	2000	2001	2002	2003	2004
Social arrears total (wages and pensions) in UAH mn	3089	1344	621	840	325	0

Source: IMF 2002 (Staff Country Report), IMF 2002 (Fiscal Snapshot); 2005 Country Report.

The situation improved more clearly in 2004—tax arrears were reduced significantly, and social arrears were eliminated. This was the result of tax reforms coinciding with strong growth, and at the same time with a strong political incentive to clear social payments in a decisive election year. Given the commitment of the post-Orange government to create a more transparent and accountable fiscal system, no new arrears emerged in 2005; although the problem of VAT refund arrears remained. After more than a decade of fiscal turmoil and deliberate distortions, the system was finally reshaped towards bringing formal rules and *de facto* behavior into closer alignment.

8.5.4. THE BUDGET PROCESS: FROM SERVING THE REGIME TO SERVING THE PEOPLE

Similar to the situation with taxation, incremental reforms of the budget system continued during the late Kuchma period, but fundamental flaws remained unaddressed, since they served the self-preservation of the hybrid regime. A further step towards improving formal rules was made with the adoption of a new budget code in 2001. However, when the new 'Orange' government took over, considerable problems with leakage from the budget were revealed, which had been particularly large in 2004 when the Kuchma government was scrambling for funds to finance its election campaign. Budget execution was eased in the 2000s, since in sharp contrast to the 1990s, revenues tended to be higher rather than lower than expected. 2004 and 2005 brought a major expansion of spending on wages and social security, which signalled that the trend of reducing the 'social' role of the state had stopped or even begun to be reversed.

8.5.4.1. THE THIRD BUDGET CODE

A new budget code was adopted in July 2001.[85] The code had received an overwhelming majority of 391 votes in the *Rada*, meaning that it was supported by virtually all factions. While the re-ordering and further regularization of the budgeting process was comparatively uncontroversial, the reform of inter-governmental fiscal relations had proven more contentious. In the fall of 2000, the president had opposed the approval of the budget code fearing that the 'presidential vertical,' i.e., presidential control over regions and districts, would be weakened by increased local autonomy in fiscal matters.[86] After lengthy consultations, a compromise had been found in early 2001.[87]

The new budget code regulated the general budgetary process by imposing a clear time table and clarifying the rights and obligations of various actors, and it introduced new rules for intergovernmental fiscal relations—while leaving the details of this to be specified by a proposed Code on Local Government.[88] Within parliament, the coordinating role of the budget committee was strengthened, giving it the right to review all draft laws and to evaluate their possible effects on the budget.[89] Also, the role of the treasury in budget execution was strengthened, limiting the possibility of incurring financial commitments for which funds were not available.[90]

Overall, consensus-building with regard to the budget code proved easier than it did for the tax code. The budget code represented a 'big step,' but one of intermediate difficulty only (see Chapter 3 regarding types of institutional change). In contrast to the tax code, distributional issues were less crucial to the budget code—apart from the reform of intergovernmental fiscal relations which had accordingly been its most contested component. The Ministry of Finance as well as the Budget Committee of parliament had an interest in clarifying the technocratic aspects of the budget. The new code helped to foster the slow process of regularization,[91] but budgeting continued to be fraught with political maneuvering and unexpected decisions.

8.5.4.2. BUDGET PROCESSES FROM 2002 TO 2005

The 2002 budget was the first to be debated after the new budget code had come into effect. The budget debate occurred during the beginning of the campaign for the March 2002 parliamentary elections and hence was politically charged. Relations between the budget committee and the government were worse than during the previous year due to the fact that Yulia Tymoshenko and her ally Oleksandr Turchynov who chaired the *Rada's* budget committee had gone into radical opposition to the president during the preceding months. The budget negotiation process was fraught with mutual accusations.[92] Furthermore, budget formulation suffered from the failure to adopt tax reform in 2001 as had originally been expected.[93] The government lost in its effort to cut out 'un-fundable' social benefits from the budget: parliament refused to go along and voted to maintain these benefits.[94]

Despite this strained situation, the new budget code "strictly disciplined the process of reconciling and approving budget priorities and discontinued the undesirable practices that used to exist before its implementation" according to the Fiscal Analysis Office.[95] Final adoption of the budget took place on December 20, 2001, continuing the series of improved timetables. Thus, the budget code is an example that improvements in formal institutions *can be* an effective first step for triggering improvements in *de facto* practices.

However, along with the shifting sands of Ukrainian politics, practices continued to harbor surprises. A year later, in the course of preparing the 2003 budget, the Communist faction leader Petro Symonenko and faction members of the SDPU suddenly accused the new chairman of the parliamentary budget committee, Petro Poroshenko, of changing line items in the budget between its adoption by parliament and its publication (to benefit Poroshenko's constituency in Vinnytsia Oblast, to the order of $9 million).[96] Poroshenko was a businessman who had entered parliament as part of the pro-Yushchenko camp in 2002, and importantly, owned the only major opposition TV channel, Channel 5. His reputation survived the allegation intact.

The 2004 budget was strongly overshadowed by the looming presidential elections; and as a result the budget process was deliberately made less transparent. Government 'pre-negotiated' the main lines of the budget with pro-presidential forces in parliament prior to the submission of the draft budget to the legislature.[97] A rather thin budget was rapidly pushed through parliament: the budget proposal was delivered to parliament in early September,[98] and was adopted after just two readings in late November. Already by January 2004, the government submitted extensive amendments.[99] Higher than expected revenue—generated from many 'urgent' privatizations while the oligarchic system was still in control (some of which were later subject to the re-privatizations discussed above)—allowed further adjustments to the budget. In September 2004, an increase in pensions which had not previously been included in the budget was decided by government resolution.[100]

The 2004 budget ended with a sizable deficit due to the expansion of spending in this election year—in marked contrast to the previous presidential election in 1999, when extra spending had remained very limited. Furthermore, the incoming Orange government revealed that substantial funds had been leaked from the budget—and at an especially large scale during the final Kuchma year. The scheme of fictitious VAT refunds was one important avenue; while procurement in the transport sector had been another.[101] The former minister of transport, Hrihorii Kirpa, committed suicide just after Yushchenko won the repeat election.[102] Abuse of remaining state-property also reached new heights with the sale of *Kryvorizhstal* several times below its real value in 2004; as well as illicit real-estate deals executed by the management department of the presidential administration.[103] The incoming administration opened numerous criminal investigations related to the abuse of public resources. The scale of these abuses showed that despite the development of the institutional system over the past years, political commands could still regularly and easily override formal rules.

Table 8.7: Revenue, expenditure, and deficit, 2002–2005

	2002	2003	2004	2005 (estimate)
Revenue/GDP	35.8	36.2	35.1	39.0
Expenditure/GDP	35.7	36.7	38.9	41.2
Deficit/GDP	0.1	–0.5	–3.8	–2.2

Sources: IMF Country Report no. 05/417; IERPC, Monthly Monitor, no. 12/2005.

Apart from leaking funds from the budget, the outgoing Kuchma government had sought to buy support by major spending increases. In September 2004, the minimum full pension was doubled to UAH 284 per month; and state sector wages grew considerably.[104] Legally, the rise in pensions was temporary, which reinforced its character as an election 'gift.'

The 2005 budget was re-written by the new government taking power in early 2005 and was then unanimously adopted by the *Rada.* The new government was strongly committed to a more 'social budget.' Consequently it made the previous pension increases permanent, and decided on further increases in social spending (especially re-establishing financial support to mothers with newborn children).[105] The deficit was planned to reach 1.6 per cent of GDP; while rising expenditures were to be met by reducing tax exemptions as well as by revisions of macro-economic indicators.

In late April 2005, Yushchenko warned that demands on the budget had been rising too strongly.[106] He, as well as some foreign observers, pointed out that 14 to 16 per cent of Ukraine's GDP went towards paying pensions, while general social expenditure reached close to 25 per cent of the total budget, particularly due to the increased pension payments.[107]

Since the government was successful at increasing revenue, it could meet these rising expenditures without too much of a squeeze on the budget in the short term. In the broader picture, 2005 marked a turn-around in Ukraine from a shrinking role of the state to a re-expanding role of the state particularly in the social sphere. However, the eventual fiscal size of the state was still evolving and volatile economic growth added considerable uncertainty.

8.5.5. CONTROL AND ACCOUNTABILITY

Under the Kuchma government, control continued to serve primarily a 'defensive' logic—and especially so in 2004. After assuming the presidency, Yushchenko promised to bring major reforms to this sphere, but these were slow to materialize in 2005, as the new regime was struggling with its internal divisions.

A first instance of control which had been developed in most post-Soviet states with the assistance of the IMF was a state treasury (State Treasury of Ukraine, STU) which centralized responsibility for executing payments in the fiscal system.[108] Created in the mid-1990s, the treasury initially handled funds for the central level of government only. In the early 2000s, coverage was successively expanded to sub-national levels.[109] While the development of the STU had been pursued by the Kuchma government, it had been separated from the Ministry of Finance, similarly to the Tax Administration; which facilitated manipulations by the political leadership when necessary.

Under the incoming Orange government, the state treasury, as well as the internal audit institution, the DKRS, and the tax and customs administration, were brought back under the control of the Ministry of Finance.[110] In its Action Plan with the EU, Ukraine made substantial commitments to improving its public financial management, and to strengthen internal and external control and audit functions; including further modernization of the treasury system, new legislation on internal financial control, and ensuring the adequate functioning of the Accounting Chamber.[111]

The Accounting Chamber continued to face difficulties in its development during the final years of the old regime. In 2001, it received the right to audit intelligence agencies.[112] In January 2002, parliament adopted a decision to broaden its mandate to cover revenue as well as expenditures—which was a key missing element, especially given the many problems with revenue, such as VAT refunds (see above). Parliament's decision involved a change to Article 98 of the Constitution (which was adopted with the required 300-vote majority).[113] However, this change was blocked by president Kuchma.[114]

In the early 2000s, the Accounting Chamber began to receive more external support from the EU as well as from UNDP, as part of efforts to strengthen overall public financial management and general accountability.[115] However, its allocated resources remained limited, and it still maintained a rather narrow focus on individual misappropriation of funds rather than taking a more systemic approach to risks. The Orange government was committed to strengthening the external audit function as part of its commitment to EU accession. However, while discussions on a new law for the Accounting Chamber were held in 2005, no new law was adopted before the basic constitutional increase of the powers of parliament which came into force in early January 2006.[116]

8.6. From Kuchma to Yushchenko: Re-tooling the state

The political change in late 2004 was an important turning point for state-development in Ukraine. The Kuchma regime had built a broadly capable, but also fundamentally distorted state, in which many elements of the 'state as a problem' were directly linked to the exigencies of a hybrid political regime. This regime had fostered the 'despotic' powers of command and control at the expense of the infrastructural powers of the state.

The 2004 mass demonstrations which led to a change in government showed that there was considerable resentment against the state system created by Kuchma; and that citizens wanted a different, and in particular a less corrupt state. This theme was also present in other 'revolutions' or secondary transitions in Georgia and in Kyrgyzstan.[117]

The Yushchenko government was committed to re-tooling this state and to developing a state oriented towards the need of society, rather than to the maintenance of power. This proved to be a difficult task, especially given the relative fragility of the new political system and of the new government itself. Some of the dysfunctionalities of the state were hard to change despite the new government's commitments to do so.

The consolidation of the new democratic regime ran into a series of obstacles in 2005. It enjoyed the support of half the citizens rather than of an overwhelming majority. The anti-Kuchma opposition which came to power in late 2004 was heterogeneous—comprising left-wing parties, market reformers, as well as defectors from the Kuchma regime. The upcoming parliamentary elections were badly timed for the new government: too late to allow capitalizing on the enthusiasm of the 'revolutionary' moment, but so early that they distracted attention from the agenda of reshaping the country and towards politicking from the very beginning. The inauspicious timing of the parliamentary elections was compounded by the challenge of constitutional changes, which would bring about further shifts in power with uncertain outcomes.

The implementation capacity of the new government was mixed: there was disagreement about what features of the old regime the new government would seek to reverse and how (re-privatization; local self-government; extent of presidential power, etc.). The new government dismissed a number of public officials, but overall public administration reform was delayed. At the same time, revenue collection improved despite a slow-down in economic growth; and since formal tax demands had been lowered by the outgoing regime, the tax administration was bound to become more regularized. Still, the government found itself in an undecided position with regard to an institution like the tax police—wanting to keep levers of power on the one hand, but being committed to re-engineer the state on the other hand.

Nonetheless, there was a process of improvements, albeit in fits and starts, which acquired a new quality under the post-Orange governments. Economic growth had already facilitated the 'normalization' of budgeting practices during the late Kuchma period; but it was the Orange revolution which led to a major, if still unfinished, cleaning up of the system.

Accountability to the public remained relatively weak—the Accounting Chamber and parliament itself did not provide an effective oversight of fiscal flows, since the AC was limited in its capacity; and the parliament had only a limited interest in providing accountability to citizens. While post-Orange governments did not immediately change this, at least there was a commitment to set things on a right path; which also attracted further support by the IFIs and increasingly the EU to improve public financial management.[118]

The new government pledged to create a more 'just state,' but initially was deeply divided over the role of the state; reflected in months of wrangling over re-privatizations, over the use of price controls and so on.[119] However, it did strive to create a more rational administration and to reduce avenues for *ad hoc* political interference; and it impressively demonstrated that the state could broaden the tax base, and used the additional funds to re-build a welfare state. Overall, the Orange revolution had a positive impact on Ukraine's state-building trajectory, but the uncertainty of the political regime continued to pose risks for developing a truly capable and well-governed state.

8.7. Summary: the state-building process in Ukraine as reflected in the fiscal sphere

This has been an account of more than a decade of state-building in Ukraine, viewed through a fiscal lens; but covering also a wide range of potential driving factors. Several issues stand out: the political regime remained unconsolidated throughout, moving from an unconsolidated democratic regime in 1992 to 1994, to an increasingly authoritarian-leaning hybrid regime between 1994 and 2004, and back to an unconsolidated democratic regime from late 2004 onwards. Power, and the rules about power remained contested. Following the adoption of the constitution in 1996, the president sought to expand his powers until around mid-2000. The "tape scandal" then set off a decline of the "Kuchma era;" this in turn also brought the proposal of a constitutional change towards a parliamentary system back onto the agenda.

Political contestation among competing elite groups in Ukraine has been marked by conflict as well as compromise. Regional differences in interests are real, but they are more a competition about which regional or sub-regional networks can dominate the national political game, rather than posing a real threat of secession. A key recurrent feature in Ukrainian politics have been shifting, frequently unexpected, and sometimes rather unholy alliances; including alliances between left-wing parties and oligarchic groups, as well as between the 'Orange' government and the Dnipropetrovsk clan. Thus, political compromise has been possible, although compromise often undermined any commitments to a political program.

Moreover, the *modus operandi* of the contested, hybrid political regime has cost people's lives and health: Gongadze and other journalists have been killed; Yushchenko was severely poisoned; and there have been numerous less prominent victims. Furthermore, the 'defensive' logic according to which Kuchma shaped the state apparatus has made the state work less well than it could have otherwise, and has made the majority of Ukrainian people worse off as a result—through years of pension arrears, oppressive and unpredictable taxation, impoverished public services, and rising corruption in the fiscal sphere and in public services.

Regarding the main driving factors and interactions, we can distinguish the following: a key initial condition was the degree of institutional erosion and economic crisis which accompanied independence. Civil and political society were in a state of flux. The Communist Party disintegrated; leaving the informal 'party of power' as the main, but rather amorphous and incoherent political group. Existing capacity was mainly used for *ad hoc* 'firefighting.' Institutional weakness fostered the rise of 'opaque groups.'

By the mid-1990s, a new institutional order began to crystallize, and the president played a key role in shaping this order. However, for his hold on power he had to rely on 'opaque groups' which gave these increasingly direct influence over the state. At the same time, visible groups, and especially political parties, still remained rather weak and very fragmented. While pursuing a path of state-building, the political leadership deliberately fostered a range of distortions which served to maintain a hybrid political regime, as reflected in the tax system.

In the early 2000s, resistance of wider society against this state system began to intensify. Models of recent second transitions in Serbia and Georgia, and domestic economic recovery facilitated mobilization. The 'Orange Revolution' of late 2004 brought a new government to power, which was committed to transform the state further in the direction of a modern, capable, and accountable state. However, achieving this vision proved challenging; not least since opaque groups retained considerable influence, but also because of internal divisions within the new government and looming constitutional change.

The interactions between institutions and various groups in the domestic arena played a key role in shaping the Ukrainian state. External influences did have an intermittent impact: in contrast to the Central Eastern European and the Baltic states, Ukraine did not have an EU accession 'anchor' to tie its state-building efforts to. The IFIs played a role, by making policy demands and by supporting the development of various elements of the institutional structure. Their policy leverage was limited in a large country such as Ukraine, and also due to the fact that debt reached problematic levels only for a few years in the late 1990s; but they had an impact by promoting the import of certain institutional models. An important moment of external influence was the political 'meddling' by Russia as well as the West in the 2004 elections, and the presence of a 'Georgian model' (the 'Rose revolution') to emulate.

The dynamic of institutional change means that the predictive value of institutional legacies has been limited. In the fiscal sphere, wide-ranging institutional transformation and creation became inevitable once the process of privatizing the economy had been started. Western influence promoted new institutional models such as a treasury system, the VAT, or the Accounting Chamber. While these institutional imports proved difficult to digest (VAT) or rather ineffective (AC), they are set to remain in place and their functioning will most likely be improved over time. Legacies therefore have had rather little impact on the institutional reforms which are being pursued, but more on how people operate, especially also in the context of weakened and distorted institutions.

The following chapters provide three comparative case studies based on a most-similar-systems design. They especially illustrate the important impact which the development of the political regime had on state- and institution-building in the post-Soviet period.

Notes

1 Melnychenko claimed to have acted on his own, which has been doubted. He sought asylum in the US after the revelation of the tapes. Only a part of the tapes has been actually transcribed. Wilson (2005b), 52. See also http://www.orangeukraine.squarespace.com/journal/2005/3/15/those-damn-melnychenko-tapes.html [accessed: February 4, 2006.]

2 See also Karatnycky (2001).

3 For example, Kuchma received millions in contributions for his 1999 re-election campaign from leading oligarchs. Wilson (2005b), 57.

4 "Kuchma says no crisis in Ukraine," *RFE/RL Newsline,* part II, February 20, 2001.

5 "Ukrainian Deputy Premier indicated for gas smuggling, tax evasion" *RFE/RL Newsline,* part II, January 16, 2001.

6 "Ukrainian anti-presidential opposition demands Tymoshenko's release," *RFE/RL Newsline*, part II, February 15, 2001.

7 "Yushchenko Advises his Successor to Pursue an Open and Honest Policy," *Interfax, Ukraine Business Report*, April 26, 2001.

8 Kinakh had been head of the committee for industrial policy (07/1998-02/2000); vice-prime minister for industrial policy (07/1995-09/1996); and vice-prime minister of Ukraine (08-12/1999).

9 "President's people, not ministers, to run ministries," *Kyiv Post*, June 1, 2001.

10 "Yushchenko initiates pro-reform election bloc," *RFE/RL Newsline,* part II, July 24, 2001. The smaller parties participating in the NSF were the Fatherland Party (*Batkivshchyna*), the Sobor Party, the Social-Democratic Party, the Republican Party, the Conservative Republican Party, and the Republican Party.

11 "Yushchenko eyeing centre," *Jamestown Monitor*, September 28, 2001 Monitor, Volume VII, Issue 178.

12 Wilson (2001).

13 "United Ukraine Faction to Become Inter-Faction Union," *Ukraine Today*, June 17, 2002. The 'For a United Ukraine' Faction split into 8 separate groups, while the SDPU (o) formed the 9th pro-presidential faction.

14 *RFE/RL Poland, Belarus, and Ukraine Report*, June 12, 2002.

15 Taras Kuzio, "Is Kuchma genuine in his political reform?" *RFE/RL Poland, Belarus, and Ukraine Report*, September 3, 2002.

16 Kutuev (2003). Yanukovych had served two prison terms in his youth in the late 1960s to early 1970s, for theft and for violence. Taras Kuzio, "Who Really Wears Pampers in Ukrainian Politics?" *Ukrains'ka pravda*, June 25, 2004.

17 See *RFE/RL Poland, Belarus, and Ukraine Report*, June 18, 2002.

18 "Ukraine's Constitutional Court Rules President Leonid Kuchma Can Run For a Third Term," *Associated Press*, December 30, 2003.

19 Matsuzato (2005), 56.

20 Taras Kuzio, "Will contradictions undermine Viktor Yanukovych's election campaign?" *Eurasia Daily Monitor*, July 8, 2004. Taras Kuzio, "Ukraine's pro-presidential parliamentary majority disintegrates," *Eurasia Daily Monitor*, September 13, 2004. Wilson (2005b), 79-81.

21 "Ukraine's Tipping Point", *Washington Post*, March 1, 2004; "Mykola Ryabchuk Discusses Paradoxes of the Post-Soviet Transition in Ukraine" 38th Annual Shevchenko Lecture, April 7, 2004.

22 Taras Kuzio, "Poll Numbers Show Yanukovych Closing the Gap", *Eurasia Daily Monitor*, May 11, 2004 (from UKL 234).

23 Taras Kuzio, "Former Security Chief reveals details about violence during Ukrainian presidential election" *Eurasia Daily Monitor*, Jamestown, June 1, 2005.

24 See International Election Observation Mission, Presidential Election, Ukraine - October 31, 2004, Statement of preliminary findings an conclusions, OSCE/ODIHR, http://www.osce.org/documents/odihr/2004/11/3771_en.pdf. [accessed: April 2, 2205]

25 Vladimir Paniotto, "Even if the Turnout was Such, as Announced by the Central Electoral Commission ...," UKL 270, November 23, 2004.

26 OSCE, International Election Observation Mission, "Presidential Election (Second Round), Ukraine - 21 November 2004," November 22, 2004; http://www.osce.org/documents/odihr/2004/11/3811_en.pdf. [accessed: April 2, 2205]

27 The earlier date would have been effective, if direct elections for local leaders had been in place by then. See Wilson (2005b), 151.

28 The strongest opposition came from the communists of whom 56 deputies abstained. UKL 338, item 4, list complied by Dominque Ariel.

29 "What did Kirpa die for—stealing millions or stealing votes?" *Ukrains'ka pravda*, December 28, 2004. Possibly, this also involved funds which had been granted by the EBRD for the renovation of railways.

30 "Former Minister's death hampers investigation into Gongadze murder," *Jamestown Monitor*, March 7, 2005.

31 Oleksandr Sviridenko, "The Constitutional Court Agreed to Increase Power of Institutions of Local Self-Administration," *Kommersant Ukraina*, September 14, 2005; Roman Olearchyk, "President slams Tymoshenko; seeks delay of constitutional reforms," *Kyiv Post*, September 14, 2005.

32 The program is available in English at http://www.kmu.gov.ua/control/en/publish/article?art_id=15998559&cat_id=15998458 [accessed: August 23, 2005].

33 Program of Tymoshenko's Government; http://www2.pravda. com.ua/archive/2005/february/3/programma.shtm [accessed: August 15, 2005]

34 The Ukrainian-Russian gas deals had traditionally relied on a mix of cash and barter payments. Russia used the Orange Revolution to increase gas prices for Ukraine; a deal on which was only reached in early 2006 after a brief 'gas war.' See "Russia/Ukraine: Does Gas Deal Signal 'Victory For Common Sense'?" *RFE/RL Newsline*, January 4, 2006.

35 EBRD, *Transition Report Update*, May 2005, 13–17.

36 World Bank, *Country Assistance Strategy Progress Report for Ukraine*, May 19, 2005.

37 Regarding these reforms, the government received also external advice from a "Blue Ribbons Commission" headed by Anders Aslund and supported by UNDP. See www.carnegieendowment.org.

38 Pensions had been sharply increased in September 2004. "Yanukovych Catching Up with Yushchenko in Presidential Race-Poll" *UNIAN*, October 6, 2004.

39 "Ukrainian Prime Minister Says Fuel Crisis is nearly over," *RFE/RL Newsline*, April 25, 2005.

40 Taras Kuzio, "Washington Concerned Ukraine May not Join WTO this Year," *Eurasia Daily Monitor*, June 15, 2005.

41 "Kiev falters in bid to reopen dubious sell-offs," *Financial Times*, May 10, 2005. See also "Yushchenko's Problems," by Elena Zvereva, *Moskovskii Komsomolets*, March 16, 2005.

42 "Ukraine set to drop Barter Trade," *International Herald Tribune*, April 11, 2005.

43 "Russia/Ukraine: Does Gas Deal Signal 'Victory for Common Sense'?" *RFE/RL Newsline*, January 4, 2006.

44 Wilson (2005b), 73–76.

45 See Taras Kuzio, "Ukrainian Authorities Target Student and Youth Election-Monitoring Groups," *Eurasia Daily Monitor*, October 13, 2004. More than 37,000 NGOs were officially registered in 2004. See *Nations in Transit*, 2005, Ukraine. While tens of thousands of NGOs were officially registered in Ukraine, the number of active NGOs and especially the number of NGOs active around political and policy issues was much smaller.

46 Tymoshenko was accused of siding with the 'Privat' group, a major Ukrainian conglomerate based in Dnipropetrovsk and active in steel and chemicals, against Pinchuk, the son-in-law of Kuchma, and main owner of the 'Interpipe' conglomerate.

47 Taras Kuzio, "Yekhanurov refers to oligarchs as 'national bourgeoisie'," *Eurasia Daily Monitor, Jamestown Monitor,* October 28, 2005.

48 Akhmetov is the owner of a holding company called Capital System Management. Large holding companies with diverse business interests are typical of oligarchic groups in post-

Soviet countries. Serhii Harmas, "The Party of Regions is Changing its Face," *Ukrains'ka pravda*, December 1, 2005.

49 Jan Maksymiuk, "Parties get down to crucial election campaign," *RFE/RL Belarus, Ukraine, and Moldova Report*, December 16, 2005.

50 In 2005, Ukraine was rated at B1 by Moody's and BB- by Standard and Poor's. This compares to a rating of Caa1 by Moody in early 2000, and at B2 in early 2002 (i.e., B1 is 3 grades above Caa1).

51 http://www.state.gov/p/eur/rls/fs/36503.htm [accessed: February 1, 2006].

52 http://www.globalsecurity.org/military/world/ukraine/election-2004-w.htm [accessed: February 1, 2006].

53 Wilson (2005), 85.

54 Aslund, "Economic Policy" (2005), reports based on sources from the Yushchenko camp that Yanukovych claimed to spend 600 million USD.

55 Similarly, overt Russian attempts at influencing the election outcome also backfired in spring 2005 in Moldova.

56 For example, UNDP set up a 'Blue Ribbon Commission' to advice on further economic reforms. See http://un.org.ua/brc/report_e/brcreport040305eng.pdf. [accessed: August 12, 2005]

57 Wolzcuk (2003).

58 Jan Maksymiuk, "Ukraine: Kyiv, Moscow vie for WTO entry," *RFE/RL Newsline*, November 3, 2005.

59 ICPS, "Political Commentary," August 2003, 8.

60 IMF, Country Report no. 05/415, Ex-Post Assessment of longer-term program engagement, 19.

61 IER, "VAT replacement," June 2004. Total tax revenue in 2003 amounted to 76 billion UAH.

62 Roman Olearchyk, "State Tax Administration Targets Opposition," *Kyiv Post*, 19 February 2004. This issue was pursued further by the new 'Orange' government in 2005: "Ukrainian President reveals illegal VAT refunds [...]," *RFE/RL Newsline*, June 16, 2005. It claimed that up to US $650m had been paid out in illegal VAT refunds by the government in 2004.

63 Aleksandra Nenadovic, "Economic Analysts Comment on the Future in Ukraine," *FirsTnews*, Kyiv, Ukraine, April 20, 2005.

64 IERPC, *Macroeconomic Forecast*, May 2005.

65 "Anatoliy Kinakh: 'I am not Satisfied with the Assessment that the Cabinet Made of itself.'" *Zerkalo Nedeli*, August 13, 2005.

66 IERPC, *Monthly Economic Monitor*, Ukraine, May and October 2005.

67 Ukrainian Ministry of Finance, "Monitoring of the fulfillment of the consolidated budget of Ukraine for January-September 2005," October 10, 2005.

68 Fred Weir, "Corruption's Grip Eases in Ukraine," *The Christian Science Monitor*, November 29, 2005.

69 IERPC, *Monthly Economic Monitor*, August 2005. Speech by President Viktor Yushchenko, UT1, Kyiv, September 20, 2005, BBC Monitoring Service.

70 IERPC, *Monthly Economic Monitor*, December 2005.

71 "Yushchenko promises to propose a new fiscal policy within 3 months," *Podrobnosti*, October 6, 2005.

72 "Yatsenyuk proposes the introduction of a moratorium on tax changes in 2006," *Podrobnosti*, October 22, 2006.

73 IMF, *ROSC Fiscal Transparency Module*, 2004 (Country Report 04/98), 29.

74 See Chamber judgments concerning France, Moldova, Portugal, Turkey and the Ukraine, October 18, 2005, http://www.echr.coe.int/Eng/Press/2005/Oct/ChamberJudgments181005.htm, [accessed: April 23, 2005].

75 http://www.ukrweekly.com/Archive/2004/290401.shtml, "Yushchenko introduces his platform," [accessed: August 22, 2005].

76 "Ukraine revenue up as tax dodging falls, Premier says," *Bloomberg*, August 19, 2005.

77 "Tax police to be liquidated in Ukraine," *Ukraine Now*, November 19, 2005.

78 "The STA on the doorstep of tax reform," *Forum*, January 31, 2006.

79 E.g. 200 out of 3000 tax officers in Donetsk oblast were dismissed.

80 "The Viktor and Yulia show," *Economist*, June 16, 2005.

81 "The results of work of organs of state tax service for seven months 2005," www.sta.gov.uk [accessed: October 20, 2005]. "Will there be mass dismissals at the STA?" *Forum*, January 31, 2006.

82 "Fishy biznes," *Kyiv Post*, July 14, 2005,

83 "Ukrainian Police Search Tycoon's Offices," http://blog.kievukraine.info/2005_08_01_kievukrainenewsblog_archive.html. [accessed: August 25, 2005]

84 Maria Vyshnya, "Reasons for Tax Arrears Accumulation in Ukraine," 2004; http://www.eerc.kiev.ua/eroc/anconference/mvyshnya.pdf. [accessed: April 14, 2005]

85 "Ukrainian Parliament Adopts Budget Code in New Wording," *Interfax, Ukraine Business Report*, June 22, 2001.

86 Interview, Leonid Kosakivskiy, former mayor of Kiev (07/1995-07/1996), at the time of the interview member of the parliamentary budget committee, December 15, 2000.

87 See for example, "Matviychuk believes in a Realistic Budget," *EED*, November 23, 2000.

88 The Code is available at http://www1.worldbank.org/publicsector/pe/BudgetLaws/Ukraine%20Budget%20Code%20_2001_.pdf. [accessed: May 23, 2003]

89 "Meet the first-born! The Budget Code about which they had talked for so long, thanks to the 'bolsheviki' [...] was adopted," *Zerkalo Nedeli*, March 24-30, 2001.

90 Before signing the Code, the president successfully demanded several changes in the code from parliament. See "Ukrainian Parliament Adopts Budget Code in New Wording," *Ukraine Business Report*, June 22, 2001.

91 IMF, *ROSC: Fiscal Transparency Module*, Country Report 04/98, 2004.

92 "Budget Politicization Grows," *Den'*, December 4, 2001.

93 "Kuchma taps new finance chief," http://www.ukrweekly.com/Archive/2002/010201.shtml [accessed: May 2, 2003]

94 *One Plus One TV*, Kiev (in Ukrainian) December 20, 2001.

95 FAO, *Budget and Fiscal Review,* March 2002, 3.

96 "2003: The Year in Review," http://www.ukrweekly.com/Archive/2004/020414.shtml. [accessed: February 13, 2004]

97 "Amid uproar, *Verkhovna Rada* passes controversial budget," http://www.ukrweekly.com/Archive/2003/490301.shtml. [accessed: February 13, 2004]

98 Taras Lanovyk, "Budget is coming soon," *KINTO Research Weekly*, September 8-12, 2003.

99 "Ukraine: Yushchenko Comments on Amending Constitution, Budget Approval," January 5, 2004 *UKRAYINA MOLODA* (via FBIS).

100 Cabinet of Ministers resolution no. 1215, September 18, 2004, On Improving Pension Provision Level, see: http://www.pension.kiev.ua/eng/Law_Base/ [accessed: March 7, 2006].

101 Roman Kupchinsky, "Ukraine government attempts to get grip on corruption," *RFE/RL Newsline*, June 14, 2005

102 "Bakai Fled Ukraine, Yushchenko's Supporters did not Go to Kirpa," *Ukrains'ka pravda,* December 28, 2004. http://www2.pravda.com.ua/archive/2004/december/28/news/21.shtml. [accessed: April 2, 2005]

103 The department was headed by Ihor Bakai, the former head of Naftohaz Ukrayiny, who acquired Russian citizenship and fled to Moscow during the Orange Revolution.

104 "Ukraine: Pre-election policies raise inflation risk," *Oxford Analytica*, October 13, 2004.

105 The latter expenditure was also motivated by Ukraine's demographic situation of declining birth rates.

106 *Ukrainian News Agency*, Kyiv, Ukraine, April 26, 2005.

107 Aslund (2005); see also IMF, "Ukraine—2005 Article IV Consultation Preliminary Conclusions of the Mission," August 2, 2005.

108 IMF, "ROSC, Fiscal Transparency Module, 2004" (Country Report 04/98).

109 "Update: Kuchma Directs Cabinet to Improve State Treasury's Services," *UNIAN*, December 7, 2002.

110 See "The DRKS on the way of reconstruction," May 25, 2005, http://www.dkrs.gov.ua/control/uk/publish/article?art_id=34477&cat_id=32243 [accessed: October 20, 2005].

111 EU-Ukraine Action Plan, adopted in February 2005 (www.kmu.gov.ua).

112 Under a new Law on Intelligence Agencies of Ukraine, adopted in March 2001. For an English translation, see "Ukraine: Text of law on intelligence services," *BBC Monitor,* April 19, 2001.

113 "Parliament Grants Accounting Chamber the Right to Control Incomes to the State Budget," *UNIAN*, January 18, 2002.

114 "Kuchma Vetoes Law that Authorizes Accounting Chamber to Control State Budget Revenues," *UNIAN*, February 8, 2002.

115 See also UNDP, "Integrity in Action: Governance Programme," no date, www.undp.org.ua. [accessed: April 2, 2005]

116 "*Verkhovna Rada* Chairman Believes Society should be Consolidated," *Ukrinform*, January 6, 2006.

117 Christopher Walker, "Waiting for the Next Tipping Point in the Former Soviet Union," *The Globe and Mail*, June 3, 2005.

118 This assessment is also based on discussions with Sergiy Kulyk, Country Program Coordinator for Belarus, Moldova, and Ukraine, World Bank, Washington DC, August 20, 2005.

119 Discussion with Oleksandr Fisun, Associate Professor at Kharkiv National University, at a panel of the American Political Science Association Annual meeting, Washington DC, September 3, 2005.

CHAPTER 9.
AVERTING INSTITUTIONAL CHANGE: THE CASE OF BELARUS

Belarus has come to be called a 'museum' of the Soviet system. It is one of the post-Soviet countries that has experienced the least degree of change. The economic structure based on commands from above and embedded in a state-set framework rather than market interaction has been preserved. A key factor for this peculiar pathway has been the weakness of a (national) opposition movement during the process towards independence. Due to this, no coherent counter-elite emerged in Belarus, and elite turnover remained minimal.[1] The one important change that has occurred is that from a party-run authoritarian system to one based on personal rule by Aliaksandar Lukashenka.[2]

Belarus poses a puzzle to many observers, in particular to those of neo-liberal instincts, because it has been economically rather successful compared to other countries in the region.[3] Regarding average growth rates in the region from 1992 to 2001, Belarus was third after Estonia and Uzbekistan—the latter being another consolidated autocracy-cum-command economy.[4] In the early 2000s when stronger growth set in across the CIS region, Belarus followed the general trend, thus showing no obvious sign of falling behind.

Furthermore, Belarus' fiscal system was relatively robust and capable, generating the highest levels of revenue of any CIS country. In the political sphere, there was substantial consolidation—within the parameters of an authoritarian regime. It has been based on the goals of preserving the old system, and—at least during periods of this state-building process—of re-integration with Russia. The preservation of the old order has important implications: it was a relatively painless way of preserving substantial state capacity, because in this way Belarus was able to avoid some of the high costs associated with large-scale change (see Chapter 3, section 2).

At the same time, there are several serious problems. Firstly, the authoritarian regime has committed a number of human rights abuses—which are believed to have included the killing of several opposition politicians. Secondly, the economic policies of president Lukashenka have often been eccentric. This has added to the general problem of sustaining a Soviet-style system in a rapidly changing external environment. Also, the relatively strong state may be over-extracting from the economy. Finally, the goal of re-integration with Russia has brought external disturbances to the Belarusian path: the Russian leadership under Putin has been rather wary of the idea of a union state and demanded 'submission' rather than the integration of equals from Belarus. Finally, Russia had already changed its state and economic system to such a degree that there was little 'fit' with the neo-Soviet Belarusian model. Possibly, however, Belarus' relatively capable state would eventually also allow a successful transformation of the state's role.

The lack of a Belarusian 'national identity' is widely regarded as a cause of Belarus' path, which is unusual at least among the Western parts of the former Soviet Union.[5] This lack of national identity is held to account both for Belarus' pro-Russian orientation, and for society's acceptance of an authoritarian regime which continues the communist 'social contract' (obedience and acquiescence for stability and social security).

9.1. Political developments: from liberalization to autocracy

During the late 1980s and the break-up of the USSR, Belarus was among the most conservative republics.[6] This conservatism was based on a relatively well-functioning Soviet system: rates of investment and economic growth were high, corruption more limited than elsewhere in the Union, and the political leadership rather popular.[7] Moreover, a Belarusian national identity was weak.[8] Accordingly, the early opposition movement was even weaker than in Ukraine: in the first multi-candidate elections in March 1990, the Belarusian Popular Front (BPF) won only 7.5 per cent of the mandates.[9] As a consequence, the ruling elite did not "find it expedient or necessary to co-opt the national-democratic agenda of their opponents."[10]

In subsequent years the turnover of political elites remained minimal. The parliament elected in 1990 stayed in session until the end of 1995 and was the last to be replaced in the entire post-communist region; while the government continued to be led by Vyacheslau Kebich, a former head of the Belarusian *Gosplan*, the former planning ministry. The most reformist politician in power was Stanislau Shushkevich, a physicist and former *prorektor* at the Belarusian State University, who was elected parliamentary chairman in September

1991.[11] However, he was removed from power in early 1994 by a vote of non-confidence in the Supreme Soviet, after accusations of corruption by a special commission headed by then parliamentary deputy Lukashenka.[12]

Following Shushkevich's ouster, a constitution providing for a strong presidency was quickly adopted. Presidential elections were held in June–July 1994. In these elections, which were internationally judged as free and fair, Lukashenka won 45 per cent of the votes in the first round (other candidates: Kebich, 17 per cent; Pazniak (BPF), 13 per cent; and Shushkevich, 10 per cent). In the second round—after accusing Kebich of corruption—Lukashenka finally won with an overwhelming 80 per cent of the vote.

After his ascendancy to power, Lukashenka did not rely on the Communist Party, which up to then had been the most potent organized political force in Belarus. Rather, the former *Kolkhoz* director adopted a personalistic style of rule based on popular appeal.[13] To this end he created strong 'presidential verticals' with direct power over various administrative structures and the regions.[14] This included strong direct presidential control over public finances (see below).

The 1995 parliamentary elections—stretching from May to December—resulted in a deep crisis of the parliamentary branch of power. In the first two rounds many seats could not be filled due to the complex voting system.[15] Finally, in the third and fourth rounds sufficient additional seats could be filled to allow the legal formation of a parliament dominated by leftist-communist forces (and without any oppositional BPF members).

In spite of its rather pro-presidential composition, the president chose to disband parliament in the wake of a referendum he initiated in 1996. This constitutional referendum extended the president's term in office from five to seven years and introduced a two-chamber parliament. The 110-member lower house (House of Representatives) was filled with a selection of deputies of the Supreme Soviet as elected in the previous year, while the 64-member upper house (Council of the Republic) was created as having 56 members elected by regional *soviets* and 8 members appointed by the president.[16]

New elections to the lower house of parliament and presidential elections were held in October 2000 and September 2001 respectively. Both votes were judged to have been unfair by the international community. In the presidential elections, the main opposition candidate was Uladzimir Hancharyk, head of the Trade Union Federation.[17]

After the presidential elections, Lukashenka continued to strengthen his direct control over all spheres of government and the economy. According to an opposition newspaper, "[t]he new Council of Ministers and the prime minister possess the same degree of independence as the puppets on NTV [a political puppet show on Russian TV ...]. The president carries out practically the whole staff policy, makes decisions on establishing ministries and committees, may grant the status of a legal entity to a department in any ministry."[18]

In October 2004, parliamentary elections were held in combination with a referendum on permitting Lukashenka to stand for a third term. According to official results of the referendum, 80 per cent of voters opted for the change; while according to independent estimates, slightly less than 50 per cent approved it. In the parliamentary elections, not a single opposition candidate was successful. Out of a total of 692 applicants, district election committees registered only 359 candidates; while those opposition candidates able to register experienced various interferences from the authorities to limit their campaigning.[19] Street protests against the official election results on October 19 were suppressed with police force. Generally, the Belarusian parliament as well as political parties have been deprived of almost all political weight (see also section 4.2 below). Presidential decrees have the force of law.[20]

The next presidential elections—in which Lukashenka will be able to stand for a third term—were scheduled for September 2006. Lukashenka and his government became increasingly nervous due to the specter of the recent 'color revolutions' which occurred in Georgia, Kyrgyzstan, and neighboring Ukraine; and were resorting to increasing oppression. At the same time, the opposition continued to be weak and divided—not least as a result of years of oppression. Opposition parties failed to unite behind a strong candidate in time in 2001.[21] In 2005, several potential opposition candidates were put into prison on various fabricated charges.[22]

President Lukashenka became an outlaw on the international scene (except in Russia, which supported his re-election), but he still appeared to enjoy substantial popular support at home.[23] Partly, this has been based on economic and especially social policies, in particular the ability to pay 'living' pensions and wages on time, in contrast to Russia and Ukraine. "Pensioners account for a large percentage of the population and are Lukashenka's bedrock of support. There are few problems with pension arrears, unlike in Russia or until recently in Ukraine, and the value of pensions has been maintained."[24]

While human rights abuses in Belarus sparked official condemnation in Europe and in the US, neither have developed effective policies to influence the situation in Belarus.[25] Restrictions on collaboration with NGOs have limited their main mode of operation.[26] At the same time, Belarus is not a country of intense interest to main Western actors, since no significant threats emanate from it, and since it does not have the significance of Ukraine in ensuring that there is no return to a Russian empire. Poland and Lithuania have sought to raise engagement with regard to Belarus in the EU; however, the anti-Russian stance which is a *leitmotif* of Poland's foreign policy in particular is at a dissonance with the still strong pro-Russian leanings among the Belarusian public.

Table 9.1: Belarus prime ministers, ministers of finance, and heads of the state control committee, 1990–2005

Prime ministers	04/1990–07/1994	Vyacheslau Kebich
	07/1994–11/1996	Mikhail Chyhir
	11/1996–02/2000	Syarhey Linh
	02/2000–10/2001	Uladzimir Yarmoshyn
	10/2001–12/2003	Henadz Navitski
	12/2003–	Syarhey Sidorsky
Ministers of finance	12/1994–01/1997	Paval Dik
	01/1997–07/1997	Mikalai Rumas (acting)
	07/1997–09/2001	Mikalai Korbut
	09/2001–	Mikalai Korbut (re-appointed)
Heads of the State Control Committee	12/1996–12/1998	Mikalai Domashkevich
	12/1998–07/2000	Andrei Kobiakov
	07/2000–	Anatol Tozik

9.2. Economic developments: preserving the command economy

Economic preconditions in Belarus were relatively better than in most other parts of the former Soviet Union at independence. The country had become highly industrialized after WWII with some diversification of production (metallurgy, chemical, food and electronics industries, car manufacturing).[27] Transport distances to Central Eastern and Western Europe are relatively short, and the population is highly educated and urbanized.[28] Like other post-Soviet countries, Belarus is dependent on Russian energy imports and its markets were predominantly in other Soviet republics, while its goods were uncompetitive on Western markets at the outset of independence.[29]

Some reforms of the economy were introduced in the early 1990s, albeit at an even slower pace than in Ukraine. Government intervention in the economy, including subsidies, remained prevalent. As the EIU noted in 1993: "Precisely because of its timid approach to market reforms, Belarus came through the tumultuous changes of 1992 in apparently better shape than some of its neighbors."[30] While GDP fell by more than 20 per cent in Lithuania in 1992, the fall was less than 10 per cent in Belarus (see Appendix, Table I.1.2).

Communist ideology and resistance to privatization was strong from the beginning. Nevertheless, some standard institutional reforms were initially undertaken: the creation of a two-tier banking system, some price liberalization, and limited privatization.[31] This gradual transformation was terminated when Lukashenka came to power. He instead began to rebuild a neo-Soviet economic system with a strong personalistic component. The president renationalized partially privatized banks and brought the Central Bank under his control (formally under the Council of Ministers).[32] This allowed the channeling of large credits to the construction and agricultural sectors, as under the Soviet system.

The agricultural sector in particular was preserved in its Soviet form. There is no private ownership of land. Prices especially for agricultural goods have been administratively fixed again since 1997.[33] However, due to continued large subsidies and the quasi-fiscal use of monetary policy—made possible by the Central Bank's dependence—inflation re-emerged as a major problem in the late 1990s, and Belarus recorded the highest levels of inflation in the CIS region for some years. However, inflation was brought back under control from 2001 onwards (see Appendix, Table I.1.3).

Savchenko, in a comparison of economic reform policies in the Baltics and Belarus, proposes an interesting argument: in the Baltics in the initial independence period, the influence of the industrial sector (of both managers and workers) on economic policies was weakened by the fact that these sectors were dominated by the Russian minority, while the central government was dominated by nationally-minded politicians.[34] In Belarus, by contrast, a considerable part of the legislators elected in 1990 were industrial managers, and they continued to have a strong and close relationship with the executive after independence. This greatly increased their potential to resist reforms.

Especially in the early 1990s, economic and political elites in Belarus must furthermore have felt vindicated in their policies by unfolding events as output was falling more rapidly in the Baltic states than in their own country. Thus, in 1994, prime minister Kebich stressed: "We managed to stem the reformist euphoria. Thanks to this, our people were not hungry, had their homes heated in the winter, produced goods, tilled the soil."[35]

The Belarusian economy remained rather successful by regional standards, officially boasting the highest growth rates of all post-Soviet countries in 1997 and 1998 (see Appendix, Table I.1.2). This has puzzled outside observers who generally saw economic reforms as the only road to success.[36] Partially, the success has been attributed to Russian subsidies (favorable terms of trade and energy credits). These subsidies have variously been estimated at US $500 million to US $1.5 billion per annum which would be equivalent to 4 to 11 per cent of the GDP.[37] The extent of subsidies decreased since the Russian crisis of 1998.[38] The loans Russia granted to Belarus were relatively small (less than US $100 million per loan).[39] In terms of gas subsidies, in 2000, Belarus paid $30 to Russian suppliers per 1000 cubic meters of gas (in general, the same price as in the neighboring Russian region), while Ukraine paid $50 and Lithuania $76, and world prices ranged between $90 and $100.[40] However, this means primarily, that Belarusian producers enjoyed the same advantageous energy prices as those in Russia. Also, the actual difference in energy prices between Ukraine and Belarus was smaller than these figures suggest, because Ukraine received around 40 per cent of its gas deliveries in fees for gas transit—a benefit it inherited from the Soviet Union. Both Belarus and Ukraine have frequently engaged in non-payments, delayed payments, and payment in barter for gas deliveries from Russia. Thus, even taking Russian subsidies to Belarus into account, the advantage of non-reform still remains an important explanatory factor. By largely preserving the old economic order, Belarus appears to have avoided considerable costs of 'disorganization' and 'reorganization.'[41]

As a result of preserving the old economic order, and in contrast to Ukraine and Russia, no strong 'oligarchs' emerged in Belarus. This has been reinforced by Lukashenka's strategy to intermittently cut down any potential alternative leaders. In 1999, Vasil Liavonau, then minister of agriculture, and Vasil Staravoitau, a prominent *Sovkhoz* director, were arrested on corruption charges. In December 2001 and January 2002, further arrests of members of the old economic elite followed. Among those arrested were Mikhail Liavonau, head of the Minsk Tractor Plant, and Leanid Kaluhin, director of the "Atlant" refrigerator plant. Both companies are flagships of the Belarusian economy.[42] Personal enrichment and tax evasion formed part of the charges brought against those arrested. The true reason behind the arrests, however, appears to be that both managers had developed some ties to the opposition and had considered running for the presidency in the fall of 2001.[43]

Moreover, due to the minimal privatization, a major precondition for the emergence of oligarchic groups was absent. By 2004, only 25 per cent of the economy had been privatized.[44] At the same time, economic policy making in Belarus rather closely resembled the Soviet pattern of a command economy.

Thus, the president decrees GDP growth, rises in the harvest and in industrial production, higher revenue collection, higher spending, a lower tax burden, a low deficit and a lowering of inflation, without mentioning how these (potentially conflicting) goals are to be aggregated and achieved.

The challenge facing such an economic system is how to achieve investments and technological modernization. In the early 2000s, strong growth in Belarus was facilitated by the revival of the CIS economies, and by strong demand from Russia.[45] Unusual for an energy-importing country, Belarus overall benefited from high oil prices, since it has large refinery capacities (at Polatsk and Mozir) and due to continued Russian energy subsidies.[46] Chemicals and fertilizer production are the strong sectors of the economy. Belarus has also substantial machine building and light industries (refrigerators, TV sets, etc.). Avoiding privatization, Belarus has thus far received relatively little foreign direct investment either from Western or Russian sources.

Belarus remained rather insulated from pressures from the international financial community. World Bank and IMF programs were suspended in 1995 when Lukashenka began to reverse the previous course of gradual reforms.[47] In 1998, Belarus restarted its contacts with the IMF. While initially hoping for new loans, the regime apparently never found it sufficiently worthwhile to change its economic policies fundamentally enough to persuade the IMF to open its purse. In 2001, a six-month monitoring program was agreed, at the end of which the IMF refused to grant any new loans. The World Bank eventually committed new loans to Belarus in 2001 after its minimum condition, a unified exchange rate, had been fulfilled. Thus, due to the absence of major programs, as well as rather low debt these Western institutions had virtually no leverage influencing the policy and institutional choices in Belarus.

As mentioned in section 1 above, there is a particular social contract in Belarus—which is absent from the other consolidated autocratic regimes in the former Soviet Union—and that is the emphasis on economic benefits for the population at large. Belarus has the lowest level of inequality among the CIS countries, and poverty is almost absent. Growth has been used to finance wage increases.[48] Especially in recent reports (2005), both the World Bank and the IMF have stressed these features of the Belarusian economy.

The sustainability of Belarus' political and economic system has repeatedly been called into question.[49] Given Belarus' geographic location and the influences and pressures resulting from it, change will be unavoidable at some point. However, the puzzle is when and how this happens. Changes in the relationship with Russia could be a trigger; but especially in the face of "color revolutions" in several CIS countries, change in Belarus has not been in Russia's interest. More inadvertently, growing Russian attempts to acquire parts of Belarus' economy could set off a greater orientation of the political leadership towards the West. While elections have led to mobilization and change in several other CIS countries, this is a more difficult potential route in Belarus, due to greater oppression, and a very weak opposition.

Table 9.2: Income and poverty in Belarus and neighboring countries

	GNI per capita 2003, in US $	GNI in PPP 2003, in US $	Life expectancy in 2002	Gini index*	Population below 2$ per day in %*
Belarus	1590	6010	68	30.4	<2
Ukraine	970	5410	68	29.0	45.7
Russia	2610	8920	66	45.6	23.8
Poland	5270	11450	74	31.6	<2
Lithuania	4490	11090	73	31.9	13.7

* Data for Belarus, Russia and Lithuania from 2000, for Ukraine and Poland from 1999.

Source: World Development Report, 2005.

9.3. Belarus' international situation

A particular feature of Belarus' state-building process was the declared intention of the government to forgo independent statehood and to form a union state with Russia. However, despite relying heavily on Russia, the Lukashenka government has nonetheless also pursued Belarusian national interests. In the early 2000s it became increasingly uncertain whether and how integration would be realized given that several deadlines for taking concrete steps towards such a union passed without progress. In 2002, President Putin suggested that Russia should absorb Belarus as one or several regions. Such a complete dissolution of Belarus went clearly beyond the intentions of Belarusian elites. Still, plans for integration, including monetary union and the drafting of a common constitution continued in 2005.

Russia, in turn, pursued a combination of political and economic interests: on the one hand, Belarus has been an important political ally and as such has received Russian subsidies. On the other hand, Russian business sought to take over economic assets in Belarus,[50] which the Belarusian government resisted, even to the point of risking a minor 'gas-war' which resulted in Russia briefly turning off Belarusian gas supplies in 2004. Overall, while Belarus is an exceptional case in the wider Eastern European region in having declared its intention to give up full statehood, *de facto,* independence has continued and is likely to continue.

Influences from the West—from IFIs and from the EU—have been rather marginal in Belarus. The Belarusian government has by and large resisted IFI advice. Foreign debt levels have remained low (see Appendix, Tables II.1.1 and II.1.2). In early 2005, Belarus fully repaid its debts to the IMF.[51] While it has sought technical advice in specific areas from the IFIs, financially and economically Belarus has relied on Russia.

In sharp contrast to Lithuania, and even Ukraine, the EU has been relatively unimportant in Belarus. While the positive incentives of the EU can be very strong in connection with accession, its incentives and sanctioning levers outside the 'accession zone' appear quite limited. The EU has protested human rights abuses in Belarus and EU countries have imposed a travel ban on high-level officials.[52]

Nonetheless, Belarus is not cut off from the West with regard to economic linkages or personal travel. About half of Belarusian exports go to countries outside the CIS; and foreign direct investment was somewhat higher per capita than in Ukraine for most years.[53] Belarusians do not face exit restrictions on travel, and many visit or work in neighboring countries.

9.4. State-society relations in Belarus

9.4.1. TRUST AND EXPECTATIONS

Trust in various institutions is generally higher in Belarus than in Ukraine and Russia.[54] Probably, this is founded on a better day-to-day performance of Belarusian institutions. Bribery and corruption are much less perceived as having increased since Soviet times than in Ukraine. Also, far fewer Belarusians than Ukrainians have suffered from the non-payment of wages: in spring 2000, 5 per cent of respondents in Belarus had not received their salaries on time during the previous 12 months compared to 32 per cent of Ukrainians.[55] This trend of relatively higher trust in Belarus appears to have continued or even strengthened over time (see Chapter 10, Graph 10.3).[56]

With regard to socio-economic expectations of the state, Belarusians and Ukrainians are rather similar. After a decade of non-transition, Belarusians are even somewhat less opposed to private ownership of large enterprises or bankruptcy of inefficient ones (see Appendix, Table II.4.1).[57] Furthermore, according to findings by White and Rose, fewer Belarusians than Ukrainians had any preference for authoritarian alternatives.[58]

Thus, expectations of the state's role in the economy do not seem to have differed vastly in Ukraine and Belarus in the beginning. By the end of the first transition decade, Belarusians were in fact more supportive of markets than Ukrainians.

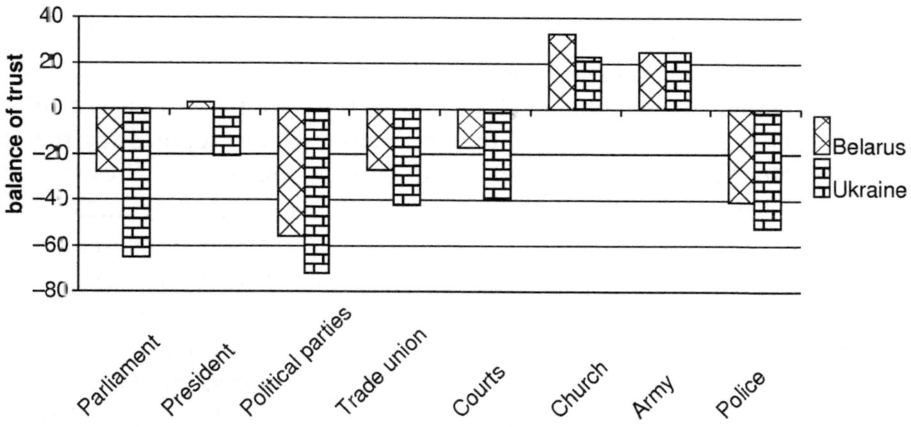

Graph 9.1: Trust in Belarus and Ukraine, 2000

9.4.2. INTERMEDIARY ORGANIZATIONS

Until about 1996, intermediary organizations (parties, trade unions, NGOs, in the wider sense, also independent media) could develop relatively freely in Belarus, although societal interest was not strong. About 1100 political and non-political organizations had registered by November 1996.[59]

However, after the authoritarian turn in Belarus from the mid-1990s onwards, intermediary organizations have been stalled in their development. Before 1997, 40 parties had emerged, while their number was reduced to 27 by January 2000 and to 17 in 2004. Membership in parties is very small, even the largest left-wing parties have only a few thousand members; and parties have been effectively marginalized in political life.[60] The more significant remaining parties are: pro-governmental—Agrarian Party, the Belarusian Communist Party, the Belarusian Patriotic Movement; opposition—Belarusian Popular

Front, the Belarusian Social-Democratic Party, the Liberal-Democratic Party of Belarus, and the United Civic Party.[61]

On January 26, 1999, President Lukashenka issued a decree ordering the re-registration of all political parties, trade unions, and other public associations. Many organizations chose not to apply while others were refused registration. At the same time, the regime started to create 'state-led' (N)GOs (youth organizations, business associations, etc.), similar to public associations existing in Soviet times.[62] In the fall of 1998, a "Belarusian Confederation of Entrepreneurs" (BCE) was set up. At its founding conference, President Lukashenka reminded those present not to think of meddling in politics, while at the same time promising support to producers.[63]

Financial audits (often conducted by the Security Council discussed in section 4.3 below) have been one of the key instruments in suppressing the activities of NGOs, in particular those with foreign financing.[64] Thus, the "Children-of-Chernobyl" organization underwent a six-month long audit in 1996.[65] In 1997, a US $3 million fine was imposed on the Soros Foundation for alleged tax evasion,[66] and in late 2000 the equipment of an independent publishing house—which had been leased from the Soros Foundation—was confiscated by the tax inspectorate (after a decision by the Supreme Economic Court).[67] Activities of foreign or foreign-supported NGOs were treated with increased suspicion since the 'revolution' in Ukraine in late 2004. The government started to target community based organizations of the Polish minority; while Poland became increasingly vocal about advocating support for regime change in Belarus, leading to a diplomatic tug-of-war in mid-2005.[68]

The most important traditional intermediary organization has been the Federation of Trade Unions of Belarus (FTUB), the successor of the communist-era umbrella organization. The FTUB claims a membership of 5 million.[69] To some extent, the lack of change in the economic structure has benefited trade unions in Belarus because it has preserved the state as a unified bargaining partner. Thus, the state and the FTUB have regularly negotiated wage deals, which have included such questions as wage indexation and income taxes.[70] Given the president's tendency to base his legitimacy on claims of protecting the people, and in particular industrial and agricultural workers, trade unions could not be disregarded.

While most commonly, trade unions have demanded higher pay or the payment of back wages,[71] their demands have also included the abolition of off-budgetary funds controlled by the presidential administration, and thus, increased fiscal transparency.[72] In September 2001, the trade union leader

Uladzimir Hancharyk stood as the main candidate of the opposition against Lukashenka. In retaliation, Lukashenka pressured the FTUB to oust Hancharyk—who eventually stepped down in early 2002 to avoid the complete destruction of the organization.[73] The government has continued in its efforts to ensure that the trade union is 'aligned' with the government and does not become an independent force.[74]

Among the most vocal parts of the population concerning taxation have been street vendors and miners—groups belonging to rather different spheres of the economy—i.e., small and private on the one hand, and large and state-owned on the other hand.[75] Both have protested against changes in taxation which threatened to worsen their respective situations. In 2000, street vendors complained about heavy fines for tax violations and high administrative pressure.[76] Lukashenka warned those striking not to voice any political demands, while at the same time meeting some of their economic demands—in the case of the street vendors, suspending fines on VAT miscalculations for half a year.[77] In early 2005, street vendors again protested, this time against the imposition of VAT payments on individual imports from Russia. In contrast to overtly political protests, the government reacted relatively responsively and promised to facilitate the procedures; the leader of the movement was, however, imprisoned for several weeks. Opposition politicians made promises of tax cuts in the run-up to the fall 2001 presidential elections. However, as these promises were combined with promises of hefty wage increases, they appeared by and large to be just as populist as those made by the incumbent.[78] Also, the opposition has criticized the lack of transparency of the entire fiscal system of Belarus.[79]

In line with a tendency to avoid changes in the economic system, Belarusian society remained structured in a rather Soviet way. Soviet-style trade unions have remained relevant as a negotiating partner for the state; and these trade unions formed part of the Soviet-post-Soviet continuity rather than of an opposition force such as 'Solidarity' in Poland. However, in recent years the relationship between the state and these intermediary organizations is becoming strained.[80] While society has remained more equal than in other CIS countries, it also remains rather atomized, without any strong intermediary organizations which would have some firm independence from the state. This is likely to pose a challenge once regime change eventually does take place since no alternative group of power holders is able to form—in contrast to Ukraine, where Yushchenko, Tymoshenko, and their associates were able to build a powerful opposition movement.

9.5. Fiscal policies

Belarus has preserved a state-managed economy with some alterations—including greater external openness (substantial trade with non-CIS countries), and a somewhat more arms-length relationship between ministries and the still state-owned enterprises. Associated with this system is a continued blurring of boundaries between the private and the government sector: the state still undertakes considerable quasi-fiscal activities by directing investments, and state-owned enterprises still maintain a social infrastructure (sanatoria, kindergartens, etc.).

The fiscal system is marked by considerable capacity in particular with regard to extraction and to an effective, top-down system of accounting and control. At the same time, the tax burden is very high relative to the level of per capita income. The executive and in particular the president can change fiscal policies at will (grant tax privileges, budget revisions); while parliament has a very minor role. Budget transparency is much more limited than in Ukraine, Russia, or Lithuania, although at least some budget data has become readily available.[81]

9.5.1. THE TAX SYSTEM

Belarus' extraction rates of above 40 per cent of GDP throughout the post-Soviet period are the highest of all countries in the region. Tax collection is highly efficient by post-Soviet standards, as shown in the study by Shaffer on statutory and effective tax rates.[82] Thus, while in 1997 the general VAT rate in Belarus, Russia, and Ukraine stood equally at 20 per cent, Belarus actually collected 9.4 per cent of GDP as VAT, Ukraine 8.1 and Russia 7.2.[83] Tax collection in Belarus appears even stronger when we consider that the country—together with Uzbekistan—has one of the smallest shadow economies in the region according to estimates by Schneider and Enste—meaning that the share of total economic activity actually covered by taxation is larger.[84]

This is not due to a better *formal* tax regime. As in Ukraine, individual tax rates and tax exemptions have changed frequently.[85] Special tax and customs privileges are enjoyed by enterprises controlled by the presidential administration, and the president grants tax privileges to specific firms.[86] As Belarus has preserved a planned economic system, actual tax payments have remained negotiable depending on the profitability of a firm or the need to preserve employment. Foreign investors were also affected by instability: for example, a major investment by Ford into a joint venture car manufacturing plant was granted an exemption from VAT payments for an 'indefinite period' in July 1997; however, after a complaint by Russia about unfair tax competition, the exemption ended three months later.[87] In line with the nature of Belarus' authoritarian regime, the president has decreed himself to be the only authority with the right to grant tax privileges on an individual basis.[88] Changes in tax rates and tax laws are likewise introduced by presidential decree.[89] In April 2002, Lukashenka issued a decree prohibiting tax and customs exemptions starting from January 2003—amounting to a decree against his own previous behavior.[90]

Taxes imposed at the local level have likewise been unstable. In 1997 the rights of local authorities to levy taxes were broadened. This led to a sudden substantial increase in local taxation. As a consequence, the national authorities decided to limit the rights of local authorities again in the following year.

The overall tax burden has been high. For example, Belarus imposed a 10 (later 7) per cent emergency tax on enterprises in addition to normal profit taxes to finance spending on the consequences of the Chernobyl disaster. In addition to basic taxes, there were numerous funds to which legal entities have to pay some 'contributions.'[91]

Marginal tax rates were lowered somewhat since the late 1990s—in agreement with the trend in other post-Soviet countries and especially in Russia. The top personal income tax rate was lowered from 50 to 30 per cent by presidential decree in 1999.[92] In July 1999, Lukashenka offered a 5 per cent flat rate tax, replacing all other types of taxes to (collective) farmers—one of his main support groups. The general profit tax rate (CIT) was reduced from 30 to 25 per cent in the same year.[93] However, when the revenue situation became strained, the government quickly re-imposed a 30 per cent rate. Then, in November 2001, the rate was lowered again from 30 to 24 per cent—bringing it in line with the rate change in Russia which had been adopted a few months earlier (see Chapter 11 below).[94] The VAT rate was lowered from 20 to 18 per cent. Furthermore, the government proclaimed a one-year moratorium on changes to tax legislation.[95]

Like elsewhere in the former Soviet Union, in his rhetoric the Belarusian president has begun to favor a lower tax burden.[96] However, this goal has often been contradicted by immediate revenue needs to finance state expenditure programs.[97] In 2003, an article by the Mises Center complained that promises of liberalizing the business environment had been a sham and that private business continued to suffer from a high tax burden.[98] In early 2004, the general part of a new tax code came into force which unified existing tax-related legislation.[99] In the same year, however, the government imposed tax targets on state-owned enterprises, specifying how much VAT and profit tax would have to be collected—and imposing personal responsibility on senior officials for meeting these.[100] While the tax burden remains high in Belarus, it did not develop excessive distortions as in Ukraine.[101]

A key explanation for the high level of tax collection is the continued system of economic control, including a state-controlled banking sector. This control system has been supplemented by societal controls encouraged by the authorities and draconian tax collection. The Belarusian tax administration is a separate ministry (the Ministry of Taxes and Levies).[102] Punishments for economic offences—which can be imposed by the State Control Committee (see below), the Ministry of Finance, tax and local authorities—are stiff.[103] A large number of companies are audited each year, and more than half of those audited are fined in some way or another. Thus, 70 per cent of audited enterprises and 60 per cent of private entrepreneurs audited in 1998 were found guilty of some violations of tax laws and were fined.[104] According to Belapan, "tax inspectors raided more than 40,000 companies or 42.4 per cent of the total number of registered companies, in the first nine months [of 2000]. Tax irregularities were discovered at 71.6 per cent of the companies inspected."[105]

Plans to create a union state with Russia had only a limited effect on the tax regime. In November 2001, Deputy Minister of the Economy, Andrei Tur, announced that the overall tax burden would be reduced by at least 5 to 6 per cent over five years, and that special budget and off-budget funds would be eliminated by 2005.[106] A unified tax code for the two countries was planned to be adopted as early as the end of 2002.[107] However, neither the significant reduction in the tax burden, nor the harmonization of the tax regime with Russia came to fruition.

9.5.2. BUDGET STRUCTURE, THE BUDGETING PROCESS AND EXPENDITURE POLICIES

The consolidated budget in Belarus is composed of the state budget and the Social Protection Fund (SPF). The state budget contains the republican (central) budget as well as regional/local budgets of 6 regions, the city of Minsk, 38 smaller cities and 141 districts (rayons).[108] There have been varying numbers of extra-budgetary funds, including a Chernobyl Fund, a Road Fund and a Fund for the Support of Agricultural Producers, to mention a few. In 1998, five of these special funds were integrated into the state budget; however, a number of "innovation funds" and other extra-budgetary funds remained.[109] Furthermore, there is a special 'presidential fund' which, however is apparently largely not financed via tax revenue, but rather with proceeds from arms sales (see section 4.4 below).[110]

The budgeting process is heavily controlled by the president with the parliament acting as a rubber-stamp institution since 1996. In 1995, a last major conflict occurred over the president's right to control and alter the way the budget is executed. The Constitutional Court declared parts of a presidential decree "On the Specification of the Budget Estimates of the Republic of Belarus for 1995 and on Provisional Measures for Cutting Budget Expenses" to be unlawful. However, the government followed the presidential instructions. From 1996 onwards, in particular after he dissolved the parliament that had been elected in 1995, the president's absolute control has not been disputed.[111]

Accordingly, budget debate and adoption periods are short in Belarus. To begin, economic parameters used for drawing up the budget are set by presidential decree. Then, it is the president rather than the government who submits the budget to parliament.[112]

For 1999, the budget was presented to parliament on January 28, was adopted by the lower house (House of Representatives) on February 4 (in the second reading), and by the upper house (Council of the Republic) on February 8. The process for the 2001 budget took place somewhat earlier: presentation and first passage in the lower house occurred on October 3, 2000, the second reading on October 12, and the adoption by the upper house on November 2. A number of extra-budgetary funds were approved later.[113] In 2004, the budget law was rushed through the sitting legislature (i.e. before the parliamentary elections) already in early October. Few changes in the budget are brought about by parliamentary debate; according to one source, any lobbying takes place either during the drafting or the implementation stage.[114] As a rule, a report on budget implementation is presented to parliament by the Minister of Finance in June of the following year. However, there seems to be very little discussion or criticism from deputies.[115]

Budget execution, like budget drafting can be altered at will by the president. In September 1999, the president revised revenue, expenditures, and the deficit upwards, allocating a part of the additional revenue to his own presidential fund.[116] In March 2000, Lukashenka decided to cut funding to state agencies by 10 per cent, channeling the money to his own reserve fund with the declared purpose of giving it to healthcare institutions.[117] In November of the same year, a revised budget was issued by presidential decree.[118] In December 2001, the 2001 budget was adjusted virtually to reality (insufficient collections) by presidential decree.[119] Overall, considerable changes to the originally adopted budget regularly occur throughout the year—and there are few formal rules on the executive's powers to change the budget during implementation.[120] In 2004, presidential decrees again led to frequent changes in the budget.[121]

Still, given strong revenue collection capacity, during the 1990s, budget execution (actual revenue and expenditures compared to planned figures) has been closer on target than in Ukraine. The budget was fulfilled at 85 per cent in 1996, under-fulfilled by less than 5 per cent in 1997, and slightly over-fulfilled in 1998.[122] However, by 2001, budget fulfillment was worsening; for the first 11 months, 80 per cent of planned revenue was collected and 78.7 per cent of planned funds spent. The populist pledge of the president to double average wages rendered the budget impossible to fulfil, and in an end-of-year decree, the president had to adjust the budget.[123] Overall, there were considerable deviations between the Annual Budget Law and the revised budget plan.[124] In 2003, several expenditure categories—particularly in the social sphere—received less financing than envisaged, despite a good revenue situation.[125]

Tax and payments arrears from the budget also exist in Belarus but were far smaller than in Ukraine or Russia in the 1990s. According to IMF data, tax arrears reached a high point of 2.1 per cent of GDP in 1996, but were then reduced to 0.1 per cent of GDP in 1999. In addition, there are deferred taxes—tax arrears negotiated with the Ministry of Finance or relevant regional bodies—amounting to around 1 per cent of GDP in 1997 and 0.2 per cent in 1999.[126] In the 2000s, tax arrears and deferred taxes again grew in Belarus, to a combined total of 1.9 per cent of GDP in 2003, but falling back to 1.3 per cent in 2004.[127]

As the tables on expenditure composition in the Appendix show (see Table II.3.2), budgetary subsidies in Belarus were the highest of all four countries in 1999—while *de facto* they were even far larger, due to the prevalent use of cheap credits. In terms of spending on social security and welfare, Belarus does not differ substantially from the other three countries which are more closely observed here. Spending on health and education has remained higher, which reflects the fact that the state has still had the means to sustain these sectors more adequately than elsewhere and that less open or creeping privatization has taken place. Spending on defense is small in Belarus, as it is in Ukraine and Lithuania, while Russia—the former superpower—has by far the largest defense budget in the group. There are some reports criticizing high internal security spending in Belarus.[128] However, allocations—in 2002, 1.6

per cent of (planned) GDP for the police and state security agencies—do not differ from spending on similar items in Ukraine. Spending on interest has remained small due to low debt levels (see Appendix, Table II.1.2). Total foreign debt amounted to only 10.5 per cent of GDP in 2000, and to less than 5 per cent of GDP since 2003.[129]

Overall, Belarus' pattern of expenditure distribution is primarily determined by its past as a communist state rather than its current authoritarian regime (high spending on communist-style welfare, education and health). Moreover, the preservation of this spending pattern forms an important element in the (self-)legitimization of the regime. At the same time, regime consolidation is an important factor which has enabled the state to preserve its extractive capacities—allowing the most generous spending programs among the CIS countries.

While Belarus' extraction and expenditure system appears rather robust, there is a peculiarity which calls its sustainability into question: no other post-Soviet country has opposed monetarist orthodoxy (i.e. keeping inflation down) as strongly as Belarus.[130] The limited independence of the Central Bank (the NBB) was abolished in several steps after 1994—steps which included corruption charges and the imprisonment of chairwoman Tamara Vinnikova, who had been initially selected by Lukashenka himself.[131] Since 1996, the NBB had been ordered to channel massive credits through state-owned banks primarily to the agricultural and construction sectors.[132] This is part of Lukashenka's authoritarian Soviet-style welfare-state regime: cheap foodstuffs and affordable housing for young families were intended to legitimize the regime among various groups.

Another feature has been Soviet-style state-ordered increases of the average wage: in 2001, Lukashenka instructed the government to raise the average wage to US $100 per month by any means available—in spite of a monitoring program agreed upon with the IMF and falling budget revenue (see above).[133] Mandated wage increases continued throughout the early 2000s reaching US $175 per month in 2004. While IFIs warned repeatedly about the impact of rapidly rising wages on Belarus' competitiveness, relatively high wages have bolstered domestic demand.

9.5.3. CONTROL

Control with regard to budget execution works relatively well in Belarus. A treasury system supervized by the Ministry of Finance was first established in late 1993 and received an overall positive review by the IMF in 2000.[134]

The Control Chamber (CC) of Belarus—as an institution supervising budget execution that was accountable to parliament—was one of the first institutions of independent Belarus established by the Supreme Soviet in December 1991. In the 1994 constitution the CC was confirmed as the main control institution.[135]

In 1996, the Control Chamber was among the institutions which were involved in attempts to limit the authority of the president, who increasingly acted as being above the law. The CC tried to audit the presidential administration and enterprises controlled by it (including *Torgexpo*). These attempts were thwarted by the president. In September-October 1996, parliament instructed the CC to audit the account opened to finance the referendum initiated by the president with the aim of changing the constitution. However, the CC was denied access to any relevant data by the Ministry of Finance.[136]

After Lukashenka had successfully pushed through constitutional changes, the CC was abolished under the altered constitution of 1996 and replaced by a newly created State Control Committee (SCC) "charged with 'monitoring a broad range of state activity'" not further specified in the constitution. While possessing extremely broad ranging powers, the SCC is accountable solely to the president who also appoints all members.[137] The president can order specific audits.[138] The SCC controls not only the use of funds as stipulated in the budget but also checks whether laws and presidential decrees are properly implemented. According to the SCC about 10 per cent of state budget and off-budget funds are misused.[139] The primary line of reporting is to the president, but reports are also shared with the government and with parliament; they are generally not made public, although several reports have been discussed in some detail by the Mises Center.[140]

Initially, the SCC was created and functioned according to presidential decrees. A law on the SCC was formally adopted by parliament only in February 2000.[141] The SCC can impose financial fines and seize property without recourse to courts.[142] The SCC has been used to harass private businesses, opposition politicians, as well as foreign NGOs like the Soros Foundation.[143] In the first five months of 1999 alone, 250 managers and officials were dismissed after inspections by the SCC.[144] A massive audit of various media was conducted in April 2000—apparently to ensure 'proper' reporting during the election campaign for the October 2000 parliamentary elections. In August-September 2000, a special temporary commission was set up, headed by the chairman of the SCC, Anatol Tozik, to conduct audits of timely wage payments at all enterprises and institutions throughout the country.[145] SCC inspections have led to the dismissal of various regional and local level officials as well as officials from the Ministry of Finance.[146] Overall, the SCC has developed into a scapegoat-finder for the president in order to blame incompetent ministers as well as profiteering 'middlemen' for the country's economic ills. At the same time, the fact that it is feared seems to have contained 'subversive informality' and petty corruption to a greater degree in Belarus than in most other post-Soviet countries at least for some time.

The president has initiated repeated anti-corruption campaigns, using them *inter alia* to punish potential political rivals. In his rhetoric, Lukashenka has gone so far as even to threaten his own minister of finance, Mikalai Korbut that he would "answer with [his] life" if any money intended for the support of agriculture was misused.[147]

Financial control in Belarus is entirely exercised from above. Formal institutions guaranteeing horizontal forms of control or a free press as a precondition for effective control from below have been severely curtailed. Until around 2000, this system appeared effective in oppressing potential opposition as well as in controlling corruption—Belarus was perceived as much less affected by corruption than Russia or Ukraine, and only somewhat worse than Lithuania. In most recent years, however, the perception of corruption in Belarus has grown considerably (see Appendix, Table II.5.1 and 5.2). Petty corruption appears to be more widespread due to strains in the social welfare system (free education and health-care). For example, as corruption related to university entry exams increased, the SCC was charged with monitoring these in 2003.[148] Also, the president and his immediate entourage are above any control and have used their positions for personal enrichment.

Trials for corruption are relatively frequent in Belarus, and at least some of them are politically motivated to purge potentially power-acquiring individuals.[149] Furthermore, maintaining intensive trading ties with more liberal economies where levels of corruption are higher, is likely to offer numerous opportunities for self-enrichment of public officials, which may be increasingly 'used.' Thus, for example, a report on corruption by the Minsk city council involved a case of procurement of trolleybuses in which a Russian company was awarded the contract although two Belarusian companies offered lower prices.[150]

9.5.4. FISCAL TRANSPARENCY

Belarus has had a large number of extra-budgetary funds and uses monetary policy to finance the deficit, which renders the true financial position of the state opaque. In particular, substantial funds allegedly flow through a 'shadow budget' under the president's direct and exclusive control (including a 'presidential reserve fund' financed through arms sales).[151] According to a *Financial Times* report from 2001 "[a]nalysts say a significant share of national reserves, including proceeds from arms sales, disappear each year into off-budget funds controlled by the president."[152] The size of this fund was disclosed for the first time during the presentation of the budget to parliament in November 2001 as Rbl 36 billion (US $2.5 million or 1 per cent of the total budget revenue). The disclosure created a major stir in parliament.[153] However, the cited size of the fund appears to be rather small. Apart from the presidential reserve fund, the president declared in 2000 that goods seized from illegal imports (on the scale of US $40 million a year) be put under the control of the presidential administration (which would sell it and channel the proceeds to the state budget).[154]

In general, more fiscal data—including relevant legislation—is being made public in recent years. However, the absence of free media as well as of free research institutions means that there is little independent commentary on or questioning of such data—which would be needed to make the data relevant for a wider public; and to reveal the true extent of extra-budgetary fiscal activity.

9.6. Belarus: the strong state that does not want to be a state

Belarus offers a counter-intuitive case of post-Soviet state-building in several ways. While it is widely regarded as one of the least viable post-Soviet states in terms of national consciousness, in terms of state capacity, it appears to be one of the most viable states in the region. Although the economy depends to some extent on subsidies from Russia, the capacity to extract from this subsidized economic pie is driven by domestic factors—the consolidation of an authoritarian political regime combined with the regeneration of a neo-Soviet state and economic system. In broad terms, Belarus provides a model of state-formation by restoration, i.e. of putting the Soviet system—which had deteriorated during the late 1980s—back to work, albeit in a modified form, rather than of transforming the role of the state (see Chapter 3, section 2).

Belarus' path of authoritarian consolidation itself contradicts at least two assumptions about the 'predisposition' to democratization: it contradicts assumptions of 'modernization theory' as well as of spatial diffusion. Belarus was one of the most developed and relatively affluent republics of the former Soviet Union, and it is geographically close to the West.[155] However, economic progress in Belarus is associated with the Soviet period, a fact which appears to have promoted support for preserving the socialist economic system. Furthermore, while weak national consciousness was not a hindrance to state-building, it has held back democratization, since national liberation was much less relevant as a potential rally-point for the opposition than in the Baltic states or Ukraine.[156] At the same time, as Goujon argues, Lukashenka has been rather successful in his populist appeal.[157]

Furthermore, the initial experience of Belarus confirmed that not undertaking reforms—i.e. not choosing institutional change in the economic sphere—can, at least for some time, be a relatively successful path. While other post-Soviet countries, including Lithuania, were reeling from the costs of undertaking all-out change and cutting off many ties with Russia, the fall of GDP in Belarus remained considerably more moderate. While this is not an argument that authoritarian rule will be more *efficient* in its economic policies,[158] it is an argument that in the specific post-Soviet configuration, keeping institutional change limited to a minimum allowed an *avoidance of costs*.[159] Industrial and agricultural enterprises could continue to produce and to rely on state subsidies if necessary, while trade unions were satisfied with timely wage payments. Economic performance, and performance in terms of maintaining social security in turn contributed to the acceptance of creeping authoritarianism.

Decision-making capacity is centralized around the president, which facilitates decision-making—but at the same time increases risks of erratic decisions. Implementation capacity and overall 'infrastructural capacity' (Mann) are rather strong by comparison with other post-Soviet countries as evinced by the continuous high levels of actual extraction as well as of relatively high levels of public service provision. Since the private sector is less relevant, fewer talented people than in neighboring countries left the state administration for higher wages elsewhere.[160] Hierarchical, top-down control is generally exercised and has kept certain aspects of the state-as-a-problem in check; but may become less effective over time as is indicated by rising corruption levels. Generally, institutional legacies have been much stronger in Belarus than elsewhere, although even here the institutional system has been modified—as evinced by the gradual lowering of tax rates, but also the creation of the State Control Committee as a new instrument of top-down control.

It is rather striking that in Belarus trust in state institutions is relatively high and in some areas even higher than in Lithuania, with a consolidated democratic regime (see also Chapter 10). At least on some dimensions, the Belarusian state appears to serve public interests, even though effective mechanisms for accountability to citizens are absent.

While there is at best minimal political accountability in Belarus, there is an implicit social contract of acquiescence to Lukashenka's rule in return for the preservation of an extensive social welfare system. As Wintrobe argues in his *Political Economy of Dictatorship,* dictators are faced with the chance of removal by force.[161] One possible solution to this problem is to elicit loyalty—either from the population at large or from powerful groups; a different solution is to rely on fear. Through populist policies, Lukashenka has clearly sought loyalty, particularly from those sections of the population with nostalgia for the communist past, i.e., older and more rural groups; while keeping elites in a situation of fear. However, facing 'color revolutions' in its regional neighborhood, the Belarusian regime has become more oppressive in the early 2000s especially against politically active groups. Heightened oppression can be effective at preventing the development of a mass opposition, but it is also likely to have a price in terms of loyalty.

While weak national consciousness has inhibited the growth of a democratic opposition in Belarus, it does not appear *per se* as a hindrance to building a capable state.[162] Rather, Belarus confirms our assumption that consolidating political power—in this case around an authoritarian regime—is a key factor for creating and maintaining capable state institutions; and the weakness of nationalism facilitated such an authoritarian path of consolidation.

In the longer term, however, the Belarusian trajectory of state-building faces important political and economic risks: politically, it faces the risk of tyranny, the key risk associated with any authoritarian regime, and possibly also of stagnation, as the impetus for modernization is stifled by fear among elites. Growing oppression is likely to reduce popular support for the regime. Moreover, when authoritarian regimes turn into tyrannies, the propensity for using the state to impair rather than support society increases, as other post-Soviet states such as Uzbekistan or Turkmenistan, and even more extreme cases such as North Korea attest to.

Overall, an eventual change of the system is very likely, while its timing and the conditions under which it will take place are more difficult to foresee. The current socialist 'ownership' state appears unsustainable in a single, relatively small country which is open to trade and travel—not least since Belarusian elites can calculate that a redistribution of property is likely to benefit them as it has their counterparts in neighboring countries. Once fundamental change begins, the challenge will be to move rapidly towards a consolidated democratic system, and to avoid a prolonged period of uncertain rule which would weaken state capacity. 'Completing' transition rapidly may be difficult given the absence of a well-organized opposition. Thus, a 'second transition' in Belarus will re-pose the challenge of accomplishing a deeper transformation of the role of the state without losing too much capacity.

Weak nationalism, combined with Lukashenka's catering to the popular nostalgia about the Soviet Union has driven the 'policy project' of integrating Belarus with Russia. However, the moment for full integration with Russia appears increasingly to have passed—possibly also as the awareness has grown that joining Russia is not equivalent to re-creating the Soviet Union. Curiously, by supporting the Belarusian economy, Russia may rather unintentionally have contributed to the consolidation of a Belarusian state. As a small state, there are good reasons for Belarus to align with some larger entity—be it Russia, or eventually the EU, as Lithuania has chosen. Nonetheless, after 15 years of sovereignty, Belarus is likely to remain on the map as an independent state.

Notes

1 National movements are not so much generally promoters of economic and political changes; but they were the most common form of strong opposition movements which emerged in the former USSR.

2 For an overview of post-Soviet Belarus see also: Korosteleva, Lawson, and March (eds.) (2003).

3 Eke and Kuzio (2000), 524: "Curiously, against all the odds, this nation-specific model of development continues to defy predictions [...], suggesting the need to re-evaluate the criteria for post-Soviet transition to democracy and the free market [...]"

4 See Zettlemeyer (1999).

5 Hill, (2005), 1-3. For a dissenting view see Leshchenko (2004).

6 See Mihalisko (1997), 237-240.

7 See Eke and Kuzio (2000), 539.

8 Silitski (2003).

9 The BFP was legally registered only in July 1991. See Eke and Kuzio (2000), 526.

10 Mihalisko (1997), 240.

11 See Karol in: Lindner and Boris Meissner (eds.) (2001), 114.

12 Mihalisko (1997), 249.

13 See Goujon (2002).

14 Mihalisko (1997), 257.

15 See Freedom House, *Nations in Transit* (1998), "Belarus".

16 Freedom House, *Nations in Transit* (2001), 102. Most foreign governments do not recognize this 'created' parliament as legitimate.

17 According to official election results, Lukashenka received 76, Honcharyk 15, and another candidate 2.5 per cent of the vote. *RFE/RL Poland, Belarus, and Ukraine Report*, vol. 3, no. 34, September 12, 2001.

18 "Belarusian president keeps tight rein on government after shake-up," *Belarusskaya Gazeta*, October 1, 2001.

19 See final report of the OSCE/ODIHR observer mission, http://www.osce.org./documents /odihr/2004/12/3951_en.pdf [accessed: April 5, 2005]

20 The 1996 constitution is somewhat vague on this; see Articles 84 and 85 of the 1996 Belarusian Constitution. See also IMF, "Report on the Observation of Standards and Codes," Country Report 04/361 (2004), 7.

21 David Marples, "Belarusian opposition debates tactics", *Jamestown Monitor*, June 20, 2005.

22 Mikalai Statkevich together with Pavel Seviarynets in May 2005 for their organization of the October 2004 protests against the parliamentary elections; Mikhail Marynich in December 2004. See "Lukashenka's Repression Machine Tightens the Screws", *RFE/RL Belarus and Ukraine Report*, June 6, 2005.

23 Mihalisko (1997), 276; Goujon (2002). In a May 2005 survey, 41% said they would again vote for Lukashenka, and 23.2% for a candidate from the democratic opposition. See http://www.iiseps.by/epress6.html [accessed: August 8, 2005].

24 Freedom House, *Nations in Transit* (2001), 110. See also Ioffe (2004) who emphasizes the relatively successful economic performance as the base for Lukashenka's domestic legitimacy.

25 The EU has imposed travel bans on selected Belarusian officials; and membership of Belarus in the Council of Europe has been refused. Bartory (2003).

26 For a critical view see also Korosteleva (2005), 54-55.

27 See Eke and Kuzio (2000), 537.

28 Urban population: 71% according to World Bank, 2002.

29 Holtbrügge (2001), 34.

30 EIU, *Country Report Belarus*, no. 1, 1993, 22.

31 EIU, *Country Report Belarus*, various issues; EBRD, *Transition Report*, various issues.

32 Mildner (2000), 17.

33 Mildner (2000), 6.

34 Savchenko (2000), 116-119. However, for Lithuania, with a much lower Russian population share, Savchenko's argument is not fully applicable (see Chapter 10).

35 Kebich in an interview with *Belaya Rus'*, May 20, 1994, quoted from Savchenko (2000), 115.

36 See IMF, Belarus, *Country Report* no. 99/143 (1999), 10. Most international institutions seem to treat the growth figures as real.

37 Mildner puts Russian subsidies at 6 to 7% per annum; Mildner (2000), 12.

38 Arkady Moshes, "Russian Policy towards Ukraine, Belarus, and the Baltic States in the Putin Era," *PONARS Policy Memo*, no. 123, April 2000.

39 "Russia tells Belarus to toe the line in economy," *Belarusskaya Delovaya Gazeta*, December 6, 2001.

40 See www.ce-review.org/00/40/belarusnews40.html [accessed: January 14, 2003].

41 See Blanchard and Kremer (1997); Poznanski (1999).

42 "Lukashenka arresting and prosecuting economic managers," *Jamestown Monitor*, January 11, 2002.

43 "Lukashenka has directors arrested," *Neue Zürcher Zeitung*, January 28, 2002.

44 See EBRD, *Transition Report*, 2001.

45 Vitaly Silitski, "Minsk Posts 10 Percent Economic Growth - True but Not Miraculous," *RFE/RL Ukraine and Belarus Report*, August 19, 2004.

46 IMF, Belarus, *Country Report* no. 05/217 (2005).
47 No new WB loans were committed to Belarus from 1996 to 2000, while disbursements on a small scale and some grant assistance continued. See www.worldbank.org.by.
48 Average wages in Belarus stood at $175 in 2004, compared to $114 in Ukraine. US State Dep., Country Reports on Human Rights for 2003 and 2004.
49 Including Hill (2005).
50 "'Privatization' in Belarus," *Jamestown Monitor*, vol. 8, no. 97, May 1, 2002: "The first major deal could be a partial sale of Beltranshaz to the Russian company Gazprom."
51 IMF, Belarus, *Country Report*, no. 05/214 (2005).
52 In connection with the disappearance of several opposition politicians since 1999 and suspicions about the deaths of several journalists.
53 On trade see UNECE, Economic Survey of Europe, 2005 no. 1, statistical Appendix, Table B. 11. The origin of FDI is not always clear, but foreign investments in Belarus are not exclusively Russian.
54 Mishler and Rose (1998), 15. Regime support in Belarus is likewise higher than in Ukraine and Russia, see Mishler and Rose (2000), 18.
55 White and Rose (2001), 6.
56 There are concerns about the reliability of surveys as political oppression increased in Belarus. However, in Russia expressions of distrust continue to be very high despite the fact that political and civic freedom has been reduced since 2000.
57 White and Rose (2001), 17.
58 White and Rose (2001), 26.
59 Tatiana Protko (Chairperson of the Belarusian Helsinki Committee), "Problems of the Formation of a Civil Society in Belarus (1995-1999)," (March 1999) www.internews.ru/iiseps/11/5.html [accessed: September 4, 2002]. Hill (2005), 6.
60 See the OSCE/ODIHR report http://www.osce.org./documents/odihr/2004/12 /3951_en .pdf [accessed: August 8, 2005].
61 An overview of political parties is provided by Korosteleva (2005). According to her, most parties only had a few hundred to a few thousand members.
62 Protko (1999).
63 "President Lukashenka pledges support for Belarusian Business," *BBC Monitoring Service*, September 30, 1998.
64 See also Eke and Kuzio (2000), 540.
65 See www.chronicle.home.by/resources/doc/ccs/9708h.htm [accessed: March 5, 2002].
66 "Soros Foundation Suspends Activities in Belarus," *RFE/RL Newsline*, May 16, 1997.
67 "Belarusian Authorities Clamp Down on Independent Printing House, Newspaper," *RFE/RL NEWSLINE*, August 23, 2001.
68 "Warsaw recalls ambassador from Minsk," *RFE/RL, Belarus and Ukraine Report*, August 3, 2005.
69 *Nations in Transit* (2001), "Belarus: Trade Unions Face Increasing Harassment," *RFE/RL report*, October 12, 2000.
70 "Independent Trade Union Gains Concessions from Government," *Belapan*, January 25, 2001.
71 "Industrial Trade Union Discontented with Low Wages," *Belapan*, May 30, 2000.
72 "Belarusian protest rally appeals to president," *Belapan*, December 7, 1998.
73 "After his 'elegant election victory' the Belarusian dictator cleans up," *FAZ*, February 2, 2002.

74 See http://www.ilo.org/public/english/dialogue/actrav/new/belarus.htm [accessed: August 8, 2005].

75 "Belarusian miners protest against new tax," *Belapan*, Nov. 16, 2001; "Belarusian businessmen protest policies on small business," *Interfax*, January 3, 2001.

76 "Belarusian leader accuses striking vendors of political agenda," *Belarusian television*, February 1, 2000.

77 "Belarusian Leader Decrees Exemption from fines for VAT Miscalculations," *Belapan*, February 23, 2000.

78 "Liberal Democrat leader announces election platform," *BBC Monitoring Service*, August 26, 2001.

79 "Belarusian draft 2002 budget lacks transparency - paper," *BBC Monitoring Service*, November 15, 2001.

80 Lukashenka has to a considerable degree based his legitimacy on providing a low but stable level of economic security. According to Maravall, "The more dictatorships claim legitimacy on the grounds of performance rather than ideology, the more vulnerable they become to economic crisis." See Maravall (1997), 6.

81 Annual budget laws and data on budget outturn since 2000 are available on the website of the Ministry of Finance, at http://ncpi.gov.by/minfin/ [accessed: August 10, 2005]. However, the budget does not cover all areas of financial activity by the state.

82 See Mark Schaffer and Gerard Turley, "Effective versus Statutory Taxation: Measuring Effective Tax Administration in Transition Economies," *EBRD Working Paper*, no. 62 (2001), 13-14.

83 See Schaffer and Turley (2001), 8.

84 Schneider and Enste (2000), Table 3.

85 Freedom House, *Nations in Transit* (2001), "Belarus," 109.

86 Mildner (2000), 18-19. A *dpa* report from November 1996 alleged that the president kept the parliament pliant by granting tax privileges to the business of MPs. "President Lukashenka adored and mocked by Belarusians," *dpa*, November 20, 1996.

87 "Lukashenka axes Ford tax breaks in Belarus," *AFP*, October 14, 1997.

88 "Belarusian lower house passes presidential edict on tax, customs privileges," *Belapan*, August 2001.

89 "Belarusian president introduces single tax for self-employed workers," *Belapan*, May 21, 2001. "Belarusian president gives farmers tax exemptions," *Belarusian TV*, March 2, 1999.

90 IMF, Report on the Observation of Standards and Codes, *Country Report* no. 04/361 (2004), 9.

91 See "Status of the Tax System," IMF, Belarus, *Country Report* no. 99/143 (1999), 131-138.

92 "Belarus Amends Personal Income Tax Law," *Interfax*, March 16, 1999. Individual income tax declarations were introduced only for persons earning above 240 minimum wages a year.

93 "Belarusian upper house approves 1999 budget," *Belarusian Radio First Program*, Feb. 8, 1999.

94 "Belarus: Profit tax to drop next year," *Belarusian TV*, November 5, 2001.

95 "President submits own 2002 draft budget to parliament," *Belapan*, November 9, 2001.

96 "Belarusian President calls for simplified tax system, fiscal restraint," *Belarusian Radio First Program*, December 23, 1998.

97 In April 2000, the president imposed a 0.5 per cent sales tax to finance the promised construction of housing. "President imposes tax on companies to fund housing construction," *Belapan*, April 5, 2000.

98 Elena Rakova, "Belarusian Small Businesses Complain about Imperfect Laws and High Taxes," Mises Center, July 2003; at http://liberty-belarus.org/download/bsm.pdf [accessed: .August 10, 2005].

99 The tax code is available at http://law.by/work/EnglPortal.nsf/6e1a652fbefce34ac2256d910056d559/6ab5450e01845f4bc2256de4005e1495?OpenDocument [accessed: August 10, 2005].

100 IPM, *Belarusian Monthly Economic Review*, June 2004.

101 World Bank, *Country Economic Memorandum*, Executive Summary, June 2005, 17.

102 The ministry maintains a website with extensive information in Russian at www.nalog.by.

103 "Belarusian president orders new penalties for economic offences," *Belapan*, January 18, 2002.

104 "Belarus: Budget Revenue BR3,100 billion short," *Belapan*, January 29, 1999.

105 "Belarus reports larger than expected tax revenues in first nine months," *Belapan*, October 27, 2000.

106 "Deputy Minister promises tax reform over the next few years," *Belapan*, November 20, 2001.

107 IMF, Belarus *Staff Country Report*, No. 00/153 (2000), 41. IMF, Belarus, *Country Report* no. 03/119 (2003), 42 and 48-63.

108 IMF, Belarus, *Country Report* no. 99/143 (1999), 11.

109 IMF, Report on the Observation of Standards and Codes, *Country Report* 04/361 (2004).

110 Eke and Kuzio (2000), 531 also mention this 'additional' budget.

111 See www.geocities.com/CapitolHill/Lobby/4631/98-1/belarus.htm [accessed: November 22, 2001]

112 "Government plans marked increase in public spending," *Belorusskaya Delovaya Gazeta*, November 6, 2001, "Belarusian president submits own 2002 draft budget to parliament," *Belapan*, November 9, 2001.

113 "Belarusian government approves social spending targets," *Belapan*, November. 24, 2000.

114 Alexander Vasilevich, "Belarus 1998 budget breakdown," *Minsk News*, 1998, http://www.geocities.com/CapitolHill/Lobby/4631/98-1/belarus.htm [accessed: November 22, 2001]. Parliamentary committees can ask for increased spending on certain areas, but have to make off-setting financing suggestions. See World Bank, "Belarus: Strengthening Public Resource Management," June 2003.

115 "Belarusian Finance Minister Reports Budget Figures to Parliament," June 8, 2000; "Lower House Approved 1998 State Budget Implementation," *Belapan*, June 8, 1999.

116 "Belarusian President signs decree increasing the 1999 budget deficit," *Belapan*, September 22, 1999.

117 "Belarusian leader cuts state management expenses in favor of Health Protection," *Belarusian TV*, March 7, 2000.

118 "Belarusian president puts cap on 2000 budget deficit," *Belarusian Radio First Program*, November 23, 2000.

119 "Belarusian president corrects underfulfilled 2001 budget," *Belarusian TV*, December 25, 2001

120 World Bank, "Belarus: Strengthening Public Resource Management," June 2003.
121 IMF, "Belarus: 2005 Article IV Consultations," June 2005.
122 *BBC*, Jan. 23, 1997; *Belapan*, January 30, 1998; *Belapan*, June 8, 1999. *BBC Monitoring Kiev Unit*, July 24, 2001.
123 "Belarusian president corrects underfulfilled 2001 budget," *Belarusian TV*, December, 25, 2001.
124 World Bank, "Belarus: Strengthening Public Resource Management," June 2003, figure 4.1.
125 Yaroslav Romanchuk, "The budget for 9 months," Mises Center, November 2003.
126 IMF, Belarus, *Country Report* 00/153 (2000), 81; and no. 97/111 (1997), 94.
127 IMF Belarus, *Country Report* no. 05/218 (2005), 25.
128 "Belarus allots 8.6 per cent of budget for security, law enforcement," *Belapan*, December 19, 2001.
129 EBRD, *Transition Report* (2000), 141.
130 See also IMF *Staff Country Report* (November 2000), 13.
131 See "Banking Revolution in Belarus," *Moscow News*, March 14, 1996, "Two from the treasury - to prison" *Belaruskaya Delovaya Gazeta*, January 16, 1997.
132 For example, banks were ordered to lend Rbl 20 trillion to the agricultural sector for the 1999 sowing campaign. IMF, Belarus, *Country Report* no. 99/143 (1999), 13.
133 "Defense spending may be cut to fulfill president's wage pledge," *Belarusian TV*, May 1, 2001. "Belarusian government faces 'terrible situation' paying public sector wages," *Belapan*, June 6, 2001.
134 IMF, Belarus, *Country Report* no. 00/153 (2000), 16.
135 Constitution of Belarus (1994), Chapter 8, Art. 137-140.
136 *BBC summary of world broadcasts, Part 1, former USSR*, October 5, 1996.
137 The first head of the SCC was Mikalai Damashkevich; in July 2000 he was replaced by Anatol Tozik.
138 "Belarusian President orders audit into National Bank," *Belarusian Television*, February 20, 1999.
139 "Belarus: Around 10 per cent of State Funds are misused - State Control Official," *Belapan*, May 22, 1999.
140 See http://liberty-belarus.org/english/20040726195140.shtml [accessed: February 5, 2005]
141 A first draft law was submitted by the president to parliament in November 1998. "Belarusian Parliament adopts draft law on State Control Committee," *Belapan*, November 18, 1998.
142 Mildner (2000), 18. In 1998, a fine imposed by the SCC was challenged by an affected company, Belnationalservice. The company head lobbied the president, rather than seeking recourse in court. www.open.by/belarus-now/cont/1998/0721/politics/bg1-pol.html [accessed: November 23, 2001].
143 See: "Chronology: Belarus Government vs the Soros Foundation" http://www.belarusian.com/chronology/soros.html [accessed: June 25, 2003].
144 At the same time, state auditors were awarded a 30 per cent salary bonus. "Belarusian Auditors receive 30-per-cent salary bonus," *Belapan*, June 25, 1999.
145 *BBC monitoring Kiev unit*, September 1, 2000.
146 *BBC summary of world broadcasts, Part 1, former USSR*, November 12, 1997. *BBC summary of world broadcasts, Part 1, former USSR*, April 8, 1998.

147 "More spending on sowing will cut funds for other projects in Belarus - minister," *Belapan*, April 20, 2001. Korbut remained still in office by 2005.

148 See Freedom House, *Nations in Transit*, "Belarus," 2004, 20-21.

149 2242 corruption cases were 'detected by law-enforcement bodies' from January to May 2005. http://www.belarusembassy.org/news/digests/061605.htm [accessed: April 25, 2006]

150 Yaroslav Romanchuk, "State of Corruption in the Republic of Belarus," Mises Center, July 2004.

151 "Dismissal," *Belapan*, December 6, 1999.

152 "Belarus returns to the international financial fold," *Financial Times*, August 3, 2001.

153 "Belarus finance minister details presidential 'reserve fund'," *Kommersant*, November 18, 2001.

154 "Presidential Administration Charged with Sales of Seized Property," *Belarusian TV*, April 3, 2000.

155 Huntington (1991); Kopstein and Reilly (2000). The distance between Minsk and Vilnius—i.e., between the capital of the most democratic and one of the most autocratic successor states of the former Soviet Union—is only 150 km.

156 In the early 2000s, people apparently did not perceive the current system as strictly authoritarian rule. Students at the Belarusian State University, International Relations Department, were clearly surprised when confronted with the Freedom House ratings putting Belarus on a par with Turkmenistan. Lecture given by the author, April, 3 2002.

157 Goujon (2002), 33, 45.

158 See Maravall (1997), 1-37.

159 See also Popov (2004), 108ff.

160 Interview with Sergeiy Kulyk, World Bank, resident representative, and Marina Bakanova, Country Economist, Minsk, May 2, 2002.

161 Wintrobe (1998).

162 Leshchenko (2004) similarly proposed that Belarus may be a case in which—according to the older European pattern—the formation of a nation follows rather than precedes the state-building process.

CHAPTER 10.
LITHUANIA: MOVING TOWARDS WESTERN MODELS

While Belarus preserved key features of the old economic order, its northern neighbor, Lithuania, is among the post-Soviet states which have reformed fastest and most thoroughly. Lithuania provides an interesting case for comparison: in terms of pre-conditions, it is the Baltic state which is most similar to the Western CIS countries, while in terms of institutional change it has taken a very different path where both speed and direction are concerned. Thus, the case of Lithuania indicates that speedy, large-scale institutional reforms were possible in a post-Soviet context.

At the same time, transition in Lithuania has been far from problem-free. Shadowy business groups and business deals have played an important role; and corruption emerged as a serious problem. These problems attest to the powerful incentives of extra-legal activity which transition unleashes. While these problems have led to considerable popular disappointment with transition, they did less damage to the formal institutional system than in Ukraine; and hence are more likely to be reigned in over time.

Furthermore, Lithuania showed greater state capacity from the outset of independence: deficits were kept comparatively small in the early 1990s, the statutory tax system was reformed early on, and an acceptable level of revenue was maintained without driving large parts of the economy into the shadows. Budgeting has been more regularized and meaningful, while control mechanisms compatible with a democratic regime were introduced earlier and have developed more fully.

Lithuania was chosen as a comparative case, because it is the Baltic state most similar to the Western CIS countries but at the same time, it varies with regard to the central explanatory variable, regime consolidation. In contrast to Belarus, consolidation has been achieved within a democratic rather than an authoritarian system; and in contrast to Ukraine or Russia, the democratic system was rapidly consolidated rather than remaining in an inchoate state.

Among the three Baltic states, Lithuania has the most in common with its Eastern Slavic neighbors. In the 19th century, Lithuania was part of the Russian Empire. It was the most backward among the Baltic states, and serfdom was abolished only in the 1860s. Modernization occurred primarily after WWII under Soviet rule.[1] To the present day, it is the most agrarian Baltic country.[2] In terms of culture, Lithuania—like Ukraine and Belarus—has been strongly influenced by Poland (and Russia). Furthermore, Lithuania is predominantly Catholic, which may arguably be closer in terms of worldviews to the Uniate and Orthodox churches than the northern Baltic Protestantism.[3] Finally, ethnic problems have played only a limited role in Lithuania—similar to the Western CIS countries.[4]

Lithuania differs most obviously from Ukraine and Belarus with regard to its previous experience as a modern independent state (1918–1940), which also means a shorter period under communist rule. By the mid-1990s, such historic differences vis-à-vis other post-Soviet states were reinforced when the EU decided to accept the Baltic states' applications for membership.

10.1. Political developments: early elite reconfiguration and after

Broad popular movements emerged in the Baltics in 1988. During the following two years *Sajudis*, the Lithuanian movement, constantly grew in political importance. In the March 1989 elections to the All-Union Congress of People's Deputies, *Sajudis* candidates won 36 out of 42 seats. In the first semi-free parliamentary elections in March 1990, *Sajudis* gained a landslide victory, winning 91 out of 141 seats in the Lithuanian Supreme Soviet.[5] Subsequently, the leader of *Sajudis,* Vytautas Landsbergis, was elected parliamentary chairman, acting as a *de facto* president.[6]

These first elections mark a major difference with Ukraine and other non-Baltic post-Soviet countries, as a real reconfiguration of elites took place early on.[7] At the same time, the Lithuanian Communist Party entered a path of rapid transformation into a left-wing social democratic party under the Gorbachev-appointed leader Algirdas Brazauskas.[8]

Lithuania became the Soviet republic that pushed most radically for independence: immediately after the 1990 elections, the *Sajudis*-dominated parliament passed a resolution declaring that Lithuanian independence had been restored. However, the expected support from the West was not forthcoming, and the Soviet leadership imposed an economic blockade on Lithuania.[9] In

January 1991, Soviet troops descended on Vilnius and 13 people died in the ensuing street fighting. After several months of tension, the failed August putsch against Gorbachev finally opened the path to independence.

In the course of 1992, the constitutional foundations for the new system were debated. As in Ukraine, the national-democratic forces—united in the *Sajudis* movement—favored a presidential constitutional model.[10] In the same year, *Sajudis* suffered two major defeats: first, a constitutional referendum in favor of a presidential constitution failed due to low participation in the spring of 1992. Secondly, in the parliamentary elections in October, *Sajudis* lost unexpectedly heavily to the ex-Communist Party, now called the Lithuanian Democratic Labor Party (LDDP) under Brazauskas. This made Lithuania the first transition country where the ex-communist party first lost and subsequently regained power in free elections. On the same day as the elections, a compromise, semi-parliamentary constitution was finally adopted by referendum.

Lithuania's system of government has a popularly elected president who holds some real power. However, in the letter of the constitution and in practice, this power is significantly more limited than in Ukraine or the other presidential post-Soviet polities. Thus, the government is appointed by the president upon approval by the *Seimas* (parliament). The *Seimas* but not the president can express no confidence in the government, while the formal act of dismissal is in the hands of the president.[11] Furthermore, while the president can issue decrees in some fields of policy-making, these decrees need to be counter-signed by the prime minister or a responsible minister who will bear responsibility for the decree.[12] *De facto,* therefore, Lithuania has functioned along the lines of a parliamentary rather than a presidential republic with its government being based on majorities in parliament. There have been no multiple sources of rule-making as in Ukraine or Russia.

The early election victory of the ex-communist party has been primarily attributed to the bad economic situation. In particular, large parts of the electorate disapproved of the very rapid privatization which had been pursued by *Sajudis*. As leading members of *Sajudis'* successor, the 'Homeland Union,' themselves admitted privatization had primarily been driven by a political logic (with the aim of creating a new class of owners), but without sufficient consideration for mechanisms which would ensure fairness and lawfulness.[13] Furthermore, under the leadership of Landsbergis, the *Sajudis* movement was widely perceived as too nationalist. As a result, the ex-communist leader Brazauskas also won the first presidential elections in January 1993; Landsbergis—the "hero" of the Lithuanian independence movement—had chosen not to run when it became clear that his chances were slim.

The LDDP government generally maintained the path of seeking EU accession and reform. In doing so, however, it swayed far from keeping its election promises which had focused on protecting the interests of workers. In the winter of 1995–96 the LDDP government lost public confidence when a major banking scandal erupted.

Thus, when the next parliamentary elections were held in 1996, the pendulum swung back: *Sajudis* which had transformed itself into the Homeland Union/Conservatives of Lithuania won 70 seats and formed a coalition government with the Lithuanian Christian Democratic Party (16 seats). While this conservative government was able to preside over the first economic upturn, it was likewise marked by several scandals and the ouster of individual ministers. Furthermore, in 1998–99, Lithuania became the Baltic country worst affected by the Russian crisis.

Both the LDDP and the Conservative periods of government went through internal instability with each camp 'using' three different prime ministers (see list below). This is primarily attributable to the difficulties of the transition period, where any government was bound to disappoint expectations and—particularly in the context of privatization—to be accused of corruption.

In early 1998, the second presidential elections took place; these were won by a returned émigré, Valdas Adamkus. Landsbergis had decided to stand this time, but his nationalism and personally rather authoritarian style still cost him electoral appeal; he lost already in the first round against Adamkus and Arturas Paulauskas, the candidate backed by the LDDP.

By 1998, Lithuania appeared to have one of the most stable and clear-cut party systems of any post-Soviet state with the two strong poles represented by the reformed communists, the LDDP, and the conservatives, who had emerged from the *Sajudis* movement. However, the system again entered a period of flux from the late 1990s onwards. The New Union (a social liberal party) was formed and the initially small Liberal Union became a major force after the ousted conservative Prime Minister Rolandas Paksas joined in. Paksas had stepped down as prime minister of the Homeland Union due to a disagreement between him and other members of government over the partial sale of the oil refinery, Mazeikiu Nafta, Lithuania's biggest and most important enterprise to the American investor Williams International.

These two newcomer parties joined forces for the October 2000 parliamentary elections: although the LDDP became the strongest party with 31 per cent of the vote (51 seats), the New Union and the Liberal Union formed a minority government supported also by the Center Union (holding a combined share of 63 seats).[14] However, this government lasted only for eight months before breaking up due to disagreement between the coalition partners *inter alia* over tax reform.

This time, the fall of a government led to a change in the parties holding power. In early 2001 the LDDP had merged with the smaller Lithuanian Social Democratic Party (LSDP) thereby acquiring the latter's more 'European style' name. In July 2001, this enlarged LSDP formed a new government under the leadership of Algirdas Brazauskas.[15]

This was the first Lithuanian government to serve a full term. Moreover, the LSDP managed to form also the next government, elected in late 2004, under Brazauskas—albeit with a much-diminished share of seats in parliament and in a coalition with several smaller, newly formed parties.[16] Apart from the LSDP this coalition included the Social Liberals, the Union of Farmers, the New Democracy Union, and the Labor Party.

While government became more routinezed, Lithuanian politics during this period nonetheless experienced heavy doses of the populism, dirty play politics, and of the post-communist business elite entering politics as seen in other transition countries. In early 2003, the populist politician and former prime minister Paksas was elected as president on a populist platform which included anti-corruption, anti-government, and anti-foreign elements, and appealing primarily to those constituencies left behind by transition especially in rural areas and small towns. Paksas made strong claims about the prevalence of corruption in Lithuania's government circles ("government thieves") but eventually it came to light that he himself was deeply involved in shady dealings.

Eventually, Paksas was impeached and removed by parliament. The investigations found that Paksas was linked to dubious privatization deals of the alcohol industry and to large-scale smuggling operations.[17] After months of international ostracism of the president, Lithuania managed to jettison Paksas after a Constitutional Court ruling and a parliamentary vote less than a months before acceding to the European Union on May 1, 2004.

Early presidential elections had to be called in mid-2004 with Valdas Adamkus and Kazimira Prunskiene, the first post-Soviet prime minister, running as the main candidates. At the peak of the election campaign, Lithuania's anti-corruption Special Investigation Service (STT) raided the offices of four political parties over allegations that five parliamentarians had been bribed in connection with a law on the energy sector.[18] The timing of this raid was widely seen as an attempt to influence the presidential elections.

A different type of linkage between business and politics was meanwhile developed by Viktor Uspaskich, one of the most successful Lithuanian businessmen of Russian origin. Uspaskich, together with other wealthy businesspeople, created a party under the label of 'Labor'—rather similar to Tyhypko's party by the same label in Ukraine. The Lithuanian Labor Party adopted a rather populist program, promising to raise pensions, cut utility prices, and (re-)introduce various social benefits. Founded in 2003, Labor became the most popular party by 2004. Labor won 41 out of 141 seats in the *Seimas* in the October 2004 elections, and eventually joined a coalition government under Brazauskas.[19]

The coalition government formed in late 2004 proved not to be entirely stable: in April 2005, Algirdas Butkevicius resigned as Minister of Finance over the issue of further tax reforms (see section 4 below); while in June 2005 Uspaskich had to step down from his post as Minister of Economy over accusations that his Russian business contacts broke ethical rules.

Rather reminiscent of Italy, Lithuania had eleven governments in as many years between 1990 and 2001. However, below the surface, where we see a frequent change of prime ministers, there was more stability: each respective political camp stayed in power for the full period (i.e., 1992 to 1996 and 1996 to 2000). Most importantly, while Lithuania was the first post-communist country in which government changed back into the hands of the communists, it was also the first to prove that these ex-communists stuck to the new rules. Thus, while there was instability at the level of government, the consolidation of (new) rules and a new democratic regime occurred early and firmly.

As a result, the Lithuanian system of government has produced much more coherent reforms than have the presidential systems of Ukraine or Russia regardless of the frequent changes in government. Furthermore, Lithuania developed a relatively mature structure of organized 'visible' interests (in comparison with other post-Soviet states) which includes not only parties but also unions and employers associations (the Lithuanian Confederation of Industrialists).[20] Also, Lithuanian interest associations have had more distance from the state/government than in Ukraine or Russia.[21] This has *inter alia* stimulated a livelier and more structured public debate on issues of taxing and spending.

However, frequent changes in governments and the electoral swings have had some detrimental effect. A related problem is that law-making was extremely rushed during the first decade of independence: particularly in the run-up to being admitted as a member to the EU, a large number of laws were adopted rather hastily (see Appendix, Table II.6.1). These laws often lacked careful formulation, coordination, as well as transparency and consultation.

Table 10.1: Lithuania—list of prime ministers, heads of state, and of the state tax inspectorate

Prime ministers	03/1990–01/1991	Kazimiera Prunskiene (LKP)
	01/1991–07/1992	Gediminas Vagnorius (*Sajudis*)
	07/1992–12/1992	Aleksandras Abisala (n/p)
	12/1992–03/1993	Bronislovas Lubys (LDDP)
	03/1993–02/1996	Adolfas Slezevicius (LDDP)
	02/1996–11/1996	Laurynas Stankevicius (LDDP)
	11/1996–05/1999	Geiminas Vagnorius (TS (LK)) (Homeland Union)
	05/1999–10/1999	Rolandas Paksas (TS (LK)) (Homeland Union)
	10/1999–10/2000	Andrius Kubilius (TS (LK)) (Homeland Union)
	10/2000–06/2001	Rolandas Paksas (LLS)
	07/2001–	Algirdas Brazauskas (LSDP) (2nd government from Nov. 2004)
Heads of state/presidents	03/1990–11/1992	Vytautas Landsbergis (Chairman of the Supreme Council)
	11/1992–02/1993	Algirdas Brazauskas (Chairman of the Seimas)
	02/1993–02/1998	Algirdas Brazauskas (President)
	02/1998–01/2003	Valdas Adamkus
	01/2003–04/2004	Rolandas Paksas (removed through impeachment)
	06/2004–	Valdas Adamkus
Heads of the state tax inspectorate	03/1995–06/1996	Petras Navikas
	07/1996–12/1996	Antanas Nesteckis
	12/1996–12/1998	Nijole Pitreniene
	03/1999–07/1999	Jaunius Ziogas
	09/1999–07/2000	Arturas Baksinskas
	07/2000–10/2000	Henrikas Tamulis
	10/2000–05/2002	Mindaugas Strumskis
	09/2002–	Violeta Latviene

An important aspect of Lithuania's development has been its commitment to and eventual acceptance of becoming an EU-accession country. Lithuania first applied for EU-membership in December 1995. Negotiations on the terms of membership started in early 2000, after the decision at the EU's Helsinki summit of December 1999 to open negotiations with all candidate countries. Since the late 1990s, the accession process had an important influence on shaping the state-building effort in Lithuania.

Early elite reconfiguration and democratic orientation among all major political forces were a further key factor, generating an early and consistent drive for creating a new institutional system.[22] Moreover, applying for EU and NATO membership—both achieved in 2004—meant that all elite groups came to share a broadly common policy orientation. Thus, there was an underlying consolidation in two regards: an agreement to stick to democratic rules as the basis of legitimate government, and a basic agreement on the new order to be built.[23]

At the same time, successful political transition and rather successful state-building in Lithuania were not unspoiled processes: the social cost of transition was substantial, and business-government links in Lithuania involve elements of corruption and state-capture; with privatization providing powerful incentives to bend formal rules.[24] However, the formal rules were reshaped faster and more successfully than in Ukraine or Russia, and they found more defenders as the impeachment of Paksas attests.

10.2. Economic developments: the great leap from communism to capitalism

Historically, Lithuania was the least industrialized of the three Baltic republics and agriculture made up 27.6 per cent of GDP in 1990. During transition, the sectoral shares in total GDP changed dramatically, with services growing from one third to two thirds of GDP.[25] While the share of agriculture in total GDP fell below 10 per cent already by 1995, agriculture continued to have twice as great a share of the labor force as the service industry.[26]

After a steep economic decline from 1990 to 1994, Lithuania began to register growth again from 1995 onwards (see Appendix, Table I.1.2). In 1994, Lithuania's GDP stood at 54.3 per cent of its 1989 level, i.e. at the CIS average for that year.[27] By 2000, Lithuania had recovered to 66 per cent (CIS average: 60.8 per cent), and growth continued to be strong in the early 2000s.

Economic policy has been marked by early rapid moves on several fundamental dimensions establishing a basic market economy framework by the mid-1990s—by which time reforms in Ukraine were only just starting. Several crucial reforms were initiated in 1990–1991—monetary reform, privatization, and the reform of the fiscal system. They were begun during a 'window of opportunity' during which *Sajudis* enjoyed broad popular support.

As a first step towards monetary reform, a National Bank of Lithuania was created in 1990. Like many other Lithuanian institutions, the bank traces its origins to the pre-war period—in this case the 1922 law on the Bank of Lithuania.[28] In May 1992, a temporary currency (*Talonas*) was issued and declared sole legal tender in September. During that year, Lithuania experienced hyperinflation (year-on-year inflation reached 1021 per cent). However, in contrast to Ukraine, inflation was reduced again relatively swiftly.

In June 1993, the *litas* was finally introduced as the permanent national currency. In order to ensure the new currency's credibility, parliament decided in March 1994 to introduce a currency board.[29] Concomitantly, inflation was reduced to 72 per cent for 1994 and moderated further in the following years.

Table 10.2: Lithuania: Ministers of finance

03/1990–02/1991	Romuldas Sikorskis
03/1991–07/1992	Elvyra Kuneviciene
07/1992–12/1992	Audrius Misevicius
12/1992–02/1995	Eduardas Vilkelis
02/1995–02/1996	Reinoldijus Sarkinas
02/1996–12/1996	Agimantas Krizinauskas
12/1996–02/1997	Rolandas Matiliauskas
02/1997–06/1999	Algirdas Semeta
06/1999–10/1999	Jonas Lionginas
11/1999–11/2000	Vytautas Dudenas
11/2000–07/2001	Jonas Lionginas
07/2001–05/2004	Dalia Grybauskaite
05/2004–05/2005	Algirdas Butkevicius
05/2005–	Zigmantas Balčytis

Privatization was particularly rapid in Lithuania, even compared to the other Baltic republics.[30] Voucher privatization was initiated in 1991. The initial goals were extremely ambitious—such as concluding the first phase by the end of 1992 (eventually, this had to be prolonged until mid-1995).[31] Emphasis on equal distribution of property was strong, although this was not always realized *de facto*. As in Russia, this rapid privatization created problems for revenue extraction (see Section 4.3). Given the political and social-engineering emphasis present in the privatization program, significant revenue was not intended nor calculated in the budget.[32]

While Lithuania reoriented its trade towards Western Europe, it remained the Baltic republic most closely linked to other post-Soviet countries, primarily Russia, Ukraine, and Belarus. As a consequence, it was also most heavily affected by the 1998 Russian crisis, experiencing a 4.2 per cent fall in GDP in

1999. However, the economy re-bounded strongly and grew at an average rate of 6.4 per cent between 2000 and 2004.[33]

As is the case with many other transition countries, Lithuania is divided into two fairly prosperous cities (Vilnius and Klaipeda) and an economically depressed countryside which has had political repercussions (see above). Unemployment hovered between 13 and 17 per cent in the late 1990s and early 2000s, eventually falling to 10.5 per cent in 2004.[34] In 2000, i.e., before a renewed spurt in growth, 13.7 per cent of the population was poor, living on less than US $2 a day.[35] The dependency ratio (the share of those not working to those working) was high, putting considerable strain on the fiscal system.[36]

Furthermore, there was a string of difficulties surrounding the Mazeikiu oil refinery, Lithuania's largest enterprise and taxpayer. A strategic share in the company was sold to an American investor in 1999 amid considerable political controversy over the terms of the deal. Then, Russian oil companies—who themselves wanted parts of Mazeikiu Nafta—refused to sign long-term oil supply contracts, triggering continued large losses. Eventually, the American investor sold its share and management rights on to Yukos, which in the course of 2002 acquired a 53.7 per cent stake in the company (while the remainder was owned by the Lithuanian government).[37] This in turn became a cause of concern when the Russian government launched its attack on Yukos in 2004.[38]

Lithuania began to attract some foreign investment already in the early 1990s, but a real take-off occurred only from 1996 to 1997 onwards. Compared to the Western CIS countries, inflows have been substantially larger, four to eight times larger than in Ukraine and in Belarus in per capita terms.[39]

While Lithuania is sometimes perceived as a laggard on economic reforms compared to Estonia, the pace of reforms was still much faster than in the Western CIS countries. The initial deep fall in GDP and the scale of social problems which emerged (unemployment, poverty) show that even a relatively well-orchestrated transition carried a high cost. Furthermore, a more rapid pace of transition meant that institutions were transformed and built while a heavy load of economic policy decision-making was continuously taking place; in the metaphor of Elster et al., this was very much an act of 'rebuilding the ship at sea.'[40]

10.3. State-society relations in Lithuania

10.3.1. INTERMEDIARY ORGANIZATIONS

As elsewhere in the former Soviet Union, intermediary organizations which would channel ideas and interests between state elites and society were initially rather weak. After the 1990 victory, a process of disintegration set in within the *Sajudis* movement. Trade unions reeled from the sudden economic downturn and the shift of employment from large, state-owned enterprises into the private sector (often in the service industries). Thus, important decisions on basic economic policies (privatization, monetary policy, the basis of fiscal policy) were made when intermediary organizations were rather weak, while general support for *Sajudis* and for the basic tenets of independence (including a return to capitalism) were strong.

Throughout the 1990s, then, a system of intermediary organizations took shape which is more developed than in any of the Western CIS countries; even though it is still far from being fully mature. As has been mentioned above, a rather strong and clear-cut party system developed in Lithuania relatively early.[41] While party membership is limited (1 to 2 per cent of the population), Miller claims that identification with distinct parties has been high from the early 1990s onwards.[42] The main parties are the Lithuanian Social Democratic Party, i.e., the communist successor party, and the Homeland Union/Lithuanian Conservatives, which emerged out of the popular movement *Sajudis*. As noted above, the New Union and the Liberal Union became major new forces in the party landscape in the late 1990s; but then they quickly diminished again after a short and poor performance in government under Paksas as Prime Minister. In 2003, a new Labor Party was founded by a group of wealthy business people which almost instantly became one of the most popular parties.[43] As in most transition countries, political parties in Lithuania came to be highly distrusted, and this process apparently opens up space for new entrants who can at least initially claim higher levels of trustworthiness.

Girnius has painted a rather bleak picture of Lithuanian political and civil society as deeply divided between ex-communists and anti-communists.[44] However, as this is an economic and ideological cleavage, it should be one that is conducive to competitive politics in the longer run. Also, citizens shared the goal of European integration with their elites: in a national referendum on EU membership held in May 2003, 91 per cent of votes were in favor, with 63.4 per cent of eligible voters participating.[45] A fundamental problem of Lithuanian politics may be rather, that the losers from transition feel that they are not well-represented by any political party; and this is reflected in the surprise successes of several new-comer parties and populist politics as pursued by Paksas as well as to a lesser degree by Uspaskich.

Lithuania has also relatively developed business associations and trade unions. The major association of large business, the Confederation of Lithuanian Industrialists (CLI), was founded as early as June 1989. Like some other organizations in Lithuania (see below), it traces its roots to the pre-war period, while *de facto* it is the successor to the Soviet era Industrialists' Association.[46] Uniting over 2700 enterprises, the CLI is "the leading lobbying group in the country."[47] Before the 1996 elections the CLI signed a deal with the Homeland Union, in which the latter promised that more loans would be allocated to industry and that corporate income tax would be lowered to 20 per cent by a conservative government.[48] After its election victory, the conservatives indeed began to advocate a reduction and eventual phasing-out of the CIT (see below). In total, there are more than 300 business associations and most small businesses are members of some organization. About 300 agricultural enterprises are united in the Lithuanian Association of Agricultural Companies. The rural population, however, appears overall to be the least well-organized and represented.

While trade unions have suffered in the economic crisis through privatization and rising unemployment, membership numbers have risen steadily and in the late 1990s about 80 labor organizations were reported to have a total of more than 200,000 members or around 14 per cent of all those employed. There are three large umbrella unions, with the Lithuanian Trade Union Confederation accounting for around 60 per cent of the unionized labor force.[49] These organizations have had an increasing voice and have been consulted in questions of crucial institutional changes such as tax reform.[50] However, as in many transition countries, trade unions in Lithuania suffer low levels of trust from the wider public (see below), and existing tripartite negotiations have had a limited coverage and impact.

With the Lithuanian Free Market Institute (LFMI), Lithuania has had a prominent think tank of economic liberalism since 1990. The LFMI first promoted radical tax reforms in 1991 when it suggested abolishing all direct taxation, which was duly rejected as impossible by the political establishment. It has promoted a flat rather than a progressive income tax (and claims to have prevented the re-introduction of a progressive scale) and has pushed for the abolition of corporate income tax. While the LFMI's liberal radicalism sits somewhat oddly with a population that is rather less radically pro-market than in Estonia—the center of post-Soviet liberalism—it has certainly been politically influential and has provided a source of public debate for which there is no equivalent in Ukraine.

Another important factor which sets Lithuania apart from the Western CIS countries is the presence of a free and relatively professional press. While unproven allegations of corruption against political opponents have been a political staple in Lithuania as elsewhere, the press, and in particular the two independent papers *Lietuvos Rytas* and *Respublika*, have covered cases of corruption in some depth. Probably as a consequence, trust in mass media is rather high.[51]

Overall, in Lithuania we find initial societal disorganization (but no large-scale disenfranchisement), followed by a phase during which Lithuania's society has become rather well-structured by post-Soviet standards. This has translated into a more developed public debate about fiscal issues than in Ukraine, for example. Rather curiously, Lithuania combines a strong ex-communist party, the LSDP, with streaks of liberalism which are rather radical by continental European standards, particularly in the debate on taxation.[52]

Corruption is still perceived as substantial in Lithuania, although the situation improved between the 1990s and the 2000s, and further incremental improvements continue to be made.[53] However, there are organized crime groups which have links to the political sphere.[54] In contrast to Ukraine or Russia, they are more clearly demarcated as 'crime groups' and as potential subjects of investigation, not as groups which can openly wield political influence. Also, they are generally balanced by relatively developed 'visible groups' and formal state structures, including a Special Investigation Service, which was set up specifically to deal with organized crime and corruption in 1997 and strengthened in 2000, but their influence poses a challenge.[55]

10.3.2. TRUST AND EXPECTATIONS

While initially, levels of trust in public institutions were rather high in Lithuania, they have fallen over time—as in most other transition countries—while still staying somewhat above the extremely low levels of trust in Ukraine or Russia. The president has been more trusted than parliament and government—a pattern that Ukraine, Russia, and Belarus also display. Trust in political parties fell very low in all four countries, although it was initially higher in Lithuania. The graphs below provide some comparisons between the target countries at different points in time.

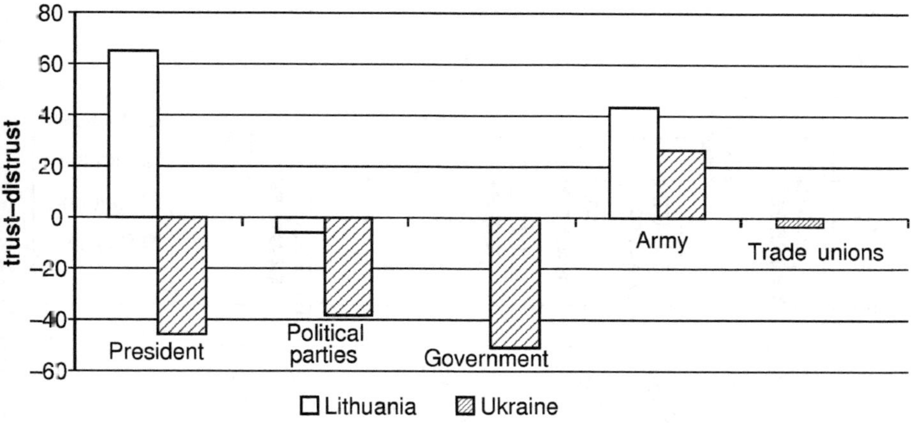

Graph 10.1: Trust in institutions, Lithuania and Ukraine, 1993–94

(The graphs show a balance of those respondents expressing some or full trust; minus the share of those expressing some or strong distrust.)

Sources: Kubicek (2000), 46; Rose and Maley (1994), 41–42. Data on government for Lithuania and data on trade unions for Ukraine is missing.

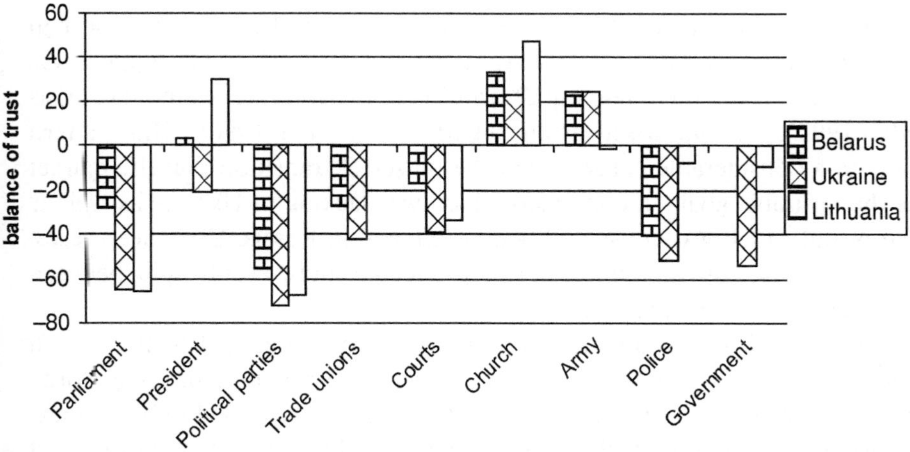

Graph 10.2: Trust in institutions, Belarus, Ukraine, Lithuania, 2000–2001

Sources: for Belarus and Ukraine: White and Rose (2001), except government Ukraine (from Socis Gallup 1999); for Lithuania: Vilmorus. No data on government for Belarus.

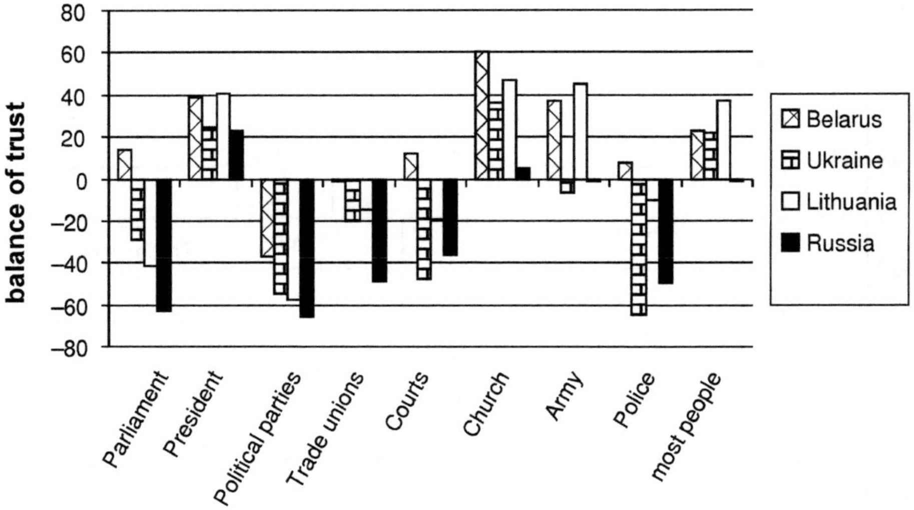

Graph 10.3: Trust in institutions, Belarus, Ukraine, Lithuania, and Russia, 2004–2005

Source: New Europe Barometer, 2004. Rose (2005) for all countries.

Support for the free market has been consistently higher in Lithuania than in Ukraine, Russia or Belarus (see Appendix, Table II.4.1). This support was initially very high, then fell rapidly during the period of economic crisis (1992-1994), and increased again slightly in the late 1990s. This pattern points to a considerable consensus at the outset of transition that the market was the desirable goal—a consensus which was lacking in Ukraine as well as Belarus and which was considerably more limited in Russia. Once deep recession had set in, Lithuanian society then became more evenly split between supporters and opponents of market reform.

Thinking back to the original proposition as formulated in Chapter 4 with regard to trust, the following observation emerges: a generally better performance of government in Lithuania than in Ukraine has so far led only to somewhat less distrust, but not really to substantially solid levels of trust. As reflected in the New Europe Barometer surveys, trust in state and societal institutions is generally low across the post-communist region. Trust is low in countries perceived as more or less corrupt and in countries with higher as well as with lower standards of living and growth rates. Across all countries 'pluralistic' political institutions, political parties, and the parliament are the least trusted; while presidents enjoy the highest levels of trust, even ahead of the church. Trust in the police and in courts is clearly higher in some of the more successful transition countries (Estonia, Hungary) than in the least successful ones; but it is still low in other good performers such as Slovenia, the Czech Republic, or Poland. Remarkably, in 2004 trust in public institutions was the highest in Belarus among all countries surveyed.[56] In Lithuania, even though economic performance and state capacity improved between 1993 and 2001, levels of trust fell, with a possible slight re-increase by late 2004.[57] Overall, therefore, the relationship between trust and state capacity appears less direct than originally assumed. While very poor performance is reflected by very low levels of trust, better performance does not necessarily result in proportionally higher levels of trust: at least not in the short to medium term. Part of the explanation may lie in the fact that any form of transition is associated both with substantial social costs and with widespread accusations of corruption, both of which have a negative impact on trust.

10.3.3. THE IMPORTANCE OF WESTERN MODELS

The strong commitment to national independence led Lithuanian citizens and elites to embrace capitalism as the economic model.[58] The presence of a strong cognitive alternative to the Soviet system contrasts with Belarus where it was absent, and Ukraine, where there was considerable confusion about which model to adopt. Furthermore, the strength of nationalism meant that relying on Russia (for cheap energy) was never an option; rather, confrontation with Russia forced institutional change in order to cope with suddenly expensive energy. At the same time, the desire to make independence secure has meant seeking to integrate with the West and consequently accepting the requirements put forth by Western organizations.[59] Initially, Western influence was strongest via the IMF, with which Lithuania concluded its first agreement in 1992.[60] Over the years, the IMF has exerted considerable external pressure to lower subsidies and to keep fiscal discipline.[61] With the acceptance of the Baltic states as candidates for EU membership, integration with the West has come to matter even more at the level of institutional change and institutional performance.[62]

The fact that Lithuania is a small country whose central goal was to rejoin Europe gave outside agents like the IMF and the EU greater leverage than in Ukraine, Belarus or Russia. At the same time, it also meant a more cooperative form of external influence. As Vaicenavičius has remarked: "The accession strategy has and will be used as an excuse for making sensible reforms that might be costly to some interest groups, but which will help society at large."[63] Furthermore, as Orenstein has argued, wanting to join the EU provided the accession countries with 'state projects' (or focal points) which all major political parties were willing to pursue. Such focal points were lacking in the non-accession post-Soviet countries; and the policies promoted by outside agents there (primarily the IMF and the World Bank) often had very little overlap with the goals and values of the societies concerned.[64]

As we will see in more detail below, the EU's influence on the fiscal system mattered in at least two respects. On the one hand, it provided some guidance for reforming the tax system—coinciding with the desire to attract foreign investment which was probably an even more important motivation. On the other hand, the EU pushed strongly for better financial controls before making large pre-accession funds available to Lithuania.[65] Thus, the EU provided significant incentives, constraints, and assistance in developing these institutional structures which reduced the possibilities for abuse of public funds. In this sense the EU also acted as an external check on Lithuania's elite. While this mechanism was far from perfect, it created a set of incentives which was absent in the non-accession countries.

10.4. Fiscal and budgetary system

In terms of overall fiscal size, the share of revenue and expenditures of GDP has been somewhat smaller in Lithuania than in Ukraine and Russia, and more than 10 per cent smaller than in Belarus (see Appendix, Table I.2.1). The size of total expenditures has hovered around 35 per cent of GDP throughout the 1990s. In 1999, expenditure briefly reached 40 per cent of GDP when the economy contracted in the wake of the Russian crisis. Thereafter, revenue and expenditure levels declined relative to the GDP to around 30 per cent, during a period of strong economic growth. By 2003, Lithuania had become the (prospective) EU member country with the lowest government expenditure.[66] Debt levels (external debt) stood at similar levels as in Ukraine—around 40 per cent of GDP in 2000, rising to 45 per cent by 2003.[67]

10.4.1. TAX SYSTEM

As has been pointed out above, the formal institutional starting point in Lithuania was the same as in Ukraine and elsewhere in the former Soviet Union, namely the Soviet tax system with numerous different rates of turnover tax and profit/loss sharing between enterprises and the state—variously described as 'confiscatory profit taxation' (Vaicenavičius) or 'soft budget constraints' on enterprises (Kornai).

The *Sajudis* government elected in March 1990 adopted a number of tax laws in mid-1990 which were understood to be provisional and would be replaced by more permanent laws once the economic situation had stabilized.[68] Thus, fundamental institutional change started a year and a half before full state independence. The list of major taxes adopted at this early stage was already that of most contemporary market economies, i.e. comprising corporate and private income taxes, payroll taxes, excise taxes, and a general turnover tax which functioned as a precursor to a fully-fledged VAT system.[69]

The next major step was the introduction of an EU-style value-added-tax in 1994.[70] Together with individual income tax and payroll taxes, VAT has since provided the most important revenue source. In 1997, the favorable VAT regime on food and energy (9 per cent instead of 18 per cent), was abolished in order to increase revenue as required by the IMF.[71] Moreover, a single tax rate of 33 per cent on personal incomes was introduced—which is high by post-Soviet as well as by international standards since under a progressive tax regime the majority of the population falls into the lower tax brackets.[72] Payroll taxes were levied at a rate first of 31 and later of 34 per cent. Overall, Lithuania shifted the tax burden heavily towards labor; while the corporate income tax rate was successively reduced from 29 to 24 to 15 per cent (see Table 10.3 below).[73]

In contrast to Russia, individual income taxes were phased in relatively fast and successfully, and became more important than corporate income taxes already by 1994.[74] By 2000, PIT was contributing 7.8 per cent of GDP, while CIT had been much reduced in importance, collecting only 0.7 per cent.[75] As the IMF observed in 1995: "The decline in tax revenue was accompanied by dramatic changes in the composition of revenue, in particular a shift in taxation from capital to labor."[76]

Further reforms of the tax system have been almost continuously on the agenda.[77] The conservative government that came back to power in late 1996 proposed cutting various taxes: reducing the VAT from 18 to 15 per cent, personal income tax to 28-30 per cent and abolishing the profit tax over a ten-year period.[78] In 1998, ambitious plans to abolish profit taxes within two years were announced.[79] However, due to the difficult revenue situation which developed in 1999, radical tax cuts were put off.[80]

The debate was renewed in 2000, and was marked by the crucial impact of external factors: Estonia had abolished its corporate income (or profit) tax from January 2000, so the question of whether it was necessary and desirable to copy its example was hotly debated.[81] However, both the IMF and the EU opposed plans to cancel the tax immediately. The IMF's primary motive was concern for fiscal stability, while the EU as a club of economies worried more about unfair tax competition.[82] Domestically, President Adamkus criticized the idea to abolish the corporate income tax as creating an unfair system in which labor would be far more heavily taxed than capital.[83] At the same time, the EU became more deeply involved in those issues of taxation which needed to be reshaped for accession (rules for levying VAT, strengthening of administrative capacity, etc.).

Table 10.3: Basic tax rates in 1993, 2001, and 2003

	1993	2001	2003
Personal income tax	18–33% (changed to 33% flat in 1994)	33% flat for main job	33% flat (to be lowered gradually to 24% by 2008)
Corporate income tax	29%; 19%	24%	15% from 1/1/2002 onwards, 13% for small enterprises and 0% for agricultural enterprises
Payroll taxes	30% employers + 1% employees; 23% farmers	31% employers + 3% employees	31% employers + 3% employees
VAT	18%	18%	18% (with exemptions)
Excise taxes		specific rates on alcohol, tobacco, and fuel	specific rates on alcohol, tobacco, and fuel
Capital gains, dividends, royalties, rentals	–	15%	15%

In summer 2001, the government coalition of the center-left New Union and the center-right Liberal Union fell apart *inter alia* over a dispute concerning how to reform the tax system. It was replaced by a left-wing government under the veteran politician Algirdas Brazauskas, which promised its own version of tax reforms. While during the October 2000 election campaign the LSDP had been calling for the reintroduction of progressive taxation of individual income, in the economic program presented by the new government this plan was changed to an increase in the tax-free minimum income.[84] Furthermore, in December 2001, parliament decided to lower the profit tax rate from 24 to 15 per cent.[85] Around the same time, in October 2001 and March

2002, new laws on VAT and on excise taxation were adopted, mainly to bring the rules and regulations in line with EU requirements.

The high taxation of labor stimulated a debate about the need for further change. The idea was to gradually bring this tax down to a flat rate of 24 per cent; but since in contrast to Ukraine or Russia most tax-payers were already captured, this was expected to result in a loss of revenue. There was disagreement about which other taxes to increase or introduce in order to make up for the expected loss. While Minister of Finance Butkevicius suggested to increase the profit tax rate for a period of two years from 15 to 19 per cent, the government as a whole initially favored the temporary introduction of a 'solidarity tax' to be levied on corporate turnover—which, however, Butkevicius claimed would be in breach of EU rules and prompted him to step down.[86]

In June 2005, the changes in the tax system were adopted largely in line with Butkevicius' proposal: a temporary social tax was added to the profit tax rate (4 per cent extra in 2006 and 3 per cent extra in 2007); the property tax base was extended to include natural as well as legal persons (at an unchanged and uniform rate of 1 per cent); and the personal income tax was to be lowered to 27 per cent from July 2006 and to 24 per cent from January 2008.[87]

The main remaining challenges in the early 2000s have been the administrative burden of taxation as well as some problems with corruption. A new tax administration law was passed in April 2004, coming into force May 1, 2004, aiming to ease the administrative burdens and to increase voluntary compliance.[88] However, due to the frequent changes in legislation in the years prior to EU accession (which included also accountancy rules related to EU approximation) tax inspectors were often not fully informed about current rules, and implementation often lagged behind formal rules.

10.4.2. THE PUBLIC DEBATE ON TAXATION

The public debate on taxation has been far more lively and structured in Lithuania than in the other three comparative cases surveyed here. The first crucial changes in the tax system, however, were undertaken by *Sajudis* during a 'window of opportunity' in mid-1990 before a structured debate had set in. Thus, according to Vaicenavičius:

At this time (early 1990s) the rapid economic liberalization and the high speed of fiscal policy reform led to a certain loss of fiscal control, if compared to both the rigid central planning system or the systems of highly developed market economies. [...] During the early transition period, by necessity there was certain haste involved in reforming fiscal policy. As noted above, fiscal policy responded to the pace and unexpected surprises of transition, and accelerating transition was the overarching public policy objective. As a result, there was a certain rush-to-reform public policies of all sorts without adequate time available for assessment, public discussion and debate of rather major policy changes. Stealth did produce rapid reform, but it also opened the door for an environment in which special interests could exert considerable influence on public policy making.[89]

The early lack of a more detailed public debate on fiscal issues continued into the first years of transition. Lazutka, who focuses on the closely related area of social policy, observes:

In the summer and autumn of 1994 very important laws were discussed in the Parliament. [...] There were some cardinal changes in these laws but they did not rouse any debates among political parties. When observing a rather severe general position of the opposition to criticize, such an agreement with respect to social policy is surprising. When a subsistence level is so low, this agreement can be interpreted only as an unpreparedness of politicians to assess social policy and propose alternative solutions.[90]

This assumption—that laws got through due to a lack of attention and proper analysis rather than general agreement—is supported by the fact that at the outset of transition, Lithuanians at large were somewhat, but not substantially more willing to support the new requirements of the state by paying higher taxes (see Appendix, Table II.4.2).

Once public debate had started and public life was beginning to restructure (with regard to interest associations), it became more difficult to adopt changes in the tax system. For example, five to six years passed between the first announcement of an intention to phase out profit taxes and a first legislative decision in this direction—about the same time span over which tax reform has been debated in Ukraine or Russia.

Finally, it is interesting to observe the type of institution-building and the direction of later changes chosen. While Lithuania in general is the most conservative among the three Baltic states, there is a strong liberal streak in the debate and in actual policy. The phenomenon of liberal(ist) tax reform, primarily the introduction of flat income taxes in post-communist countries—

Estonia, Lithuania, Slovakia, Russia, Ukraine—has caught international attention.[91] It provides an interesting reflection on legacies: while being a long standing liberalist idea, the flat income tax has not been introduced in any of the traditionally liberal Anglo-Saxon countries but in former communist countries. This indicates that institutional reform can go *against* the grain of existing legacies and can be more a reaction to the dismantling of an old order and the need to create something radically different. While, as I have explained above, the absence of personal income taxation in the previous system posed problems for the introduction of such a system, it also meant that there was no ingrained progressive system and consequently little resistance to radical change.[92] In this vein we may also note that the flat tax experiment took hold in new states rather than in continuous post-communist states such as Hungary or Poland.

A very low flat tax rate was chosen in the weaker post-communist states such as Russia and Ukraine, as is discussed in more detail in Chapters 5 and 11, where the rationale was to bring people back into the tax-net who were evading higher taxes. This 'gamble' of radically lowering rates paid off in the form of higher revenue from personal income taxation in these weaker states—in a way in which it would not in well-established systems in which most people are already covered by existing progressive taxes. In a relatively more capable state like Lithuania, a simple flat tax was also introduced, but at a much higher rate (33 as compared to 13 per cent).

10.4.3. ADMINISTERING AND EVADING TAXES

While Lithuania moved early on to a reasonably well-structured statutory tax system, the actual capacity to extract still suffered in the early 1990s. Thus, we can observe that the ratio of revenue to GDP fell more steeply in Lithuania than in the other two Baltic countries (in spite of initially roughly similar tax rates).[93] This was attributable to the hasty privatization process pursued in the early 1990s, in particular with respect to collecting indirect taxes (GET/VAT and excises). The IMF stated in 1995 that "the Lithuanian tax administration lacks the expertise to track the new private sector firms accurately."[94] In 1995, president Brazauskas held that "there are no bigger problems in our country than tax evasion and abuse of authority."[95] On public television he exhorted business people to pay their taxes so that adequate pensions could be paid by the state. Also, considerable problems with corruption among the tax inspectorate were assumed to exist. Thus, according to a 1995 survey among Lithuanian and foreign business people, representatives of the tax inspectorate and the customs service were judged to be the most corrupt of all bureaucrats.[96] Furthermore, we can observe that the heads of the tax inspectorate have changed even more often than prime ministers in Lithuania, indicating that there was little satisfaction with the performance of the department (see Table 10.1).[97]

Estimates of the shadow economy in Lithuania for 1994–95 vary between 25 and 40 per cent (while for Ukraine, the two estimates are 47 and 54 per cent).[98] Vaicenavičius gives an estimate of 40 per cent for the mid-1990s.[99] Data on the willingness of Lithuanians to pay taxes is extremely contradictory. According to one poll, tax evasion was even more accepted in Lithuania than in Ukraine and Russia.[100] According to a different poll taken about a year earlier, Lithuanians overwhelmingly said that paying one's taxes and never cheating on social security was very important.[101]

From 1995 onwards, the situation began to improve.[102] That year, a new tax administration law was passed in line with EU requirements, which included a separation of tax policy and tax administration functions. In 1996, the incoming Stankevicius government decided to cancel penalties concerning tax payments accrued by enterprises from 1992 to 1994, provided the enterprises paid their previous and current tax debt in full.[103] Furthermore, Stankevicius sacked the head of the tax inspectorate after widespread complaints in the press about controversial interpretations of tax laws and discrimination among business people.[104] The new head of the inspectorate, Nesteckis, announced a policy of "helping rather than controlling" taxpayers.[105] At the same time, a new law aiming to better control cash payments was introduced.[106]

In 1997, a tax police was set up to curb tax evasion.[107] It was placed under the Ministry of Internal Affairs (rather than the Ministry of Finance, under which the tax inspectorate was located), and was given the right not only to check private enterprises (for double bookkeeping and other evasion schemes), but also to investigate violations by the state tax inspectorate and the customs service.[108] Furthermore, fines for purposeful evasion and evasion by mistake were differentiated and sharply increased for the former category (i.e. in cases where companies use double or technically altered cash registers, falsify their data, etc.).[109] Also in 1997, a first cooperation agreement with the tax service of another state—Latvia—was concluded in order to increase control over tax evasion.[110] A trilateral agreement of all three Baltic countries followed in June 1999.[111] Regionally, tax offices were re-organized along functional lines and their number was reduced from 56 to 10 in 1999.

At the end of the first decade of transition, the EU judged Lithuania to be relatively efficient with regard to collecting taxes—while further improvements, data collection and information sharing on the one hand, and a move towards more cooperative relations with taxpayers on the other hand were put in place in the early 2000s as required by the EU.[112] Other indicators, such as the ranking on the Corruption Perceptions Index, point in the same direction of an improving situation with regard to corruption and the shadow (i.e. non-taxed) economy. In 2001, the shadow economy was estimated at 20 per cent of the GDP—half its share of five years earlier.[113] This stands in contrast to Ukraine and Russia, which were still having major problems with getting businesses 'out of the shadows.'

Still, some problems relating to the tax system were similar to those encountered in Ukraine: thus for example, firms used fake exports in order to claim VAT refunds, and due to the high tax burden on labor a considerable shadow labor market emerged.[114] In contrast to Ukraine, tax reductions were generally not seen as the primary measure to address this problem.[115]

Having a workable and fairly clear legal tax system in place has allowed Lithuania to concentrate on improving the tax administration from the mid-1990s onwards. Moreover, in contrast to Ukraine, Russia, and Belarus, the tax administration has not been compromised by large-scale political abuse. As a result, a fairly high level of revenue has been collected without choking off the development of business as is widely reported in Ukraine.

Table 10.4: World Bank, Investment Climate Survey, 2002

	Lithuania	Belarus	Ukraine	Russia	Estonia
Tax rates as a major constraint in %	36.5	47.0	39.6	24.6	16.7
Tax administration as a major constraint in %	19.8	44.2	34.9	31.8	4.5

Source: World Bank

As the figures from the 2002 Investment Climate Survey of the World Bank show, Lithuania differed from the other three cases studied here by bringing the problem of the tax administration better under control and making it less burdensome on investors. At the same time, businesses in Lithuania still saw the tax administration and especially tax rates as more of a problem than in Estonia, the regional "reform leader."

10.4.4. BUDGET STRUCTURE AND BUDGETING PRACTICE

The first budget law was adopted in late June 1990, three months after Lithuania had unilaterally declared independence from the Soviet Union. During 1991, Lithuania stopped transferring resources to the union budget. Having one's own budget was part and parcel of the drive for independence.

The general government budget consists of the state budget and 56 local budgets. The basic budget structure was created through the budget law of 1990 and the constitution adopted in 1992, i.e., early in transition. The proliferation of extra-budgetary funds (from 4 in 1992 to 30 by 1998) allowed some flexibility during the transition but also resulted in a lack of control over these earmarked funds.[116] These problems eventually began to be addressed in 1998–2000 when a new organic budget law was formulated. In 1998, revenue-sharing between the state and local budgets was re-organized on the basis of a revenue-sharing formula suggested by the World Bank, replacing yearly negotiations between local and central governments. In 2000, a new organic budget law was adopted under the guidance of EU recommendations which introduced program budgeting (see below). Medium-term, five-year planning periods were introduced and the number of extra-budgetary funds was reduced from 22 to 4 (now made up of the social insurance fund, the health insurance fund, the privatization fund, and the fund for the closure of the Ignalina nuclear power plant).

The approval of the budget by parliament has generally been more orderly than in Ukraine. Budgets were usually passed in early December.[117] Since governments in Lithuania are based on parliamentary majorities, budget negotiations are more conciliatory and involve more consultations with parliamentary factions than in Ukraine.[118] Furthermore, the existence of a system of party discipline ensures that interests are aggregated within the parliament, thus keeping specific demands by individual MPs on the budget in check.[119]

As elsewhere in the former Soviet Union, the Ministry of Finance was initially rather weak as an organizational institution. In the course of transition, then, its role was considerably strengthened vis-à-vis other ministries. For example, on the basis of IMF advice, responsibility for macro-economic forecasting as well as for fiscal policy-making was transferred to the Ministry of Finance by the mid 1990s.[120] A treasury system was first created in 1995–96;[121] by 2001 there was a single unified treasury account, but extra-budgetary funds were not yet covered, and according to Butkevicius, the treasury system still needed further improvement.[122]

According to the constitution, changes in the budget (cuts, increases, shifts between expenditure categories) have to be approved by parliament.[123] In the early 1990s, during the period of highest uncertainty, the Ministry of Finance used the crude but effective method of cash-rationing: expenditures were only made to the extent that revenue was actually coming in, with cuts being made across the board (rather than by evaluating expenditure needs).[124] Furthermore, sequestration (i.e. repetitive budgeting) was used regularly until 1996 and again in 1999.[125] This reflects Wildavsky's point that repetitive budgeting is a feature of poor and uncertain countries. The high uncertainty during the initial transition period was a challenge for Lithuania's state capacity, and one with which the state coped relatively well—although in 1999 ongoing struggles in the political arena hampered decision-making for coping with the ripple effects of the Russian crisis. Overall, the period of fundamental economic turmoil in Lithuania was relatively short, and in the early 2000s, strong growth facilitated budgeting as the state could spend more, rather than having to cut back on expenditures.

From the beginning, expenditure discipline was much tighter in Lithuania than in Ukraine or Russia. Very large deficits (of more than 10 per cent of GDP) never occurred.[126] Although revenue collection was at times difficult in the early 1990s, it was much closer to the target than in Ukraine.[127] Furthermore, in contrast to Russia and Ukraine, where off-sets were used extensively, Lithuania collected its revenue in cash.[128] Budget execution (overall and of broad expenditure categories) has also been much closer on target than in Ukraine, except in 1999.[129] Overall, therefore, a basically functioning and meaningful budget process was established rather early on during Lithuania's independence and transition.

During the deepest economic slump, Lithuania experienced budget deficits of up to 5.5 per cent of the GDP (in 1994). Furthermore, Lithuania never accumulated substantial arrears in pensions and wages. With the return of economic growth, the situation improved, and in 1997 the idea of formulating a constitutional amendment to outlaw budget deficits was proposed by Prime Minister Vagnorius.[130] No law was adopted at this stage, but governments started to define deficit-free budgets as a goal. However, in 1999, when the first deficit-free budget was planned, the worst result of the post-independence era was recorded and the budget deficit reached 8.6 per cent.[131]

Several things went wrong in 1999. Firstly, the budget had been based on overly optimistic assumptions about GDP growth.[132] Secondly, the governing coalition of the conservatives was badly organized, with two changes of prime ministers in one year, which delayed the government's reaction to the crisis spreading from Russia. Furthermore, the conservatives were reluctant to give up the popular program of savings restitution—which, however, proved too costly for the budget. When early in the year the IMF suggested raising taxes, the government refused to consider the proposal.[133] Throughout the year, revenue fell short of what had been budgeted, but only in October 1999 did the parliament finally decide that expenditures should be cut—and allowed the Ministry of Finance to decide on further reductions if necessary. Eventually, the incoming government under Andrius Kubilius reached a decision to freeze the savings compensation program arguing that the program—initiated by Kubilius' own party—was simply unaffordable to the country in the current situation.[134]

For 2000, the IMF strongly pressured the government to keep the deficit down. This had initially been planned at 6.5 per cent of GDP in order to cover considerable outlays related to the sale of Mazeikiu Nafta, the country's large oil refinery, to a foreign investor (for which the government promised to provide a US $350 million long-term loan).[135] Eventually, two large cuts were made by eliminating the planned LTL 700 million savings restitution from the 2000 budget, as well as by lowering agricultural subsidies.[136] In subsequent years, deficits were kept low, facilitated by strong economic growth.

During most years, the relationship between the parliament and especially the parliamentary budget committee and the government appears to have been relatively cooperative—certainly more so than in Ukraine. Several politicians have held both the position of head of the budgetary committee and minister of finance at some point in their political careers.[137]

About half of Lithuania's budget is spent on health, education, and social security, while another third is spent on the judiciary, police, and defense. Spending on education is higher than in Ukraine and Russia.[138] As for defense, Lithuania had to increase its spending in order to meet NATO accession requirements. Social welfare payments comprise just over a quarter of public expenditures. However, the social welfare fund has been facing serious financial difficulties due to under-reporting of wages, as well as due to high dependency ratios. In 2000, pay roll contributions were raised from 31 to 34 per cent of wages.[139]

A major spending decision was taken by the conservative government in 1996 to pay compensation on the savings lost during hyperinflation in 1992—an extremely popular as well as a costly policy move. By the late 1990s, savings had mostly been restored to pensioners, but not to other groups. Plans were discussed to use the funds to be used for restitution to younger people—mainly proceeds from privatization—in order to reform the pension system and to introduce a fully-funded scheme.[140] However, as mentioned above, the whole program had to be frozen in 1999 when revenue fell short, and was not reactivated.

10.4.4.1. FROM BASIC TO ADVANCED REFORMS: THE IDEA OF PROGRAM BUDGETING

The idea to reform the budget law was developed in 1998 under the conservative government and was particularly promoted by Andrius Kubilius who became prime minister in 1999.[141] As Kestutis Skiudas, advisor to Kubilius explains, reforming and strengthening the state became one of the main goals during the second half of the 1990s—and budgetary reform was regarded as a center piece in this process.[142] Kubilius himself has stressed that his aim was to make ministers think strategically rather than focus all their attention on day-to-day matters, as he found strategic thinking to be strongly lacking upon becoming prime minister.[143]

Budget reform was oriented on a model of program budgeting taken from Canada, implying that ministries (and other spending agencies) were required to present and defend their entire spending program together with budget requests.[144] The broad idea was to escape the 'ratcheting' effect described by Wildavsky, i.e. the fact that in normal years, spending units receive approximately the same level of funds as in the previous year, plus or minus an increment depending on the overall availability of resources. Instead, the budget would become useable as a strategic plan.[145] As with regard to tax reform, the specific content of budget reform in Lithuania was oriented on a non-EU model.[146] Program budgeting as a reform idea originated in the 1960s in the US; but its impact on budget systems initially remained limited.[147] As part of the public sector reform wave of the 1990s ('New Public Management'), program budgeting was revived as a reform idea, and increasingly also 'exported' to transition and developing countries.

In Lithuania, the intent was to strengthen the accountability of appropriation managers, i.e., of those who use budgetary funds, by requiring them to present reports on the performance of the funds used in the previous year, as well as to develop strategic plans for the following budget period.[148]

In principle, all political forces supported the reform; however, as Butkevičius, the incoming head of the budgetary committee in 2001 acknowledged, there were problems with the implementation of such an ambitious change in budgeting practices.[149] Strategic policy making and the use of performance assessment had some impact, but could not obliterate the fact that budget allocations are flexible only within limits, and also that political interests and maneuvers affect budgets and the public administration in many ways which can undermine 'best practices.'[150]

Overall, given the initial shock of a substantial economic crisis, budget discipline has been reasonably good in Lithuania—even if the rhetoric of a balanced budget proved to be unrealistic. The consolidated parliamentary system produced considerably more coherence and consensus in the process of drafting, passing and executing budgets than in Ukraine. Having such a reasonably well-functioning system allowed Lithuania to move on to a more advanced stage of reforms, i.e., trying to introduce a more strategic way of budgeting. These advanced reforms are challenging in any country, but they show that by the late 1990s, Lithuanian political elites had overcome the emergency stage of state-building and were beginning to address the question of how to build an effective, flexible, and modern state. While EU accession was an important motor for reform, Lithuania, as other accession countries, looked also beyond existing EU member states for institutional models.

10.4.5. FINANCIAL CONTROL AND CORRUPTION

Two main factors were driving the Lithuanian system of financial controls forward from 1990–92 onwards: the first was the memory of the old institutional system and the second, becoming stronger over time, was related to external demands that came primarily from the EU. At stake was a change from a Soviet system, which explicitly worked without a *public* accountability of its institutions, to one which would ensure such an accountability.

The main (external) element of financial control in Lithuania is the State Control (*Valstybes Kontrole*), Lithuania's supreme audit institution. The State Control (SC) explicitly defines itself as founded in 1919, i.e., at the time of the first modern independent Lithuanian state, when a State Control Institution was set up, which was then abolished in 1940 in the wake of Soviet occupation. The resurrection of the State Control began immediately after the declaration of independence in 1990, with the adoption of a new law on state control and the appointment of Kazimieras Uoka as its head. Thus, a basic control institution was created roughly six years earlier than in Ukraine. Being able to reach back to historical models allowed greater speed in building institutions at various levels in Lithuania; and it was also widely used as a source of legitimization for these institutions.

Approximately from 1992 onwards, the SC was functional, but continued to be in a constant process of re-organization with major changes and amendments to the legal base occurring in 1995, 1998, 2001, and 2003. In the early years, staff appointments were often based on the political criterion of 'patriotism' rather than professionalism. Later, the emphasis on professionalism increased, although the institution faced the problem of competing with auditing firms in the private sector for qualified personnel.[151]

The State Control is an independent state body which reports to and is accountable to parliament. Its head is proposed by the president and appointed by parliament for a five-year term. In 1999, this led to conflict between the president and parliament, when president Adamkus was asserting greater powers of his office and nominated a candidate the parliament would not accept; but eventually a compromise was found.

The competencies of the Lithuanian control institution are broader than those of its Ukrainian counterpart. Thus, it has a mandate to monitor revenue as well as expenditures, it controls privatization results, and it has the authority to audit all institutions and bodies which receive or manage state funds (including the Central Bank), as well as enterprises in which the state holds at least half of the voting shares. Thus, in October 2000 the State Control published a report heavily critical of the sale of the main shipping line (LISCO), demanding that the privatization deal be annulled, which consequently was what occurred. According to Jacevičius, in the 1990s, monitoring privatization deals occupied about half of the State Control's time and resources.[152] In 2003, the auditing of municipal budgets and of EU financial assistance were added to the State Control's mandate.

Apart from the broader mandate than that of the supreme audit institution in Ukraine, the Lithuanian State Control also benefited from a more conducive public environment, and in particular a free and professional press. As many of those interviewed emphasized, Lithuanian politicians, state-institutions, and state-run companies have developed a self-interest in not drawing media criticism, which has helped to foster a culture of public accountability. However, this still remains imperfect, as the various scandals which occurred in the 1990s and 2000s attest.

Two of the greatest problems of the State Control were its 'politicized' nature and its initially rather inquisitive character. Thus, under the first Law on State Control politicians as well as the State Prosecutor (the institutional legacy of the powerful Soviet *Prokurator*) had the power to request specific audits.[153] This link was formally abolished by the new Law on State Control adopted in late 2001. Moreover, from around 1996 the State Control benefited from intensive institution-building support from the EU, which helped to move from narrowly checking compliance to a more broadly defined control of performance.

External assistance included intensive reviews of the State Control's mandate and institutional structure, as well as the provision of technical assistance from a range of Western European supreme audit institutions provided via twinning programs.[154] EU recommendations and requirements (not least for controlling prospective large amounts of pre-accession aid) resulted in a strategic development plan of the institution as well as in the new 2001 Law on State Control.

Furthermore, the EU pushed for the establishment of a complete system of internal audit within all government ministries and agencies.[155] Good internal audit systems are a key component of a well-functioning control and audit system within the state. In 1998 less than half of state institutions had systems of internal control, but this figure rose to over 90 per cent by January 2001.[156] Still, the 2001 progress report on EU accession stressed that substantial further progress was needed in making internal control effective. Subsequently, a new Law on Internal Control and Internal Audit was formulated and adopted in late 2002. The last 'Comprehensive Monitoring Report' by the EU on Lithuania before accession acknowledged substantial progress, while still pushing for further strengthening of administrative capacities.[157]

A third important element in the state's institutional accountability system is a strong parliamentary committee on financial issues which hears and follows up on reports from the audit institutions. On recommendations from the EU, a specialized Audit Sub-Committee of the Seimas Committee on Budget and Finance was created in 2002; and in late 2004 this was transformed into the Seimas Audit Committee.

Despite the early creation of a rather strong control institution with a broad mandate, corruption has been a major problem in Lithuania as elsewhere in former Soviet countries. A major corruption scandal involving high-level government officials emerged in the winter of 1995–1996 when two major banks—the Innovation-Bank and the Litimpex Bank—collapsed. Subsequently, it was revealed that several politicians had received special interest rates on their accounts; furthermore, they had been warned to withdraw their funds before the banks declared bankruptcy.[158] The impeachment and removal of president Paksas from office in 2004 brought to light the fact that corrupt links between businesses and political groups were still a serious problem.

There have been some positive trends in tackling corruption and rent-seeking; with outside pressures and incentives playing an important role.[159] Thus, Lithuania improved its rating on the CPI from rank 50 in 1999 to rank 38 in 2001, with a more or less stable rating over the following four years. In contrast, Ukraine hovered at the bottom of the list, although it was rated as slightly improved in 2005; while Russia was rated as gradually improving during the early Putin period, but then as worsening again in 2005 (see Appendix, Table II.5.1).

In mid-2002, a National Anti-Corruption program was adopted by the Seimas. Already in 2000, Transparency International opened a chapter in Lithuania, promoting assessments and public debate on corruption;[160] and the government set up a Special Investigation Service in 1997 to work towards uncovering and preventing corruption. Initially under the Ministry of Interior, the SIS was based on a new law in 2000, making it accountable to the president and parliament directly.

Overall, in contrast to Russia and Ukraine, Lithuania had two major advantages with regard to developing an audit and control system compatible with a democratic political regime: 1) the pre-existence of historical models of control which provided a focal point and allowed the early institutionalization of a control mechanism in the form of the SC; 2) this was followed up by the emergence of an outside actor (the EU) which demanded improvements in transparency and control in the sphere of public finance and with which there was a high general readiness to comply since accession was the key national goal. Finally, in contrast to Belarus, control is not only exercised by government over the administration, but there is also control by the governed over their elites—i.e., democratic accountability—even if this still remains far from perfect.

10.5. State capacity and its determinants in Lithuania

Overall, state capacity was higher and developed more quickly after independence in Lithuania than in Ukraine, with regard to all three dimensions: decision-making, implementation, and control. Furthermore, in Lithuania, the state developed fewer dysfunctional aspects. In contrast to Belarus, in Lithuania state-building was linked to pursuing changes in the role of government. Within this broadly positive development, there have still been substantial problems related to populist politics on the one hand, and opportunities for illicit enrichment by state elites during transition on the other hand which have had negative impacts on the state.

This broad assessment is reflected in the three dimensions of state capacity which have been analyzed. With regard to regular decision-making, Lithuania has done reasonably well with regard to adopting budgets on time; and with the exception of 1999, budgets have been relatively realistic (see section 4.4

above). Furthermore, important decisions about institutional change were made in the initial as well as in latter phases of independence.

Implementation has been reasonably good. Thus, when the economy went into turmoil in the early 1990s, the government kept expenditure under control using crude but effective methods.[161] There were problems with implementing taxation in a rapidly changing economy, but gradually the situation has improved. Thus, by 2001, the shadow economy was down to about 20 per cent of GDP—and thus coming within the 'normal' OECD range.[162]

The difference in building a system of control was particularly stark in comparison to Ukraine: an (external) accounting institution with wide-ranging powers was already established during the first phase of independence. This was then re-enforced by EU accession requirements and institution-building assistance for a 'clean' public sector, and by the presence of a free and investigative press. Thus, Lithuania developed both managerial control within the state, and accountability of those in government to the public (as shown by several turnovers in government).

The Lithuanian state is not free of dysfunctional aspects: corruption is still considerably more prevalent than, for example, in Estonia, and trust in key institutions, especially in parliament and in political parties, is rather unexpectedly low. However, political, social, and state structures appear to address remaining problems and are likely to be able to reduce these over time.

Two key factors appear to have driven this development of a capable and relatively well-governed state in Lithuania—the early consolidation of a democratic regime on the one hand, and the positive external incentive of EU accession on the other hand. From the very start, all political forces were broadly in agreement on the acceptance both of fundamental rules and also, fundamental goals (independence, integration with Western clubs). Early elite reconfiguration was overall propitious, especially since the communist party transformed itself rather than disappeared and supported independence, as well as transformation. Already the 1992 elections brought the ex-communist party back to power, reminding both sides of the need to be accountable to voters.

A further positive feature was that Lithuania developed a parliamentary system of government, which broadly worked in the context of relatively well-defined parties. As the examples of Ukraine and Russia show, presidential or mixed presidential-parliamentary systems can engender problems for state-building. Presidents and prime ministers have competed for power, and presidents have used prime ministers to shift the blame for poor performance. Furthermore, parliaments and presidents have mutually blocked each other's decision-making, especially when competencies were still being defined; and have engaged in competitive rule creation (i.e., decrees vs. laws).

In Lithuania, in contrast, government is based on a parliamentary majority. Hence there were no multiple sources of law-making, and the budgeting process has generally been smoother. Nonetheless, fairly well-developed parties were present in Lithuania to make its parliamentary system operable—without which the risk of developing 'feckless pluralism' may be substantial.[163]

With regard to political consolidation, it is important to distinguish between instability at the governmental and the regime level. Governments were relatively instable in Lithuania, with ten prime ministers holding office during the first ten years of independence, but this was mitigated by the fundamental agreement on key policies. Furthermore, while prime ministers changed frequently, respective political parties or coalitions lasted. Still, government instability had some negative consequences, as it shortened the time-horizon of key government personnel and their opportunities for seeing reforms through, as the example of the reforms suggested by the Kubilius government shows.

Regular elections, a relatively strong civil and political society and a free, investigative press have provided a balance to political consolidation, providing an emerging system of overall accountability. Furthermore, the self-restraint by elites at the outset of transition and the will to create institutions providing checks and balances, as well as the presence of outside 'supervision,' have all interacted to ensure that in Lithuania the 'state-as-a-problem' overall has been kept in check considerably better than in Ukraine.

Beyond political consolidation, the second important factor which enabled Lithuania's overall successful state-building was the emergence of the EU-accession option from the mid-1990s onwards. Thus, in contrast to assumptions that international integration damages state-building prospects, in Eastern Europe the specific prospect of regional integration into the EU has benefited those new states in the region that were accepted as 'accession countries' and eventually as new member states. Aiming at accession has supported a rapid modernization of administrative structures which otherwise might have proceeded considerably slower—even though, as Nakrosis reminds us, pre-accession assistance has not been a panacea and has been limited by domestic constraints in several areas.[164] Furthermore, the need to adopt an avalanche of laws in the run-up to accession has also involved overly rapid adoption of legislation.

The EU has been an external actor with considerable leverage and has pushed for the adoption of effective control mechanisms over public finances. Corruption and the abuse of power by elites has been a major problem in all post-communist countries. While general democratic consolidation has helped to address such dysfunctionalities, EU accession has provided a crucial additional impetus to rapidly establish structures which could contain corruption and the misuse of funds.

A factor which supported the overall successful state-building was the previous experience of independent statehood. This experience had two effects: firstly, in Lithuania, all political forces, including the communists, rallied early behind the goal of independence. Secondly, due to this experience, domestic models for building state institutions were available. This facilitated the legitimization of an institutional structure, as the examples of the SC and the Central Bank show—even if what remained were ideas rather than administrative experience. Furthermore, the strong drive for independence meant a rejection of the notion of reliance on Russia, and thus forced the rapid establishment of problem-solving capacity on the part of the new policy-makers. In this sense, pre-Soviet legacies contributed to state-building in Lithuania.

At the same time, it is interesting to observe that in terms of state-building models and constituent institutional elements, Lithuania has 'experimented' in ways which cannot be attributed either to domestic legacies or to EU models. Examples are the introduction of a flat income tax, the debate about abolishing corporate income taxes, and the introduction of program budgeting based on Canadian models. Lithuania, like all post-Soviet countries, opened up to the outside world during a period when new ideas of public management were gaining ground. Lithuania's regional neighbor Estonia has taken the role of a front-runner of liberalism, providing a model which has been important in Lithuanian public debates. These debates and the adopted institutional changes show that some rather radical reforms may be easier to realize in the post-Soviet realm than in traditional OECD countries. As ingrained patterns of institutional legacies and interests based on these had anyway been weakened by transition, the range of options for reform opened far wider than in 'stable state' countries. Thus, while the legacies of previous independent statehood were important for Lithuania's state-building process in a broad sense, at the more detailed level institutional choices have deviated from legacies to a rather unexpected degree.

Overall, among the four cases studied here Lithuania has been most successful at establishing a capable and well-governed state, due to a mixture of political consolidation around rules (despite some instability at the government level), a historical memory of independent statehood, and the positive external impact of the EU. The institutional structure which has emerged is far from perfect, and further work especially on reducing corruption remains.[165] However, the key accomplishment of creating a state based on a democratic regime has been achieved.

Notes

1 Nørgaard and Johannsen (1999), 35.
2 See Table 1, "Basic structural indicators," Introduction.
3 Nørgaard and Johannsen (1999), 48.
4 The Russian minority accounted for 8.5% of the population in Lithuania, but 30.4% in Latvia, and 25.6% in Estonia; in Ukraine 21%. In contrast to Latvia and Estonia, there were few obstacles to acquiring Lithuanian citizenship. Savchenko has argued that ethnic cleavages may have facilitated economic reforms in Estonia and Latvia since Russians were concentrated among the industrial workforce. Savchenko (2000); Haavisto (1997).
5 See www.essex.ac.uk/elect/electer/lt_er_nl.htm [accessed: June 25, 2002].
6 Krickus (1997), 297.
7 On other post-Soviet cases, especially Georgia, see Wheatley (2003).
8 See Tauber (1997).
9 Mygind in Haavisto (1997), 23.
10 Nørgaard and Johannsen (1999), 62–63.
11 Constitution of Lithuania, Article 101, also articles 67, 9 and 84.
12 Constitution of Lithuania, Article 85.
13 Interview with J. Razma and Kestutis Skiudas, Homeland Union, Vilnius, July 26, 2001.
14 T. D. Clark and N. Prekevicius: "Political Turmoil within Institutional Stability." (Annual Report on Lithuania 2000), *Transition Online*, http://archive.tol.cz/countries/litar00.html [accessed: February 18, 2001].
15 "Lithuania: Analysis - Parliament Approves New Government," *RFE/RL features*, July 12, 2001.
16 In 2004, the LSDP won 31 out of 141 seats in the Seimas. The largest share of seats (41) was taken by the newly formed Labor party which entered into a coalition with the LSDP.
17 Virgis Valentinavicius, "One Populist Down, others yet to come," *Transition Online*, April 13, 2004. "The Lithuanian Way: A Botch-Job in the Baltics," *Economist*, January 15, 2004.
18 Rokas Tracevskis, "A curious case of timing," *Transition Online*, June 28, 2004.
19 Labor was the preferred party for 34.2 per cent of respondents while around 12 per cent of respondents each preferred the Conservatives and the LSDP. See "Political-Economic Report," *International Business Network*, Lithuania, November 2004 to January 2005.
20 Nørgaard and Johannsen (1999), 70–71.
21 For example, in July 1992, several business associations publicly requested that the Vagnorious government step down. "Non-confidence in the Vagnorius Cabinet," *RusData DiaLine-BizEkon News*, July 9, 1992.
22 Almost half of Sajudis 36 founding members had communist party backgrounds, so elite reconfiguration is more appropriate than 'change.' Krickus (1997), 295.

23 See also: Abdelal (2001), Chapter 4: "Lithuania: Towards Europe and the West," 84-85.

24 Similar problems can be found also in many other "successful" transition countries such as Poland or the Czech Republic.

25 Nørgaard and Johannsen (1999), 111.

26 Clark and Prekevicius (2000).

27 UNECE, *Economic Survey of Europe*, no. 1 (2001), 254.

28 See www.lbank.lt/Eng/about/ANDA.HTM [accessed: March 4, 2002].

29 Lainela and Sutela in Haavisto (1997), 92.

30 Mygind in Haavisto (1997), 47-51.

31 Maldeikis (1996), 15.

32 See EBRD, 2001.

33 Vaicenavičius (1999), 8-11.

34 IMF, Lithuania, Country Report no. 05/123.

35 WDR, *World Development Indicators*, 2005.

36 In late 2004, 29 per cent of respondents in a survey were pensioners; levels in Belarus, Ukraine, and Russia were likewise high (29, 32, and 27 per cent respectively). *New Europe Barometer* (2004).

37 See "Russia's Yukos to control Lithuanian Oil Concern after Buyout," *RFE/RL Newsline*, August 21, 2002 and "[...] as Lukoil, Yukos make their own overtures," *RFE/RL Newsline*, part I, September 6, 2002.

38 See "Lithuanian Prime Minister dismisses speculation over Mazeikiai Oil," *RFE/RL Newsline*, 30 January 2004. Yukos' share in Mazeikiu is owned by a Dutch subsidiary, rather than Russian Yukos directly. The sale of Yukos' shares in Mazeikiu remained unresolved in 2005.

39 EBRD, *Transition Report Update*, May 2005, Table A7.

40 Elster, Offe, and Preuss (eds.) (1998).

41 See also Miller at al. (2000), 462.

42 Miller et al. (2000).

43 Krupavicius (2004).

44 Girnius (1999), 51-66.

45 Krupavicius (2004), 1060.

46 The alleged origin is the Union of Lithuanian Traders, Industrialists and Handicraftsmen founded in April 1930. See www.lpk.lt/aboutLPK.html [accessed: March 4, 2002]; Krickus (1997), 316.

47 Freedom House, *Nations in Transit*, 2000.

48 "Lithuanian Industrialists to Demand Half of Country's Loans from Conservatives," *Baltic News Service*, October 9, 1996.

49 Set up in 2002 following a merger between the Lithuanian Trade Union Unification and the Lithuanian Trade Union Center. *European Industrial Relations Observatory Online*, 2004.

50 Freedom House, *Nations in Transit* (2000), 250.

51 Krickus (1997), 322-323. Rose reports about 13 per cent 'complete trust' and 65 per cent 'general trust' for late 1996. *New Baltic Barometer III*, question 87.

52 Thus, for example, a former prime minister, Andrius Kubilius, called anybody advocating progressive income taxes "in short supply of common sense." "New Lithuanian government sworn in amid attacks on its plans," *Lithuanian Radio*, July 12, 2001.

53 See Map of Corruption in Lithuania 2004, http://www.transparency.lt/tyrimai.php [accessed: August 10, 2005]; Bertelsmann Foundation, "Country Report Lithuania," *Bertelsmann Transformation Index 2006*, http://www.bertelsmann-transformation-index.de/175.0.html [accessed: October 2, 2006]

54 Juska and Johnstone (2004).

55 See www.stt.lt

56 *New Europe Barometer* (2004).

57 The data for 2001 and 2004 are not fully comparable.

58 See Krickus (1997), 309.

59 Thus, for example, Landsbergis appealed in March 1993 to the president not to sign the budget adopted by parliament because it contained a deficit which would "contribute to Lithuania being compromised in the eyes of the West." "President signs budget law for 1993 despite Landsbergis' objection," *Lithuanian Radio*, March 4, 1993.

60 "Memorandum on Economic Policy," *Radio Vilnius*, September 4, 1992. Lithuania became a member of the IMF on April 29, 1992.

61 "IMF threatens suspension of credits to Lithuania if deficit is not tackled," *ITAR-TASS*, May 12, 1994. In the last quarter of 1994, the IMF actually withheld a tranche of the Extended Fund Facility (EFF) because of a higher than agreed upon budget deficit. EIU, *Country Report Lithuania* (3rd quarter 1995), 32; the budget was brought back in line and IMF credits were resumed in 1995.

62 See also: Nakrosis (2000).

63 Vaicenavičius (1999), 18.

64 Orenstein (2001).

65 See Regular Reports by the EU commission, various years, chapter 28 (financial control). SIGMA, *Peer Review of the State Control of Lithuania*, October 5, 2000, www.vkontrole.lt/dokumentai/sigma_en.html [accessed: August 23, 2001].

66 World Bank, *Investment Climate Assessment*, December 2004.

67 IMF Country Report no. 05/123, 2005.

68 "Head of Seimas finance committee on hopes for new taxes," *Respublika*, April 29, 1994.

69 Vaicenavičius (1999), 3.

70 Before, a general excise tax had existed which was charged at the same rate of 18%. The VAT became effective from May 1, 1994. "VAT start-up date delayed again," *East European Business Law*, April 1, 1994.

71 EIU, *Lithuania Country Report* (2nd quarter 1997), 33.

72 The initial tax exempt minimum was fixed at LTL127 (~US $32), while the average wage in 1994 stood at LTL 327. IMF, Lithuania, *Staff Country Report* no. 95/82 (1995), 22, 80.

73 From 29 to 24% in 2000, to 15% from 2002 onwards.

74 The relatively low level of CIT collections is mainly attributable to exemptions: according to the IMF, in 1994, out of 116,000 registered firms, 30,000 enjoyed some kind of tax exemption. IM, Lithuania, *Staff Country Report* no. 95/82 (1995), 20–21.

75 This trend is also critically observed in Lazutka (1997), 233.

76 IMF, Lithuania *Staff Country Report* No. 95/82 (1995), 20.

77 "Lithuanian Finance Minister, Western Investors Mull Taxes," *Baltic News Service*, March 9, 1998.

78 "Vagnorius and IMF Representative Discuss Tax Policy of New Government," *Baltic News Service*, December 11, 1996.

79 "Lithuania to Eliminate Profit Tax in 2 Rather than 10 Years," *Baltic News Service*, June 18, 1998.
80 "Lithuanian Govt Putting Off Tax Reforms," *Baltic News Service*, November 20, 2000.
81 Elena Leontjeva, "Lithuania's Tax Reform Overshadowed by Estonia," www.freema.org/Articles/Corptax.phtml [accessed: March 4, 2002]. In Estonia, only profits which are paid out are taxed, while profits which are re-invested are not.
82 "Profit Tax Repeal May Not be Lithuania's Pot of Gold," *Baltic News Service*, March 12, 2001.
83 "Lithuanian President Questions Scrapping of Legal Persons' Profit Tax," *Baltic News Service*, April 19, 2001.
84 "New Lithuanian government sworn in amid attacks on its plans," *Lithuanian Radio*, July 12, 2001.
85 "Lithuania's profit tax bill passes 2nd reading in parliament," *Baltic News Service*, December 18, 2001.
86 "Lithuanian finance minister quits over coalition's tax reforms," April 19, 2005. http://www.eubusiness.com/Finance/050419090609.t65uvmsp [accessed: September 11, 2005].
87 "Lithuania prepares for the new tax reform," *Norcous and Partners*, August 28, 2005.
88 World Bank, *Lithuania - Investment Climate Assessment*, Draft Report, December 2004.
89 Vaicenavičius (1999), 8.
90 Lazutka (1997).
91 See "The Flat Tax Revolution," *The Economist*, April 14, 2005.
92 See also: Kornai, Haggard and Kaufman (eds.) (2001).
93 Algis Zvirblis, "Tax Policy and Reform of the Taxation System," in Buracas et al. (1997), 322.
94 IMF, Lithuania, *Staff Country Report* No. 95/82, 21.
95 "Lithuanian President, Government discuss tax collection," *Baltic News Service*, April 6, 1995.
96 "Corruption rules supreme in Lithuania says World Bank," *TASS*, September 29, 1995.
97 For an overview over the state of Lithuanian tax administration around 1997, see World Bank, *Lithuania: An Opportunity for Economic Success*, vol. 2, 211-238.
98 Schneider and Enste (2000).
99 Nørgaard and Johannsen (1999), 120; Vaicenavičius (1999), 4.
100 "Lithuanians Distinguished in Europe for Low Awareness of Civic Values," *Baltic News Service*, November 20, 2000.
101 Loftsson, Choe, and Ahlquist, *Baltic Barometer*, series no. 1, question 38.
102 See also EBRD *Transition Report*, November 1995.
103 "New law eases companies' tax arrears," *Interfax*, March 21, 1996.
104 "Lithuania's chief tax administrator sacked," *Baltic News Service*, June 5, 1996.
105 "Lithuania's new chief tax inspector set to change style of work," *Baltic News Service*, July 11, 1996.
106 EIU, *Lithuania Country Report* (4th quarter 1996), 36.
107 "Lithuania establishes tax police," *Baltic News Service*, February 6, 1997.
108 It has a staff of 100 police officers and 50 accountants. "Tax Police Observes Signs of Money Laundering in Lithuania," *Baltic News Service*, January 20, 1998.
109 "Lithuania tightens sanctions for tax evasion," *Baltic News Service*, February 14, 1997.
110 "Latvian, Lithuanian Tax Administrations to cooperate," *Baltic News Service*, May 8, 1997.
111 "Baltic Tax Authorities Sign Cooperation Accord," *Baltic News Service*, June 3, 1999.

112 Short Overview of recent Developments in Tax Legislation and Tax Control, State Tax Inspectorate, November 3, 2004.

113 See www.freema.org/Projects/Survey02-2.phtml [accessed: January 13, 2003].

114 "Finance Minister Dudenas sees no economic crisis," *Veidas*, August 4, 2000.

115 Interviews with Algirdas Butkevičius, incoming head of the Seimas budgetary committee and with Kestutis Škiudas, assistant to Andrius Kubilius, Vilnius, July 26, 2001.

116 Vaicenavičius (1999), fn. 1. Extra-budgetary funds can help to maintain funding for certain services during periods of crisis (such as road funds ensuring road maintenance). However, they reduce coherence of the budget.

117 EIU, *Lithuania Country Report* (1st quarter 1995), 39; EIU, *Lithuania Country Report* (1st quarter 1996), 39; "Lithuanian parliament narrowly approves 1998 budget," *dpa*, December 2, 1997. The 1990 budget law does not specify when the government has to submit the draft budget to parliament.

118 "Lithuania to Have Balanced Budget only in Year 2000," *Baltic News Service*, June 18, 1998.

119 Interview with Remigijus Simasius, Policy Analyst, Lithuanian Free Market Institute, Vilnius, July 31, 2001.

120 Interview with Andrius Želionis, Deputy Director of the Budget Department in the Ministry of Finance, Vilnius, July 25, 2001.

121 The Law on the State Treasury was adopted in December 1994. IMF, Lithuania, *Staff Country Report* no. 95/82 (1995) , 67.

122 Interview, July 26, 2001.

123 Interview, Andrius Želionis, Deputy Director, Budget Department, Ministry of Finance, July 25, 2001.

124 IMF, Lithuania, *Staff Country Report* No. 95/82 (1995), 22, 24.

125 IMF, Lithuania, *Staff Country Report* No. 98/92 (1998), 7; see also Evans and Evans (2001), 944.

126 Hans Aage, "Public Sector Development: Difficulties and Restrictions," in: Haavisto (1997), 110.

127 "Lithuania Tops Budget Target by LTL 45 million," *Baltic News Service*, February 6, 1998.

128 Interview with Remigijus Simasius, Policy Analyst, Lithuanian Free Market Institute, Vilnius, July 31, 2001. Dzintra Sakevičienė, Deputy Director, Fiscal Policy Department, Ministry of Finance, July 31, 2001.

129 See Evans and Evans (2001), 945.

130 "Lithuanian Budget Will Have no Deficit by 1999," *Baltic News Service*, December 15, 1997; Vaicenavičius (1999), 14.

131 "Lithuanian Parliament Adopts Balanced Budget," *Interfax*, December 3, 1998.

132 *De facto* GDP contracted by 4.2 per cent. GDP growth estimates are difficult in a transition situation. Not only governments but also the IMF has made erroneous assumptions about growth. See Helbling, Mody, and Sahay (2004).

133 "Government rejects IMF proposal on taxes," *Lithuanian Radio*, February 11, 1999.

134 "Budget Woes, Devaluation Threat Weigh on Lithuanian Economy," *Baltic News Service*, December 3, 1999. "Einigung zwischen dem IMF und Litauen," *NZZ*, December 16, 1999.

135 "IMF, World Bank officials urge Lithuania to narrow budget gap further," *Lithuanian Radio*, December 7, 1999.

136 "Lithuania: Review 2000," *Europe Review World of Information*, September 19, 2000.

137 Jonas Lionginas, Minister of Finance in 1999 and in 2000–2001 and head of the parliamentary committee from 2004; Algirdas Butkevicius, head of the committee in the early 2000s and minister of finance from May 2004.
138 For a comparison of expenditures on health-care and education across all transition countries, see World Bank, *Transition: The First Ten Years*, World Bank: Washington, D.C. (2002), 85–86.
139 "Litauen," *Wirtschaftslage und Reformprozesse in Mittel- und Osteuropa, Sammelband 2000*, [Economic situation and reform processes in Central and Eastern Europe] Bundesinstitut für Außenhandelsinformationen (2000), 111.
140 Vaicenavičius (1999), 16.
141 Interview with Jurgis Razma, MP for the Lithuanian Conservative Party, July 26, 2001.
142 Interview with, Kestutis Škiudas, Advisor to A. Kubilius Vilnius, July 26, 2001.
143 Interview with Andrius Kubilius, former Prime Minister, Chairmain of the Faction of the Conservative Party, Member of the Budget and Finance Committee, Vilnius, July 31, 2001.
144 Program budgeting has been a 'reform tool' introduced in a number of countries to encourage explicit linking of expenditures to outcomes, and strategic discussions about priorities.
145 See also IMF, Lithuania, *Staff Country Report*, 98/92 (1998), 18.
146 "Lithuania Changes Structure of Budget," *Baltic News Service*, April 15, 1998.
147 Premchand (1981).
148 See Law on the Budget Structure, Art. 5, Art. 32.
149 Interview with Algirdas Butkevičius, MP for the LSDP, (incoming) head of the budgetary committee, Vilnius, July 26, 2001.
150 SIGMA, *Lithuania: Public Service and the Administrative Framework Assessment*, Paris, 2003.
151 Interview with Juozas Vytas Jacevičius, Deputy Auditor General and Remigijus Pužauskas, Head of the Division of Control, Examination, Prevention, and Methodology, Supreme Auditing Chamber (Valstybes Kontrole), July 24, 2001.
152 Interview with Juozas Vytas Jacevičius, Deputy Auditor General, July 24, 2001.
153 See Law on State Control (1995), Art. 9.
154 See SIGMA, "Peer Review of the State Control of Lithuania," October 5, 2000 www.vkontrole.lt/dokumentai/sigma_en.html [accessed: August 23, 2001].
155 KOM (2000), *2001 Regular Report on Lithuania's Progress Towards Accession.*
156 Communication by the SC, July 2001; Commission Document SEC(2001) 1750; *2001 Regular Report on Lithuania's Progress Towards Accession*, 101.
157 EU, Comprehensive *Monitoring Report on Lithuania's Preparations for Membership*, 2003.
158 "Red sleaze and a super-crash," *Süddeutsche Zeitung*, February 9, 1996,
159 See, for example, the reports by the EC's and the Council of Europe on corruption issues, Evaluation Report (2002) and Compliance Report (2004), Greco Eval I Rep (2002) 1E Final and Greco RC-I (2004) 6E.
160 GRECO, *Evaluation Report on Lithuania*, Strasbourg: March 2002.
161 IMF, Lithuania, *Staff Country Report* 95/82 (1995), 22.
162 See www.freema.org/Projects/Survey02-2.phtml [accessed: January 13, 2003].
163 Way (2003).
164 Nakrosis (2000), 47–49.
165 See Evans and Evans (2001).

CHAPTER 11.

THE 'AUTHORITARIANIZING' ROUTE TO RECOVERY: THE CASE OF RUSSIAN TAX REFORM

As indicated in the introduction, this chapter has a narrower angle focusing on a specific puzzle which serves to highlight the main hypotheses of this research. The primary puzzle is the adoption of tax reform in two stages in 1998 and 2000–2001. Why was it possible to adopt a major tax reform in Russia at this point in time while such reform continued to be blocked in Ukraine? The two countries faced similar problems with regard to their extractive systems, including an economic elite which benefited from tax privileges—which made its businesses profitable and kept potential competitors in check.[1] If anything, the obstacles to tax reform appeared *greater* in Russia than in Ukraine due to Russia's federal nature, and the power of large oligarchic groups, which controlled vast resource wealth.[2]

This chapter explores the relevance of two key factors: the consolidation of political power, and changes concerning the 'opaque' networks (i.e., the oligarchic groups). As we have seen in the cases of Belarus and Lithuania, early consolidation of power allowed the creation of relatively more capable states than in Ukraine, albeit based on diametrically opposed political regimes. However, in Russia, as in Ukraine, initially a hybrid, and uncertain regime emerged.[3] Competing interests proliferated within a federal framework and stimulated by the process of privatization, while mechanisms for aggregating interests in such a way as to foster state-building were weak.

The questions raised here are the following: Why did tax reform become possible in 1998–2000? In particular, was power consolidation a significant factor in this process, and to what extent did the influence of 'opaque' groups and external pressures play a role? In answering these questions, this chapter traces the pathway of re-building state capacities after a prolonged period of deterioration involving a shift from a hybrid to an increasingly authoritarian regime.

11.1. The stage: political power and oligarchic groups

There are many accounts of the political events, the evolution of the political system, and the political economy of democratization and marketization in Russia.[4] As in the case of other post-Soviet countries, the Russian Federation emerged as an independent state after the collapse of the Soviet Union in December 1991, with Boris Yeltsin as president. Like the other countries, Russia was affected by the collapse of former Soviet structures, and a steep decline in GDP (see Appendix, Tables I.1.1 and I.1.2). However, there are also significant factors—structural conditions as well as initial policy choices—which set Russia apart. Regarding structural factors, Russia as the former imperial center had greater human resources and policy-making experience available in Moscow than existed in Kyiv or Minsk, let alone Bishkek or Dushanbe. At the same time Russia 'inherited' higher expenditures: it assumed most Soviet debt, and it had the highest military spending in the region (see Appendix, Table II.3.4). Russia is the only federal state to emerge from the former Soviet Union; and its geographic expanse is vast.[5] This carries important implications for fiscal reforms, since regions are more powerful actors than elsewhere and have their own interests in the fiscal system. Despite economic decline, Russia continued to be the dominant political and economic power in the post-Soviet region with a GDP more than twice as large as all other post-Soviet countries combined.[6] Furthermore, Russia has enormous wealth in natural resources and the relevance of natural resources in the revenue base is assumed to affect the nature of a state.[7]

In terms of post-Soviet developments, there are two crucial differences when compared to Ukraine. The first was the early decision to privatize rapidly and extensively. This triggered a rapid 'primary accumulation of capital' and 'oligarchization,' which was more pronounced and generated an initial greater shift of power away from the state than in Ukraine. The second difference was the earlier and more clear-cut movement towards a presidential system. A key event was the 1993 stand-off between the president and the parliament which the latter lost. Consequently, a constitution stipulating a very strong presidency was adopted.[8] However, the Russian president also had to contend with more 'power competition' from the federal regions and from large business groups. Some regions (and their governors) gained considerable weight, and a system of "asymmetric federalism" developed with some regions enjoying more autonomy than others.[9] Furthermore, from 1996 to 2000, Russia was governed by a weakened and seriously ill president Yeltsin.

As Kounov and Sitnikov have argued, although the president was stronger in Russia than in Ukraine, the distribution of responsibility for the budget and other matters of economic policy-making was still structured in such a way as to generate mutual irresponsibility rather than (encompassing) presidential control.[10] The role of the president developed in a rather unique way in 1999–2000 with the handing over of power from Yeltsin to Putin. In contrast to Yeltsin, whose main political aim was to end communism, Putin made the re-building of the Russian state a key goal of his presidency.[11] Especially in the early years of his presidency, he was very popular; and unlike a majority of strong post-Soviet presidents did not engage in personal enrichment.[12] As a result, he could shift from relying on a narrow business-financial elite (which had financed Yeltsin's re-election in 1996) towards reliance on popularity.[13] Under Putin's early presidency, a number of reform laws were adopted;[14] but his primary concern was with the state rather than with economic reforms *per se*.

The political order which Putin sought to build was more an authoritarian than a democratic one; but this was combined with a greater drive for modernization—of the public administration, of the regulatory regime—than in Belarus or in Uzbekistan.[15] Putin's effort at re-building the state and reviving the economy ran into several difficulties: entrenched interests particularly in the regions, the scale of state dysfunctionality which had emerged as a result of Soviet and post-Soviet institutional deterioration, and the fall-out from the war in Chechnya—which initially had served to make Putin popular.

From the start, Putin sought to consolidate power.[16] This coincided with a consolidation of the legislature which strongly benefited the president: the Duma elected in late 1999 saw a small increase in the number of factions (from 7 to 9), but it was much more pro-presidential than its predecessor. The Unity faction, which was jumpstarted as a party supporting the president, managed to become the second largest faction in parliament (see Table 11.1). Subsequently, Unity took leading positions on important committees, and successfully forged shifting alliances to the left and right for the passage of crucial legislation submitted by the president.[17] Furthermore, Unity formed an increasingly close coalition with the Fatherland party (of Luzhkov and Primakov) since 2001; and the two parties merged in early 2002 (adopting the label Unified Russia).[18]

An important factor in consolidating presidential power has been the high level of public support for Putin, whose work has continuously been approved by about 70 per cent of the population.[19] Despite this, economic policies approved under Putin have generally not been populist: a new labor law lowered the standards of protection, and with a new flat income tax rate the state gave up on taxing higher incomes progressively.

The Putin government was confirmed in the 2003 Duma and the March 2004 presidential elections. In the Duma elections, Unified Russia won a large share of the votes and an even larger share of seats (300 out of 450); while the communists were reduced to 52 seats. Only four factions won seats.[20] In March 2004 Putin was re-elected with 71.2 per cent of the vote—an almost 20 per cent increase over his 2000 election result.[21]

Table 11.1: Distribution of seats in the Duma after the 1999 elections

	List seats	SMD seats	Total seats	Factions Feb. 2000	Seats Jan. 1996
Reform factions:					
Union of Rightist Forces	24	5	29	32	n/a
Yabloko	17	5	22	21	46
Centrist/pro-governmental:					
Unity	64	9	73	81	n/a
People's Deputy	–	–	–	58	n/a
Fatherland-All Russia (OVR)	36	32	68	45	n/a
Russia's Regions	–	–	–	38	41
Opposition forces:					
Liberal Democratic Party	17	2	19	17	51
Communist Party	67	55	124	89	149
Agro-Industrial Group	n/a	2	2	41	n/a
Other		115		19	
Total	*225*	*225*		*441*	

Source: Smith and Remington (2001), 150 and 143. Note: The Agro-Industrial group, People's Deputy, and Russia's Regions were factions formed after the new Duma convened in order to represent deputies elected from SMDs, many of whom had been nominated by parties which failed to receive seats in the PR ballot.

Table 11.2: Russian prime ministers, 1992–2005

06/1992–12/1992	Yegor Gaidar (acting)
12/1992–03/1998	Viktor Chernomyrdin
03/1998–08/1998	Sergey Kiriyenko
08/1998–09/1998	Viktor Chernomyrdin
09/1998–05/1999	Yevgeny Primakov
05/1999–08/1999	Sergey Stepashin
08/1999–05/2000	Vladimir Putin
05/2000–02/2004	Mikhail Kasyanov
03/2004–	Mikhail Fradkov

The year 2004 was dominated by two political events: the court case against Mikhail Khodorkovsky and the terrorist attack in Beslan. The first negatively affected the confidence of domestic and foreign investors; while the second event reduced the confidence of citizens in the president. In early 2005, Putin was less trusted as president than his colleagues in Belarus, Lithuania, and Ukraine (see Graph 11.2 below).[22] The Beslan attack and the report by presidential envoy to the Southern Federal District, Dmitry Kozak, revealed to what extent the situation in Chechnya and its neighboring regions in the North Caucasus was out of control. Nonetheless, in the course of 2005, Putin's high domestic approval ratings returned again.[23]

11.2. The economic background to reform

During the early 1990s, Russia experienced a deep economic crisis. As in Ukraine, the budget deficit ballooned and inflation shot up. From 1995–96 onwards, relative stabilisation set in, but this was accompanied by 'virtualization.' As the government sharply reduced expenditures, inter-enterprise arrears began to mount as government subsidies were cut. In particular, domestic industries and agriculture stopped paying energy suppliers. The government in turn did not allow energy companies to cut off their debtors; rather, it accepted non-payment of taxes by energy companies and provided them with lucrative export deals.[24] As part of stabilization, the Central Bank sought to keep the exchange rate to the US dollar within a certain band.

Initially, public sector debt was taken up by domestic private banks in the form of short term treasury bills, known as GKOs (*Gosudarstvennoe Kratkosrochnoe Obyazatelstvo*). From 1997 onwards, Russia began to borrow more from international lenders and some of it at short term. In August 1998, the whole system collapsed when Russia became unable to either borrow more or extract sufficient additional revenues to pay for its debt obligations. The Central Bank tried to maintain the managed exchange rate, in the process losing further foreign reserves. While the relative weights of the different causes are subject to debate, there is agreement that four related factors contributed: high budget deficits in the early and mid-1990s, short-term borrowing at (increasingly) high interest rates, volatile and falling oil prices in 1998, and the withdrawal of funds from the treasury bill market by non-residents following the Asian financial crisis.[25]

The consequences of the crisis were that the ruble had to be steeply devalued, the government declared a default on domestic debt and a moratorium on paying principle on debt to international lenders. Contrary to expectations, however, the economic situation began to show rapid improvement from 1999 onwards. The sharp devaluation gave a boost to Russian exporters as well as to import-substituting industries, for example, in food processing. Rising profitability of the enterprise sector together with rapidly rising oil prices (see Graph 11.1) helped to overcome the fiscal crunch. Russia began to register rapid economic growth, amounting on average to 6.2 per cent between 1999 and 2004 (see also Appendix, Table I.1.2).

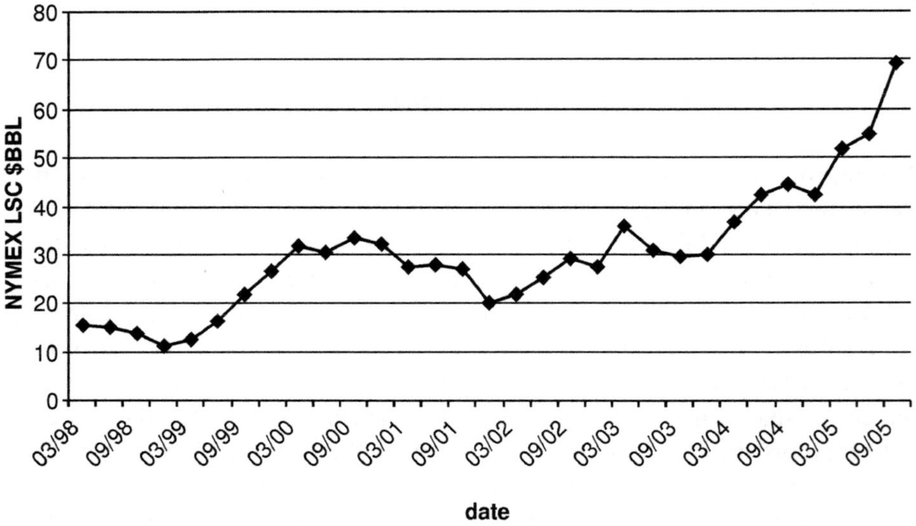

Graph 11.1: Fluctuation of world oil prices, 1998–2005

Source: http://octane.nmt.edu/marketplace/prices/default.asp

11.2.1. PRIVATIZATION—REDISTRIBUTING WEALTH AND POWER

The lawlessness and corruption which surrounded the massive transfers of property into private hands in all the transition countries was particularly prevalent in Russia. According to the EIU: "Russian privatization has proceeded far more rapidly—but in a much more disorganized fashion—than in most other transition economies."[26] As McFaul has stressed, privatization took place without the proper state institutions for control being in place.[27] State income from privatization was low: Gray claims that between 1992 and

1996 assets with market value estimated at US $50–60 billion in the oil and gas sector were privatized for less than US $1.5 billion.[28]

Privatization took place in three stages in Russia. The first stage lasted from 1992 to 1994. During this stage, most small enterprises were privatized through local property committees. In the fall of 1992, vouchers were distributed to citizens for purchasing shares in medium and large enterprises. This 'privatization' often did not result in clear private ownership structures.[29]

The second stage in the privatization process was the "loans-for-shares" program in 1995, and 1996. According to the official plan, banks would provide long-term loans to government and as collateral would receive controlling stakes in large state-owned enterprises. In reality, this scheme provided Russian banks with an opportunity to acquire the gems of Russian industry at very low prices.[30] The "loans-for-shares" privatization period was a phase of rapid 'oligarchization' or concentration of economic (and by extension political) power in the hands of a few individuals and their holding companies.

Since the late 1990s, the pace of privatization of remaining state assets slowed down and in some sectors there is a noticeable tendency to maintain (or re-expand) state-ownership.[31] This concerns primarily the transportation of energy (Transnefteprodukt), gas (Gazprom), some interest in the oil sector (Rosneft), and Unified Energy Systems (UES) all of which remained wholly or partially state-owned.[32]

Oligarchic groups reached the apex of their influence during the 1996 presidential election campaign and immediately afterwards.[33] In the 1998 financial crash, several oligarchs lost parts of their resource base. During the 2000 presidential elections, oligarchs were less needed, since Vladimir Putin enjoyed sufficient levels of popularity.[34] In his first 'State of the Nation' address, Putin explicitly stated that the pervasive influence of 'shadowy groups' would no longer be tolerated. Two formerly highly influential figures—Vladimir Gusinsky and Boris Berezovsky—left the country in the following months.[35] In the fall of 2003, Yukos head Mikhail Khodorkovsky was arrested; and was eventually sentenced to nine years in prison in May 2005.

Nonetheless, "big business groups" are still widely assumed to contribute to "the Kremlin" and to pro-presidential political parties.[36] As Jones Luong and Weinthal have argued, the original oligarchic groups of Russia began to transform themselves into more rule-supporting business groups particularly since the shock of the 1998 crisis.[37] The Russian state under Putin on the one hand demanded that business groups contribute taxes to the state; but as the Yukos case indicates, on the other hand, it did not necessarily support those companies which were on a path to introducing more transparent corporate governance practices.

Through years of economic crisis and reforms benefiting primarily a small circle of insiders, Russian society suffered a high cost: in 2000, 24 per cent of the population was living on less than 2 dollars a day, and the measured level of inequality was higher than in all other transition countries.[38] In 2005, after several years of high growth, 17.8 per cent of the population was still living under the official poverty line, and around 40 per cent perceived themselves as poor according to public opinion polls.[39]

Thus, in the early 2000s political power became more consolidated and more structured. Furthermore, there were signs that the 'oligarchs' of the mid-1990s lost some of their influence; but to some extent they were replaced by a different type of shadowy structures around the still state-controlled companies. Moreover, massive redistribution of wealth had taken place in Russia, which was likely to mark Russian society and the Russian state for the coming decades.

11.3. State-society relations

According to Reddaway and Glinski, the relationship between citizens and post-Soviet elites in Russia was transformed "from a state of considerable cohesion and expectation that defined the public mood in the late 1980s to its current state of pervasive mistrust and apathy, tinged only with desperate popular hope that Putin might perform some miracles."[40]

Trust in public institutions has fallen to low levels; however, approval rates for the Russian president improved again during 2005 according to surveys.[41] Remarkable is also the low trust in 'most people,' which has a positive balance in Belarus, Ukraine, and Lithuania, but a slightly negative balance in Russia.

With regard to expectations concerning state-market relations, public opinion shifted from cautious support for a market system towards increasing scepticism and opposition. By late 2004, Russians were the most clearly in favor of state ownership in enterprises among the countries surveyed by the New Europe Barometer, and 62 per cent of those surveyed believed that the state should be responsible for the material security of individuals—a higher share than in Belarus.[42]

Organizations which are held to be important intermediaries between the state and society in established democracies have been among the least trusted in Russia. By 1998, 7 per cent of respondents trusted political parties, 14 per cent trade unions, and the level of distrust increased further over time.[43]

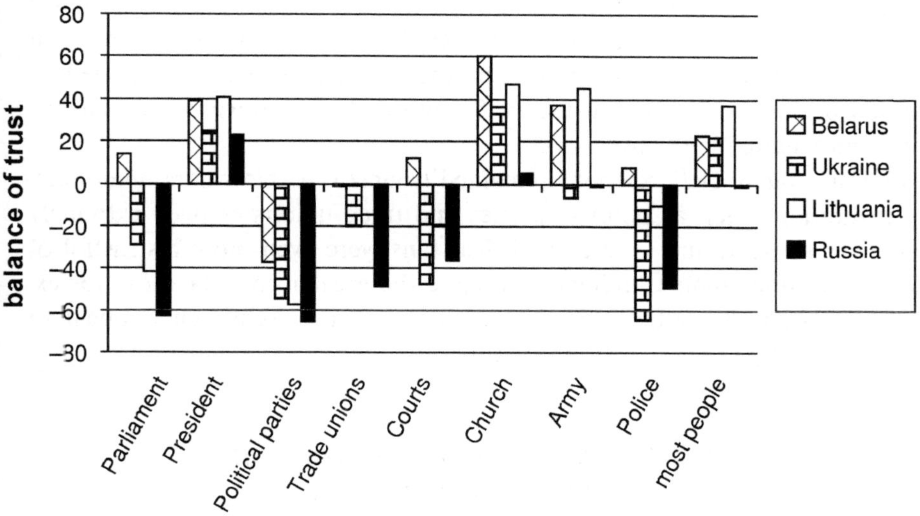

Graph 11.2: Levels of trust in public institutions, 2004–2005

Source: Rose, New Europe Barometer 2004.

Russia has had fewer and rather more stable parties than Ukraine. On the left of the spectrum are the Communists, and in the center is the smaller but still rather stable Yabloko. Alongside these, some important parties have been created top-down to function as a support base for powerful politicians—most notably Our Home is Russia, and Unity/Unified Russia. The constitutional structure with a relatively weak parliament and governments that depend on the president has not helped to promote the development of strong and programmatically well-defined parties.[44] At the same time the creation of top-down parties was significantly more successful in Russia than in Ukraine—where such parties were set up, but failed at the polls. Also, the relationship between the president and the communists became more cooperative in Russia.[45]

The largest trade union organization is the Federation of Independent Trade Unions, which is a Soviet-successor organization.[46] More than half of all workers allegedly belong to the various member-unions of the Federation. However, trade unions are neither trusted by the population nor have they been effective with regard to policy-making: the opposition of the Federation to the introduction of a unified social tax (see below) was by and large ignored.[47]

The biggest business association is the Russian Union of Industrialists and Entrepreneurs (RUIE). Similar to the UUIE in Ukraine, the RUIE unites Russia's big business. Furthermore, the RUIE was strengthened when Putin began to use it as a main negotiating partner and also when it was joined by the new business class from about 2000 onwards (while previously it had predominantly united 'red' directors).[48]

Overall, state-society relations remained troubled. As elsewhere, intermediary institutions such as political parties and trade unions enjoyed extremely low levels of trust, and in late 2004, Russians were even more distrustful of these institutions than Ukrainians—despite the greater consolidation, for example, in the party system. Moreover, 'statist-socialist' sentiments appear to have remained particularly strong in Russia.

11.4. Fiscal crisis and tax reform: surveying explanations

The tax system in Russia prior to tax reform had many features similar to Ukraine in the mid-1990s. Existing problems were compounded by the federal structure and the fact that a politically weak center was not able to ensure that regions would collect and pass revenues on to the federal budget.

Busse as well as Pirttilä argue that social norms contributed to the problem of collecting revenues.[49] According to this moral- and trust-centered explanation, the state and state institutions were regarded as adversaries—which could be legitimately cheated. However, as discussed above, trust was low in many post-communist countries, including Ukraine and Lithuania; and low trust by itself did not lead to fiscal crisis even if it makes tax collection more difficult.

Another problem that has been pointed to was the weak administrative capacity.[50] With the change from a state-owned economy to an economy based on more numerous and smaller enterprises as well as private banks, financial flows became more difficult to monitor. However, as in Ukraine, while Russia's Tax Service was initially unprepared for a market economy, it was rapidly built up into a large organization by international comparison. Thus, in 1998, 185,000 people were employed in the Tax Service, and another 40,000 in the Tax Police, while the figure for the US Internal Revenue Service stood at about 90,000 employees.[51] Furthermore, tax inspectors had considerable discretion in employing tax rules; and the tax police became a rather powerful organization.[52] Thus, while there were many problems with the tax administration, by the late 1990s the problem was more about how this administration was used, rather than a weak organization *per se*.[53]

Treisman and Shleifer, as well as Easter have argued that various elite bargains undermined tax collections in Russia.[54] Treisman in particular points to central-regional relations as a key factor in Russia's fiscal crisis. He argues that due to the nature of tax-sharing between the federal and regional budgets, tax offices in the regions often had insufficient incentives to collect and properly channel funds for the federal budget.[55] With regard to privileges overall, Russian tax ministers repeatedly complained about the levels of state revenue lost.[56] According to Sokolowski, "frequently, the President would award *l'goty* (tax breaks, discounts or exemptions) to favored sectors, groups of enterprises or individual enterprises."[57]

These accounts of the fiscal roots of the 1998 financial crisis fit well with the overall interpretation proposed in this study that the lack of consolidation and integration of the political regime was at the heart of the problem. This lack of consolidation had particularly far-reaching consequences in the setting of a federal structure and of oligarchs controlling a significant share of Russia's vast natural resources. Furthermore, tax reform initially seemed more difficult than in Ukraine since the federal system meant that there were additional important veto-players, represented in particular in the Federation Council, the upper chamber of parliament, which had to approve any fundamental tax reform.

Remarkably, reforms were passed nonetheless, and the downward spiral of a disintegrating institutional structure was reversed, with tax reform being one of the initial key steps. Nonetheless, the scale of the challenge to re-build the Russian state was enormous; and the way in which Putin and the post-Yeltsin political elite set about it had a number of problematic aspects as will be discussed in the concluding section.

11.5. From drag to leap: the gestation and eventual success of tax reform

The Russian tax reform package—the so called Tax Code—was passed in two main stages, followed by several further tax reductions. The first part of the code was passed in July 1998, during the build-up of the Russian financial crisis. This part mainly deals with definitions and the relationship between taxpayers and tax authorities. The second part was passed in July 2000, with further chapters adopted in 2001 and beyond. Part two of the code deals with specific taxes, the tax base and tax rates, including the famous introduction of a 13 per cent flat tax on income. The first part was passed after a gestation period of several years during a moment of financial crisis. The second part, which had more decisive distributional consequences, was passed during the early stages of power-consolidation under Putin.

11.5.1. THE GESTATION PERIOD DURING EARLY INDEPENDENCE

The initial Russian tax system emerged in 1991–1992, and included the replacement of turnover taxes by VAT and the introduction of a personal income tax.[58] In subsequent years, innumerable changes to tax rules and laws were issued by various bodies (laws, presidential decrees, instructions by the Tax Service, etc.)—a situation similar to that in Ukraine.[59] At the same time, successive governments began to promise a comprehensive tax reform.[60]

By the mid-1990s, tax reform began to be addressed more seriously. A first fully-fledged Tax Code was worked out under the leadership of deputy minister of finance Sergei Shatalov by late 1995. The drafting process was severely criticized, since most stakeholders—tax-payers, the tax administration, and even parliamentarians—as well as the wider public had not been consulted.[61]

In the run-up to the presidential elections in July 1996, tax reform was put on hold, while tax arrears were allowed to mount—according to Sokolowski an 'informal tax holiday' driven by heightened political uncertainty.[62] This was followed by an attempt to claw back some of the lost revenue after the elections: in late 1996, and *inter alia* urged by the IMF, an "Emergency Commission" (VČK) headed by first deputy prime minister Chubais was set up to enforce tax collection, in particular from large tax debtors such as energy companies (Gazprom, LUKOIL, Sibneft, etc.).[63] However, the stock of tax arrears remained rather constant,[64] and the commission was widely seen as yet another failed attempt to enforce revenue collection.

11.5.2. GETTING PART I THROUGH

In March 1997, Yeltsin declared tax reform to be the top priority of his second term, and appointed Anatoly Chubais as minister of finance.[65] As a key external actor, the IMF again demanded more reforms—after Yeltsin had been successfully re-elected and the communist threat had passed.[66] The government soon submitted a new draft Tax Code to the Duma proposing some tax reductions to be offset by canceling various privileges (for a summary of the suggested changes in tax rates, see Table 11.4); but similar to the situation in Ukraine in 1997, the draft was disproved by various political forces.

Reformist Duma deputies criticized the draft Code for being far from 'revolutionary,' while other deputies claimed that the cancellation of privileges would worsen the economic situation. *Yabloko* opposed the draft, arguing that it would favor big industrial groups.[67] Communists warned that a higher tax-burden was being shifted onto consumption which would hit the poor the hardest, and that the likely revenue losses would lead to further cuts in social spending.[68]

Eventually, the executive threatened the Duma with dissolution if it did not pass the Code. A majority of deputies relented and voted in favor of the Code at a first reading on June 19 (laws need to be approved in three readings to be adopted).[69] However, after returning from summer recess, deputies took their revenge and submitted over 4000 proposed changes to the Code.[70] On top of this legislative filibuster, *Yabloko* threatened the government with a non-confidence vote. The executive backed down and withdrew the Code.

In the fall of 1997 a conciliatory council with representatives from the Duma, the Federation Council, and the government was set up to rework the draft Code.[71] In November, Yeltsin dismissed Chubais as minister of finance and replaced him with Mikhail Zadornov, a member of *Yabloko* and until then chairman of the Duma's budgetary and tax committee, and one of the sharpest critics of the government's draft Tax Code.[72]

The governments of wealthy regions—led by Moscow and its powerful mayor Yuri Luzhkov—opposed the Tax Code claiming that it would deprive them of their fair share of the revenue.[73] Various other groups remained distrustful of the effects which a 'big-leap' change in the rules would bring. Voices from the tax administration warned that rapid implementation would be impossible or even harmful. Business circles were likewise cautious. *Kommersant Daily*—one of Russia's main business newspapers—commented in late 1997:

> There will be no Code in Russia next year, and that is good for taxpayers. It is good because the Code, in its current form, would bring us only one thing—a tougher tax system. [...] It would be accomplished not by imposing new taxes or raising old taxes but by increasing the high-handedness of the authorities, first of all the tax agencies. After all, existing tax legislation has a

definite framework. It may be harsh and unfair, but it does exist. But from the Code, one often is at a loss to figure out exactly what taxes one is supposed to pay, how much and to whom. And by Russian tradition, everything that cannot be figured out is interpreted in favor of the budget.[74]

Table 11.3: Ministers of Finance of the Russian Federation, 1992–2005

10/1991–12/1992	Egor Gaidar
12/1992–02/1994	Boris Fyodorov
02/1994–10/1994	Sergey Dubinin
11/1994–08/1996	Vladimir Panskov
08/1996–03/1997	Aleksandr Livshits
03/1997–11/1997	Anatoly Chubais (acting)
11/1997–03/1998	Mikhail Zadornov
04/1998–08/1998	Mikhail Zadornov (re-appointed)
09/1998–04/1999	Mikhail Zadornov (re-appointed)
04/1999–05/2000	Mikhail Kasyanov
05/2000–	Aleksey Kudrin (re-appointed in March 2004)

In early 1998, a re-worked government Code was submitted. Some earlier criticism had been worked into the new government proposal, in particular the concerns raised by *Yabloko*, whose members were now leading the Ministry of Finance, including a greater fit with the Civil Code as well as a more substantial overall lowering of tax rates (see Table 11.4).[75]

Again, the IMF was pressing for the passage of the code; moreover—among the brewing financial crisis—key international rating agencies called for tax reform and improved revenue collection if Russia wanted to avoid a downgrade of its rating.[76]

In March 1998, amid crisis-signals emanating from Asia, Yeltsin dismissed prime minister Chernomyrdin. He appointed Sergey Kirienko, a young businessman without political clout, who was initially rejected by the Duma. In the midst of this government crisis, the Tax Code—this time supported by the budget and tax committee—was adopted at a first reading by a wide margin of 312 to 17.[77] A week later, the Duma finally confirmed Kirienko in order not to risk dissolution.[78]

As the crisis loomed larger and larger, the government desperately sought new funds from the IMF and suggested an emergency plan to increase revenue. In this situation, the first part of the Tax Code—dealing with definitions, taxpayers rights and duties, etc.—was finally passed in early July.[79] Already then, the newly appointed minister of taxation, Boris Fyodorov, immediately started to demand changes to Part I since he regarded it as too lenient on tax-payers.[80] At the same time, several 'emergency' laws, a new tax on gambling and an imputed tax on small businesses as well as the introduction of a 5 per cent sales tax, were quickly pushed through the Duma.[81] The second part of the Code, however, dealing with tax rates, deductible costs etc. was left for further work.[82]

Table 11.4: Tax rates changes suggested in draft tax code

	1997 draft (June)	1998 draft Tax Code	Nov. 1998 Boos (STS)	Final changes (2000/01)	Status 2004
VAT	raised from 20 to 22 per cent	20 per cent 10 per cent preferential	14 per cent 1999 10 per cent 2000	20 per cent 10 per cent preferential	18 per cent 10 per cent preferential
PIT	12 and 30 per cent	12 and 30 per cent	to be discussed	13 per cent flat rate	13 per cent flat
Profit Tax (CIT)	35 per cent	30 per cent (18 per cent for small businesses)	30 per cent	24 per cent	24 per cent
Sales Tax	to be introduced at 5 per cent	3 per cent		5 per cent (to be phased out Jan. 1, 2004)	–
Other key provisions		tax authorities can impose fines only after court ruling	contributions to pension fund lowered from 28 to 19% of wages	regressive unified social tax; 35.6% on annual incomes below R100,000; (20%, 10% intermediary rates); 5% for income higher than R600,000 (2% from 2002 onwards)	unified social tax reduced to a marginal rate of 26%

On July 20, the IMF announced a major new loan of US $11.6 billion to Russia.[83] A considerable share of this money was used by the Central Bank in a desperate attempt to prop up the ruble. By August 17, this attempt had failed. The ruble was left to devalue and lost more than 60 per cent of its value against the dollar in the following weeks; which in turn triggered the collapse of several banks. A moratorium on payments on all foreign loans was declared. On August 23, Yeltsin sacked the Kirienko government and eventually Yevgeny Primakov was confirmed as the new prime minister.

11.5.3. THE BATTLE FOR PART II OF THE TAX CODE

In the aftermath of the crisis, more and more high-level politicians began to call for radical tax reductions.[84] However, there was no agreement on how to proceed, with the newly created Ministry of Taxation and the Ministry of Finance proposing different options. Georgii Boos, the minister of taxation, suggested a radical lowering of the VAT to 10 per cent within two years.[85] In view of strained resources and the need to assure the IMF that more revenue would be collected, the Ministry of Finance opposed this plan and instead favored the re-introduction of export taxes on gas and oil.[86] While hitherto strongly advocating tax reform, the financial crisis made the IMF now more cautious with regard to any radical lowering of tax rates.[87]

Table 11.5: Heads of the State Tax Service/tax ministers of the Russian Federation

11/1991–02/1993	Igor' Lazarev
03/1993–03/1996	Vladimir Gusev
03/1996–04/1997	Vitalii Artyukhov
04/1997–05/1998	Aleksandr Pochinok
05/1998–09/1998	Boris Fyodorov
09/1998–05/1999	Georgii Boos
05/1999–08/1999	Aleksandr Pochinok
08/1999–05/2000	Aleksandr Pochinok (re-appointed)
05/2000–03/2004	Gennadii Bukaev
03/2004–	Analtoly Serdyukov (acting 03–07/2004)

Source: www.cityline.ru/politika/prav/gns.html; in December 1998, the Russian State Tax Service was transformed into the Ministry for Taxes and Collections (*Ministerstvo po nalogam i sboram*) by presidential decree.

In 1999, the search for a successor to Yeltsin dominated the political scene, distracting the government from further tax reform. Also, the prime-minister-carrousel kept turning: in May 1999, Yeltsin replaced prime minister Primakov by Sergey Stepashin, and in August, Stepashin was replaced by Vladimir Putin. Similar to Kirienko a year earlier, Putin—coming from the intelligence services—had not been a leading political figure before this appointment. In the Putin government, Mikhail Kasyanov was appointed minister of finance and Aleksander Pochinok head of the Ministry of Taxation.

Elections to the Duma took place in December 1999, resulting in a significant shift of power towards centrist and pro-governmental forces (see section 1 above). During the election campaign, taxes were a key issue. All parties essentially supported lower corporate tax rates, a reduction of exemptions, as well as simplification and more stability in the tax system. The communists proposed to extract more from the natural resource sector; and advocated a progressive income tax with a top rate of 45 per cent.[88] Most other relevant parties with reasonably clear economic programs (SPS, OVR, *Yabloko*)[89] favored a flatter or flat income tax rate.[90]

The Duma elections were followed by the shock of Yeltsin's New Year's address: on December 31, 1999, Boris Yeltsin announced his departure, and the appointment of prime minister Putin as acting president. The anointment worked: in March 2000, Putin was confirmed as president in popular elections winning in the first round with 52.9 per cent over his closest rival, the communist Zyuganov, who received only 29.2 per cent.

The result of the Duma and presidential elections created the preconditions for 'big-leap' tax reform. The newly elected Duma was far more likely than its predecessor to pass a comprehensive reform,[91] while the new president was committed to re-building the Russian state and to pursue reforms towards this end.[92] In late May 2000, the government submitted the proposal of a 13 per cent flat rate income tax (as a key element of Part II of the Tax Code) to parliament.[93]

While pushing for Part II of the Tax Code, the government also sought substantial modifications of Part I as adopted in 1998 in order to reduce the liberal provisions on taxpayers' rights;[94] in particular, it proposed stricter rules for controlling transfer pricing (i.e. the use of artificially low prices between subsidiaries of the same company), and for determining a taxpayer's resident status.[95]

By July 2000, after lengthy negotiations,[96] the government succeeded in achieving the final adoption of Part II in the Duma.[97] The major innovation was the 13 per cent flat rate income tax, along with a regressive unified social tax.[98] Two major taxes, profit taxes and property taxes, as well as a new tax regime for the fuel and energy sector were left out of the package to be dealt with at a later date.

In order to enter into law, Part II still had to pass the Federation Council, composed of regional governors and heads of regional parliaments. Serious opposition was expected not only because of the tax changes themselves, but also because the government concomitantly sought a significant reduction of the powers of regional governors.[99] Furthermore, regions were set to lose tax revenue from the VAT of which they had been receiving a significant share, as well as revenue from the turnover tax.

Contrary to expectations, Part II was passed in the Federation Council by a large margin of 115 for, 23 against and 5 abstentions on July 26, 2000. This unexpected result had two sources. Firstly, the Federation Council was losing veto power due to the increased co-operation between the president and the Duma. According to the constitution, if the FC rejects a law, the Duma may override this rejection with a two-thirds majority (300 out of 450 deputies). It was precisely in this way that a law granting the president the right to dismiss regional governors had been adopted earlier in July 2000.[100]

Secondly, it was helped by the concentration of revenue in a few regions: in 2000, only 19 out of 89 regions were contributing more to the central budget than they received. Thus, while especially Moscow opposed the tax reform,[101] other regions, who received budget subsidies, could be pressured to go along with tax reform.

Moreover, when the first chapters of Part II entered into force in January 2001, the Russian fiscal situation had already turned from a cause of disaster to optimism. After collapsing in 1998, revenues had bounced back rapidly. This was due to a combination of changes in commodity prices and rising exports as well as import substitution due to devaluation, policy changes such as the re-introduction of export taxes on commodity exports in early 1999, and increased compliance, in particular with regard to cash payment of taxes.[102] At the same time, expenditures had been sharply reduced by nearly 8 per cent of GDP between 1998 and 2000 (see Appendix, Tables I.2.2 and II.4.4).

Several changes to existing parts of the Tax Code were adopted in 2001. Most importantly, it passed additional chapters on the profit tax and on the energy sector tax regime.[103] The profit tax rate was lowered from 35 to 24 per cent to be divided between the federal, regional, and local budgets and deduction possibilities were expanded.[104] For energy companies, royalties and a mineral-resource tax were replaced by a unified tax on the production of raw materials.[105] Taxation was moved closer to the source of production in order to reduce incentives for transfer pricing within vertically integrated energy companies.[106] In compensation for a higher formal tax burden, energy companies gained greater predictability since the government reduced its discretionary power over export tariffs and linked tariffs to the development of international commodity prices.[107]

Throughout the early 2000s, the trend towards further tax reductions continued. The general VAT rate was reduced from 20 to 18 per cent in 2004. Simplified tax regimes for small businesses and for agriculture were introduced in 2003 and in 2004 respectively.[108] The social tax, a major source of revenue collecting around 7 per cent of GDP, was reduced from a marginal rate of 35.6 to 26 per cent starting on January 1, 2005. The combined reduction of the formal tax burden was very substantial over these years. High oil prices made such reductions 'affordable' as the revenue from royalties and the export taxes had risen briskly since the early 2000s; while now the IMF began to warn against overly low taxation and the risk to revenues if oil prices were to fall sharply.[109]

11.5.4. WHAT MADE 'BIG LEAP' INSTITUTIONAL REFORM POSSIBLE IN RUSSIA?

Why did big-leap institutional change become possible in Russia in 1998 and 2000–2001, but not in Ukraine—given that the debate about such reform had started at a similar time in both countries, and despite the fact that the obstacles to major reform seemed larger in Russia than in Ukraine?

As in Ukraine, from about 1995 there was agreement that taxation required fundamental reform, but initially there was no agreement on the type of reform. Also, as in Ukraine, the first plans were developed exclusively inside the government without consultation—a method of preparing decisions that proved unworkable in a semi-democratic system. From 1996–97 onwards, tax reform was debated more openly, and after Zadornov's move from parliament to government, the two sides cooperated more closely, and many of *Yabloko's* suggestions were incorporated into Part I of the Tax Code.

The trigger for passing the first part of the Tax Code in 1998 was the financial crisis. At this moment, external demands for reform also played a role as the government was desperate for additional funds. With regard to Part II of the Tax Code, however, there was no close connection to external demands. While Russia had negotiated a new IMF loan in July 1999 (of US $4.5 billion), only the first tranche of this was ever paid. Throughout 2000, negotiations about a further loan continued, but due to its trade and budget surplus, Russia rather started to pay back previous loans and become less reliant on new injections of money.[110] Overall, therefore, the IMF's leverage over the timing and type of Russian tax reform was limited after 1998.

Regarding other external influences, international private rating agencies exerted some pressure in 1998 in tandem with the IMF's, but much less so in

2000 when the economy was much improved. Thus, while there is considerable disagreement over how crucial external factors were for Russia's transition process up to 1998—and how harmful their influence was to the economy—and ultimately the state, after 1998 the influence of external actors became much more limited.[111]

A very different international factor was the sharp rise in world-market prices for oil and gas from 1999 onwards. From an average of $20 per barrel, the price of crude oil rose to more than $60 per barrel in 2005. While this created risks of making the economy overly dependent on the energy sector, the extra revenue allowed the government to lower the rates of almost all taxes significantly.[112] This assisted in reducing the shadow economy substantially—which would be advantageous both to the state and the economy in the longer run.[113]

Thus, while international factors had some impact, the consolidation and development of political power appears as the key factor which allowed a 'big-leap' institutional change particularly in 2000. As set out in section 1, Putin's personal popularity gave him substantial 'autonomy' from powerful 'opaque' groups which Yeltsin had been beholden to. Furthermore, the 1999 Duma elections changed the relationship with parliament. Because big-leap institutional change requires parliamentary approval in the semi-democratic post-Soviet states, the executive-legislative relationship was important—as demonstrated in 1997 when tax reform stalled even after being passed in the first reading by the Duma.

The Duma elected in 1999 was more pro-govermental, and left-wing forces lost influence. This is important not because left-wing forces posed a risk of returning to the past, but because they tended to block the creation of new institutions—often playing into the hands of 'opaque' networks which benefited from a de-institutionalized situation. Furthermore, the Duma supported the president in reining in the regions and in reducing the power of the Federation Council.[114]

'Opaque' networks, including powerful business groups, did not block the tax reform. There are several reasons: most importantly, the political executive had become much less dependent on them. As with the regions, the government used a strategy of 'divide and rule:' while some oligarchs were put under pressure (Boris Berezovsky, Vladimir Gusinsky; later Mikhail Khodorkovsky), others were allowed to become actively involved in the policy drafting process (for example, Vladimir Potanin).[115] There were also some incentives for these networks to accept reform.[116] As the government showed an increasing determination to reduce privileges and loopholes, general reform became more attractive. At the same time, after a prolonged period of institutional deterioration, the Russian government decided to lower its demands on citizens and businesses rather decisively, in particular with regard to direct taxation (income tax, profit tax, and social security tax), thus offering a reform which was overall beneficial to businesses.

The tax administration was a third potential important player in tax reform. However, different from Ukraine, the Russian tax service was deeply divided between federal and regional/local loyalties. Furthermore, heads of the tax service changed frequently throughout the 1990s (see Table 11.5 above) and hence did not develop the same power as Azarov did in Ukraine in the late 1990s.[117]

Regarding state-society relations, fiscal reform reflects a marginalization of society, rather than a post-Soviet social contract. The criticism of the unions towards the unified (and regressive) social tax, the low flat income tax rate and the rises in excise taxes—higher excise taxes on gasoline were widely expected to lead to higher consumer prices—was largely disregarded.[118] Furthermore, according to a survey, 53 per cent of Russians were against the flat-rate income tax.[119] However, by 1998—after yet another shock and another period of rapidly deteriorating living standards—it had become amply clear that social protests would not pose a threat to the government or to elites in general. Overall, the Tax Code was a 'contract' imposed by the elites, which has however, gained legitimacy as it was widely seen as working.

11.5.5. THE CONSEQUENCES OF INSTITUTIONAL RE-BUILDING

As argued in Chapter 4, section 2, institutional change and the constellation of players interact over time. The rise of Putin and the changes in the Duma, i.e., altering constellation of players, made tax reform possible. What then, did this major institutional change imply for further developments in Russia?

Several authors have suggested that formal reform is less relevant than often assumed;[120] also in Russia itself there was considerable doubt that new formal rules would bring decisive improvements.[121] Furthermore, a 'big leap' change necessarily involves uncertainty about its effects, and can potentially even result in a weakening of state capacity.

Firstly, the formal tax system as it had developed in the early 1990s—overly complex, giving the tax administration large discretionary powers, and with high tax rates relative to economic capacity—had been widely identified as an important cause of economic problems in Russia.[122] Thus, the tax system increased the 'state as a source of problems' (see Chapter 2, section 2) for the economy and for society. The reduction of tax rates and the clarification of rules was therefore a clear improvement.

Secondly, formal institutional reform is the logical first step which the state can take.[123] Bad formal rules are often the origin of subversive informal behavior; hence, improving formal rules makes sense even, or especially in a situation of pervasive informality (while it can be difficult to 'get it right'). The replication of several elements of the Russian tax reform in other post-Soviet countries indicates that this formal reform was regarded as useful. At the same time, it is important to note that the Russian tax reform took place alongside a range of other reforms (judicial reform, re-assertion of central power over the regions, etc.); and it seems very likely that the effectiveness of a formal reform depends on parallel improvements in other parts of the institutional structure.[124]

Thirdly, the choice of reform involved a downward revision of direct taxation of wages and profits. In this sense, formal reform *followed* the informal practice of paying less tax than was formally due.[125] Thus, there was a good potential for successful implementation.[126] In fact, the collection of personal income tax improved despite the cut in marginal rates: revenue from income taxes rose from 2.4 per cent of the GDP in 2000 to 3.3 per cent in 2002 and continued at this level.[127] Still, among policy makers there was a perception that the problem of underreporting wages was not fully solved, and as a consequence, in 2004 the decision was taken to lower social security contributions as well.[128]

By 2002, Russian tax rates were seen as a major constraint by 25 per cent of respondents to a survey compared to 40 per cent in Ukraine (see Chapter 10, Table 10.4). From 2002, the inflow of foreign direct investment became more significant (see Table II.2.1 and Graph II.2.1 in the Appendix). At the same time, the tax system was still used as a political instrument, most spectacularly in the case of Yukos.

Apparently, improved formal rules contributed to narrowing the formal-informal gap to some extent. Russia's scores on two indices capturing corruption improved between 2000 and 2004: from 2.1 to 2.8 (out of a 1 to 10 scale) on the Corruption Perceptions Index of TI, and from 9.7 to 29.1 on a 0 to 100 scale in the World Bank Institute's governance indicators. Among other CIS countries only Armenia scored better than Russia on both indicators (as did all three Baltic states).[129] However, this perceived progress was still very tentative: for 2005, Russia's CPI rating worsened again somewhat; and the shadow economy was still estimated to stand at around 40 per cent of the GDP—unchanged since 2000.[130]

The deliberate shrinking of the state through tax reform has been associated with a strengthening, rather than with a further weakening of the state (see Chapter 2, section 3). Nonetheless, given the degree of deterioration of the institutional system and the size and federal structure of Russia, the task of bringing about a sustained recovery of state capacity still appears daunting. As a 2005 OECD study argues:

> [. .] progress in rebuilding state capacities has been very uneven. Since 1998, there has been a dramatic strengthening of the state's extractive capacities—its ability to tax—and of its rule-making capacity. The latter largely reflects increasing executive dominance of the legislature. However, the same cannot be said of rule enforcement.[131]

The legacy of prolonged Soviet and post-Soviet institutional deterioration is not easily overcome.[132]

Overall, the tax reforms undertaken since 1998 have been steps towards strengthening the state as a provider of solutions and have reduced it as a source of problems. However, as argued in Chapter 4, 'late consolidators' face larger obstacles to creating capable and well-governed states since more deterioration has taken place than in 'early consolidators'—and this was reflected in the continued high levels of corruption and associated governance problems which Russia continued to face.

11.6. From prolonged deterioration to unfinished recovery: the Russian path of state-building

This chapter looked at tax reform in Russia as a case of late and partial recovery of state capacity after a prolonged period of institutional deterioration and state weakness. State capacity had deteriorated considerably during the early and mid-1990s due to similar factors as in Ukraine and to the additional strains emanated by the federal structure and an earlier and more rapid privatization.

The process of tax reform shows that the consolidation, increased development and integration of political power played a crucial role in producing a 'big leap' reform. Additional factors, such as the unfair distribution of revenues across regions, and a latent interest of businesses in reform helped to 'cajole' the cooperation of stakeholders and potential veto players alike.

Most importantly, political consolidation was based on increasingly authoritarian tendencies. This involved the successful top-down creation of a political party—Unity/Unified Russia—which supported the executive and its approach to re-establishing state capacity against potential veto players (wealthy regions, 'opaque groups'). Similar efforts at building such a party in Ukraine, in contrast, consistently failed (see Chapters 6 and 7). The shift towards a more authoritarian mode of state-building, furthermore, enjoyed popular support—which in turn increased the autonomy of the executive. Interestingly, this support was not based on the satisfaction of redistributive expectations, as in Belarus. Rather, it appears to have resulted from the deep frustration with the preceding chaos and state-malfunctioning during the more democratic government under Yeltsin. Overall, Putin has sought to steer a path of authoritarian consolidation while maintaining the trappings of an electoral democracy. This path involves advantages—such as increasing decision-making capacity—as well as risks, including the question of leadership transition which will arise again in 2008.

Moreover, its natural resource wealth remains a challenge for the development of a capable and especially of a well-governed state in Russia. While some of the initial 'wild-capitalism-oligarchs' have lost power, a new class of 'statist-oligarchs' controlling energy enterprises is developing as part of the Putin regime. Furthermore, the increase in revenue from natural resources enabled tax reform, but the economy overall, and the fiscal system in particular are becoming dependent on exports of natural resources, and hence on prices in international markets.

The radical fiscal reform which Russia adopted generally marks a break with the past; while the support for an authoritarian regime can be linked to its past—but it is also a reaction to the institutional erosion which the more democratic period of government came to be associated with. In 1998, Russia's vulnerability to the international economy—resulting from an incapable state—became apparent during the financial crisis and triggered a search to improve the state. However, the effort at re-building the state which emerged was very much driven by domestic factors, including the unexpected handover of the presidential office in late 1999.

Considerable risks to the development of a more capable state remain. President Putin has repeatedly reminded the Russian parliament of some of these in his annual addresses. These include a large but still very unreformed bureaucracy slowly emerging from years of underfunding; threats of secession and terrorist attacks emanating from the North Caucasus, which have been worsened by the presence of corruption in the security apparatus, as well as by authoritarian approaches to conflict-solving; and last but not least the powerful risks of the 'natural resource curse.' Thus, efforts at re-building state capacity and at improving the quality of the state remain far from finished, and subject to considerable uncertainty.

Notes

1 Interview, Alexei Makrushin, Senior Economist, Center for Economic and Financial Research, Moscow, June 10, 2002.
2 Treisman (1999).
3 See Higley, Bayulgen, and George (2001), 14–16.
4 On Russia's political and economic transformation see: Reddaway and Glinski (2001); Treisman and Shleifer (2000); Smith (1999); Granville and Oppenheimer (eds.) (2001); White, Pravda, and Gitelman (eds.) (2001); Gaddy and Ickes (2002); Shevstova (2003); Lynch (2005).
5 Population density (8.4 inhabitants per sq km) is low by European standards, but it is more than twice as high as in Canada (3.6 inhabitants per sq km), which has a similar geographic division into warmer and colder regions.
6 In 2004, Russia had a GDP of around $580 billion, while all other post-Soviet countries, including the Baltic states, had a combined GDP of around $215 billion.
7 Moore (2004).
8 See McFaul (2001), 194–204, 207–227.
9 McFaul (2001), 328–331.
10 Kounov and Sitnikov (1999), 6–14.
11 In his annual speeches to the Federal Assembly, Putin has emphasized three themes: the power and the role of the state, economic reform, and social policy. See Elena Chinyaeva, "Putin's state of the nation address," *Russia and Eurasia Review*, May 27, 2003. For the full text of the annual addresses since 2000, see www.kremlin.ru.
12 Close Putin aides control major industries which still have significant state ownership, but there is less of the tendency seen during the Yeltsin years, as well as in Ukraine under Kuchma or in Kazakhstan under Nazarbayev to personally enrich family members. See "Putin's advisers control over $200 billion in key industries," *RFE/RL Newsline*, July 27, 2005.
13 Interview with Andrey Ryabov, Scholar-in-Residence, Carnegie Center, Moscow, June 27, 2002. Other interviewees agreed with this perception.
14 Ahrend and Tompson (2005).
15 See Putin's interesting rhetoric in his April 2005 address to the Federal Assembly: "You know that in the last five years we have had to tackle difficult tasks to prevent the degradation of state and public institutions in our country. At the same time, we had to create the foundation for development in the next few years and decades. We cleared the debris together [...] [T]he stabilization policy [...] has reached the limit of its effectiveness. It must be replaced with a policy oriented towards the future. And for that, we must have an efficient state. However, despite many positive changes, this key problem has not been solved so far." www.kremlin.ru.

16 Holmes (2001); Smyth (2002). Interview with A. Ryabov, Scholar-in-Residence, Moscow, Carnegie Center, June 27, 2002.

17 See Shevtsova (2003), 181–182.

18 "Fatherland, Unity Fade Away," *RFE/RL Newsline*, February 11, 2002. The third party which joined Unified Russia was the All-Russia Movement.

19 See Russian Centre for Public Opinion and Market Research (VCIOM) at www.wciom.ru. See also Kounov and Sitnikov (1999b), 9.

20 Unified Russia, the Communists, the Liberal Democratic Party (LDPR), and Motherland. Neither the Union of Rightist Forces (SPS) nor *Yabloko* cleared the 5 per cent threshold for party list seats.

21 In the 2000 presidential elections, Putin received 52.94 per cent of the vote. See www.fci.ru. The OSCE's assessment of the elections for 2004 is more critical than in 2000. However, it also acknowledges that there was very likely a popular majority favoring the incumbent. See http://www.osce.org/odihr-elections/14519.html [accessed: January 31, 2006].

22 *New Europe Barometer,* 2004.

23 Georgiy Ilichev, "Putin 2005 surpasses Putin 2004," *Izvestiya*, September 23, 2005.

24 Herrera (2001), 146–47.

25 See Alexei Medvedev, "Non-residents and the Russian Financial Crisis of 1998," *BOFIT Discussion Paper*, 6/2001.

26 EIU, *Country Profile, Russia*, 2000–2001, 25.

27 McFaul (1995).

28 Gray (1998). See also Willerton Jr. in White et al. (2001), 36. Ahrend and Tompson argue against this view that many of the companies which were privatized were in bad shape and that their claim to valuable natural resources was often ill-defined. Ahrend and Tompson (2005), 31.

29 See Herrera (2001), 151.

30 An important role in this loans-for-shares program was played by so-called FIGs—Financial Industrial Groups (often dominated by a bank)—which were officially encouraged and registered. See http://stars.coe.fr/doc/doc99/edoc8294.htm.

31 Ahrend and Tompson (2005), 22–23.

32 "Putin's Advisers control over $200 billion in key industries," *RFE/RL Newsline*, July 27, 2005.

33 See also Frye (2001), 8.

34 Two bankers, Roman Abramovich and Aleksandr Mamut, took part in financing Putin's election campaign. See "Putin to meet oligarchs," *RFE/RL Newsline*, July 28, 2000.

35 See also Willerton Jr. in White et al. (2001), 36–38.

36 Alexander Ryklin, "The Kremlin has failed to cleanse Russian politics of big business," *Johnson's Russia List*, January 23, 2003.

37 Jones Luong and Weinthal (2002).

38 World Development Report, World Development Indicators, 2005. Russia's reported gini-coefficient measuring expenditure inequality stood at 45.6 per cent; even war torn and poor countries like Tajikistan, or oil-rich countries like Azerbaijan registered lower inequality than Russia (34.7 and 36.5 respectively).

39 "Despite rising incomes, almost half of Russians feel poor," *RFE/RL Newsline*, June 23, 2005.

40 Reddaway and Glinski (2001), 625.
41 WCIOM, *Press Release* no. 304, September 30, 2005. Rose (1999), SPP 320, 21; Mishler and Rose (1998), 15.
42 *New Europe Barometer,* 2004, section E.
43 Rose (1999), no. 320, 21.
44 Hough (2001), 177–183. Richard Sakwa, "Parties and Organised Interests," in: White, Pravda, and Gitelman (eds.) (2001), 84–107.
45 Higley et al. (2001), 19.
46 See www.fnpr.ru [accessed: March 11, 2002]. Freedom House, *Nations in Transit* (2001), 318.
47 See: Sergei Blagov, "Unions lash out at tax reforms measures," *Asian Times Online*, June 13, 2000; Kubicek (2002), 610.
48 Interview with Andrey Ryabov, Scholar-in-Residence, Carnegie Center, Moscow, June 27, 2002.
49 Jukka Pirttilä (1999); Busse (2000).
50 Tanzi (1998).
51 Boris Fyodorov, newly appointed head of the Ministry for Taxes, June 26, 1998, *Official Kremlin Int'l News Broadcast*. On the IRS, see www.irs.gov.
52 "Taxes in Russia," *Russian Economic Trends*, December 1997; also: Hainsworth and Tompson (2002). "Tax Police get more powers," *RFE/RL Newsline*, April 19, 2000.
53 Interestingly, the powerful, but allegedly highly corrupt tax police was dissolved in March 2003. See "President consolidates security agencies," *RFE/RL Newsline*, March 11, 2003.
54 See Treisman and Shleifer (2000), Chap. 6, 113–136; Easter (2001).
55 Treisman (1999).
56 In 1997 Aleksandr Livshits claimed annual losses of US $30 billion. *Kommersant*, February 20–21, 1997.
57 Sokolowski (2001), 560.
58 The "Law on the Principles of the Tax System" had been adopted in December 1991.
59 "Real Tax Reform in Russia—at long last?" *Russian Economic Trends*, July 2000. "Press Conference with Deputy Minister of Finance Mikhai Motorin Regarding the New Tax Code," *Official Kremlin Int'l News Broadcast*, April 15, 1998.
60 "State Duma and Commodity Producers Work out New Tax Code," *TASS*, July 15, 1994. EIU, *Russia Country Report* 2000/01, 26.
61 "Government Approves Tax Code," *Moscow News*, December 22, 1995. "Tax Reform: Tortuous Road to Equity," *Current Digest of the Post-Soviet Press*, February 7, 1996.
62 Herrera (2001), 147; Sokolowski (2001), 560.
63 The name of the Commission "VeCheka"—reminiscent of the precursor of the KGB (see also Chapter 5, section 1)—was intentional "aggressive symbolism" according to Reddaway and Glinski, signalling that the bureaucracy was re-claiming control. Reddaway and Glinski (2001), 535.
64 Reddaway and Glinski (2001), 535. IMF, Russia, *Country Report no. 99/100*, 1999, 60.
65 Cited after Reddaway and Glinski (2001), 541.
66 "IMF Says No Loan without Tax Code," *Moscow Times*, April 4, 1997; "IMF head calls on Russian deputies to pass new Tax Code," *BBC Summary of World Broadcasts*, April 4, 1997.
67 "Russian parliament passes tax code in first reading," *AFP*, June 19, 1997. According to some reports, the oil lobby had directly participated in drafting legislation concerning the

extraction of natural resources. "Poor Regions Hardest Hit By Tax Code," *Moscow Times*, September 30, 1997.

68 "Are We Achieving Prosperity on the Shoulders of our Citizens?" *Trud*, July 8, 1997.

69 "Communists sound tough on govt, despite passing tax code," *TASS*, June 21, 1997.

70 Samoylenko (1998), 2. "Yeltsin Delays Tax Code in Duma Truce," *Moscow Times*, October 22, 1997. "5000 amendments to Tax Code submitted as of now - Seleznyov," *TASS*, November 1, 1997.

71 Such councils have come to be widely used to negotiate agreements on legislation between the two chambers of parliament and representatives of the president and government. See Remington (2001), 57–58.

72 "Moscow mayor calls for nationwide debate of Tax Code," *TASS*, November 21, 1997. According to Reddaway and Glinski, getting Zadornov to accept a government post was a coup by Chernomyrdin. Zadornov left *Yabloko* when he became a government member. (2001), 544, 576.

73 "Moscow City govt to struggle against new Tax Code - Luzhkov," *TASS*, October 10, 1997.

74 "What there will be instead of a Tax Code," *Kommersant-Daily*, October 23, 1997, 1.

75 "Tax Code Point Man Sees July Approval," *Moscow Times*, February 4, 1998. "Russian Governments wants to finish amending draft tax code by February," *Interfax*, January 24, 1998.

76 "Acting PM Pledges to Boost Tax Revenues," *Interfax*, April 2, 1998.

77 "Russian parliament approves new tax code on first reading," *AFP*, April 16, 1998.

78 A few days earlier, Kirienko had promised Russia's energy companies that they would not be broken up and that tax relief would compensate for falling oil prices. "Tax relief planned for Russian oil and gas companies," *Bloomberg*, April 25, 1998.

79 "Russian Duma passes general section of Tax Code," *TASS*, July 3, 1998.

80 "Tax Czar splashes into Rough Water," *Los Angeles Times*, July 5, 1998.

81 "Russian Tax Overhaul," *NPR Morning Edition*, July 17, 1998. "Russia woos IMF with austere tax reforms Kiriyenko threat to resign if MPs reject budget," *Daily Telegraph,* July 2, 1998. The new sales tax—lambasted by communist deputies as "against the people"—was made much less widely applicable than initially intended. "Russia's Duma rejects tax reforms," *The Financial Post*, July 17, 1998.

82 "Russia's Duma Approves Tax Code as IMF Deadline Nears," *Bloomberg News*, July 16, 1998.

83 Reddaway and Glinski (2001), 599.

84 "Tax chief plans to introduce 20 per cent income tax rate," *TASS*, July 1, 1998. "Chernomyrdin wants tax reform now," *United Press International*, September 1, 1998. The energy companies meanwhile lobbied for further tax cuts: "Russia's Yukos Seeks Tax Cuts on Oil From Unprofitable Wells," *Bloomberg*, October 16, 1998.

85 "Russia appoints taxman to push reform," *United Press International*, September 29, 1998.

86 "Russian Budget, Tax Problems to Frustrate Debt Restructuring," *Interfax*, December 2, 1998; "Russia's tax-raising Plan Goes Easy on Oil, Gas Producers," *Bloomberg News*, December 9, 1998.

87 "IMF approves Key Points of Russia's Planned Tax Reforms," *Interfax*, February 12, 1999.

88 "State Duma approves plan to lower tax rate to 39%," *The Russia Journal*, October 4–10, 1999.

89 SPS: Union of Right Forces (reformist), OVR: Fatherland - All Russia (centrist).

90 "Economic Programmes and Policy: Where is Russia Heading?" *Russian Economic Trends*, January 2000.

91 "High-Ranking Duma Official, 'First Part of Tax Code is Serious Step to Improve Investment Climate in Russia,'" *Ros Business Consulting Database*, March 14, 2000.

92 "Putin unveils plan to slash tax rates," *The Russia Journal*, May 29-June 04, 2000. A more business-friendly tax regime was promoted by German Gref, Putin's main economic advisor and Minister of Economic Development and Trade. Also, Sergei Shatalov, the "father of Russian tax reform" returned to the government as first deputy Minister of Finance.

93 "Walking on the Spot," *Segodnya*, May 26, 2000.

94 "Amendments to Tax Code approved by Russian government," *TASS*, April 13, 2000; "Russian Government Approves Amendments to Tax Code," *Bloomberg* News, April 13, 2000.

95 "Cabinet Approves Amendments to Tax Code," *Interfax*, April 20, 2000.

96 "Duma Passes Tax Code II on 1st Reading," *St. Petersburg Times*, July 7, 2000. Part II has been passed chapter by chapter; some chapters were adopted in 2000, and some in 2001. For an English translation of the two parts of the tax code see: http://www. garweb.ru/project/mns/en/law/garweb_law/10800200/10800200-001.htm http://www.garweb.ru/project/mns/en/law/garweb_law/10800200/10800200-029.htm [accessed: January 24, 2003].

97 253 deputies voted in favor, 92 against, and 2 abstained. *Prime-TASS*, July 19, 2000.

98 "Duma approves New Tax Code," *Moscow News*, July 26, 2000.

99 "Senate May Drag Feet in Passing Tax Code," *St. Petersburg Times*, July 25, 2000. Governors and heads of regional legislatures would lose their ex-officio seats in the Federation Council which would be taken by one appointee of the regional legislature and one of the regional executive.

100 "Lower House gives president right to dismiss regional leaders," *RFE/RL Newsline*, July 19, 2000.

101 Shleifer and Treisman (2000), 132-34. "Moscow mayor slams Russian tax code reform," *Ekho Moskvy*, July 26, 2000.

102 "Minister: New Tax Code Won't Stop Collection," *Moscow Times*, February 7, 2001. Collections amounted to Rbl 613 billion, 1.8 times more than in 1999. See also IMF, Russian Federation, *Staff Country Report*, no. 00/145 (2000), 59-72.

103 The measure was adopted with strong support (330 deputies in favor, 5 against). "Duma backs cut in profit tax to 24 per cent," *RFE/RL Newsline*, June 25, 2001.

104 7.5, 14.5, and 2 per cent respectively, with a permission for regions to grant preferential rates no lower than 10.5 per cent.

105 Set at 16.5 per cent of gross revenue; to be shared at a ratio 80 to 20 between the center and the regions.

106 "Tax Code bill set to bolster investment, but requires redraft," *The Russian Journal*, June 22-28, 2001.

107 "Duma passes oil tax bill in 2nd reading," *Reuters*, July 8, 2001. Heinrich and Pleines (2001), 15.

108 IMF, Russian Federation, *Country Report* no. 04/314 (2004).

109 IMF, Russian Federation, *Country Report*, 04/316 (2004), 57-59.

110 "Russia gives IMF more than it receives," *RFE/RL Newsline*, January 4, 2000. "IMF head says Russia needs no loan, urges reforms," *Johnso's Russia List*, October 11, 2001.

111 See Wedel (1998); Reddaway and Glinski (2001); Ganev (2001) argues against this.
112 According to IMF calculations, a $1 change in oil prices per barrel has an effect of 0.33 per cent of GDP in revenue collection. IMF, Russian Federation, *Country Report* 04/314 (2004).
113 A good discussion of the impact of rising oil prices on revenues and on fiscal policy is provided by Spilimbergo (2005).
114 The highly unequal division of revenue among regions allowed the executive to use a strategy of 'divide and rule:' it promised the poor regions more transfers and a more equal distribution of resources, and thus won their support against the strict opposition of rich regions—headed by Moscow. "Tax reform instead of devaluation," *Segodnya*, July 27, 2000.
115 "The work on the draft law on profit tax of organizations will be continued," *Prime-TASS*, February 19, 2001.
116 Jones Luong and Weinthal (2002).
117 The Russian STS was also used to pressure independent media during election campaigns; but it did not develop into a state within the state. See Freedom House, *Nations in Transit* (2001), 315.
118 "Russian trade unions today organized protest against government plans to introduce a single social tax," *Prime-TASS*, June 1, 2000.
119 *Prime-TASS*, July 10, 2000; citing a survey conducted by VTsIOM.
120 On the debate about the relevance of formal institutions, see: Carey (2000).
121 "The tax code—no panacea," *Vesti*, February 11, 2000.
122 Grafe and Richter (2001), 148-149.
123 According to Hainsworth and Tompson: "[...] the approach to tax reform [...] is promising. Simplifying the system and lowering rates should make it easier to bring actual practice in line with formal rules." Hainsworth and Tompson (2002), 294-95.
124 This was also argued by Yelena Nikolayenko, Center for Fiscal Policy, Deputy Director and Leading Consultant, interview, Moscow, June 21, 2002.
125 See also Leitzel (2003), 41.
126 Even though there was still distrust as to whether this formal downward revision would be stable over time. "The president promised not to raise taxes," *Segodnya*, February 14, 2001.
127 Institute for the Transition Economy, 2002 Report, p. 66, Table 7 (www.iet.ru). IMF, Russian Federation, *Country Report* 04/314 (2004). "Tax collections have risen by a third," www.strana.ru [accessed: October 18, 2001]. Ivanova et al., "The Russian Flat Tax," 2005.
128 IMF, Russian Federation, *Country Report*, no. 04/314 (2004), 58-62; "Flat Tax might be Raised," *RFE/RL Newsline*, 19 February 2004.
129 Transparency International, www.transparency.org. The WBI's rating is a composite of other existing indicators. Both WBI's and TI's indicators are perception and survey based.
130 "Russian Shadow Economy Makes up to 40% of Legitimate GDP – Research," *MosNews*, October 5, 2005.
131 OECD 2005, 40.
132 "Old Tax Habits Die Hard in Russia," *Transition Newsletter*, vol. 13, no. 6 (2002), 33-34; "Russian Businessmen still Manage to Cheat the State," *Pravda.Ru*, August 23, 2002.

CHAPTER 12.
CONCLUSION

State-building in the former Soviet Union has been a messy affair. On the one hand, there are a lot of failings: corruption runs high in most countries, the 1998 Russian crisis was a spectacular instance of state failure, and overall, only the Baltic countries have achieved the goal of building capable as well as accountable states based on consolidated democratic regimes. On the other hand, there is some degree of success: all post-Soviet states have established their own state structures and the specter of state collapse which haunted the region during the initial state-building period in the mid- to late 1990s has largely receded. While there are still many dysfunctional aspects of the state, there have also been real efforts at improving the state as a source of solutions—in some cases initiated top-down, and in others demanded by growing opposition movements.

State-building and the wider context of system transition have been dynamic processes, still ongoing more than a decade after the break-up of the Soviet Union. A steep and protracted decline has been followed by considerable but uneven and incomplete recovery; and societies and institutions are still recovering from crisis and upheaval.

There are important risks: apart from the Baltic countries, no consolidated democratic regimes have emerged in the region. In the countries which experienced 'colored revolutions,' eventual consolidation of democratic regimes is not an outcome that can be taken for granted. As this study has shown, regimes which remain unconsolidated harbor negative implications for the capacity and quality of states. The consolidated authoritarian regimes which have emerged in several countries have benefited state capacity in some respect, but there are indications that the quality of their public administrations and their legitimacy is deteriorating. Furthermore, in several of these countries, the state may come under severe strain during eventual moments of leadership succession, or challenges from dissatisfied populations.

This conclusion summarizes the central findings emerging from this study. Section 1 reviews how the state has evolved as a source of solutions and of problems in the four case studies, and comments on the effects which state malfunctioning has had on societies. Section 2 sums up the importance of institutional erosion; and of the political regime as the core for subsequent state-building efforts. The early consolidation of democratic or authoritarian regimes enabled state-building; while political fragmentation and contestation hindered state-building efforts.

Section 3 revisits other factors which have been considered in this research, in particular Soviet legacies, the level of development, and international economic integration. Legacies and the level of development broadly shape the background against which state-building takes place, but neither of these two factors *a priori* determines state-building trajectories.

Section 4 draws implications from this research for three fields of debate: institution building and institutional change, transition theory, and state-building. The material and findings of this research point to ways in which institutionalist concepts can be extended so as to become applicable to instances of non-incremental change and of declining levels of institutionalization. Regarding transition theory, a central concern of this study is to contribute to building stronger links between the consideration of regime transitions and of state-building and state reform processes. Finally, the section offers some reflections on how the analysis of post-Soviet state-building processes can contribute to a comparative research agenda on states and state-building.

12.1. States as problems and solutions

As set out in Chapter 2, on the one hand, states are needed as solutions to the collective action challenges which modern, complex societies face—and consequently societies suffer when the state is (suddenly) weakened. On the other hand, states themselves are a potential source of problems: they may become too immobile as in some stable, highly developed countries; or they may become dysfunctional due to deliberate abuse by uncertain regimes and to the associated state capture by narrow and opaque groups, which has been a key risk in transition countries; or they can be turned into machines for oppression, a key risk that has been associated with authoritarian forms of government.

Both aspects of the state have proven major challenges in post-Soviet state-building processes. Especially until the mid- to late 1990s, states as providers of solutions shrank dramatically, while deliberate distortions and state capture led to a proliferation of corruption and rent-seeking with numerous negative implications for societies. At the same time, there has been considerable variety among post-Soviet states both with regard to the degree of 'state-shrinkage' and to the types and degrees of state dysfunctionalities, depending on the way in which regime transition and other factors affected the state-building process.

This duality of the state also has important implications for state-building prescriptions: strengthening the state without addressing state capture and dysfunctionalities means nurturing an unfair state machine, while fighting dysfunctionalities such as corruption without enhancing state capacity is likely to be futile.

Amongst the post-Soviet states analyzed here, the way in which the state operates is still evolving. In Russia, the state has become less of a problem in some areas—such as taxation—and more in others, as it is seeking to control society in an authoritarian mode to an increasing extent. In Belarus, the state has been relatively capable, and has provided a specific range of solutions to society; however, over time oppression has increased, and so have other elements of the state as a problem, especially corruption. The 'Orange revolution' in Ukraine has triggered an attempt to re-orient the state, turning it into more of a source of solutions and less a source of problems. However, the results of these efforts are still uncertain, as the distortions created by the Kuchma regime, and the opaque groups on which it relied have become well entrenched during a decade and a half of 'captured' state-building.

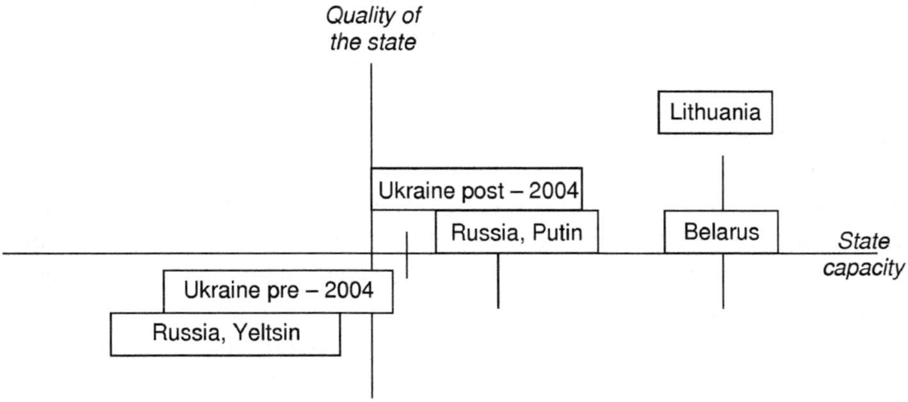

Graph 12.1: The state as a problem and solution – Belarus, Lithuania, Russia, Ukraine

Graph 12.1 maps the four cases against the two aspects of the capacity and quality of the state, also reflecting the changes which have taken place in Ukraine and in Russia in 2004 and since 2000 respectively. Relatively, Lithuania has the most capable and well-governed state, although there is still room for further improvement of both aspects. The Belarusian state is capable, but its quality of governance contains positive as well as problematic aspects, and may be deteriorating. In Ukraine and Russia, shifts in the political regime have brought about improvements in the capacity and quality of the state—but the improvements are still incomplete and uncertain in both cases.

12.1.1. WEAK AND DYSFUNCTIONAL STATES: CONSEQUENCES FOR SOCIETIES

This study has focused on the causes rather than the consequences of state capacity, because, as argued in the introduction, the causes have not been sufficiently explored in most existing accounts. However, because we take an interest in states not as ends in themselves, but as important elements in fostering the welfare and prosperity of societies, in this conclusion I want to comment briefly on the consequences of post-Soviet state-building problems.

Both aspects of the state—as a provider of solutions and as a source of problems—are important with regard to consequences for society. In some post-Soviet countries, particularly those combining poor economies with high political fragmentation and contestation (e.g., in Tajikistan, Kyrgyzstan, Georgia, Moldova), the state as a provider of solutions has been failing almost completely at least for some time and at least in some parts of the territory, while the remaining disintegrated state institutions have become mostly a source of problems (such as police, customs, and tax officials extracting bribes, or even actively involved in illegal activities). In other cases, including Ukraine, the state continuously provided some range of solutions to society but has been unreliable in doing so, for example, allowing pension and wage arrears to accumulate, or allowing bribery to proliferate in public service provision. Nearly everywhere, dysfunctionality pervaded many areas of state activity, and has, at best, been slowly rolled back.

A central effect of the reduction of the state as a solution and the increase of the state as a source of problems is the tendency to generate rising inequality and poverty. This is accentuated in a post-communist context where the state previously was very encompassing, including its roles as an employer, and as the *de facto* owner of most assets. Those groups which previously relied on the state for an income (pensioners, and recipients of social assistance, but also those working in the 'budgetary sphere'—teachers, health-care workers, civil servants, etc.) were for the most part made worse off. Ukrainian lawmakers adopted an elaborate welfare state immediately after independence, but in fact hyperinflation meant that life-time savings were wiped out over night, while legal welfare entitlements far exceeded available budgetary resources (see Chapters 6 and 7).

In most post-Soviet countries, more than 30 per cent of the population became poor, falling below national poverty lines. In Russia, poverty and inequality increased sharply despite the fact that Russia remained one of the relatively wealthiest post-Soviet republics; and in Ukraine poverty became very widespread by the late 1990s.[1] In the weakest and economically poorest post-Soviet states, 50 per cent and more of the population fell into poverty. In 1999, Ukraine's per capita income was close to that of Côte d'Ivoire, Honduras, or Sri Lanka; while Russia was on a par with Peru and Tunisia.[2]

Table 12.1: Human Development Indicators for the post-Soviet region, 1987–2003

	USSR 1987*	1990	1995	2000	2003
Armenia	0.920*	0.737	0.698	0.735	0.759
Azerbaijan		–	–	–	0.729
Belarus		0.787	0.751	0.774	0.786
Estonia		0.814	0.795	0.833	0.853
Georgia		–	–	–	0.732
Kazakhstan		0.767	0.721	0.731	0.761
Kyrgyzstan		–	–	–	0.702
Latvia		0.799	0.765	0.812	0.836
Lithuania		0.823	0.787	0.828	0.852
Moldova		0.739	0.682	0.665	0.671
Russian Fed.		0.817	0.770		0.795
Tajikistan		0.696	0.629	0.630	0.652
Turkmenistan		–	–	–	0.738
Ukraine		0.799	0.747	0.754	0.766
Uzbekistan		–	0.679	–	0.694

Source: UNDP. *The HDI for the USSR for 1987 is not fully comparable to those for later years, while the data for 1990–2003 is fully comparable.

As Table 12.1 shows, the human development indicator for all post-Soviet countries deteriorated significantly between the late 1980s and the mid-1990s, and only the Baltic states maintained a high level of human development (i.e., above 0.8). In a global perspective, reversals in human development are highly unusual during the period since 1975—and apart from the former Soviet Union have only occurred in some African countries such as Zimbabwe or Lesotho.[3]

The state as a source of problems made people worse off, at the same time as helping members of the political and economic elite to enrich themselves by skewing state actions in their own favor (unfair privatizations, tax privileges, etc.). As a result, inequality increased, and considerably more so in the former Soviet Union than in Central Eastern Europe.[4] This is exemplified by Ukraine in the late 19990s, when oligarchs received millions in assets from the state at 'discount' prices, while pensions dropped to below the subsistence minimum, and were often not paid for months.

Above and beyond economic insecurity, physical insecurity also increased due to corruption and low pay levels in the police and the army. Citizens could expect little or no help when they became victims of a crime, and the risk of terrorist attacks especially in Russia grew due to corruption in the security apparatus.

The dissolution of the Soviet state and the dismantling of its oppressive apparatus brought advantages: post-Soviet societies have greater freedom of choice and especially of interaction with the rest of the world. Civic and political freedom have increased, although they are still limited in most parts of the former Soviet Union. The stagnation of the late Soviet period was replaced by disorder, but also a dynamism which has been welcomed especially by younger, better educated people. But the failure to establish capable, well-governed states in the majority of post-Soviet countries has imposed high costs and has delayed the benefits from transition for a majority of citizens in these countries for the past 15 years.

Overall, state dysfunctioning in the context of transition has had substantial negative effects on post-Soviet societies, and these effects will take a long time to overcome. In many countries of the former Soviet Union, state malfunctioning and its consequences have generated deep distrust, and frustration with the state as reflected in opinion surveys presented in the empirical chapters; and some search for better leadership, albeit in different ways and under different auspices, as the increasingly diverging trajectories of Ukraine and Russia demonstrate.

12.2. Institutional deterioration and the importance of the political regime

As suggested in Chapter 4 (Graphs 4.1 and 4.4), there is a crucial interaction between the level of institutionalization, on the one hand, and the behavior and structuring of actors, on the other. Experience from some countries elsewhere suggests that *in extremis* an overarching institutional order can break down completely for years, or even decades. Afghanistan has not, essentially, had a unified institutional order across its territory since 1979; while in Somalia there has not been an institutional order since 1992. In both cases it has proven extremely difficult to re-establish a new order after a prolonged period of institutional breakdown.

Institutional erosion was the common starting point of post-Soviet state-building, and it meant that old constraints and incentives had become weakened or dissolved essentially since the last 1980s, while new ones were not yet in place (see Chapter 5). Institutional deterioration had important implications due to the weakening of institutional constraints on actors. A particular feature of post-communist countries is the way in which the weakening of institutional constraints coincided with the opportunity to distribute the accumulated wealth of these economies, from flats to factories, and from agricultural land to vast natural resources; which especially benefited a narrow elite section of society. Due to this coincidence, the weakening of institutions had a particularly strong impact on the redistribution of power among groups in society.

The 'fate' of regime transition in post-Soviet countries was important for the way and the speed at which capable institutional systems could be re-established. As Graph 4.3 in Chapter 4 set out, the political regime is at the core of the state. The political center of the state is the 'seat' of decision-making as well as of exercising control over the administration. Therefore, regime transition and the (non-)consolidation of a political regime after the end of communism had important implications for the state-building processes and for re-building a new institutional system.

As analyzed in Chapter 5 and corroborated by the case studies, countries which early on consolidated either democratic or authoritarian regimes preserved better fiscal discipline during the phase of economic crisis than those with unconsolidated regimes. They have tended to construct more capable fiscal systems, have kept corruption in check better, and have maintained stronger economies than states based on unconsolidated regimes.

Generally, a new institutional order was more rapidly re-established in those post-Soviet cases in which the consolidation of a new regime occurred early on. This happened in Lithuania, as well as in the other Baltic states, where nascent democratic regimes began re-building institutions as early as during the struggle for independence. In Belarus an autocratic regime was consolidated in the mid-1990s and supported a conservative course of rebuilding a modified socialist state. Ukraine and Russia, in contrast, both developed unconsolidated, hybrid political regimes that faced challenges from several quarters: a rising oligarchy, unreformed communists, as well as low popularity, and a lack of credible political parties which could have provided a base for political debate and regime-building. During the 1990s, neither the consolidation of a democratic nor of an authoritarian regime was possible.

In Lithuania as well as Belarus, control over taxing and spending during early independence was stronger and less marked by overrunning than in Ukraine and Russia, or other countries with unconsolidated regimes. But reflecting the difference in regime type, the institutional mechanisms used in Lithuania and Belarus have been different. In Lithuania, taxing and spending was based on an evolving elite consensus embedded in a parliamentary system in which broader parts of the population had at least a potential voice. Labor bears a heavy burden in terms of direct and indirect taxation, but in turn benefits from a relatively capable and well-governed state.

The consolidation of democracy furthermore means that different elements of control and accountability can reinforce each other: the State Control (Lithuania's SAI) which reports and is accountable to parliament, a free press which picks up and discusses governance problems, and an increasingly organized society—even if many citizens are quite disenchanted by the political class as reflected in public opinion polls.

In Belarus, political consolidation centers around a single leader who is feared by the elites, but apparently enjoyed considerable popular legitimacy among society at large. Lukashenko used repeated anti-corruption campaigns, focusing on accusations of abuse of public funds, to keep elites in a state of fear, and at the same time relied on populist appeal to the majority of citizens. The system of revenue extraction could rely on a still largely state-controlled economy. The Belarusian parliament has been robbed of all but the most marginal control over the budget, and in this way competing demands on state funds are shut out, allowing the top executive to decide about where to allocate funds in order to increase its own legitimacy. The president has brought control over public funds directly and exclusively under his personal command.[5] Thus, in this consolidated autocracy various institutional elements interact, producing an overall rather effective fiscal system. A key risk to Belarus' state-building trajectory is that 'secondary transitions' in neighboring Ukraine and elsewhere are threatening to the regime. As a consequence, the balance is shifting between relying on considerable popular support versus relying on force and fear.

Overall, albeit employing different mechanisms, Lithuania and Belarus both have relatively high state capacity by regional standards. Still, there are considerable problems in both cases: in Belarus, the quality of the state is good with regard to delivering public services, but it is worse on the dimension of giving citizens a voice, and with respect to modernizing the state.[6] In Lithuania, the overall quality of the state is the highest among the four cases, but there have been frequent turnovers of government, and a sequence of political scandals—which have had a negative effect on trust in state institutions.

Ukraine and Russia both suffered from an initial lack of political consolidation. Initially, power became deeply contested between the parliament and the president. Also, in both countries the ex-communists had split up into those supporting and profiting from reforms, and those fervently opposed to building a capitalist system. At the same time, the presidents of both countries relied increasingly on narrow groups in the 1990s. Furthermore, in Russia president Yeltsin fell ill, leaving various actors grabbing for the reins of power during the initial state-building period.

Consequently, in both countries a situation emerged in which the state did not collapse, but became highly dysfunctional and delivered much fewer solutions to society than were needed in a situation of transition. In both countries, tax reform was debated for years without results, although the existing tax systems were recognized as highly dysfunctional and as a key obstacle to economic recovery as well as to the provision of social services. In Russia, furthermore, the fiscal crisis became especially acute because power had become more dispersed due to early privatization and the federal structure—eventually bringing about the 1998 financial crisis.

In Russia, the eventual reaction has been a move towards greater authoritarianism; while in Ukraine it has been a shift towards greater democratization. In Russia, a new president came to the helm in 2000 who promised to strengthen the state. This promise proved to be a popular proposition in a society which had experienced a rather traumatic transition, and especially since Russians still mourned the loss of empire and grandeur at the international level. In turn, popularity helped the new president to gain greater autonomy, since he had to rely less on powerful interest groups than his predecessor Yeltsin.

The move to greater authoritarianism in Russia was accompanied by a (top-down) restructuring of the political party landscape, especially in terms of which political parties were represented in parliament. This reinforced the move towards greater decision-making capacity at the central state level—which also allowed for a reversal in the previous trend towards 'asymmetric' federalism.

Under Putin, several 'big leap' reforms were adopted, of which fundamental tax reform was the 'opening act' (Chapter 11). The trend towards a more authoritarian regime in Russia coincided with a steep rise in prices for oil and gas which has brought a windfall of extra resources for the state. Furthermore, there has not only been an increase in the capacity, but at least in some respects also in the quality of the state: the tax burden has become more evenly distributed, and the somewhat better functioning of regulation has improved the business climate, even though much room for further improvement remains.[7]

Still, it is uncertain to what extent greater authoritarianism will provide a solution to Russia's state-building challenges. There are contradictory signs: despite its authoritarian leanings, the government under Putin is pursuing a modernization of the state which also aims at developing a more service-oriented behavior of the bureaucracy.[8] However, by international surveys corruption is recorded as rising again after declining between 2000 and 2004 (see Table II.6.2., Appendix). Furthermore, the increasingly authoritarian form of rule suppresses the civic liberties necessary to develop an effective demand for better governance.

Ukraine took the opposite direction away from a hybrid regime with the 'Orange revolution' in late 2004. While the Kuchma regime had rebuilt some elements of state capacity, it had also distorted the state, and had allowed considerable state capture by opaque groups in return for support to the president. Thus, in 2003, Ukraine followed Russia's lead in adopting several tax policy measures, but widespread problems with tax privileges remained, and in 2004, large funds were siphoned from the budget via the VAT refund system to finance the Kuchma–Yanukovych election campaign.

Subsequent to the 'Orange revolution' the new government promised and set out to reform the state, and to develop a state 'for the people.' However, during the first year of the Yushchenko government, the democratic regime remained unconsolidated. It was under considerable pressure from internal discord, the continuing strength of the oligarchic networks, popular disappointment, as well as looming constitutional changes and parliamentary elections. Consequently, while post-Orange governments made some spectacular achievements, such as increasing tax and other revenue considerably despite a marked slow-down in economic growth, in many areas the reform of the state lacked orientation and drive, leading to widespread feelings of disappointment and disillusionment.

From the analysis of these four post-Soviet cases, we can conclude that among countries with similar structural conditions, it is the presence of political consolidation and the type of political regime that have a decisive impact on whether, and within what timeframe, capacity is established in new states. Furthermore, the type of political regime being consolidated will have decisive effects on the kind and quality of the state being built—i.e. whether it ultimately relies on top-down control, or on checks and balances as well as accountability to citizens. Hybrid, unconsolidated regimes offer relatively greater political and civic freedom than authoritarian regimes, but they are particularly vulnerable to state capture by oligarchic groups and tend to be marked by abuses of the state apparatus, undermining the quality of the state.

12.2.1. THE ROLE OF GROUPS AND INTERMEDIARY ORGANISATIONS

Social groups and intermediary organizations such as political parties are important: they affect the initial development of the political regime, and their opportunities are in turn affected by the emerging political and state institutions, as proposed in Chapter 4, and traced in the empirical chapters.

Elite reconfigurations at the outset of transition differed markedly across the four cases and gave shape to different political regimes, hence shaping initial state-building trajectories. These in turn affected the further reconfiguration of groups. In Lithuania, a new elite group emerged out of the national opposition. At the same time, the former communist elite remained a 'visible' group, and transformed itself into a strong ex-communist party. Further new political groupings—mainly based on the new more or less 'legitimate' business class—emerged during the process of transition and state-building. In Belarus, the communist establishment remained in place, but became 'subjugated' to a former rather minor functionary; while the national opposition remained weak and without the popular appeal which it enjoyed in Lithuania.

In Russia, the Communist Party fragmented into different parts and networks —some pushing for economic reform, and others who eventually refounded a Communist Party and became staunch opponents of reform. The democratic opposition allied with those ex-communist networks favoring 're-form.' In contrast to the non-Russian republics, nationalism was not an issue galvanizing the democratic opposition.

In Ukraine, the communist elite also split. The upper echelons of the former communist system formed an 'old boys' network which distributed spoils and positions, but without the enthusiasm for 'economic reform' brandished in Russia. A sizable, but non-transformative national opposition emerged, as did a number of political parties based on developing business 'clans.' This chequered pattern of aspiring new elites evolved into a game of shifting alliances with limited time horizons. Both in Russia and in Ukraine, but much less so in smaller Belarus and Lithuania, national level constellations were supplemented by and, to differing degrees, related to regional constellations and power bases.

In Ukraine as well as in Russia, a result of the distorted state-building based on hybrid regimes has been the emergence of extremely wealthy oligarchs, who in turn began to play an important role in politics, and hence in shaping the future rules of the game. In both countries, however, other groups have eventually also sought a role: the emerging middle class in Ukraine, and the security structures—enjoying broad popular support—in the case of Russia.

Lithuania is the only one among the four cases scrutinized more closely in which we see a clear rise of 'visible' groups and a relatively well-structured party system during the first two phases of independence. This is combined with a free press which has been able to report on alleged cases of corruption in depth. These factors have combined to keep more 'opaque' powers in check.[9]

In Belarus, in contrast, 'opaque' interest groups other than the immediate entourage of the president could not rise to the fore. Thus, there are no oligarchs in Belarus. However, 'visible' groups are likewise weak. New parties and civil society have been oppressed, while 'old' Soviet organizations such as the Trade Union Federation have remained in a state of relative dependence. As a result, Belarus resembles the situation of a 'stationary bandit' in Olson's terms, which has allowed the building of a relatively capable state from above. As all wider groups are relatively weak, however, the risk of tyranny has grown over time.

In Ukraine and in Russia, 'opaque' interest groups acquired the strongest influence. The respective moves of these two countries towards a more democratic and a more authoritarian regime have involved changes in the role of different groups. In Ukraine, groups representing the middle class, or 'civil society,' have become more prominent, wresting the government from politicians close to oligarchic groups. However, the effectiveness of post-Orange government has been hampered by continued fragmentation and in-fighting, as well as by regional divisions. In Russia, the ascendancy of President Putin is widely equated with the re-assertion of groups based on the former and current security apparatus over oligarchic 'robber barons.'[10] 'Visible groups'—political parties and social organizations—have become less fragmented than in Ukraine, but at the same time have become more dependent, moving their roles more towards top-down transmission belts than bottom-up avenues of interest aggregation.

In both countries, these shifts in group constellations have brought about changes in the functioning of the state: in Russia, since 2000 a number of important reforms have been adopted in the fiscal and other spheres, which previously appeared impossible. 'Opaque' groups have retreated, and had to accept tax reforms; so the *problematique* of state capture has lessened.

In Ukraine, the government under Yushchenko sought to improve the capacity and especially the quality of the state. It has been somewhat successful at shifting the rules in favor of broader social interests, but improvements in the quality of the state have still been vulnerable to reversals. Nonetheless, the 'Orange revolution' has created a new level of expectations about what the Ukrainian state can do for its citizens and a different atmosphere about whom politicians must be responsive to: the December 2004 elections, beginning with the campaign period, generated markedly more socially oriented policies than are present in Russia. This is well-illustrated by the evolution of the welfare state in the two countries: average pensions reached slightly higher levels in Ukraine than in Russia in 2005—despite the fact that per capita incomes were more than two and a half times higher in Russia.[11]

In summary, the original reconfiguration of elites and the evolution of former communist parties had a decisive impact by shaping the emerging new regimes. This in turn affected the state-building process, the way in which wealth and power was redistributed, and the opportunities for state capture by 'oligarchic' groups. More than a decade into independence, the composition and power of different groups and the relevance of intermediary organizations continues to evolve.

12.2.2. UNTRUSTED STATES

While trust in public institutions is rather low in all four cases, we see that it is relatively higher in the consolidated systems of Lithuania and Belarus (see Chapter 10, Graph 10.3).[12] Interestingly, trust in state institutions tends to be highest on average in Belarus among a number of post-Soviet and Central Eastern European countries. Authoritarian Belarus appears to still deliver some of the public goods which people expect of the state.

Overall, trust appears more as a re-active phenomenon, rather than a driving factor. For example, tax compliance has improved over time both in Russia and in Ukraine despite continuing low levels of trust in the state. Similarly, greater state capacity in Poland than in Russia or Ukraine is not matched by or based on higher trust. Hence, any direct causal flow from trust to state capacity appears relatively weak and appears to the main direction of causation flow from the provision of a social order to more trust. The example of Poland is also a reminder that even states with comparatively high levels of capacity can lose trust when the political game becomes too blatantly self-serving.[13]

12.3. Setting the background: legacies, international integration, and the level of development

The range of analysis of this study confirms that the consolidation of the political regime is a key factor driving state-building in post-Soviet countries. However, as proposed in the framework in Chapter 4, and evinced by the empirical findings, political consolidation does not stand in isolation. Institutional legacies and the level of development form a background which gives a broad shape to opportunities and constraints. International economic integration played a role, but where state weakness is a problem, this is predominantly related to domestic factors.

12.3.1. INSTITUTIONAL LEGACIES AND THE LIMITS OF PATH-DEPENDENCY

Many accounts of post-communist developments emphasize the importance of institutional legacies and 'path-dependency.'[14] However, assumptions that legacies are deceisive appear simplistic in a situation of fundamental change. Legacies do not restrict post-Soviet state building to a specific path or a very limited set of options. The empirical evidence of this study clearly shows that countries enter different trajectories despite similar legacies; and that institutional development can diverge considerably from anything that went before it.

Section 2 has summarized the importance of institutional deterioration. Deterioration appears to reinforce some legacies at the same time as weakening others. For example, the legacy of basic social protection dissolved in the former Soviet Union to a far greater extent than in Central Eastern Europe. In contrast, the legacy of a cumbersome and unresponsive bureaucracy remained strong. Similarly, networks between the bureaucracy and 'well-connected' parts of business remained or developed into more pernicious forms, especially when the political regime was unconsolidated and governments used the bureaucracy 'defensively'—as in the case of the tax administration in Ukraine, documented in Chapters 7 and 8.

In general, by dismantling the Soviet economic system, the majority of post-Soviet states were pulled into a wave of institutional change as many communist institutional templates became irrelevant for governing in the context of a largely privately-owned economy. Moreover, institutional 'evolution' has been driven by copying existing models from elsewhere; and importantly, by the way in which different power-holders interacted.

Still, while legacies are not dominant relative to all other factors, they are not irrelevant. Legacies in particular have given shape to common problems across the region, but the capacity of and incentives for how societies and elites have sought to solve these problems have differed. All post-Soviet countries faced the challenge to re-invent their tax policies and tax administrations. However, the solutions found to this challenge have differed: maintaining a socialist ownership state combined with gradual adjustments to regional trends in Belarus, rather radical innovation in Lithuania and the other Baltic states, the creation of distorted and dysfunctional systems in Ukraine and Russia, followed by a downward adjustment of rules after the first decade of state-building. As a result of these differing adjustments of formal rules, the evolution of informal institutions has likewise differed, with the worst kinds of evolution—economic and fiscal 'virtualization,' the spread of tax privileges, arrears, corruption and political abuses of the tax administration—appearing in the half-reformed, distorted systems of Ukraine and Russia in the 1990s.

An exclusive focus on institutional legacies can obscure our understanding of institutional changes that go *against* rather than *along* established paths, such as the introduction of a flat income tax. As we saw in Chapter 5, while fiscal rules have diverged and re-converged over time, they have moved ever further away from those of the previous system.

Overall, legacies form part of the background conditions, but are refracted by institutional deterioration as well as by other factors, especially the shifting influences of various groups, but also by the process of 'importing' institutional models.

12.3.2. THE LEVEL OF DEVELOPMENT

The impact of the level of development on state-building efforts has not been at the center of this inquiry, as the study has focused on four cases which started off from broadly similar levels of development. However, the broad relevance of this factor was explored in Chapter 5. As Graphs 5.5 and 5.8 showed, the fiscal size of the state and the level of development are (loosely) related among the countries of the former Soviet Union, and, on average, revenues and expenditures have shrunk more in poorer than in richer post-Soviet countries. However, the impact of the level of development appears to be weaker with regard to indicators of the capacity and quality of the state, such as the ability to control post-independence deficits and to contain corruption.

One relevant mechanism by which the level of development affected state-building in post-Soviet countries is that the poorest former republics lost especially from the USSR's dissolution as previously they enjoyed fiscal and other forms of subsidies from wealthier parts. Since 1991, some poor parts of the former Soviet Union appear to have fallen into a trap of weak stateness combined with very low per capita incomes (e.g. Kyrgyzstan, Tajikistan, Moldova).

By global comparison, poorer countries on average appear to run a higher 'risk' of weak state capacity, as well as of governance quality problems.[15] However, countries can defy this risk: literature on developmental states in East Asia suggests that very capable states can emerge even in poor countries, and can drive a transformation of the economy within relatively short periods of time.[16] Thus, similar to legacies, the level of development appears to shape opportunities, but it does not determine the capacity and quality of the state. A deeper understanding of how the level of development matters for state-building in the post-Soviet universe would, however, require a research design more closely focused on this question.

12.3.3. INTERNATIONAL ECONOMIC INTEGRATION

All post-Soviet countries entered independence at the same time, and thus were confronted with the same broad process of increasing international integration. Furthermore, all had some interaction with crucial international institutions such as the IMF: and all non-Russian post-Soviet states had to define their relationship with Russia. I therefore proposed that there may be common pressures emanating from the international sphere, and especially from the international economic system, on the state-building processes.

In Chapter 5, we found two trends pointing to a potential impact from the international realm: the substantial decrease in the fiscal size of the state, and the marked trend of reducing fiscal deficits in post-Soviet countries from the late 1990s onwards after initial international borrowing was 'interrupted' by the 1998 Russian financial crisis.

These trends, however, still appear to be primarily driven by domestic factors, most of all, economic crisis and the degree of political consolidation and resulting state capacity. In countries with less capable states, revising tax rates and total tax collections downward was a necessary response, to narrow the formal-informal discrepancy, and to overcome distortions that inhibited economic recovery. Beyond these elements of similarity, external influences and the relationship of post-Soviet countries with the outside world have varied considerably.

In Lithuania, initial institutional reforms were reinforced by a second phase of reform connected to the demands of EU accession. At the same time, Lithuania became the economically most internationally integrated country of the four states—from trade, to debt, to foreign direct investment (see Appendix, Tables II.2.1, II.3.1). Overall, Lithuania is on the road to becoming an effective and flexible state which is well-integrated into the international economy. Belarus, while located in the same regional neighborhood, has resisted pressures (and more limited incentives) from the West, and has rather pursued reliance on Russia—while still maintaining a low-level relationship with the IFIs and gradually increasing trade with non-CIS countries. This has so far enabled it to maintain a restored Soviet economic system, which has been a key pillar in preserving and restoring state capacity, and in developing a rather old-fashioned strong state.

With regard to Ukraine, and even more so Russia, their size and especially Russia's geopolitical importance have limited the leverage of international actors such as the IMF. Russia was negatively affected by its partial integration into international financial markets in 1998, but the source of the crisis lay more in the domestic than in the international realm. The foremost problems of state-building for Russia lie in recreating state capacity and salvaging some quality of the state after a prolonged period of disorganization. Nonetheless, both Russia and Ukraine have economies that rely heavily on the export of a narrow range of goods—oil and gas in the case of Russia, and steel in the case of Ukraine, which potentially exposes their revenue systems to shocks emanating from international markets.

In contrast to assumptions that the pressures of globalization would inhibit state-building, we find that *state-building has taken place* and that it has followed a variety of paths which cannot be accounted for by uniform external pressures.[17] Thus, the example of Lithuania conforms to Evans's view that *state competency is a precondition* for (successful) participation in the global economy.[18] At the same time, governments are challenged and have to react to the conditions in international markets, and this challenge is growing as the international integration of post-Soviet countries intensifies. The majority of post-Soviet countries since 2000 have used the opportunity of growth (and high prices for natural resources) to reduce their external debts. In the case of Russia this reduction was swift and far-reaching.[19] Furthermore, in Russia's case, rising oil prices have been an asset for state-building, which has *inter alia* facilitated tax reform, but they also remain a risk. Overall, the way in which international factors affect the state-building process is shaped by domestic choices, external opportunities and constraints, and by interactions between the domestic and the external sphere.

12.4. Wider implications: conceptualizing institutional change, regime change, and state-building

What do the findings from this study imply for the key strands of comparative research which it has drawn from? There are three main areas of implications: the first relates to the conceptualization of institutional change; the second is the 'neglected link' between regime transitions and state-building; and the third relates to the comparative study of state-building processes.

12.4.1. CONCEPTUALIZING INSTITUTIONAL CHANGE

The findings of this study have several implications for institutional theory. The majority of empirical applications of institutionalist thinking have focused on OECD countries where the initial aim was to explain the persistence of different institutions among developed countries. Thus, institutional concepts were applied to relatively stable, incrementally evolving systems.[20] As a result, the potential of institutional approaches to account for instances of non-incremental change and for processes of institutional breakdown and re-creation remained under-explored.

This study yields several suggestions with regard to how institutionalist concepts may be enhanced to capture the situation of institutional systems during periods of heightened instability. First of all, apart from analyzing the *direction* of instances of institutional change (e.g., from a German to a more Anglo-Saxon structure of state-industry relations), we also need to pay attention to changes in the *level* of institutionalization, i.e. whether institutions are functioning or are eroded. Thus, privatization in the context of a capable and accountable government and public administration differs from privatization in the context of limited capacity, state capture, and high levels of corruption. Changes in the *level* of institutionalization in turn shape and generate other institutional changes, such as reduction of the welfare state in Russia as a consequence of a weakened extractive capacity, or they can lead to a heavy emphasis on re-asserting control (e.g. introducing a tax police).

Secondly, the experience of post-Soviet state-building highlights the interdependencies between various elements of an institutional system, and the challenges that arise when several elements are weak or dysfunctional. For example, introducing a value-added tax creates a useful revenue source and moves countries closer to European standards, but its administration has proven challenging in Ukraine and other countries where fraud is widespread and the capacity of courts to deal with fiscal cases is limited. Similarly, the work of the Accounting Chamber in Ukraine has had little effect during the first decade of its existence due to institutional competition with the DKRS, the 'entrenched' internal control and audit institution, and due to a lack of interest by parliamentarians to exercise real control over the budget. Concepts of institutional change therefore need to capture how overall institutional systems emerge and evolve, and how they do so after major shocks.

Thirdly, some suggestions regarding the complexity of the relationship between formal and informal institutions emerge. North and others have proposed that informal institutions tend to change more slowly than formal ones, implying that formal institutional change would be retarded by informal 'stickiness.' The situation in post-Soviet states suggests that informal institutions can also change more rapidly than formal ones when these erode and become less binding. 'Subversive' informality has proliferated on a considerable scale across the region, and most so in the countries where formal institutions became weakest or most distorted. For example, the weakening and distortion of the tax system led to the built-up of arrears in Ukraine in the late 1990s; which in turn led to the proliferation of informal practices such as offsets and the hand-steering of expenditures during revenue shortfalls. Hence, if a system erodes but formal reform is delayed, informal rules spread. Once informal institutions are sharply divergent from formal ones, it can then become very challenging to re-establish any binding formal rules.

As Leitzel has argued, the prevalence of informality may lead to an adjustment of formal rules towards the existing informal arrangement.[21] Generally, such 'downward' adjustments—if well-planned, coherent, and implying the re-establishment of lower but stronger formal constraints—may be a useful strategy for closing the formal-informal gap and re-increasing state capacity. They can also be a signal of a commitment towards more even-handed, rather than selective enforcement of rules. However, adjusting the state downwards may also reinforce social inequalities which emerged during transition, for example when the state gives up attempts at progressive taxation and formalizes fee-based education and health-care.

12.4.2. CLOSING THE LINK: REGIME TRANSITIONS AND STATE-BUILDING

Transition theorists generally regard stateness as a precondition for democratization.[22] Linz and Stepan imply that full democracy cannot be established in a dependent entitity (such as Hong Kong), and that there needs to be some agreement about the polity, i.e. about citizenship rules and eligibility as voters. However, in most post-Soviet countries all current inhabitants at the point of independence could claim citizenship, while paradoxically the two most exclusionary countries with regard to citizenship, Estonia and Latvia, have been among the best in consolidating democracies.

This research considers the opposite direction of the relationship, from political regime transition to the (re-)building of state capacity. The key argument is that transitions which do not result in regime *consolidation* cause problems with establishing state capacity and with developing states of sound quality, particularly in a situation of new statehood. These problems are compounded by poor management of the economic transformation, which is associated with weak and uncertain regimes. Establishing (and consolidating) democratic systems of government in parallel with building new states is demanding and has not been successful in most parts of the former Soviet Union. It has proven especially difficult without the kind of incentives that highly supportive neighborhoods such as the EU have offered to accession countries.

Furthermore, where democratization is perceived to be associated with the absence of rules—anarchy or anomie—or with highly unfair rules, dissatisfaction with a malfunctioning state can become an important reason why support for democratization falters, as appears to have happened in Russia. This risk is not limited to the situation of the former Soviet Union, but potentially also affects other cases of ongoing democra-tization-cum-state-building (e.g., Afghanistan, Iraq, former Yugoslavia), as well as state reform and democratization processes in existing but weak and dysfunctional states elsewhere.

State- and regime-building necessarily entail risks for societies and their elites whichever trajectory they initially seek to embark on (see Chapter 4, Graph 4.4). To some, chosing a consolidated authoritarian regime may seem preferable in a situation of new statehood, since the likelihood of such a regime generating a capable state appears higher. However, as stressed in the framework and in the case study on Belarus, even when it is in fact possible to consolidate an authoritarian regime, this trajectory always entails the risk of turning towards tyranny, and of a declining quality of the state over time. Tyranny in its most extreme forms may even deploy the state to destroy society; and in more limited versions may shift substantial resources from public services to oppression. Hence, while authoritarian regimes can provide a better basis for building capable states than hybrid regimes, they may also turn into something worse. Therefore, societies 'run a risk' when acquiescing to an emerging authoritarian regime in the hope that it will bring about an effective state.

While the second trajectory in Graph 4.4 is the 'optimal outcome'—an effective state based on a well-functioning democratic regime—the risk for societies in pursuing this route is to land inadvertently on trajectory 3 or 4, that is, developing a fragmented and contested regime with either more democratic or more authoritarian leanings. In the former Soviet Union, hybrid regimes have been the most common result of regime transitions—with negative consequences for the capacity and quality of states.[23] Uncertain hybrid regimes have gone to considerable lengths in abusing the state and especially the tax and spending system in their efforts at 'political survival.'[24]

Hybrid regimes, furthermore, allowed the rise of oligarchic groups which captured parts of state activity, and which increasingly came to dominate the political arena itself. Governments did invest in building aspects of state-capacity, but using a 'defensive' rather than a 'supportive' logic; building top-down presidential verticals, and mechanisms for top-down, selective control.

Once a hybrid regime is in place, seeking a move towards democratic consolidation appears to be the best but nonetheless challenging option.

Success in pursuing such a shift in trajectory requires a focus on what a democratic regime has to deliver in order to improve state capacity (e.g. suitable decision-making structures, constructive interplay and institutional avenues for actors to re-inforce a well-governed state). In Ukraine, the move from a hybrid towards a more democratic, but as yet unconsolidated regime has brought improvements in how the state operates, but has not resulted in a clear break-through. In Georgia and Moldova, which have been the other two more democratic regimes in the CIS region, state capacity and the quality of the state have been uneven at best.[25] Successfully moving towards a trajectory of state-building and state reform based on a democratic regime remains challenging, especially after years of state-building affected by the distortions introduced by the 'defensive logic' of uncertain hybrid regimes.

To support such changes more effectively, strengthening the links between the logic of democratization and of state-building should also become a central concern to external actors who provide advice and assistance. Furthermore, it would benefit from greater interaction between scholars interested in states and those interested in democratization processes. For example, from a statist perspective, Brusis and Dimitrov stress the need to strengthen the executive in order to better co-ordinate policy-making and to ensure strong constraints against overspending.[26] Democratization theorists, in contrast, tend to be distrustful of overly strong central executives.[27] Ongoing efforts at state and regime reform in the former Soviet Union and elsewhere would benefit from such a more intense dialogue, between statist and democratization theorists about trade-offs, risks, and pathways of institutional development.

12.4.3. REFLECTIONS ON THE COMPARATIVE STUDY OF STATE-BUILDING

This study has considered state-building in one region, the former Soviet Union, focusing on its Western part in particular. How does this feed into comparative studies of state-building across different time periods and regions?

Similar to democratization, one can think of state-building as having occurred in a number of 'waves.' The first wave in modern times was the formation of states in Western Europe as comparatively analyzed by Tilly and his co-researchers, focusing on state-building from the early modern period.[28] The last century and a half have witnessed a number of state-building waves: in the

19th century—in Latin America, around WWI—in Australia, the Middle East and the Balcans, after WWII—in Africa and Asia, since the end of the Cold War—in the former USSR, the former Yugoslavia. Furthemore, there is a most recent 'wave' of state-rebuilding subsequent to state collapse and/or invasion—Afghanistan, Iraq, Somalia, and elsewhere. As this list indicates, wars and the dissolution of empires have played a key role in spawning state-building processes.

Compared to other waves of state-building, post-Soviet state-building has been marked by an absence of wars of independence, the (relative) absence of external threats to statehood, as well as the relatively limited external involvement in state-building, and, finally, the presence of rather strong legacies of modern stateness (but not statehood, at least for most republics!), i.e., the established presence of modern state structures (including the presence of a bureaucracy, of state-organized health and education systems, etc.).

The relative absence of wars of independence is beneficial, since these can generate deep political divisions. The absence of external threats to statehood primarily means that post-Soviet states are unlikely to disappear from the map even if their states are internally weak. However, some theorists presume that a degree of external challenge can also promote state-building, since it 'encourages' actors to strengthen the state (rather than to exploit it for particularist interests).[29] Armenia may come closest to a case of state-building against perceived threats from Azerbaijan and from Turkey, and it has the second highest rating on government effectiveness among the non-Baltic states according to the World Bank's governance indicators.[30] However, Russian threats to state-building in Moldova or Georgia have not contributed to a strengthening of the state in either country.

Compared to most recent cases of state-building, for example in the Western Balcans, post-Soviet state-building has occurred without a dominant involvement by outside actors.[31] Donor projects have supported various elements of institution-building, but their influence has been comparatively limited and external actors have not directly assumed any government functions (although they have engaged in public service provision especially in the poorest post-Soviet states). Moreover, apart from the Baltic states, the influence of EU norms and processes has been limited—although it may grow in the context of the EU's Neighborhood Policy initiated in 2003.[32] Thus, the finding of this research that external factors have played a marginal rather than a key role in state-building is likely to be rather different for other state-building processes.

The pre-existence of stateness has various implications. Societies in post-Soviet states expect the provision of state services—such as law and order, social services and public infrastructure—as reflected in the surveys cited in the empirical chapters. Post-Soviet societies have been relatively dependent on the existence of services provided by the state (a quintessential example is the extremely centralized heating system due to which most citizens cannot themselves decide when to begin or end the heating season). Overall, high expectations, dependency on state services, and frustration at state malfunctioning appear to have had an impact on the evolution of political regimes, but in diverging ways: in Russia, they may have promoted the acceptance of increasing authoritarianism under Putin; while in Ukraine, Georgia, or Kyrgyzstan such sentiments appear to have motivated social protest and 'secondary transitions.'

A comparative view of state-building also serves as a reminder that the relative progress in post-Soviet state-building is not a reason for complacency: in a number of poor countries, states have broken down several decades after gaining independence, rather than during the initial phase, frequently after prolonged erosion of the fiscal system and the civil service. This specter is particularly relevant for those countries in which low levels of capacity are combined with low levels of economic development.

Finally, the comparative view serves as a reminder that building effective and reasonably well-governed states is challenging, and has been a constant struggle in many places. The process of state-building is still ongoing in the former Soviet Union. Belarus, Ukraine, and Russia may follow the lead of Central Eastern Europe and achieve relatively capable states based on democratic regimes; but such an eventual trajectory is by no means certain.

Notes

1 See World Development Report (2005), Indicators, Table 2.

2 See World Development Report (2000), Indicators, Table 1.

3 In Zimbabwe, the HDI stood at 0.64 in 1985 and fell to 0.505 by 2003; in Lesotho it declined from 0.571 in 1990 to 0.497 in 2003. In the vast majority of middle and low income countries the indicator improved at least gradually but constantly over time.

4 Gini coefficients, which are a widely used measure of inequality, rose from around .2/.25 to .4 and higher in most post-Soviet countries; while they remained at .3 or below in Central Eastern Europe. There are doubts as to whether these figures fully reflect the extent of inequality, as the wealth of the small group of newly super-rich is likely not fully captured. World Bank (2000) and (2005).

5 Fairbanks (2001) describes a similar pattern for the consolidated Central Asian autocracies.

6 Despite the authoritarian character of the political regime, the government is not entirely untransparent. Belarus publishes data and information on its budget; see http://ncpi.gov.by/minfin/; however, given the presence of a state-controlled economy, not all financial government activity is captured in the budget.

7 See the three rounds of the Business Environment and Enterprise Performance Survey (BEEPS) conducted by the World Bank and the EBRD in 1999, 2002, and 2005.

8 OECD (2005), 6–9. Putin, "Annual Address to the Federal Assembly," April 25, 2005 (www.kremlin.ru).

9 See also Huang (2002), 5–7.

10 Kryshtanovskaya and White (2003).

11 GNI per capita stood at $3410 in Russia, and at $1260 in Ukraine in 2004. See WDR (2006), Indicators, Table 1.

12 Since survey data is not always fully comparable, it is impossible to make exact statements in this regard, but the general comparison appears valid.

13 "Finance scandal rocks Poland," *BBC News*, February 8, 2002; "A fresh scandal in breaks in Poland," *The Economist*, October 21, 2004; "Poland 2003: School for Scandal," *Transition online*, April 2004.

14 Lynch (2005); Crawford and Lijphart (eds.) (1997); Johnson (2001).

15 Poorer countries are more likely to be at the bottom of governance ratings such as TI's Corruption Perceptions Index than richer ones, although as pointed out also in Chapter 5, there is considerable variation also within income groups.

16 Evans (1995); Leftwich (2000).

17 Evans (1997) has argued against the idea of a "presumed invariant" negative effect of globalisation on stateness from a theoretical perspective.

18 Evans (1997), 69.

19 From 90 per cent of the GDP in 1999 to 33 per cent of the GDP in 2004 (see Appendix, Table II.1.2).

20 Hall and Soskice (2001); Thelen (2002); Scharpf (2000). The seminal formulation by North was formulated more broadly; but empirical applications have tended to focus on advanced industrial countries.

21 Leitzel (2003).

22 Linz and Stepan (1996), 16–24.

23 See map of Freedom House; also: recent research on democratization in other regions. Villalon and VonDoepp (2005).

24 Ames (1987).

25 The Freedom House indicators on governance indicate a declining trend in governance for Georgia and Moldova in recent years. The World Bank's indicators on government effectiveness and control of corruption show some variation but without real progress with regard to government effectiveness, and worsening levels of corruption in the 2000s compared to the late 1990s. See www.freedomhouse.org; and http://info.worldbank.org/governance/kkz2004/mc_indicator.asp.

26 Brusis and Dimitrov (2001).

27 Fish (2000).

28 Tilly (ed.), 1975.

29 Leftwich (2000), 154.

30 See http://info.worldbank.org/governance/kkz2004/. For 2004, out of a rank from 0–100 Russia receives a score of 48.1 and Armenia of 41.8 (against 28.4 for Ukraine).

31 The Baltic states have seen the most external involvement, from the EU in general and their Scandinavian neighbours in particular. However, this still differs from the neo-colonialism observable in Bosnia-Herzegovina and Afghanistan.

32 European Commission, European Neighbourhood Policy - Strategy Paper, COM(2004) 373 final.

APPENDIX

Section I:
All former Soviet Union countries

I.1 GENERAL MACRO-ECONOMIC DATA

Table I.1.1: GDP levels in post-Soviet countries, 1989–2004

	1989	1990	1991	1992	1993	1994	1995	1996	1997	1998	1999	2000	2001	2002	2004
ic states	*100*	*97.2*	*87.9*	*68.0*	*59.8*	*57.8*	*59.1*	*61.5*	*66.7*	*69.9*	*69.5*	*73.7*	*78.3*	*82.8*	
nia	100	91.9	82.7	71.0	65.0	63.7	66.4	69.0	75.7	79.2	78.7	84.3	88.6	93.6	112
ia	100	102.9	89.9	61.1	54.1	55.3	54.7	56.8	61.5	64.4	66.3	70.8	76.2	80.6	90
uania	100	96.7	91.2	71.8	60.2	54.3	56.1	58.7	63.0	66.2	63.6	66.0	70.0	74.1	89
	100	*96.8*	*89.0*	*71.3*	*63.9*	*54.3*	*51.2*	*51.4*	*52.9*	*54.4*	*57.0*	*60.8*	*65.3*	*69.6*	
enia	100	94.5	83.5	48.6	44.3	46.7	49.9	52.8	54.6	58.6	60.5	64.1	70.3	79.3	98
rbaijan	100	88.3	87.7	67.9	52.2	41.9	37.0	37.4	39.6	43.6	46.8	52.1	57.1	63.1	72
rus	100	98.1	96.7	87.4	80.8	71.4	63.9	65.7	73.2	79.4	82.1	86.8	91.0	95.2	111
rgia	100	84.9	67.0	36.9	26.1	23.4	24.0	26.7	29.5	30.4	31.3	31.9	33.3	35.1	45
akhstan	100	99.0	88.2	83.5	75.8	66.2	60.8	61.1	62.1	60.9	62.6	68.6	78.0	85.4	103
yzstan	100	104.8	96.5	83.2	70.3	56.2	53.1	56.9	62.5	63.9	66.2	69.8	73.5	73.2	80
dova	100	97.6	80.5	57.2	56.5	39.0	38.5	36.2	36.8	34.3	33.2	33.9	36.0	38.6	44
sian Fed.	100	97.0	92.2	78.8	71.9	62.8	60.2	58.2	58.7	55.8	58.9	64.2	67.4	70.2	82
kistan	100	100.2	91.7	62.1	52.0	40.9	35.8	29.8	30.3	32.0	33.1	35.9	39.5	43.1	69
menistan	100	101.8	97.0	82.5	83.7	69.2	64.2	68.5	60.7	65.0	76.0	83.6	90.3	98.4	112
ine	100	96.4	88.0	79.3	68.0	52.5	46.1	41.5	40.2	39.4	39.3	41.6	45.4	47.3	57
ekistan	100	99.2	98.7	87.7	85.7	81.2	80.5	81.9	86.1	89.9	93.9	97.6	102.0	106.3	115

Source: UNECE, Economic Survey of Europe, 2003 (1), Table B.1; for 2004: EBRD, Transition Report (2005).

Table I.1.2: GDP growth in post-Soviet countries, 1989–2004

	1989	1990	1991	1992	1993	1994	1995	1996	1997	1998	1999	2000	2001	2002	2003	20
Armenia	14.2	–7.4	–11.7	–41.8	–8.8	5.4	6.9	5.9	3.3	7.3	3.3	6.0	9.6	12.9	13.9	10
Azerbaijan	–4.4	–11.7	–0.7	–22.6	–23.1	–19.7	–11.8	1.3	5.8	10	7.4	11.1	9.9	10.6	10.8	10
Belarus	8	–3	–1.2	–9.6	–7.6	–12.6	–10.4	2.8	11.4	8.4	3.4	5.8	4.1	4.7	6.7	11
Estonia	8.1	–6.5	–13.6	–14.2	–8.8	–2	4.3	3.9	10.6	4.7	0.6	7.1	5.0	5.8	5.1	5
Georgia	–4.8	–12.4	–20.6	–44.8	–25.4	–11.4	2.4	10.5	10.8	2.9	3.0	2.0	4.5	5.4	11.1	8
Kazakhstan	–0.4	–0.4	–11	–5.3	–9.3	–12.6	–8.2	0.5	1.7	–1.9	2.7	9.8	13.2	9.5	9.2	9
Kyrgyzstan	8	3	–5	–19	–16	–20.1	–5.4	7.1	9.9	2.1	3.7	5.1	5.3	–0.5	6.7	7
Latvia	6.8	2.9	–10.4	–34.9	–14.9	2.2	–0.9	3.7	8.4	4.8	2.8	6.8	7.7	6.1	7.5	8
Lithuania	1.5	–5.0	–5.7	–21.3	–16.2	–9.8	3.3	4.7	7.3	5.1	–3.9	3.8	5.9	6.7	9.0	6
Moldova	8.5	–2.4	–17.5	–29.1	–1.2	–31.2	–1.4	–5.9	1.6	–6.5	–3.4	2.1	6.1	7.2	6.3	7
Russia	0	0	–5.5	–18.6	–13.0	–13.5	–4.1	–3.4	0.9	–4.9	5.4	8.3	4.9	4.3	7.3	7
Tajikistan	–2.9	–1.6	–7.1	–29	–11	–18.9	–12.5	–4.4	1.7	5.3	3.7	8.3	10.3	9.1	10.2	1
Turkmenistan	–6.9	2	–4.7	–5.3	–10	–17.3	–7.2	–6.7	–11.3	5	16	17.6	12.0	5.1	7.7	7
Ukraine	4	–4.0	–10.6	–9.7	–14.2	–22.9	–12.2	–10	–3.2	–1.9	–0.2	5.9	9.1	4.6	9.4	12
Uzbekistan	3.7	1.6	–0.5	–11.1	–2.3	–4.2	–0.9	1.6	2.5	4.4	4.1	4.0	4.5	4.2	1.5	6

Source: EBRD (2002), for 2002: EBRD Transition Update, May 2003.

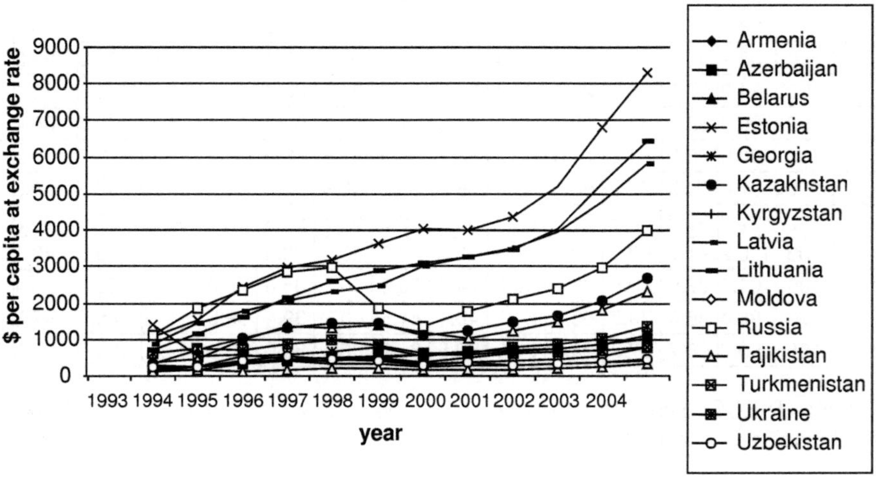

Graph I.1.1: Income per capita, 1994–2004

Source: EBRD, Transition Report, various years.

Table I.2.1: General government revenues,* in % of GDP 1993–2004

	1993	1994	1995	1996	1997	1998	1999	2000	2001	2002	2003	2004
Armenia	28.2	27.6	19.9	17.6	19.7	20.7	22.7	19.6	17.1	18.8	17.8	16.0
Azerbaijan	40.6	33.8	17.6	17.6	19.1	19.6	18.5	21.2	22.1	28.0	27.7	27.3
Belarus	52.6	46.0	36.1	39.4	43.6	43.3	44.6	45.8	44.9	44.6	45.8	46.2
Estonia	30.1	39.1	40.3	39.0	39.8	39.3	38.1	35.7	35.4	36.6	38.5	38.8
Georgia	9.7	16.1	7.1	13.8	14.3	13.7	15.4	15.3	16.3	15.8	16.4	21.8
Kazakhstan	21.1	10.7	16.9	13.2	13.5	18.0	17.9	21.9	22.5	21.7	23.0	26.0
Kyrgyzstan	24.6	26.7	24.8	23.9	23.9	24.4	24.0	18.5	20.4	22.8	22.2	22.6
Latvia	na	36.1	37.6	37.7	37.7	39.5	37.4	34.6	32.8	32.9	33.7	35.4
Lithuania	30.1	32.6	32.3	29.6	31.7	31.6	31.6	30.1	29.6	29.3	28.2	27.4
Moldova	20.5	30.4	26.5	23.5	33.9	33.1	27.1	30.7	29.1	30.0	30.4	34.7
Russian Fed.	36.3	34.7	34.1	33.5	37.1	33.4	35.1	38.8	38.7	37.6	36.6	38.6
Tajikistan	33.3	44.5	15.7	13.2	13.7	12.0	13.5	13.6	15.2	16.7	17.2	17.9
Turkmenistan	15.3	16.9	20.5	16.6	25.4	22.0	19.4	25.8	23.3	21.1	24.5	25.9
Ukraine	38.3	43.7	40.1	36.7	38.8	36.0	33.8	33.4	33.5	36.0	36.7	35.6
Uzbekistan	36.0	29.2	34.6	34.3	30.1	31.1	29.3	31.1	33.9	35.6	39.3	32.3

* comprising central and local/regional level budgets and extra-budgetary funds

Source: EBRD, Transition Report, various years.

Table I.2.2: General government expenditures, in % of GDP, 1993–2004

	1993	1994	1995	1996	1997	1998	1999	2000	2001	2002	2003	2004
Armenia	82.9	44.1	28.9	26.1	25.5	25.6	30.1	25.9	20.9	19.3	18.9	16.0
Azerbaijan	55.9	45.9	22.5	20.3	20.8	23.7	23.6	20.8	18.7	27.7	28.3	26.5
Belarus	57.8	47.3	43.0	41.2	44.8	43.9	46.4	45.9	46.8	44.7	45.3	46.2
Estonia	40.1	40.5	41.5	40.5	37.6	39.6	40.4	36.3	35.0	35.5	36.0	38.8
Georgia	35.9	23.5	12.3	21.1	21.0	19.1	22.1	19.4	18.2	17.8	18.7	19.5
Kazakhstan	25.2	18.4	20.8	18.6	20.4	26.1	23.1	22.8	23.4	22.1	24.0	23.3
Kyrgyzstan	39.9	32.4	42.1	33.4	33.0	33.8	35.8	29.9	25.9	28.0	27.3	27.1
Latvia		40.5	41.5	39.5	41.0	43.3	44.1	42.0	37.2	34.9	35.7	35.4
Lithuania	35.4	37.4	36.8	34.2	33.7	38.1	40.2	33.2	31.1	30.8	31.7	27.4
Moldova	28.0	36.3	39.6	38.7	43.2	38.7	36.4	30.2	29.3	31.3	33.3	35.7
Russian Fed.	43.6	45.1	40.2	42.4	45.1	41.4	38.4	35.8	34.6	36.9	35.7	33.6
Tajikistan	54.2	52.2	20.8	19.0	17.0	15.8	14.9	19.2	18.4	19.2	19.1	20.7
Turkmenistan	19.4	19.2	23.1	16.3	25.3	24.6	19.4	25.3	22.6	21.1	26.3	28.0
Ukraine	54.5	51.4	48.0	39.9	44.2	38.7	36.1	34.5	34.4	35.6	37.7	40.2
Uzbekistan	46.4	35.3	38.7	41.6	32.5	33.1	32.0	30.4	36.0	37.2	39.9	32.0

Source: EBRD, Transition Report, various years.

Table I.2.3: General government deficit, in % of GDP, 1993–2004

	1993	1994	1995	1996	1997	1998	1999	2000	2001	2002	2003	2004
Armenia	–54.7	–16.5	–9.0	–8.5	–5.8	–4.9	–7.4	–6.3	–3.8	–0.4	–1.2	–1.7
Azerbaijan	–15.3	–11.2	–3.1	–2.4	–4.0	–4.9	–4.7	–0.6	–0.4	–0.5	–1.2	0.8
Belarus	–5.5	–3.5	–2.7	–1.6	–0.7	–0.3	–2.2	–0.6	–1.9	–1.8	–1.4	0.0
Estonia	na	1.3	–1.3	–1.5	2.2	–0.3	–4.6	–0.7	0.4	1.4	3.1	1.8
Georgia	–26.2	–7.4	–5.3	–7.3	–6.7	–5.4	–6.7	–4.0	–2.0	–2.0	–2.5	2.3
Kazakhstan	–4.1	–7.4	–3.4	–5.3	–7.0	–8.0	–5.2	–1.0	4.7	2.6	4.7	2.7
Kyrgyzstan	–14.4	–11.6	–17.3	–9.5	–9.2	–9.5	–11.9	–9.6	–5.5	–5.3	–5.0	–4.5
Latvia	na	–4.4	–4.0	–1.8	0.3	–0.8	–3.9	–3.3	–1.6	–2.7	–1.5	–0.8
Lithuania	–5.3	–4.8	–4.4	–4.5	–1.8	–5.8	–8.6	–2.8	–2.0	–1.6	–1.9	–2.5
Moldova	–7.5	–19.2	–13.1	–15.2	–14.1	–5.7	–5.4	–2.6	–0.5	–2.0	1.1	0.4
Russian Fed.	–7.3	–10.4	–6.1	–8.9	–8.0	–8.0	–3.3	3.0	2.9	0.6	1.1	5.0
Tajikistan	–22.3	–10.1	–6.1	–5.8	–3.3	–2.7	–3.1	–5.6	–3.2	–2.5	–1.8	–2.7
Turkmenistan	–4.1	1.7	0.4	0.3	–0.2	–2.6	0.0	0.3	0.7	0.2	–1.8	–2.1
Ukraine	–16.2	–8.7	–6.1	–3.2	–5.4	–2.8	–2.4	–1.1	–0.9	0.1	–0.7	–4.6
Uzbekistan	–18.3	–4.4	–4.1	–7.3	–2.2	–3.3	–2.6	–2.2	–2.1	–1.5	–0.6	0.4

Source: EBRD, Transition Report, various years.

I.3 INITIAL ELITE CHANGE AND REGIME DEVELOPMENT

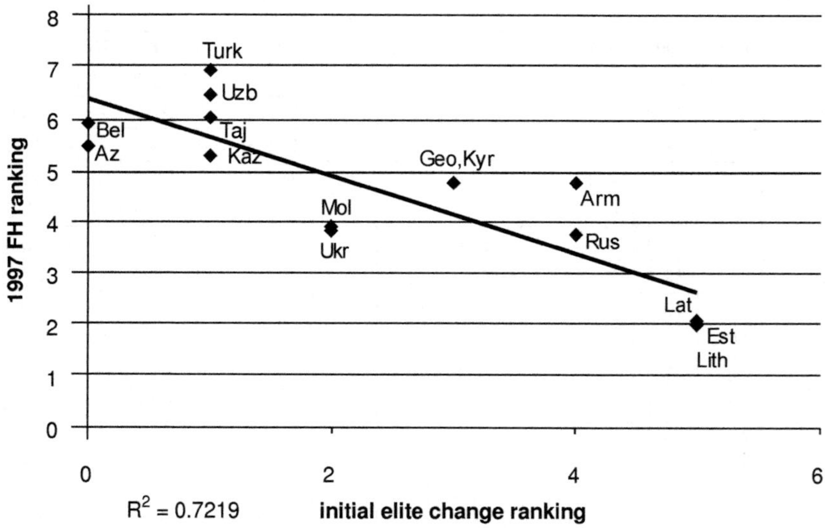

Graph I.3.1: Initial elite change and 1997 regime

Source: elite change ranking from Fish (1998), 49.

Section II: Ukraine, Belarus, Lithuania, Russia

Table II.1: GNI per Capita 1990–2004, PPP in current $

	1990	1995	1998	2002	2004
Belarus	4310	3190	4220	5500	6900
Lithuania	9230	6180	7990	10190	12610
Russian Fed.	8320	5870	5770	8080	9620
Ukraine	7080	3890	3590	4800	6250

Source: World Development Indicators.

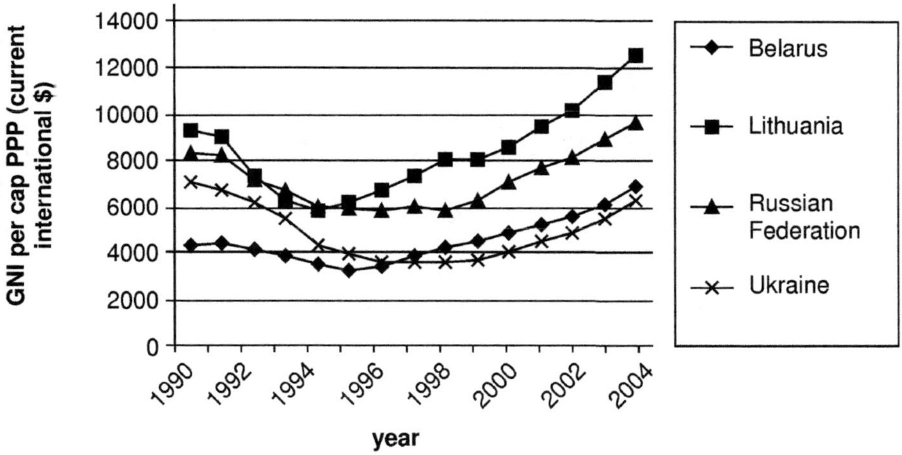

Graph II.1: GNI per capita 1990–2004, PPP in current $

II.1: EXTERNAL DEBT

Table II.1.1: Total debt stock, in US $ million, 1992–2004

	1992	1993	1994	1995	1996	1997	1998	1999	2000	2001	2002	2003	2004
us	–	969	1,297	1,694	1,105	1,171	1,154	1261	1265	1381	1655	1615	1351
ania	56	333	503	770	1,258	3,262	3,741	4,529	4,884	5268	6,199	8,342	10,466
an Fed.	73,652	112,440	122,342	121,735	126,685	127,705	177,710	177,100	160,027	152,500	147,400	175,300	192,966
ne	551	3,855	5,636	8,429	9,538	11,133	13,071	13,941	12,166	12,098	13,555	14,578	20,157

Source: World Bank, Global Development Finance.

Table II.1.2.: Debt to GDP in %, 1992–2004

	1992	1993	1994	1995	1996	1997	1998	1999	2000	2001	2002	2003	2004
Belarus	–	27.7	25.7	14.7	6.6	7.0	6.7	10.4	12.1	11.2	11.3	9.1	5.9
Lithuania	–	–	12.4	22.8	26.4	32.8	33.3	41.9	43.0	43.6	44.1	45.8	47.0
Russian Fed.	–	–	49.6	43.8	39.7	38.4	70.2	90.3	62.5	48.2	41.4	40.6	33.2
Ukraine	–	12.8	21.9	21.6	20.2	20	29.6	42.8	37.8	31.8	30.1	29.4	31.1

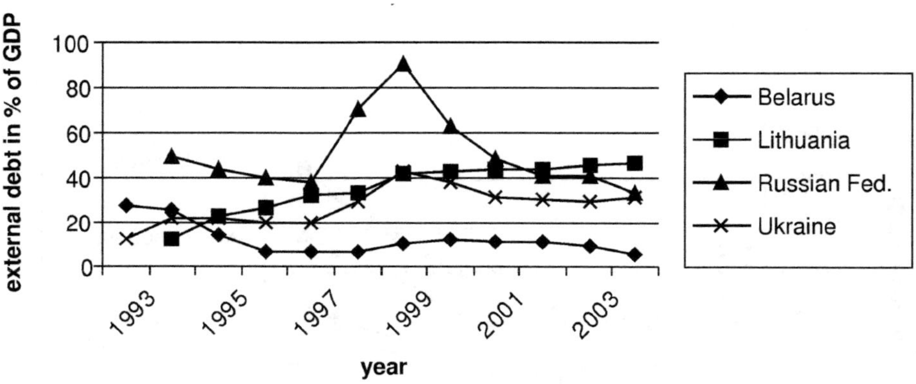

Graph II.1.1: External debt to GDP, 1993–2004

II.2: FDI INFLOWS

Table II.2.1: FDI inflows 1995–2004, in million $, per capita in $

	1995	1996	1997	1998	1999	2000	2001	2002	2003	2004
Belarus	15	73	200	149	444	119	111	247	172	169
per cap	*1.5*	*7.1*	*19.6*	*14.6*	*44.4*	*11.9*	*11.1*	*24.7*	*17.4*	*17.2*
Lithuania	73	152	355	926	486	379	446	732	179	773
per cap	*19.7*	*41.1*	*95.9*	*250.3*	*131.4*	*102.4*	*120.5*	*209.1*	*51.1*	*227.4*
Russia	2065	2579	4865	2762	3309	2714	2748	3461	7958	11672
per cap	*13.9*	*17.4*	*33.0*	*18.9*	*22.7*	*18.6*	*16.9*	*23.8*	*54.9*	*80.6*
Ukraine	267	521	623	743	496	595	792	693	1424	1715
per cap	*5.2*	*10.1*	*12.3*	*14.7*	*10.0*	*12.0*	*15.9*	*14.4*	*29.9*	*36.2*

Source: UNECE, Economic Survey of Europe (2001; 2003). These figures report only inflows (not subtracting outflows) and differ from those in the EBRD Transition Report.

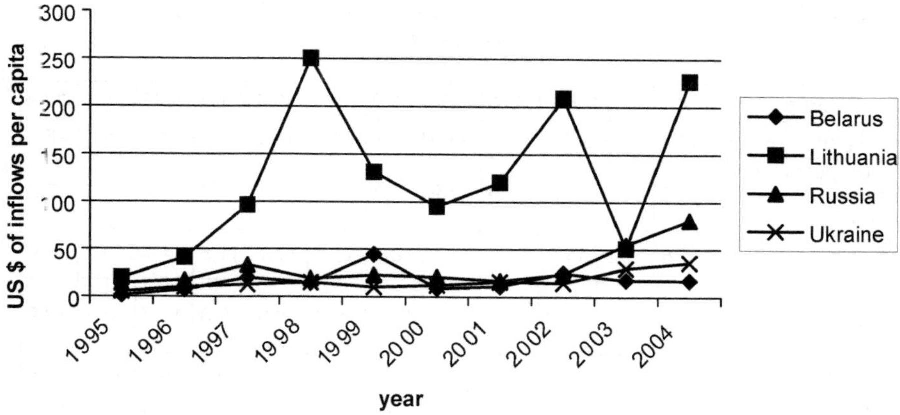

Graph II.2.1: FDI per capita inflows, Belarus, Lithuania, Russia, Ukraine

II.3 REVENUE AND EXPENDITURE COMPOSITION

Table II.3.1: Revenue and expenditure composition Ukraine, 1993–2004 (in % of GDP)

Ukraine	1993	1994	1995	1996	1997	1998	1999	2000	2001	2002	2003	2004
eral gov. rev	42.4	41.9	37.8	36.7	38.8	36.0	33.8	35.1	35.0	35.8	36.2	35.1
es on income and t	11.5	14.7	11.8	10.0	10.9	9.5	8.9	8.7	9.0	9.3	10.4	8.8
which profit tax	–	–	–	–	–	5.5	4.9	4.5	4.1	4.3	5.1	4.8
sion Fund Revenues	9.0	7.7	7.7	8.6	9.1	8.7	8.3	7.6	7.9	6.3	6.4	6.8
s on sales of goods services	14.8	12.9	9.8	9.2	10.9	11.3	11.0	9.9	9.0	8.9	7.8	7.4
l Gov. Exp.	46.9	48.1	42.5	39.9	43.4	38.4	36.1	36.4	36.6	35.7	56.7	38.9
cation & health	8.0	10.2	10.1	8.7	9.5	7.9	6.7	7.1	7.7	7.8	8.1	7.6
cation	4.0	5.4	5.4	4.9	5.3	4.4	3.6	4.2	4.7	4.6	4.6	4.3
th	4.0	4.8	4.7	3.8	4.2	3.5	3.0	2.9	3.0	3.2	3.5	3.3
al security and welfare	20.5	14.0	16.2	13.6	14.8	14.0	12.7	13.4	14.1	15.5	14.7	16.5
nse	1.8	1.8	1.9	1.5	1.6	1.3	1.2	1.3	1.5	1.3	1.3	1.4
ic order and safety	–	–	1.8	1.1	1.3	1.6	1.4	1.8	2.1	2.1	2.1	2.2
est payments	–	1.1	1.5	1.6	1.8	2.3	2.4	3.1	2.1	–	1.0	0.9
oreign debt	–	0.6	0.4	1.0	0.8	0.7	1.4	1.7	1.3	–	0.9	0.6

Source: IMF, staff country reports, various years; and IMF, Government Finance Statistics, various years.

Table II.3.2: Revenue and expenditure composition Belarus, 1993–2004 (in % of GDP)

Belarus	1993	1994	1995	1996	1997	1998	1999	2000	2001	2002	2003	2004
General gov. revenue	54.3	47.5	42.7	40.8	44.9	45.1	46.1	45.8	44.9	44.6	45.8	46.2
Taxes on income and profits (incl. Chernobyl surcharge)	13.5	13.8	9.7	6.9	7.9	8.3	8.2	7.8	7.7	6.4	6.5	7.2
Social security and payroll taxes	12.8	9.8	11.9	11.2	11.1	10.7	10.7	11.1	11.5	11.4	10.7	11.0
Taxes on goods and services (VAT, excises, fuel tax)	18.1	18	12.8	15.9	18.6	18.3	20.3	14.6	13.3	12.7	13.2	12.9
Expenditures	56.2	50	44.6	42.7	46.1	45.6	47.9	45.9	46.8	46.4	47.2	46.2
Social protection	11.9	11.2	12.9	13	13.3	13	12.7	–	13.2	13.4	12.6	12.3
Education and health	10.5	11.1	10.4	11.2	13	11.9	11.3	11.2	11.6	11.5	11.3	11.3
Defense	1.2	2.3	1.6	1.2	1.7	1.5	1.3	1.0	1.1	1.0	1.0	1.0
Public order	–	–	–	1.6	1.4	1.3	1.4	1.8	1.9	1.8	1.8	1.9
Interest payments	0.8	0.4	0.9	0.7	0.7	0.8	0.7	0.9	0.7	0.5	0.5	0.5

Source: IMF, staff country reports, various years; and IMF, Government Finance Statistics, various years.

Table II.3.3: Revenue and Expenditure Composition Lithuania, 1993–2004 (in % of GDP)

Lithuania	1993	1994	1995	1996	1997	1998	1999	2000	2001	2002	2003	2004
General gov. rev	28.8	32.4	32.3	29.6	32.6	32.7	32.1	30.3	29.6	29.9	30.0	31.4
Tax on income and profits	10.7	10.5	9.3	8.5	6.7	9.3	9.3	8.4	7.8	7.5	8.0	8.1
Of which taxes on companies	5.5	3.5	2.3	1.9	1.6	1.3	0.8	0.7	0.5	0.6	–	1.9
Taxes on individuals	5.2	7.0	7.0	6.6	5.1	5.1	8.5	7.8	5.2	4.9	–	4.9
Payroll tax	6.5	8.8	8.4	8.3	11.5	7.8	6.8	7.1	7.0	6.7	6.6	6.7
Taxes on goods and services	8.3	8.5	11.6	9.9	11.8	13.0	12.6	11.4	11.3	11.6	11.0	10.8
Of which VAT/GET	6.5	6.8	8.2	7.2	8.7	8.4	8.1	7.6	7.3	7.4	–	6.3
General gov. exp.	34.9	35.0	36.8	34.2	34.4	38.1	40.2	33.2	31.1	30.8	31.1	33.6
Defense	0.7	0.5	0.5	0.6	0.8	1.0	1.2	1.4	1.7	1.8	1.8	1.9
Education & health	7.8	9.3	9.3	8.8	7.5	7.9	7.8	7.3	10.8	10.2	9.6	10.5
Education	4.6	5.6	5.6	5.4	5.8	6.4	6.5	5.9	6.3	6.2	5.9	5.9
Health	3.2	3.7	3.7	3.4	–	–	–	–	4.5	4.0	3.7	4.6
Social security and welfare	–	–	–	10.8	11.1	11.7	12.7	12.2	10.4	9.9	9.6	9.9
Interest payments	0.0	0.1	0.4	0.5	1.0	1.5	1.8	1.7	1.6	1.3	1.2	1.1

Source: IMF, staff country reports, various years; and IMF, Government Finance Statistics, various years.

Table II.3.4: Revenue and expenditure composition Russia, 1992–2004 (in % of GDP)

Russia	1992	1993	1994	1995	1996	1997	1998	1999	2000	2001	2002	2003	2004
General gov. rev.*	41.0	39	34.6	34.1	33.5	39.3	34.4	33.6	36.9	37.3	37.6	36.6	32.3
Profit & income taxes	10.5	12.4	10.9	10.0	7.2	7.0	5.7	5.9	7.8	8.5	7.6	7.4	8.6
Profit taxes	8.2	9.8	8	7.6	4.6	4.0	3.1	3.7	5.4	5.6	4.3	–	5.2
Personal income tax	2.3	2.6	2.9	2.4	2.6	3.0	2.6	2.4	2.4	2.9	3.3	–	3.4
Taxes on goods and services	11.8	7.9	8.2	8.5	10.0	9.4	9.0	11.7	9.2	10.5	10.1	9.8	7.9
VAT	10.4	6.7	7.0	6.9	7.2	6.8	6.3	6.3	6.3	7.1	6.9	6.6	6.4
Excises	1.4	1.2	1.2	1.6	2.8	2.6	2.7	5.0	2.3	2.7	2.5	2.6	1.5
Taxes on trade (export taxes and import tariffs)	2.4	3.1	1.6	1.9	1.3	1.2	1.7	1.9	3.1	3.7	3.0	3.4	5.1
Payroll taxes	10.9	8.6	9.0	8.0	8.1	9.9	8.7	8.6	7.9	8.0	8.8	8.5	–
General gov. exp.*	47.4	44.3	45	40.2	42.4	47.8	42.5	36.7	33.7	34.6	37.0	35.5	27.8
Defense	4.5	4.2	4.6	3.1	3.3	3.2	2.2	2.6	2.6	2.7	2.7	2.7	2.6
Education & Health	6.0	7.2	7.7	6.5	6.7	7.6	6.3	6.3	5.1	5.4	6.3	6.0	5.2
Education	3.5	4.1	4.5	3.7	3.9	4.3	3.6	3.2	2.9	3.2	3.8	3.6	3.5
Health	2.5	3.1	3.2	2.8	2.8	3.3	2.7	3.1	2.2	2.2	2.5	2.4	1.7
Social protection	9.5	8.9	9.8	9.4	10	12	12	9	8.5	10.1	11.7	10.9	9.6
Public administration	–	–	–	–	–	1.7	1.1	1.0	1.0	1.2	1.4	1.4	1.3
INTEREST payments	0.7	2	2	3.6	5.9	4.7	4.5	6.3	4.6	2.8	2.2	1.8	1.4

Source: IMF, country reports, various years; IMF, Government Finance Statistics, various years; Russian statistical office (2004); Ivanova et al. 2005.

* Including federal, regional, local levels and extra-budgetary funds

II.4: ATTITUDES TO THE MARKET AND TO PAYING TAXES

Table II.4.1: % saying that free market right for the country's future

	1991	1994	1997
Lithuania	87	55	65
Ukraine	43a	38	32b
Russia	58	25	29b
Belarus	38a	32	48b

a=1992 b=1996
Source: Blanchflower (2000).

Table II.4.2: % willing to pay more taxes for new state requirements (1992)

	Yes	No	Undecided	DK
Lithuania	18.2	61.8	14.8	5.2
Russia	16.9	61.7	12	9.2
Ukraine	10.8	70.3	11	7.9

Question: If the Russian [Ukrainian] [Lithuanian] government requires more revenue to meet its new responsibilities (in connection with an increase in its powers), are you willing to pay the higher taxes or new fees for services provided?

Source: Miller, Reisinger, and Hesli, New Soviet Citizen Survey, 1992, 2000.

II.5: PERCEIVED CORRUPTION

Table II.5.1: Corruption Perception Index Ratings (rank) for Belarus, Lithuania, Russia, and Ukraine 1999–2005

	1999	2000	2001	2002	2003	2004	2005
Belarus	58	43	no data	36	53	74	107
Lithuania	50	43	38	36	41	44	44
Russia	82	82	79	71	86	90	126
Ukraine	75	87	83	85	106	122	107

Source: Transparency International.

Table II.5.2: Corruption Perception Index Ratings (score) for Belarus, Lithuania, Russia, and Ukraine 1999–2005

	1999	2000	2001	2002	2003	2004	2005
Belarus	3.4	4.1	no data	4.8	4.2	3.3	2.6
Lithuania	3.8	4.1	4.8	4.8	4.7	4.6	4.8
Russia	2.4	2.1	2.3	2.7	2.7	2.8	2.4
Ukraine	2.6	1.5	2.1	2.4	2.3	2.2	2.6

Source: Transparency International; on a scale from 1 (most corrupt) to 10 (free of corruption).

II.6: NUMBER OF LEGAL ACTS PER YEAR

Table II.6: Legal Acts (laws, decrees) in Belarus, Lithuania, Ukraine, Russia, 1992–2001

	1992	1993	1994	1995	1996	1997	1998	1999	2000	2001
Belarus										
– laws adopted by parliament	78	77	72	64	69	120	100	117	97	70
– presidential ordinances and decrees (1)	–	–	261	429	484	576	555	632	644	726
Lithuania										
– laws adopted by parliament	91	148	220	270	402	418	321	358	558	390
Ukraine										
– laws adopted by parliament	122	132	129	153	203	196	166	296	297	240
– presidential decrees	603	598	811	1173	1268	1323	1334	1521	1261	1157
– orders (*posta-nova*) of the cabinet of ministers	718	1076	863	1047	1917	1433	2044	2335	1890	1790
Russia										
– federal Laws	–	–	79	228	163	156	193	229	168	193
– presidential decrees	–	–	1807	790	1240	938	1038	1048	1214	748

Source: Belarus Legislation Databank (courtesy of Sergey Latushkin); Lithuania: http://www3.lrs.lt/n/eng/DPaieska.html; Ukraine: www.rada.kiev.ua/laws/pravo/new/; Russia: http://law.optima.ru.

Section III: Ukraine-Parliamentary election results and factions, 1994–2002

Table III.1: 1994 parliamentary elections and factions in 1995

Parties/ political camp	Parliamentary elections 1994 mandates won*	Factions 1995	
		factions/groups	seats
Left			
Communist Party (CPU)	86	Communist Faction	90
Socialist Party (SPU)	14	Socialist Faction	27
Peasants' Party (SelPU)	19	Group "Agrarians of Ukraine"	48
Center			
Party of Democratic Revival	4	Group "Reforms"	36
Labor Party	4	Interregional Group of deputies	31
Civic Congress (GKU)	2		
Social Democratic Party (SDPU)	2		
National Democratic			
Rukh (NRU)	20	Rukh Faction	27
Ukrainian Republican Party (URP)	8	Group "Statehood"	30
Radical Nationalist			
Ukrainian National Assembly (UNA)	1		
Congress of Ukrainian Nationalists (KUN)	5		
Others			
Other parties	5	Group "Unity"	31
Deputies without party affiliation	168	Group "Center"	33
		Group of Independent Deputies	29
		deputies without faction	22
Vacant seats	112		46
Total	**450**		**450**

Table III.2: Parliamentary elections 1998 and factions by 2001

Parliamentary elections 1998				Factions, Jan 2001	
party/pol. camp	**seats: party lists**	**seats: direct mandates***	**total seats won**	**factions**	**seats**
Left					
Communist Party	84	40	124	Communists	111
Bloc of Socialists/Peasant (SelPU)	29	5	34	Left-center	16
Progressive Socialists	14	1	15	PSP und SelPU	dissolved Feb. 2000
other left	0	1	1		
Center					
Greens	19	0	19	Greens	17
People's Democrats (NDP)	17	6	23	People's Democrats (NDP)	20
Hromada	16	4	20	Hromada	dissolved
Social Democratic Party (united) SDPU (o)	14	3	17	SDPU (o)	33
Agrarian Party	0	4	4	Fatherland	32
Soyuz	0	1	1	Regional Renaissance	35
Christian-Democratic	0	2	2	Working Ukraine (TU)	48
Party of Regions	0	1	1	Solidarity	23
				Jabloko (Apple)	14
Liberal-democratic					
Reforms and Order	0	3	3	Reforms and Order	15
National-democratic					
Rukh	32	14	46	Rukh-Kostenko	23
National Front	0	6	6	Rukh-Udovenko	17
Other/independents					
Other parties	0	6	6	"between factions"	45
Independents	0	128	128		
Total	**225**	**225**	**450**		**449**

* Figures for SMDs are according to nomination, not party affiliation

Source: Central Election Committee of Ukraine, http://www.cvk.ukrpack.net/.

Table III.3: Parliamentary elections and factions 2002

	Parliamentary elections 2002				Factions 2002	
	percent-age (%): party lists	**seats: party lists**	**seats: direct man-dates**	**total Seats won**	**original factions, May 2002**	**factions Septem-ber, 2002**
Left						
Communist Party	*20.0*	59	6	65	64	63
Socialist Party	*6.9*	20	2	22	22	21
Agrarian Party	–	–	–	–	formed later	16
Democratic opposition						
Our Ukraine		70	42	112	119	109
Bloc Yulia Tymoshenko	*7.3*	22	0	22	23	23
Pro-presidential parties/blocs						
For a United Ukraine	*11.8*	35	65	100	178	9
Working Ukraine (TU)	–	–	–	–	formed later	40
People's democrats (NDP)	–	–	–	–	formed later	17
Regions of Ukraine	–	–	–	–	formed later	37
European Choice	–	–	–	–	formed later	18
Democratic Initiative	–	–	–	–	formed later	18
Democratic Union	*0.9*	–	4	4	–	–
People's Will	–	–	–	–	formed later	17
Narodnii Vybor (People's Choice)	–	–	–	–	formed later	15
SDPU (o)	*6.3*	19	5	24	31	35
Other parties	*17.1*	–	5	5	–	–
Self-nominated (candidates)	–	–	96	96	–	–
Independents (deputies)	–	–	–	–	13	12
Total	***93.9***	**225**	**225**	**450**	**450**	**450**

Source: Central Election Commission of Ukraine, http://www.cvk.ukrpack.net/.

BIBLIOGRAPHY

Abdelal, Rawi. *National Purpose in the World Economy.* Ithaca: Cornell University Press, 2001.

Alesina, A., Ricardo Hausmann, Rudolf Hommes, and Ernesto Stein. *Budget Institutions and Fiscal Performance in Latin America.* Washington D.C.: Inter-American Development Bank, 1999.

Alt, James and Kenneth Shepsle (eds.). *Perspectives on Positive Political Economy.* New York: Cambridge University Press, 1990.

Ames, Barry. *Political Survival. Politicians and Public Policy in Latin America.* Berkeley: University of California Press, 1987.

Andrle, Vladimir. *A Social History of Twentieth-Century Russia.* London: Edward Arnold, 1994.

Ardant, Gabriel. "Financial Policy and Economic Infrastructure of Modern States and Nations." In: C. Tilly (ed.), *The Formation of National States in Western Europe.* Princeton: Princeton University Press, 1975: 164–242.

Aristotle. *Politics* (edited by Stephen Everson). Cambridge: Cambridge University Press, 1988.

Aslund, Anders. "The Case for Radical Reform." *Journal of Democracy*, vol. 5, no. 4 (1994): 63–74.

————. "Eurasia Letter: Ukraine's Turnaround." *Foreign Policy*, no. 100 (1995): 125–143.

————. "Tax Policy After Communism," Carnegie Endowment for International Peace. Draft, February 18, 2001, at: www.carnegie.ru/english/Projects/Reports /Economics/mar01/leo-Aslund-E.doc [accessed: September 12, 2002].

————. "The Economic Policy of Ukraine after the Orange Revolution." *Eurasian Geography and Economics*, vol. 46, no. 5, 2005: 327–353.

Aslund, Anders and Georges de Ménil (eds.). *Economic Reform in Ukraine: The Unfinished Agenda.* Armonk: M. E. Sharpe, 2000.

————. "Introduction: Reform Dilemmas." In: Aslund and de Ménil (eds.). *Economic Reform in Ukraine: The Unfinished Agenda.* Armonk: M. E. Sharpe, 2000: 3–25.

Banaian, King. *The Ukrainian Economy since Independence.* Cheltenham: Edward Elgar, 1999.

Bardhan, Pranab. "Corruption and Development: A Review of Issues." *Journal of Economic Literature*, vol. 35, no. 3 (1997): 1320–1346.

Batory Foundation. *Belarus: Reform Scenarios.* Warsaw: Stefan Batory Foundation, 2003, at http://www.batory.org.pl/doc/wybor_a.pdf [accessed date:.April 15, 2005].

Beissinger, Mark. "Elites and Ethnic Identities in Soviet and Post-Soviet Politics." In: Alexander Motyl (ed.), *The Post-Soviet Nations: Perspectives on the Demise of the USSR.* New York: Columbia University Press, 1992: 141-169.

————. "State Building in the Shadow of an Empire-State." In: Karen Dawisha and Bruce Parrott (eds.), *The End of Empire? The Transformation of the USSR in Comparative Perspective.* Armonk: M. E. Sharpe, 1997: 157-185.

Beyer, Jürgen, and Jan Wielgohs. "On the Limits of Path Dependency Approaches for Explaining Post-socialist Institution Building: in Critical Response to David Stark." *East European Politics and Societies*, vol. 15, no. 2 (2001): 356-388.

Beyme, Klaus von. "Institutional Engineering and Transition to Democracy." In: Jan Zielonka (ed.), *Democratic Consolidation in Eastern Europe.* Vol. 1. Oxford: Oxford University Press, 2001: 3-24.

Birch, Sarah. *Elections and Democratization in Ukraine.* Basingstoke: Macmillan Press, 2000.

Blanchard, Oliver, and Michael Kremer. "Disorganization." *The Quarterly of Economics*, vol. 112, no. 4 (1997): 1021-1126.

Bönker, Frank. "Initiating and Consolidating Economic Reform: a Comparative Analysis of Fiscal Reform in Hungary, Poland, and the Czech Republic, 1989-1999." In: Beyer, Wielgohs, Wiesenthal (eds.), *Successful Transitions: Political Factors of Socio-Economic Progress in Post-Socialist Countries.* Baden-Baden: Nomos, 2000: 121-138.

Braithwaite, Valerie, and Margaret Levi. *Trust and Governance.* New York: Russell Sage Foundation, 1998.

Broadman Harry et al. *Building Market Institutions in South Eastern Europe.* Washington D.C.: World Bank, 2004.

Brunner, Georg. "Industrial Law." In: Hans-Hermann Höhmann, Michael Kaser, and Karl Thalheim (eds.), *The New Economic Systems of Eastern Europe*, Londen: Hurst, 1975: 501-526.

Brusis, Martin, and Vesselin Dimitrov. "Executive Configuration and Fiscal Performance in Post-Communist Central and Eastern Europe." *Journal of European Public Policy*, vol. 8, no. 6 (2001): 888-910.

Bubnova, Nina and Lucan Way. "Trends in Financing Regional Expenditures in Transition Economies: The Case of Ukraine." *World Bank Discussion Paper*, no 378, 1998.

Buchanan, James, and Richard Musgrave. *Public Finance and Public Choice: Two Contrasting Visions of the State.* Cambridge: The MIT Press, 2000.

Bunce, Valerie. "Rethinking Recent Democratization: Lessons from the Postcommunist Experience." *World Politics*, vol. 55, no. 2 (2003): 167-192.

————. *Subversive Institutions. The Design and the Destruction of Socialism and the State.* Cambridge: Cambridge University Press, 1999a.

————. "The Political Economy of Post-Socialism." *Slavic Review*, vol. 58, no. 4 (1999b): 756-793.

Buracas, A. (ed.). *Lithuanian Economic Reforms: Practice and Perspectives.* Vilnius: Margi Rastai, 1997.

Burgess, Robin and Nicholas Stern. "Taxation and Development." *Journal of Economic Literature*, vol. XXXI (1993): 762–830.

Busse, Eva. "The Embeddedness of Tax Evasion in Russia." In: Ledeneva and Kurkchiyan (eds.), *Economic Crime in Russia*. The Hague: Kluwer Law International, 2000: 129–143.

Caporaso, J. and D. Levine. *Theories of Political Economy*. Cambridge: Cambridge University Press, 1992.

Carey, John. "Parchment, Equilibria, and Institutions." *Comparative Political Studies*, vol. 33, no. 6–7 (2000): 735–761.

Carothers, Thomas. "The End of the Transition Paradigm." *Journal of Democracy*, vol. 13, no. 1 (2002): 5–21.

Chandler, Andrea. "Social Policy and Political Discourse in Post-Soviet Ukraine." *Journal of Ukrainian Studies*, vol. 21, no. 1–2 (1996): 191–212.

Cheasty, Adrienne, and Jeffrey M. Davis. *Fiscal Transition in Countries of the Former Soviet Union: An Interim Assessment*. Washington D.C.: IMF, 1996.

Checkel, Jeffrey. "Institutional Dynamics in Collapsing Empires: Domestic Structural Change in the USSR, Post-Soviet Russia and Independent Ukraine." *ARENA Working Paper*, no. 99/2, 1999.

Christian, David. "The Supervisory Function in Russian and Soviet History." *Slavic Review*, vol. 41, no. 1 (1982): 73–90.

Clemens, Elisabeth, and James Cook. "Politics and Institutionalism: Explaining Durability and Change." *Annual Review of Sociology*, vol. 25 (1999): 441–466.

Clement, Hermann, Michael Knogler, and Alexej Sekarev. *Verschärfte Wirtschaftskrise in der Ukraine*. München: Osteuropa-Institut, Working Paper, no. 161, 1993.

Commander, Simon, Irina Dolinskaya, and Christian Mummsen. "Determinants of Barter in Russia: an Empirical Analysis." *Journal of Development Economics*, vol. 67, no. 2 (2002): 275–307.

Connor, Walter. "Social Policy Under Communism." In: Kapstein and Mandelbaum (eds.), *Sustaining the Transition*. New York: Council on Foreign Relations, 1997: 10–45.

Cornia, Giovanni Andrea, and Vladimir Popov (eds.). *Transition and Institutions: The Experience of Gradual and Late Reformers*. Oxford: Oxford University Press, 2002.

Crawford, Beverly, and Arend Lijphart (eds.). *Liberalization and Leninist Legacies*. Berkeley: University of California, 1997.

Cuddy, M., and R. Gekker (eds.). *Institutional Change in Transition Economies*. Aldershot: Ashgate, 2002.

Cummings, Sally, and Ole Norgaard. "Conceptualising State Capacity: Comparing Kazakhstan and Kyrgyzstan." *Political Studies* 52 (2004): 685–708.

Dabrowski, Marek, Marcin Luczynski and Malgorzata Markiewicz. "The Phases of Budgetary Reform." In: Aslund and de Ménil (eds.), *Economic Reform in Ukraine: The Unfinished Agenda*. Armonk: M. E. Sharpe, 2000: 113–142.

D'Anieri, Paul, Robert Kravchuk, and Taras Kuzio. *Politics and Society in Ukraine*. Oxford: Westview Press, 1999.

D'Anieri, Paul. "The Last Hurrah: The 2004 Presidential Elections and the Limits of Machine Politics." *Communist and Post-Communist Studies*, vol. 38 (2005), 231–249.

Darden, Keith. "Blackmail as a Tool of State Domination: Ukraine under Kuchma." *East European Constitutional Review*, vol. 10, no. 2-3 (2001): internet-edition.

————. "Graft and Governance: Corruption as an Informal Mechanism of State Control." *Leitner Program Working Paper*, no. 02, Yale University, 2002.

Dauderstädt, Michael. *Ukraine*. Friedrich Ebert Stiftung: Politikinformation Osteuropa Online, no. 79, 1999.

Dawisha, Karen, and Bruce Parrott (eds.). *The End of Empire? The Transformation of the USSR in Comparative Perspective*. Armonk: M. E. Sharpe, 1997a.

————. *Democratic Changes and Authoritarian Reactions in Russia, Ukraine, Belarus and Moldova*. Cambridge: Cambridge University Press, 1997b.

Dean, James. *Why Most Measures of the "Unofficial Economy" are Systematically Wrong: With Illustrations from Ukraine*. Paper for the Friedrich Ebert Stiftung and the Instituza Javne Financije, October 2002.

Diamond, Larry. "Thinking about Hybrid Regimes." *Journal of Democracy*, vol. 13, no. 2 (2002): 21-35.

DiMaggio, Paul, and Walter Powell. "The Iron Cage Revisited: Institutional Isomorphism and Collective Rationality." *American Sociological Review*, vol. 48 (1983): 147-160.

Dyczok, Marta. *Ukraine: Movement Without Change, Change Without Movement*. Amsterdam: Harwood Academic Press, 2000.

Easter, Gerald. "Personal Networks and Postrevolutionary State Building: Soviet Russia Reexamined." *World Politics*, vol. 48 (1996): 551-78.

————. *The Fiscal Crisis of the Post-Communist State: Structural Origin and Transition Legacy*. Manuscript, April 2001.

————. "Politics of Revenue Extraction in Post-Communist States: Poland and Russia Compared." *Politics and Society*, vol. 30, no. 4 (2002): 599-627.

EBRD, *Transition Report*, various years.

EBRD, *Transition Report Update*, various years.

Ebrill, Liam, and Oleh Havrylyshyn. *Tax Reform in the Baltics, Russia, and Other Countries of the Former Soviet Union*. Washington, D.C.: International Monetary Fund, 1999.

Eke, Steven, and Taras Kuzio. "Sultanism in Eastern Europe: The Socio-Political Roots of Authoritarian Populism in Belarus." *Europe-Asia Studies*, vol. 52, no. 3 (2000): 523-547.

Elster, Jon. *Nuts and Bolts for the Social Sciences*. Cambridge: Cambridge University Press, 1989.

Elster, Jon, Claus Offe, and Ulrich Preuss. *Institutional Design in Post-Communist Societies. Rebuilding the Ship at Sea*. Cambridge: Cambridge University Press, 1998.

Evans, Peter, Dieter Rueschemeyer, and Theda Skocpol (eds.). *Bringing the State Back In*. Cambridge: Cambridge University Press, 1985.

Evans, Peter. "The State as Problem and Solution: Predation, Embedded Autonomy, and Structural Change." In: Stephan Haggard and Robert Kaufman, *The Politics of Economic Adjustment*. Princeton: Princeton University Press, 1992: 139-181.

Evans, Peter. *Embedded Autonomy: States and Industrial Transformation*. Princeton: Princeton University Press, 1995.

————. "The Eclipse of the State? Reflections on Stateness in an Era of Globalization." *World Politics*, vol. 50, no. 1 (1997): 62–87.

————. "Transferable Lessons? Re-examining the Institutional Prerequisites of East Asian Economic Policies." *Journal of Developmental Studies* vol. 34, no. 6 (1998): 66–86.

Evans, Anne, and Gord Evans, "Improving government decision-making systems in Lithuania and Latvia." *Journal of European Public Policy*, vol. 8, no. 6 (2001): 933–959.

Fairbanks, Charles. "Disillusionment in the Caucasus and Central Asia." *Journal of Democracy*, vol. 12, no. 4 (2001): 49–56.

Farrell, Henry and Colin Crouch. "Breaking the Path of Institutional Development? Alternatives to the New Determinism." Cologne: *MPfG Discussion Paper* 02/05, 2002.

Fish, Steven M. "The Determinants of Economic Reform in the Post-Communist World." *East European Politics and Societies,* vol. 12, no. 1 (1998): 31–78.

————. "Postcommunist Subversion: Social Science and Democratization in Eastern Europe and Eurasia." *Slavic Review*, vol. 58, no. 4 (1999): 794–823.

————. "The Executive Deception: Superpresidentialism and the Degradation of Russian Politics," in: Valerie Sperling (ed.), *Building the Russian State*. Boulder: Westview Press, 2000: 177–192.

Fukuyama, Francis. "The End of History?" *The National Interest*, Summer 1989.

————. *State-Building. Governance and World Order in the 21st Century*. Ithaca: Cornell University Press, 2004.

Gaddy, Clifford, and Barry Ickes, *Russia's Virtual Economy*. Washington D.C.: Brookings Institution Press, 2002.

Gaidys, Vladas. "Attitudes towards the Economic System in the Baltic States: Past, Present, Future." In: Karin Junefelt and Martin Peterson (eds.), *Cultural Encounters in East Central Europe*. Stockholm: Forskningsradsnämnden, 1998: 61–73.

Ganev, Venelin. *Postcommunism as a Historical Episode of State-Building: A Reversed Tillyan Perspective*. Kellogg-Institute, Working Paper no. 289, November 2001.

Gel'man, Vladimir. "The Unrule of Law in the Making: the Politics of Informal Institution Building in Russia." *Europe-Asia Studies*, vol. 56, no. 7 (2004): 1021–1040.

Gibson, James. "Political and Economic Markets: Changes in the Connections Between Attitudes Towards Political Democracy and a Market Economy Within the Mass Culture of Russia and Ukraine." *Journal of Politics*, vol. 58, no. 4 (1996): 954–984

Gill, Graeme. *The Origins of the Stalinist Political System*. Cambridge. Cambridge University Press, 1990.

Gillis, Malcolm. "Towards a Taxonomy of Tax Reform." In: Malcolm Gillis (ed.), *Tax Reform in Developing Countries*. Durham: Duke University Press, 1989: 7–26.

Girnius, Kestutis. "Democracy in Lithuania." In: Mary Kaldor, and Ivan Vejvoda (eds.), *Democratization in Central and Eastern Europe*. London: Pinter, 1999: 51–66.

Goldscheid, Rudolf. "A Sociological Approach to Problems of Public Finance." In: Alan Peacock and Richard Musgrave (eds.), *Classics in the Theory of Public Finance*, London: Macmillan, 1994: 202–213.

Gonciarz, Andzrej, and Victor Pynzenyk (eds.). *Open Budget 1999 for Ukraine*. Kyiv: TACIS Services, 1999.

Gordon, Claire. "Institutions, Economic Interests and the Stalling of Economic Reform," in: Neil Robinson (ed.), *Institutions and Political Change in Russia*. Basingstoke: MacMillan, 2000: 106–129.

Goujon, Alexandra. "Le 'Loukachisme' ou le Populisme Autoritaire en Biélorussie." *Politique et Sociétés*, vol. 21, no. 2 (2002): 29–50.

Grafe, Clemens, and Kaspar Richter. "Taxation and Public Expenditure." In: Brigitte Granville and Peter Oppenheimer (eds.), *Russia's Post-Communist Economy*. Oxford: Oxford University Press, 2001: 131–172.

Granville, Brigitte and Peter Oppenheimer (eds.). *Russia's Post-Communist Economy*. Oxford: Oxford University Press, 2001.

Gray, Dale. "Energy Sector Tax Reform in Russia and Other Former Soviet Union Countries." *Finance and Development*, vol. 35, no. 3 (1998).

Grindle, Merilee. *Challenging the State: Crisis and Innovation in Latin America and Africa*. Cambridge: Cambridge University Press, 1996.

————. *Good Enough Governance: Poverty Reduction and Reform in Developing Countries*. Cambridge: Harvard KSG, 2002.

Grodeland, Ase, Tatyana Koshechkina and William L. Miller. "'In theory correct, but in practice ...': Public Attitudes to Really Existing Democracy in Ukraine, Bulgaria, Slovakia and the Czech Republic." *Journal of Communist Studies and Transition Politics*, vol. 14, no. 3 (1998): 1-23.

Grossman, G. "The Second Economy of the USSR." *Problems of Communism*, vol. 26, no. 5 (1997).

Grzymala-Busse, Anna and Pauline Jones Luong. "Reconceptualizing the State: Lessons from Post-Communism." *Politics and Society,* vol. 30, no. 4 (2002): 529–554.

Haavisto, Tarmo (ed.). *The Transition to a Market Economy: Transformation and Reform in the Baltic States*. Cheltenham, Edward Elgar, 1997.

Haggard, Stephan, and Robert Kaufman (eds.). *The Politics of Economic Adjustment*. Princeton: Princeton University Press, 1992.

Hainsworth, Richard, and William Tompson. "Tax Policy and Tax Administration in Russia: The Case of the Banking Sector." *Post-Communist Economies*, vol. 14, no. 3 (2002): 277–298.

Halbach, Uwe. "Drogenstroeme durch den GUS-Raum: Symptom und Ursache von Instabilitaet," *SWP-Studie* no. 47, (2004).

Hall, John and John Ikenberry. *The State*. Minneapolis: University of Minnesota Press, 1989.

Hall, John (ed.). *The State*: *Critical Concepts*, vols. I and II. London and New York: Routledge, 1994.

Hall, Peter, and David Soskice. *Varieties of Capitalism*. Oxford: Oxford University Press, 2001.

Hansen, John, and Vira Nanivska. "Economic Growth with Equity: Ukrainian Perspectives." *World Bank Discussion Paper*, no. 407, 1999.

Haran', Oleksandr. "Die Linken Parteien in der Ukraine [The Left Parties in Ukraine]." *BIOST Report*, no. 27, 2000.

Harter, Stefanie, and Gerald Easter (eds.). *Shaping the Economic Space in Russia.* Aldershot: Ashgate, 2000.

Hausner, Jerzy, Bob Jessop, and Klaus Nielsen (eds.). *Strategic Choice and Path-Dependency in Post-Socialism: Institutional Dynamics in the Transformation Process.* Aldershot: Edward Elgar, 1995.

Havrylyshyn, Oleh, Marcus Miller and William Perraudin. "Deficits, inflation and the political economy of Ukraine." *Economic Policy*, vol. 19 (1994): 354-401.

Havrylyshyn, Oleh. "The Political Economy of Delayed Reform in Ukraine." In: Sharon Wolchik, and Volodymyr Zviglyanich (eds.), *Ukraine: The Search for a National Identity.* Lanham: Rowman and Littlefield, 2000: 49-68.

Helbling, Thomas, Ashkoka Mody, and Ratna Sahay. "Debt Accumulation in the CIS-7 Countries: Bad Luck, Bad Policies, or Bad Advice?" *IMF Working Paper*, no. 04/93, 2004.

Heinrich, Andreas, and Heiko Pleines. "Steuerlast und Steuerverhalten russischer Wirtschaftsbranchen, Teil II: Besteuerung der russischen Öl- und Gasindustrie [Tax Burden and Tax Behaviour of Russian Economic Sectors, Part II: Taxation of the Russian Oil and Gas Industry]," Forschungsstelle Osteuropa an der Universität Bremen, *Working Paper* no. 28, 2001.

Hellman, Joel, Geraint Jones, Daniel Kaufmann, and Mark Schankerman, "Measuring Governance, Corruption, and State Capture." *Policy Research Working Paper*, no. 2312, World Bank, 2000.

Hellman, Joel, Geraint Jones, and Daniel Kaufman. "'Seize the State, Seize the Day'. State Capture, Corruption, and Influence in Transition." *Policy Research Working Paper*, no. 2444, 2000.

Herrera, Yoshiko. "Russian Economic Reform 1991-1999." In: Zoltan Barany and Robert Moser (eds.), *Russian Politics.* Cambridge: Cambridge University Press, 2001: 135-174.

Herron, Erik S. "Causes and Consequences of Fluid Faction Membership in Ukraine." *Europe-Asia Studies*, vol. 54, no. 4 (2002): 625-40.

Higley, John, Oksan Bayulgen, and Julie George. "Political Elite Integration and Differentiation in Russia." In: Anton Steen and Vladimir Gel'man (eds.), *Elites and Democratic Development in Russia.* Oslo: Faculty of Social Sciences, University of Oslo, 2001: 4-21.

Hill, Ronald, and Peter Frank. *The Soviet Communist Party.* London: Allan and Unwin, 1981.

————. *Communist Politics under the Knife.* London: Pinter Publishers, 1990.

————. "Post-Soviet Belarus: In Search of Direction," In: Stephen White, Elenea Korosteleva, and John Löwenhardt, *Postcommunist Belarus.* Oxford: Rowman and Littlefield, 2005: 1-15.

Hinrichs, Karl, Herbert Kitschelt, and Helmut Wiesenthal (eds.). *Kontingenz und Krise* [Contingency and Crisis]. Frankfurt/Main: Campus, 2000.

Hinton, Hugh. "Explaining Policy Choices in Transition Economies: Models of Economic Policy in Ukraine." *International Journal of Economic Development*, vol. 2, no. 1 (2000): 67-108.

Hintze, Otto. "Formation of States and Constitutional Development." In: Felix Gilbert (ed.), *The Historical Essays of Otto Hintze.* New York: Oxford University Press, 1975.

Hirschhausen, Christian von. "Industrial Restructuring in Ukraine Seven Years After Independence: From Socialism to a Planning Economy?" *Communist Economies and Economic Transformations*, vol. 10, no. 4 (1998): 451-465.

Hirschman, Albert. *Exit, Voice, and Loyalty. Responses to Decline in Firms, Organizations, and States*. Cambridge: Harvard University Press, 1970.

Hobson, John. *The State and International Relations*. Cambridge: Cambridge University Press, 2000.

———. *Beyond the State*. Cambridge: Polity Press, 1995.

Holmes, Stephen. "What Russia Teaches Us Now: How Weak States Threaten Freedom." *The American Prospect*, vol. 8, no. 33 (1997): 30-39.

Holtbrügge, Dirk. "Inflationäres Wachstum, Resowjetisierung und außenwirtschaftliche Isolation. Die Wirtschaftliche Entwicklung der Republik Belarus." In: Lindner, Rainer, and Boris Meissner (eds.), *Die Ukraine und Belarus in der Transformation: eine Zwischenbilanz* [Ukraine and Belarus in Transformation: A Preliminary Assessment]. Köln: Verlag Wissenschaft und Politik (2001): 33-49.

Huang, Mel. *Wannabe Oligarchs: Tycoons and Influence in the Baltic States*. Conflict Studies Research Centre, May 2002.

Huntington, Samuel. *Political Order in Changing Societies*. New Haven: Yale University Press, 1968.

———. *The Third Wave*. Norman: University of Oklahoma Press, 1991.

Hutchings, Raymond. *The Soviet Budget*. London: Macmillan, 1983.

Hyden, Goran, Julius Court, and Kenneth Mease. *Making Sense of Governance: Empirical Evidence from Sixteen Developing Countries*. Boulder: Lynne Rienner, 2004.

IMF Staff Country Reports, various.

Ioffe, Grigory. "Understanding Belarus: Economy and Political Landscape." *Europe-Asia Studies*, vol. 56, no. 1 (2004): 85-118.

Ishaq, Mohammed. "The Ukrainian Economy and the Process of Reform." *Communist Economies and Economic Transformation*, vol. 9, no. 4 (1997): 501-517.

Ishiyama, John, and Ryan Kennedy. "Superpresidentialism and Political Party Development in Russia, Ukraine, Armenia, and Kyrgyzstan." *Europe-Asia Studies*, vol. 53, no. 8 (2001): 1177-1191.

Ivanova, Anna, Michael Keen, and Alexander Klemm. "The Russian Flat Tax Reform." *IMF Working Paper* no. 05/16, 2005.

Johnson, Juliet. "Path Contingency in Postcommunist Transformations." *Comparative Politics*, vol. 33, no. 3 (2001), 253-274.

Johnson, Simon, John McMillan, and Christopher Woodruff. "Entrepreneurs and the Ordering of Institutional Reform: Poland, Slovakia, Romania, Russia and Ukraine Compared." *Economics of Transition*, vol. 8, no. 1 (2000): 1-36.

Jones Luong, Pauline, and Erika Weinthal. "Resource Wealth and Institutional Change: The Political Economy of Tax Reform in Russia." *Leitner Working Paper*, no. 8, Yale University, 2002.

Jowitt, Ken. *New World Disorder*. Berkeley: University of California Press, 1992.

Kakwani, Nanak. "Income Inequality, Welfare and Poverty: An Illustration Using Ukrainian Data." *Policy Research Working Paper*, no. 1411, World Bank, 1995.

Kapstein, Ethan and Michael Mandelbaum (eds.). *Sustaining the Transition: The Social Safety Net in Postcommunist Europe*. New York: Council on Foreign Relations 1997.

Karatnycky, Adrian. "Meltdown in Ukraine." *Foreign Affairs*, vol. 80, no. 3 (2001): 73-86.

Karl, Terry. *The Paradox of Plenty*. Berkeley: University of California Press, 1997.

Karl, Terry Lynn. "Economic Inequality and Democratic Instability." *Journal of Democracy*, vol. 11, no. 1 (2000): 149-156.

Katkus, Anzelmas. *Lietuvos Valstybes Kontrole* [The Lithuanian State Control]. Vilnius: Leidykla, 1994.

Kaufmann, Daniel, Aart Kray, and Pablo Zoido-Lobató. "Governance Matters II, Updated Indicators for 2000/2001." *Policy Research Working Paper*, no. 2772, World Bank, 2002.

Kitschelt, Herbert. *Post-Communist Economic Reform. Causal Mechanisms and Concomitant Properties*. Paper presented at the APSA Annual Meeting, San Francisco, August 29, 2001.

Kjaer, Anne Mette. *Governance*. Cambridge: Polity Press, 2004.

Knight, Jack. *Institutions and Social Conflict*. Cambridge: Cambridge University Press, 1992.

————. "Models, Interpretations, and Theories: Constructing Explanations of Institutional Emergence and Change." In: Jack Knight and Itai Sened (eds.), *Explaining Social Institutions*. Ann Arbor: University of Michigan Press, 1995: 95-119.

Kobrinskaya, Irina. "Russian Foreign Policy in the post-Soviet space: New Priorities for New Challenges?" *PONARS policy memo,* no. 332, 2004.

Kopstein, Jeffrey, and David Reilly. "Geographic Diffusion and the Transformation of the Post-Communist World." *World Politics*, vol. 53 (2000): 1-37.

Kornai, János. "The Soft Budget Constraint." In: Kornai, *Vision and Reality, Market and State*. Hempstead: Harvester Wheatsheaf, 1990.

Kornai, Janos, Stephan Haggard, and Robert Kaufman (eds.). *Reforming the State: Fiscal and Welfare Reform in Post-Socialist Countries*. Cambridge: Cambridge University Press, 2001.

Kornai, Janos, and Rose-Ackerman, Susan (eds.). *Building a Trustworthy State in Post-Socialist Transition*. New York: Palgrave Macmillan, 2004.

Korosteleva, Elena, Colin Lawson, and Rosalind March (eds.). *Contemporary Belarus: Between Democracy and Dictatorship*. London: Routledge Curzon, 2003.

Kotkin, Stephen, and András Sajó (eds.). *Political Corruption in Transition*. Budapest: Central European University Press, 2002.

Kounov, Andrei, and Alexei Sitnikov. "Economic Legislation of the Duma: The Role of Organisational Structure." *Russian Economic Trends*, vol. 8, no. 2 (1999): 14-21.

Kounov, Andrei, and Alexei Sitnikov. "The 'Constitutional Economy' of Russia: Political Roots of Economic Problems." *Russian Economic Trends*, vol. 8, no. 4 (1999): 6-14.

Krasner, Stephen. "Approaches to the State." *Comparative Politics*, vol. 16, no. 2 (1984): 223-246.

———. *Sovereignty: Organized Hypocrisy*. Princeton: Princeton University Press, 1999.

Krickus, Richard. "Democratization in Lithuania." In: Karen Dawisha and Bruce Parrott (eds.), *Democratization and Authoriatrianism in Postcommunist Societies*. Cambridge: Cambridge University Press, 1997: 290–333.

Krupavicius, Algis. "Lithuania." *European Journal of Political Research*, 43 (2004): 1059–1069.

Kryshtanovskaya, Olga and Stephen White. "Putin's Militocracy." *Post-Soviet Affairs*, vol. 19, no. 4 (2003): 289–306.

Kubicek, Paul. "Post-Soviet Ukraine: In Search of a Constituency for Reform." *Journal of Communist Studies and Transition Politics*, vol. 13, no. 3 (1997): 103–126.

———. "Authoritarianism in Central Asia: Curse or Cure?" *Third World Quarterly*, vol. 19, no. 1 (1998): 29–43.

———. *Unbroken Ties. The State, Interest Associations, and Corporatism in Post-Soviet Ukraine*. Ann Arbor: The University of Michigan Press, 2000.

Kutuev, Pavlo. "Kuchma's Midterm: Success or Failure?" *Russian and Eurasian Review*, vol. 2, no. 2, January 21, 2003.

Kuzio, Taras. *Ukraine, State and Nation Building*. London: Routledge, 1998.

———. Robert Kravchuk, and Paul D'Anieri (eds.). *State and Institution Building in Ukraine*. Basingstoke: Macmillan, 1999.

———. *Ukraine: Perestroika to Independence*. London: Macmillan (2nd ed.), 2000.

Laidi, Z. "Does Globalisation Threaten the State? Thesis on the Fractal State." *Cambridge Review of International Affairs*, vol. 15, no. 3 (2002): 393–405.

Lazutka, Romas. "Restructuring Social Security." In: Antanas Buracas (ed.), *Lithuanian Economic Reforms: Practice and Perspectives*, Vilnius: Margi Rastai (1997): 215–241.

Leftwich, Adrian. *States of Development*. Cambridge: Polity Press, 2000.

Legeida, Nina. *Measurement of the Fiscal Deficit in a Transition Economy, Case of Ukraine 1995-1999*. MA thesis in Economics at the Kyiv-Mohyla Academy, http://www.eerc.kiev.ua/research/matheses/2000/pdf/Legeida.pdf (quoted as Legeida 2000).

Leitzel, Jim. *Russian Economic Reform*. London: Routledge, 1995.

———. *The Political Economy of Rule Evasion and Policy Reform*. London: Routledge, 2003.

Leshchenko, Natalia. "A Fine Instrument: Two Nation-Building Strategies in Post-Soviet Belarus." *Nations and Nationalism*, vol. 10, no. 3 (2004): 333–352.

Levi, Margaret. *Of Rule and Revenue*. Berkeley: University of California Press, 1988.

Levitsky, Steven and Lucan Way. "The Rise of Competitive Authoritarianism." *Journal of Democracy*, vol. 13, no. 2 (2002): 51–66.

Li, Hongyi, Xu, Lixin Colin, Zou, and Heng-Fu. "Corruption, Income Distribution, and Growth." *Economics and Politics*, vol. 12, no. 2 (2000).

Lindner, Rainer, and Boris Meissner (eds.). *Die Ukraine und Belarus in der Transformation: eine Zwischenbilanz* [Ukraine and Belarus in Transformation: A Preliminary Assessment]. Köln: Verlag Wissenschaft und Politik, 2001.

Linz, Juan and H. E. Chehabi (eds.). *Sultanistic Regimes*. Baltimore: Johns Hopkins University Press, 1998.

Linz, Juan and Alfred Stepan. *Problems of Democratic Transition and Consolidation: Southern Europe, South America, and Post-communist Europe*. Baltimore: Johns Hopkins University Press, 1996.

Loftsson, Elfar, Yonhyok Choe, and Anders Ahlquist. *Baltic Barometer*. series no. 1, University College, Sweden, 1999.

Lynch, Allen. *How Russia is not Ruled*. Cambridge: Cambridge University Press, 2005.

Luzik, Peter. *International Experience in Tax Reform and Lessons for Ukraine*. Edinburgh: Center for Economic Reform and Transformation (CERT), Heriot-Watt University (1999), 37.

Lytvyn, Vladimir. *Ukraina: Politika, Politiki, Vlast'*. Kyiv: Alternativy, 1997.

Maldeikis, Eugenijus. "Privatisation in Lithuania: Expectations, Process and Consequences." *CERT Discussion Papers*, Edinburgh: Heriot-Watt University, February 1996.

Mandibura, Viktor. "Optimising the Personal Income Taxation Mechanism Is a Prerequisite of Developing a Civilised Market." UEPLAC, *Ukrainian Economic Trends* (December 1999): 36–43.

Mann, Michael. "The Autonomous Power of the State: Its Origins, Mechanisms and Results." In: John Hall (ed.). *The State: Critical Concepts*. London: Routledge, 1994: 331–385.

March, James, and Johan Olsen. *Rediscovering Institutions. The Organizational Basis of Politics*. New York: The Free Press, 1989.

Marin, Dalia. *The Vanishing Barter Economy*. November 2002, http://www.vwl.uni muenchen.de/ls_marin/papers/replyickes.pdf.

Markwick, Roger D. "What Kind of State is the Russian State - If there is One?" *Journal of Communist Studies and Transition Politics*, vol. 15, no. 4 (1999): 111–130.

Martinez-Vazquez, Jorge, and Robert McNab. *The Tax Reform Experiment in Transitional Countries*. Georgia State University, International Studies Program; Andrew Young School of Policy Studies, Working Paper no. 00-1, January 2000.

Martinez-Vazquez, Jorge, and Jameson Boex. *Budgeting and Fiscal Management in Transitional Countries*. Georgia State University, International Studies Program; Andrew Young School of Policy Studies, Working Paper no. 00-6, September 2000.

Maravall, José María. *Regimes, Politics, and Markets*. Oxford: Oxford University Press, 1997.

Matsuzato, Kimitaka. "Semipresidentialism in Ukraine." *Demokratizatsiya*, vol. 13, no. 1 (2005): 45–58.

McFaul, Michael. "State Power, Institutional Change, and the Politics of Privatization in Russia." *World Politics*, vol. 47 (1995): 210–43.

————. *Russia's Unfinished Revolution*. Ithaca: Cornell University Press, 2001.

Mel'ota, Iryna, Ulrich Thiessen, and Tetyana Vakhnenko. "Fiscal and Regulatory Causes of the Shadow Economies in Transition Countries: The Case of Ukraine." Institute for Economic Research and Policy Consulting, *Working Paper*, no. 9, August 2001.

Mendelson, Sarah Elizabeth. "Democracy Assistance and Political Transition in Russia: Between Success and Failure." *International Security*, vol. 25, no. 4 (2001): 68–106.

Mickiewicz, Ellen and Ada Finifter. "Redefining the Political System of the USSR: Mass Support for Political Change." *American Political Science Review*, vol. 86 (1992), 857–74.

Migdal, Joel. *Strong Societies and Weak States: State-Society Relations and State Capabilities in the Third World*. Princeton: Princeton University Press, 1992.

Migdal, Joel, Atul Koli, and Vivienne Shui (eds.). *State Power and Social Forces, Domination and Transformation in the Third World*. Cambridge: Cambridge University Press, 1994.

Mihalisko, Kathleen. "Ukrainians and Their Leaders at a Time of Crisis." *RFE/RL Research Report*, vol. 2, no. 31 (1993): 54–62.

————. "Belarus: Retreat to Authoritarianism." In: Karen Dawisha and Bruce Parrott (eds.), *Democratic Changes and Authoritarian Reactions in Russia, Ukraine, Belarus and Moldova*. Cambridge: Cambridge University Press (1997): 223–281.

Mildner, Kirk. "Belarus: Kritische Überlegungen zu Politik und Wirtschaft des Lukaschenko-Regimes." *Berichte des Bundesinstituts für ostwissenschaftliche und internationale Studien*, 2000.

Miller, Arthur, William Reisinger, and Vicki Hesli. *New Soviet Citizen Survey, 1992: Monitoring Political Change*. Ann Arbor: Interuniversity Consortium for Political and Social Research [distributor], 2000.

Miller, Arthur, Gwyn Erb, William Reisinger, and Vicki Hesli. "Emerging Party Systems in Post-Soviet Societies: Fact or Fiction?" *The Journal of Politics*, vol. 62, no. 2 (2000): 455–490.

Mishler, William, and Richard Rose. "Trust in Untrustworthy Institutions: Culture and Institutional Performance in Post-Communist Societies." *Studies in Public Policies*, no. 310, Glasgow: University of Strathclyde, 1998.

————. "Learning and Re-learning Regime Support: the Dynamics of Post-communist Regimes." *Studies in Public Policy*, no. 326, Glasgow: University of Strathclyde, 2000.

Mitra, Pradeep, and Nicholas Stern. "Tax Systems in Transition." *World Bank Policy Research Working Paper*, no. 2947, 2003.

Molchanov, Mikhail. "Ukraine and the European Union: a Perennial Neighbour?" *European Integration*, vol. 26, no. 4 (2004): 451–473.

Moore, Mick. "Revenues, State Formation, and the Quality of Governance in Developing Countries." *International Political Science Review*, vol. 25, no. 3 (2004): 297–319.

Motyl, Alexander. *Dilemmas of Independence: Ukraine after Totalitarianism*. New York: Council on Foreign Relations Press, 1993.

————. "Structural Constraints and Starting Points. The Logic of Systemic Change in Ukraine and Russia." *Comparative Politics*, vol. 29, no. 4 (1997): 433–447.

Musgrave, R. and P. Musgrave. *Public Finance in Theory and Practice*. New York: McGraw-Hill, 1976.

Nagy, Piroska. *The Meltdown of the Russian State*. Cheltenham: Edward Elgar, 2000.

Nahaylo, Bohdan. *The Ukrainian Resurgence*. London: Hurst, 1999.

Nakrosis, Vitalis. "Assessing Governmental Capabilities to Manage European Accession: The Case of Lithuania." *EUI Working Paper* (RSC), no. 2000/58.

Nanivska, Vira. "NGO Development in Ukraine." In: Ann Lewis (ed.), *The EU and Ukraine*. London: The Federal Trust, 2002: 81-92.

Nettl, J. P. "The State as a Conceptual Variable." *World Politics*, vol. 20 (1968): 559-92.

Newcity, Michael. *Taxation in the Soviet Union*. New York: Praeger, 1986.

Nørgaard, Ole, and Lars Johannsen. *The Baltic States after Independence*. Cheltenham, Edward Elgar, 1999.

Nørgaard, Ole. *Economic Institutions and Democratic Reform*. Cheltenham: Edward Elgar, 2000.

North, Douglass, and Barry Weingast. "Constitution and Commitment: The Evolution of Institutions Governing Public Choice in Seventeenth-Century England." *Journal of Economic History*, vol. 49, (December 1989): 803-832.

North, Douglass. *Institutions, Institutional Change, and Economic Performance*. Cambridge: Cambridge University Press, 1990.

————. "A Framework for Analysing the State in Economic History." In: John Hall (ed.), *Critical Concepts* (1994): 325-334.

Nove, Alec. *The Soviet Economic System*. Boston: Allen and Unwin (3rd ed.), 1986.

Nunberger, Barbara (with contributions by Luca Barbone and Hans-Ulrich Derlien). *The State After Communism*. The World Bank: Washington D.C., 1999.

Nye, Joseph S., and John D. Donahue. *Governance in a Globalizing World*. Washington D.C.: Brookings Institution (2000).

O'Donnell, Guillermo. *On the State, Democratization and Some Conceptual Problems*. Kellogg Institute, Working Paper Series, University of Notre Dame, WP no. 192, April 1993.

O'Donnell, Guillermo. "Delegative Democracy." *Journal of Democracy*, vol. 5, no. 1 (1994): 55-69.

OECD. *Regulatory Reform in Russia. Government Capacity to Ensure High Quality Regulation*. Paris: OECD, 2005.

Offe, Claus. *Modernity and the State*. Cambridge: Polity Press, 1996.

Olson, Mancur. *The Logic of Collective Action*. Cambridge: Cambridge University Press, 1965.

————. *Capitalism, Socialism, and Dictatorship. Outgrowing Communist and Capitalist Dictatorships*. Manuscript, College Park, 1997.

Onis Z. and Aysan A. F. "Neoliberal globalisation, the nation-state and financial crises in the semi-periphery: a comparative analysis." *Third World Quarterly*, vol. 21, no. 1 (2000): 119-139.

Orenstein, Mitchell A. "State Projects: Their Presence and Absence in Postcommunist Transitions." Paper presented at the conference on *State-Building in Post-Communist States: Toward Comparative Analysis*, Yale University, April 27-28, 2001.

Ott, Alexander. "Präsident, Parlament, Regierung - Wie Konsolidiert ist das System der obersten Machtorgane? [President, Parliament, Government - How Consolidated is the System of the Highest Power Organs?]." In: Gerhard Simon (ed.), *Die neue Ukraine* [The new Ukraine]. Köln: Böhlau Verlag, 2002: 75-98.

Peters, Guy. *The Politics of Taxation*. Cambridge MA: Blackwell, 1991.

Pierson, Paul. "Increasing Returns, Path Dependence, and the Study of Politics." *American Political Science Review*, vol. 94, no. 2 (2000a): 251-267.

———. "The Limits of Design: Explaining Institutional Origins and Change." *Governance: An International Journal of Policy and Administration*, vol., 13, no. 4 (2000b): 475-499.

Pigenko, Vladimir, Charles Wise, and Trevor Brown. "Elite Attitudes, and Democratic Stability: Analysing Legislators' Attitudes towards the Separation of Powers in Ukraine." *Europe-Asia Studies*, vol. 54, no. 1 (2002): 87-107.

Pirttilä, Jukka. *Tax Evasion and Economies in Transition: Lessons from Tax Theory*. BOFIT (Bank of Finland) Discussion Papers, 1999, no. 2.

———. "Fiscal policy and structural reforms in transition economies." *Economics of Transition*, vol. 9, no. 1 (2001): 29-52.

Pleines, Heiko, Oksana Sobko. "Die Entwicklung der ukrainischen Wirtschaft 1992-96." *Osteuropa-Wirtschaft*, vol. 42, no. 4 (1997): 437-453.

Polomski, Krysztof. *Tax Systems in the Selected Transition Economies: An Overview*. Warsaw: Center for Social and Economic Research, Studies and Analyses no. 181, 1999.

Popov, Vladimir. "Circumstances versus Policy Choices: Why Has the Economic Performance of Soviet Successor States Been So Poor?" In: McFaul and Stoner Weiss (eds.), *After the Collapse of Communism*. Cambridge: Cambridge University Press, 2004: 96-129.

Poterba, James, and Jürgen von Hagen. *Fiscal Institutions and Fiscal Performance*. Chicago: University of Chicago Press, 1999.

Potter, B., and J. Diamond. "Building Treasury Systems." *Finance and Development*, vol. 37, no. 3 (2000).

Poznanski, Kazimierz. "Post-Communist Transition as Institutional Disintegration: Explaining the Regional Economic Recession." *Acta Oeconomica*, vol. 50, no. 1-2 (1999): 1-36.

Prezworski, Adam, and Henry Teune. *Logic of Comparative Social Inquiry*. New York: Wiley, 1970.

Protsyk, Oleh. "Troubled Semi-Presidentialism: Stability of the Constitutional System and Cabinet in Ukraine." *Europe-Asia Studies*, vol. 55 no. 7 (2003): 1077-1095.

———. "Constitutional Politics and Presidential Power in Kuchma's Ukraine." At www.policy.hu/protsyk/Publications/PPCfinalwebversionMay05.pdf (2005). [Accessed: August 12, 2006]

Prunskiene, Kazimira. "The Importance of Social and Political Stability for Integration into Europe: Lithuania's Case." In: Lars Hedgaard and Bjarne Lindström (eds.), *The NEBI Yearbook 1998* (North European and Baltic Sea Integration). Berlin: Axel Springer, 1998: 47-53.

Putnam, Robert. *Making Democracy Work. Civic Traditions in Modern Italy*. Princeton: Princeton University Press, 1993.

Pynzenyk, Viktor. "A Path to Ukrainian Reforms." In: Anders Aslund and Georges de Ménil (eds.), *Economic Reform in Ukraine*. Armonk: M. E. Sharpe, 2000: 78-93.

Reddaway, Peter, and Dmitri Glinski. *The Tragedy of Russia's Reforms*. Washington D.C.: United States Institute of Peace Press, 2001.

Robinson, Neil (ed.). *Institutions and Political Change in Russia*. Basingstoke: Macmillan, 2000.

———. *Russia: A State of Uncertainty*. London: Routledge, 2002.

Roberts, Cynthia, and Thomas Sherlock. "Bringing the Russian State Back In. Explanations of the Derailed Transition to Market Democracy." *Comparative Politics*, vol. 31, no. 4 (1999): 477–498.

Rose-Ackerman, S. *Corruption and Government. Causes, Consequences, and Reform.* Cambridge: Cambridge University Press, 1999.

Rotberg, Robert (ed.). *When States Fail: Causes and Consequences*. Princeton: Princeton University Press, 2004.

Roth, Jürgen. *Der Oligarch: Vadim Rabinovich bricht das Schweigen* [The Oligarch: Vadim Rabinovich breaks his silence]. Hamburg: Europa Verlag, 2001.

Savchenko, Andrew. *Rationality, Nationalism, and Post-Communist Market Transformations: A Comparative Analysis of Belarus, Poland and the Baltic States*. Aldershot: Ashgate, 2000.

Schaffer, Mark and Gerlad Turley. "Effective versus Statutory Taxation: Measuring Effective Tax Administration in Transition Economies." Centre for Economic Reform and Transformation, Heriot Watt University, *CERT Discussion Papers*, no. 8, 2000.

Scharpf, Fritz W. *Institutions in Comparative Policy Research*. Cologne: MPIfG Working Paper 00/3, 2000.

Schedler, Andreas. "What is Democratic Consolidation?" *Journal of Democracy*, vol. 9, no. 2 (1998): 91–107.

Schedler, Andreas, Larry Diamond and Marc Plattner (eds.). *The Self-Restraining State: Power and Accountability in New Democracies*. Boulder, London: Lynne Rienner, 1999.

Schneider, Friedrich. "The Size and Development of the Shadow Economies of 22 Transition and 21 OECD Countries." *Discussion Paper Series*, no. 514, Institute for the Study of Labour, June 2002.

Schneider, Friedrich, and Dominik Enste. "Shadow Economies around the World: Sizes, Causes, and Consequences." *IMF Working Paper*, no. 00/26, February 2000.

Schumpeter, Joseph. "The Crisis of the Tax State." In: *The Economics and Sociology of Capitalism* (ed. by Richard Swedberg). Princeton: Princeton University Press (1991): 99–140.

Sekarev, A. "Ukraine: Crisis on the Basis of Vague Economic Policy." *Problems of Economic Transition*, vol. 37, no. 9 (1995): 40–56.

Shearer, D. *Industry, State, and Society in Stalin's Russia 1926–1934*. Ithaca: Cornell University Press, 1996.

Shelley, Louise. *Policing Soviet Society. The Evolution of State Control.* Routledge: London, 1996.

Shen, Raphael. *Ukraine's Economic Reform*. Westport: Praeger, 1996.

Shevtsova, Lilia. *Putin's Russia*. Washington, D.C.: Carnegie Endowment for International Peace, 2003.

Shlapentokh, Vladimir. *Public and Private Life of the Soviet People*. New York: Oxford University Press, 1989.

Shlapentokh, Vladimir. "Standard of Living and Popular Discontent." In: Michael Ellman and Vladimir Kontorovich (eds.), *The Destruction of the Soviet Economic System*. Armonk: M. E. Sharpe, 1998: 30–40.

Shleifer, Andrei, and Daniel Treisman. "A Normal Country: Russia after Communism." *Journal of Economic Perspectives*, vol. 19, no. 1 (2005): 151–174.

Silitski, Vital. "Explaining post-communist authoritarianism in Belarus." In: Korosteleva et al. (eds.), *Contemporary Belarus*. London: RoutledgeCurzon, 2003: 36–52.

Simis, Konstantin. *USSR: The Corrupt Society*. New York: Simon and Schuster, 1982.

Simon, Gerhard (ed.). *Die neue Ukraine* [The new Ukraine]. Köln: Böhlau Verlag, 2002.

Sinelnikov, Sergei, and Konstantin Reznikov. "Budget Crisis in Russia." *CASE Studies and Analyses*, no. 46, 1995.

Sinitsina, Irina. "Бедность и социальная политика в странах СНГ [Poverty and social policy in CIS countries]." *CASE Studies and Analyses*, no. 316, 2006.

Smith, Gordon B. (ed.). *State-Building in Russia*. Armonk: M. E. Sharpe, 1999.

Smith, Steven, and Thomas Remington. *The Politics of Institutional Choice: The Formation of the Russian Duma*. Princeton: Princeton University Press, 2001.

Smyth, Regina. "Putin's Tightrope: Maintaining Support in the Face of Domestic and International Policy Demands." *PONARS Policy Memo*, no. 242, January 2002.

Sokolowski, Alexander. "Bankrupt Government: Intra-Executive Relations and the Politics of Budgetary Irresponsibility in El'tsin's Russia." *Europe-Asia Studies*, vol. 53, no. 4 (2001): 541–572.

Solchanyk, R. "Ukraine: The Politics of Reform." *Problems of Post-Communism*, Nov./Dec. 1995: 46–51.

Solnick, Steven. "The Breakdown of Hierarchies in the Soviet Union and China: A Neoinstitutional Perspective." *World Politics*, vol. 48 no. 2 (1996): 206–239.

————. *Stealing the State. Control and Collapse in Soviet Institutions*. Cambridge: Harvard University Press, 1998.

Solomon, Peter and Todd Foglesong. "The Procuracy and the Courts in Russia: A New Relationship?" *East European Constitutional Review*, vol. 9, no. 4 (2000): (internet edition).

Sperling, Valerie (ed.). *Building the Russian State. Institutional Crisis and the Quest for Democratic Governance*. Boulder: Westview Press, 2000.

Spigler, I. "Public Finance." In: M. C. Kaser and E. A. Radice, *The Economic History of Eastern Europe 1919-1975*. Vol. II, Oxford: Clarendon Press, 1986.

Spilimbergo, Antonio. "Measuring the Performance of Fiscal Policy in Russia." *IMF Working Paper*, no. 05/241, Washington D.C., 2005.

Srivastava, Vinayak. *The Separation of the Party and the State*. Aldershot: Ashgate, 1999.

Stark, David, and László Bruszt. *Postsocialist Pathways: Transforming Politics and Property in East Central Europe*. Cambridge: Cambridge University Press, 1998.

Steinmo, Sven. *Taxation and Democracy: Swedish, British, and American Approaches to Financing the Modern State*. New Haven: Yale University Press, 1993.

Stiglitz, Joseph. *Redefining the role of the state: What should it do? How should it do it? And how should these decisions be made?* Keynote Address, 10th Anniversary of the MITI Research Institute, Tokyo, 1998.

Strauch, Rolf and Jürgen von Hagen (eds.). *Institutions, Politics and Fiscal Policy*. Boston: Kluwer, 2000.

Stroev, Egor, Leonid Bliakhman, and Mikhail Krotov. *Russia and Eurasia at the Crossroads: Experience and Problems of Economic Reforms in the Commonwealth of Independent States*. Berlin: Springer Verlag, 1999.

Tauber, Joachim. "Die Auseinandersetzung mit der kommunistischen Vergangenheit in Litauen [Dealing with the Communist Past in Lithuania]." *Bericht des BIOst* No. 28/1997.

Tanzi, Vito (ed.). *Fiscal Policies in Economies in Transition*. Washington D.C.: IMF, 1992.

————. *Transition to Market: Studies in Fiscal Reform*. Washington D.C.: IMF, 1993a.

————. *Fiscal Policy and Economic Restructuring in Economies in Transition*. Washington D.C.: IMF, 1993b.

————. "Essential Fiscal Institutions in Selected Economies in Transition." *Discussion Paper Series,* Collegium Budapest, 1998.

Teriokhin, Serhyi. "Tax Policy." In: Aslund and de Ménil (eds.), *Economic Reform in Ukraine: The Unfinished Agenda*. Armonk: M. E. Sharpe, 2000: 144-164.

Thelen, Kathleen. "How Institutions Evolve: Insights from Comparative-Historical Analysis." In: James Mahoney and Dietrich Rueschemeyer (eds.), *Comparative-Historical Analysis in the Social Sciences*. Cambridge: Cambridge University Press, 2002.

Thiessen, Ulrich. "Zur Reform des Steuersystems, der Sozialabgaben und der Staatsausgaben in Osteuropa: Das Beispiel der Ukraine [On the reform of the tax system, social contributions, and the state budget in Eastern Europe: the example of Ukraine]." *Vierteljahreshefte zur Wirtschaftsforschung*, vol. 66, no. 3-4 (1997): 395-411.

————. "Presumptive Taxation for small enterprises in Ukraine." *IER Working Paper*, no. 6, 2001. Available at http://www.ier.kiev.ua/English/WP/2001/WP_6_eng.pdf [accessed: November 23, 2002].

————. "Powerless Against the Shadow Economy? The Case of Ukraine." DIW, *Economic Bulletin* 2/2002. Available at www.diw.de/english/publikationan/bulletin/docs/eb02/n02_02feb_2.html [accessed: November 23, 2002].

Thomson, Janice. "State Sovereignty in International Relations: Bridging the Gap Between Theory and Empirical Research." *International Studies Quarterly*, vol. 39 (1995), 213-233.

Tilly, Charles (ed.). *The Formation of National States in Western Europe*. Princeton: Princeton University Press, 1975.

Treisman, Daniel. "Russia's Tax Crisis: Explaining Falling Revenues in a Transitional Economy." *Economics and Politics*, vol. 11, no. 2 (July 1999): 145-169.

Treisman, Daniel, and Andrei Shleifer. *Without a Map: Political Tactics and Economic Reform in Russia*. Cambridge: MIT Press, 2000.

Treisman, Daniel. "Russia Renewed?" *Foreign Affairs*, vol. 81, no. 6 (2002): 58-72.

Tsebelis, George. *Veto Players: How Political Institutions Work*. Princeton: Princeton University Press, 2002.

Ukrainian-European Policy and Legal Advice Centre (UEPLAC), *Ukrainian Economic Trends*. Brussels: TACIS-Program, various issues.

UNDP. *The Shrinking State: Governance and Sustainable Human Development*. New York: UNDP (Regional Bureau for Europe and the CIS), 1997.

Vachudova, Milada. *Europe Undivided*. Oxford: Oxford University Press, 2005.

Vaicenavičius, Rimantas. *Lithuanian Fiscal Policy: Experience and Challenges*. Research Report Prepared for the Conference Lithuania: From Transition to Convergence, Vilnius, September 1999.

Valovaya, Tatyana. "The Post-Soviet Space in the Era of Pragmatism." *Russia in Global Affairs*, no. 2 (2005).

Van de Walle, Nicolas. *African Economies and the Politics of Permanent Crisis 1979-1999*. Cambridge: Cambridge University Press, 2001.

Vavilov, Andrey, and Oleg V. Vyugin. "The Financial Situation of the Soviet Economy Through the Prism of the Income of the Population and Enterprises." *Economic Systems*, vol. 15, no. 2 (1991): 195–209.

Vorndran, Oliver. "The Constitutional Process in Ukraine: Context and Structure." *Research Papers in Russian and East European Studies*, No. REES 97/3, December 1997.

Waldner, David. *State Building and Late Development*. Ithaca: Cornell University Press, 1999.

Wallerstein, Immanuel. *The Modern World System: Capitalist Agriculture and the Origins of the European World Economy in the Sixteenth Century*. New York: Academic Press, 1974.

Way, Lucan. "Weak States and Pluralism: The Case of Moldova." *East European Politics and Societies*, vol. 17, no. 3 (2003): 454–482.

Weber, Max. *Staatssoziologie*. Second, reviewed and amended edition, Berlin: Duncker and Humboldt, 1966.

Wedel, Janine. *Collision and Collusion: The Strange Case of Western Aid to Eastern Europe 1989-1998*. New York: St. Martin's Press, 1998.

Weimer, David L. (ed.). *The Political Economy of Property Rights*. Cambridge: Cambridge University Press, 1997.

Wheatley, Jonathan. *The Problems of Post-Soviet Regime Change: Dynamic and Static Elements of the Georgian Regime 1989-2001*. PhD thesis, EUI Florence, March 2003.

White, Fidelma, and Kathryn Hollingsworth. *Audit, Accountability and Government*. Oxford: Clarendon Press, 1999.

White, Stephen, John Gardner, and Georg Schöpflin. *Communist Political Systems*. New York: St. Martin's Press, (2nd ed.), 1987.

White, Stephen, Alex Pravda, and Zvi Gitelman (eds.). *Developments in Soviet and Post-Soviet Politics*. London: Macmillan (2nd edition), 1992.

————. *Developments in Russian Politics 5*. Basingstoke: Palgrave, 2001.

White, Stephen, and Richard Rose. "Nationality and Public Opinion in Belarus and Ukraine." *Studies in Public Policy*, no. 346, Glasgow: University of Strathclyde, 2001.

White, Stephen, and Ian McAllister. "Putin and His Supporters." *Europe-Asia Studies*, vol. 55, no. 3 (2003): 383–399.

White, Stephen, Elena Korosteleva, and John Loewenhardt (eds.). *Post-Communist Belarus*. Lanham: Rowman and Littlefield, 2005.

White, Stephen, Paul Lewis, and Judy Batt (eds.). *Developments in Central and Eastern European Politics 3*. Duke: Durham University Press, 2003.

Whitmore, Sarah. *State Building in Ukraine: The Ukrainian Parliament, 1990–2003*. London and New York: RoutledgeCurzon, 2004.

————. "Faction Institutionalization and Parliamentary Development in Ukraine." *Journal of Communist Studies and Transition Politics*, vol. 19, no. 4 (2003): 41–64.

Wildavsky, Aaron. *Budgeting. A Comparative Theory of Budgetary Processes*. Boston: Little, Brown and Company, 1975.

————. *Budgeting and Governing*. New Brunswick: Transaction Publishers, 2001.

Willerton, John P. *Patronage and Politics in the USSR*. Cambridge: Cambridge University Press, 1992.

Wilson, Andrew. *Ukrainian Nationalism in the 1990s. A Minority Faith*. Cambridge: Cambridge University Press, 1997.

Wilson, Andrew and Sarah Birch. "Voting Stability, Political Gridlock: Ukraine's 1998 Parliamentary Elections." *Europe-Asia Studies*, vol. 51, no. 6 (1999): 1039–1068.

Wilson, Andrew. "Ukraine's New Virtual Politics." *East European Constitutional Review*, vol. 10, no. 2–3 (2001): internet edition.

Wilson, Andrew. *Virtual Politics. Faking Democracy in the Post-Soviet World*. New Haven: Yale University Press, 2005a.

Wilson, Andrew. *Ukraine's Orange Revolution*. New Haven: Yale University Press, 2005b.

Wintrobe, Robert. *The Political Economy of Dictatorship*. Cambridge: Cambridge University Press, 1998.

Wise, Charles and Trevor Brown. "The Separation of Powers in Ukraine." *Communist and Post-Communist Studies*, vol. 32, no. 1 (1999): 23–44.

Wittkowsky, Andreas. *Fünf Jahre ohne Plan: Die Ukraine 1991–96* [Five Years without (a) Plan]. Hamburg: Lit-Verlag, 1998.

Wolchik, Sharon, and Volodymyr Zviglyanich (eds.). *Ukraine: The Search for a National Identity*. Lanham: Rowman and Littlefield, 2000.

Wolczuk, Kataryna. *The Moulding of Ukraine: The Constitutional Politics of State Formation*. Budapest: Central European University Press, 2001a.

————. "Ukraine: Tormented Constitution-Making." In: Jan Zielonka (ed.), *Democratic Consolidation in Eastern Europe*. Oxford: Oxford University Press, 2001b: 243–268.

————. "Ukraine's Policy Towards the European Union: A Case of 'Declaratory Europeanization'." Warsaw: Stefan Batory Foundation (2003), available at http://www.batory.org.pl/ftp/program/forum/eu_ukraine/ukraine_eu_policy.pdf [accessed: March 15, 2004].

Woo-Cumings, Meredith (ed.). *The Developmental State*. Ithaca: Cornell University Press, 1999.

World Bank. *Ukraine: Restoring Growth with Equity*. World Bank Country Study, Washington D.C.: World Bank, 1999.

————. *Making Transition Work for Everyone: Poverty and Inequality in Europe and Central Asia*. Washington D.C.: World Bank, 2000.

————. *Transition, The First Ten Years, Analysis and Lessons for Eastern Europe and the Former Soviet Union*. World Bank: Washington D.C., 2002.

————. *Eastern Europe and the Former Soviet Union: Growth, Poverty, and Inequality*. Washington D.C.: World Bank, 2005.

Yekhanurov, Yuri. "The Progress of Privatization." In: Aslund and de Ménil (eds.), *Economic Reform in Ukraine: The Unfinished Agenda*. Armonk: M. E. Sharpe, 2000: 189–214.

Yushchenko, Viktor. "Monetary Policy in the Transition to a Market Economy." In: Aslund, Anders and Georges de Ménil (eds.), *Economic Reform in Ukraine. The Unfinished Agenda*. Armonk: M. E. Sharpe, 2000: 94–110.

Yurhelevych, Serhiy, and Maurice Downey. "Taxing Problems." UEPLAC, *Ukrainian Economic Trends*, December 2000: 42–49.

Zartman, William (ed.). *Collapsed States: The Disintegration and Restoration of Legitimate Authority*. London: Lynne Rienner, 1995.

Zettelmeyer, Jeromin. "The Uzbek Growth Puzzle." *IMF Staff Paper*, vol. 46, no. 3, September/December 1999.

Zimmer, Kerstin. "*Khozyaistvenniki* and Political Machines in Donetsk: Economic and Political Regionalism in Ukraine." Marburg: paper presented at the ECPR conference, September 2003.

van Zon, Hans. "Neo-Patrimonialism as an Impediment to Economic Development: The Case of Ukraine." *Journal of Communist Studies and Transition Politics*, vol. 17, no. 3 (2001): 71–95.

INDEX

For Product Safety Concerns and Information please contact our EU representative GPSR@taylorandfrancis.com Taylor & Francis Verlag GmbH, Kaufingerstraße 24, 80331 München, Germany

Batch number: 10703952

Printed by Printforce, the Netherlands